Weaving Words into Worlds

Edited by

Caroline Durand-Rous
Margot Lauwers
OIKOS-CRESEM, University of Perpignan, France

Series in Literary Studies

VERNON PRESS

www.vernonpress.com

In the Americas:
Vernon Press
1000 N West Street, Suite 1200
Wilmington, Delaware, 19801
United States

In the rest of the world:
Vernon Press
C/Sancti Espiritu 17,
Malaga, 29006
Spain

Series in Literary Studies

Library of Congress Control Number: 2023932404

ISBN: 978-1-64889-893-8

Also available: 978-1-64889-649-1 [Hardback]; 978-1-64889-784-9 [PDF, E-Book]

Cover design by Vernon Press. Cover image by Margot Lauwers.

Table of Contents

Acknowledgments

Sincere thanks are due to family, friends, and colleagues at the University of Perpignan and around the world for moments of sharing us with computers and books, a lot; for enriching discussions and debates during international conferences or more intimate coffee moments and/or for concrete help: Bénédicte Meillon for her endless encouragements, her belief in us, her astute comments and her invaluable help on the last section of this book and her foreword; Serenella Ioviono for her listening skills, good humor, and sage advice; Karen Houle for her inspiring discussions, poetry, and friendship. Thanks, finally, to our authors for their patience and incredibly rich contributions. Our thanks to the editors and publishers at Vernon Press for allowing this to be printed.

Foreword

Bénédicte Meillon

This great volume comes as the third spinoff of the international ecopoetics conference organized in Perpignan in 2016. As such, it is tightly interwoven with the two preceding volumes, *Lieux d'enchantement : approches écocritiques et écopoét(h)iques des liens entre humains et non-humains*, coedited by Meillon, Bénédicte et Margot Lauwers (2018), and *Dwellings of Enchantment: Writing and Reenchanting the Earth*, edited by Bénédicte Meillon (2020). All three books have emerged from that one single event bringing together roughly a hundred scholars and ecopoets from all across the world, themselves braiding many different stories, myths, theories, and sciences that we, humans, have co-created in our constant interactions with the more-than-human world since the dawn of humanity. Reflecting upon how the many stories we tell directly influence the world we live in, each of the contributions in this international volume directs our attention to the constant, ecopoetic weaving of word to world at work via the many entanglements between mind, matter, and meaning, whether on a local or a global scale. It encapsulates how the words, stories, and concepts we humans articulate as we try and make sense of the world we inhabit give part of its shape to the web of ecological relations that we depend on for our own survival. It seeks to cast light on the disenchanting and reenchanting powers of stories and poiesis in general—as stories retain the power to make us either become oblivious to and destroy, or to feel and honor the many, complex ties between the multitudinous nature cultures intertwined within the fabric of a multispecies world always in the making.

The title the co-editors and I have thought up for this book, "*Weaving Words into Worlds*," is itself an entanglement of some of the many different strands of ecopoetic thinking that illumines the power at the heart of both the metaphor and actual craft of weaving. It presents ecoliterary creation—the poeming or wording of linguistic material into ecopoetic fabric, whether in the form of prose or poetry— as a creative craft that cannot be disentangled from the other ways in which we inhabit the world. Some of the first strands knotted together in the title for this volume originate in Leslie Marmon Silko's dialogic novel *Ceremony* (1977), which tells a multifaceted story of healing. Interweaving many different types of textuality in the fabric of her postcolonial, dialogic novel—from myths, poems, and chants, to prose—, Silko meanwhile foregrounds the archetypal figure of Spider Woman. Also referred to as "Thought-Woman" in Pueblo cosmogony, this creation Goddess is held to possess the power of spinning the world into a web of sacred relations out of pure thinking. As words materialize onto the pages of Silko's novel, framed as it is by poems that read halfway between chants and myths, the overall impression is that the entire fabric of the literary work results from the spinning of Spider Woman's web of thinking, or singing: "Ts'its'tsi'nako, Thought-Woman,/ is sitting in her room/and whatever she thinks about/appears./ [...] Thought-Woman, the Spider,/ named things and/ as she named them/ they appeared./ She is sitting in her room/thinking of a story now/ I'm telling you the story/she is thinking." (1) In the highly metatextual, eponymous poem that follows, Silko underscores the value and power of stories, stories which, as we hold on to and regenerate them via dynamic storytelling, in turn, nurture us, providing food for us to thrive on even in the midst of destruction:

> I will tell you something about stories,/ [...]They aren't just entertainment. [...] They are all we have, you see, all we have to fight off illness and death./ You don't have anything if you don't have the stories./ [....] He rubbed his belly. I keep them here/ [he said]/ Here, put your hand on it/ See, it is moving. There is life here for the people./ And in the belly of this story/ the rituals and the ceremony is still growing. (2)

As Paula Gunn Allen explains, in Keres cosmogony, although "Spider Woman's Keres name is translated as Thought Woman [...] it can be better understood if translated as Creating-through-Thinking Woman." (1986 98) Thus, both Silko and Gunn Allen help unravel the material ties between thinking, story-telling, and world-mattering.

In her introduction to the stories collected in her anthology, *Spider Woman's Granddaughters* (1989), Paula Gunn Allen insists that traditional stories "are woven of elements that illumine the ritual tradition of the storyteller's people, make pertinent points to some listener who is about to make a mistake or who has some difficulty to resolve, and hold the listeners' attention so that they can experience a sense of belonging to a sturdy and strong tradition." (1) As we are now faced with global warming, accelerated biodiversity erosion, and as, according to the science on climate change, we now stand on the edge of many uncertain tipping points, many of us ecocritics and ecopoeticians, together with first peoples across the world, are still calling attention to the urgent need to reentangle the many forms of sciences and stories that have emerged across centuries, across cultures and across disciplines, so that traditional and postmodern ecological knowledges might be braided together into meaningful stories capable of guiding us onto more reasonable paths than the ecocidal ones modern science and myths have led us onto. As we are presently dealing with again another planetary crisis in the wake of the Covid pandemic, it is more than obvious that our future hinges on the stories we will tell as we may or may not reweave the story of humanity within the vibrant textures of all of other-than-human nature—whether the latter be apprehended in the form of a virus, of the wild animals that we poach, or the forests that are the latter's habitats and which we keep encroaching upon in so many, destructive ways. Gunn Allen's take on the dynamic power of storytelling captures much of the ecopoetic venture that forms the collective endeavor in this book. "The aesthetic imperative," she argues,

> requires that new experiences be woven into existing traditions in order for personal experience to be transmuted into communal experience; that is, so we can understand how today's events harmonize with communal consciousness. We use aesthetics to make our lives whole, to explain ourselves to each other, to see where we fit in the scheme of things (1989 7).

In her previous eponymous book dedicated to the concept of the Sacred Hoop—itself a variant on the metaphor of all life forms being interwoven and spun into a web—Gunn Allen writes of "the Old Woman Spider who weaves us together in a fabric of interconnection" (1986 11). From the standpoint of humans, the dynamic breath of life and the breath of storytelling are enmeshed. As Gunn Allen puts it,

> [the] tribes seek—through song, ceremony, legend, sacred stories (myths), and tales—to embody, articulate, and share reality, to bring the isolated, private self into harmony and balance with this reality, to verbalize the sense of majesty and reverent mystery of all things, and to actualize, in language, those truths that give humanity its greatest significance and dignity. To a large extent, ceremonial literature serves to redirect private emotion and integrate the energy generated by emotion within a cosmic framework. (1986 55; emphasis mine)

I believe the same is true for ecopoiesis, whether in prose or poetry, whether fictional or whether in the form of nonfiction nature writing. Indeed, what Paula Gunn Allen explains about traditional storytelling also provides a precious lens for ecopoetics:

The artistry of the tribes is married to the essence of language itself, for through language one can share one's singular being with that of the community and know within oneself the communal knowledge of the tribe. In this art, the greater self and all-that-is are blended into a balanced whole, and in this way the concept of being that is the fundamental and sacred spring of life is being given voice and being for all. (1986 55)

As many of the contributions in this book demonstrate, like most indigenous peoples whose oral traditions are still alive, ecopoets "do not content themselves with simple preachments of this truth, but through the sacred power of utterance, they seek to shape and mold, to direct and determine, the forces that surround and govern human life and the related lives of all things" (1986 55–56). In this very concrete way, then, ecopoiesis, like much indigenous storytelling, is an ongoing process of material weaving of world to word, and back to world again.

Another strand of the title for this book, itself entangled in many ways with ancient, traditional Goddess mythologies and ceremonies, comes from ecofeminism. The centrality of the metaphor of weaving, a craft often practiced by women, appears clearly in the titles of the first anthologies of pioneer ecofeminist theory, such as *Weaving the Visions: New Patterns in Feminist Spirituality*, edited by Judith Plaskow and Carol P. Christ (1989), and *Reweaving the World: The Emergence of Ecofeminism*, edited by Irene Diamond and Gloria Feman Orenstein (1990). In his essay collected in the latter, cosmologist Brian Swimme refers to Charlene Spretnak's work on weaving. One of the pioneers of ecofeminism, Spretnak has connected the scientific discoveries of cosmic expansion and phenomenal entanglements with the metaphor of weaving long honored in many traditional cultures. "In fact," says Swimme,

nothing is more obvious than Spretnak's assertion that weaving is a fundamental dynamic of this universe. Picture it: from a single fireball, the galaxies and stars were all woven. Out of a single molten planet, the hummingbirds and pterodactyls, and gray whales were all woven. What could be more obvious than this all-pervasive fact of cosmic and terrestrial weaving? Out of a single group of microorganisms, the Krebs cycle was woven, the convoluted human brain was woven, the Pali Canon was woven, all parts of the radiant tapestry of being. Show us this weaving? Well, it is impossible to point to anything that does not show it, for this creative interlacing energy envelops us entirely. Our lives, in truth, are nothing less than a further unfurling of this primordial ordering activity. (20)

According to Swimme, one of the reasons why this metaphor of weaving makes so much sense from an ecofeminist point of view may be that "[women] are beings who know from the inside out what it is like to weave the Earth into a new human being." (21) Referring to both Spretnak's and Gunn Allen's seminal work, Brian Swimme hopes that in bringing together indigenous, ecofeminist and scientific worldviews, we may "teach our children at a young age the central truth of everything: that the universe has been weaving itself into a world of beauty for 15 billion years.[...] We will teach that their destinies and the destinies of the oak trees and all the peoples on Earth are wrapped together. That the same creativity suffusing the universe suffuses all of us, too." (22)

It is in this crucial sense that the present book matters, as it examines the intricate interweaving of human creativity with other-than-human wor(l)ds. To take up the vision expressed by Cherokee thinker Dhyani Ywahoo as to how to actively renew the Sacred Hoop, the collected essays in this volume demonstrate how it is that "the knowledges of our voices, thoughts, and actions are weaving beauty around the land. There is a harmony; there is a song. All things move in a circle" (274). As the contributions collected in this volume show, ecopoetics helps us "realize the circle of life and the wheel of cause and effect. [...] In this industrial age, which has been described as paternalistic, we see how moving away from the circle and working more in components, there is a loss of continuity and a forgetfulness of how what one does affects the Earth" (276). Each of the chapters in its own way acts as a reminder that, still as Dhyani Ywahoo has put it, "[seeing] all in relationship, in the circle, is part of the planetary healing" (276). Teaching us again how to reweave creative thinking and writing, this volume and the ecopoetic works of art they examine can be imagined as one of those "[great lakes] sending forth endless ripples of compassion and care" (279). In the face of the many, interrelated, global crises we are facing, the ecopoetic studies here included provide an antidote to the current tendency where—to take up Dhyani Ywahoo's diagnosis of how much of the Sacred Hoop has been broken— "many people abdicate self-empowerment by withdrawing their energies" (278). Like the previous two books that have emerged from the 2016 Perpignan conference dealing with an ecopoetics of "Dwellings of Enchantment," *Weaving Words into Worlds* gives concrete evidence of how writers and scholars from all over the world can actively interweave their thinking, voices, and craft with the songs and creativity of the more-than-human world, "attuning to one another, working as a team, knowing that in the circle each person has a unique and necessary function" (278). It helps us believe in and work toward "the possibility of the Sacred Hoop being rebuilt," as envisioned by Ywahoo in her timeless essay.

Finally, the title of this collection is also meant as a tribute to Scott Knickerbocker's enlightening study, *Ecopoetics: The Language of Nature, the Nature of Language* (2012). In his introduction, Knickerbocker recollects how his thirteen-month-old's tentative yet imperfect speech, as he was trying to name the trees around him, was the child's first engagement in "the old human habit of weaving world to word" (1). As Knickerboker elaborates, ecopoiesis produces an essential form of "sensous poesis," which he defines as "the process of rematerializing language specifically as a response to nonhuman nature" (2). I would say that this book, in the wake of Scott Knickerbocker's deep and subtle unraveling of the workings of ecopoiesis, also suggests a positive answer to the latter's starting question, as he wondered whether "language, despite its mediating function between the human and nonhuman [could] weave us to nature?" (2) Gathering a dazzling array of voices and perspectives across many different cultures, traditions, and literary genres, the impressive volume at hand chants back in a polyphonic and multispecies chorus: Yes, language offers a way of threading ourselves back into the sensuous fabric of the world! Yes, ecopoetics can help us reweave word to world. Yes, ecopoetics can pave the way toward rewor(l)ding.

Works Cited

Allen, Paula Gunn. *The Sacred Hoop: Recovering the Feminine in American Indian Traditions.* Boston: Beacon Press, [1986], 1992.

—, ed. *Spider Woman's Granddaughters.* Boston: Beacon Press, 1989.

Diamond, Irene, and Gloria Feman Orenstein. *Reweaving the Wounds: The Emergence of Ecofeminism.* San Francisco: Sierra Club Books, 1990.

Knickerbocker, Scott. *Ecopoetics: The Language of Nature, the Nature of Language.* Amherst and Boston: University of Massachusetts Press, 2012.

Meillon, Bénédicte, ed. *Dwellings of Enchantment: Writing and Reenchanting the Earth. Dwellings of Enchantment: Writing and Reenchanting the Earth.* Washington, D.C.: Lexington Books, Rowman & Littlefield "Ecocritical Theory and Practice," 2020.

Meillon, Bénédicte and Margot Lauwers, eds. *Lieux d'enchantement : approches écocritiques et écopoét(h)iques des liens entre humains et non-humains.* Crossways Journal. n°2.1, July 2018.

Plaskow, Judith and Carol P. Christ, eds. *Weaving the Visions: New Patterns in Feminist Spirituality.* New York: HarperCollins Publishers, 1989.

Silko, Leslie Marmon. *Ceremony.* New York: Penguin Books, 1977.

Swimme, Brian. "How to Heal a Lobotomy." *Reweaving the Wounds: The Emergence of Ecofeminism,* edited by Irene Diamond and Gloria Feman Orenstein, San Francisco: Sierra Club Books, 1990, pp. 15–22.

Ywahoo, Dhyani. "Renewing the Sacred Hoop." *Weaving the Visions: New Patterns in Feminist Spirituality,* edited by Judith Plaskow and Carol P. Christ, New York: HarperCollins Publishers, 1989, pp. 274–280.

Introduction

Caroline Durand-Rous and Margot Lauwers

OIKOS-CRESEM, University of Perpignan, France

The post-humanist era we are witnessing has constantly been redefining humans in order to re-inscribe them in a history that would no longer be conceptually separate from that of nature. Indeed, for nearly forty years, scientific discoveries and fields such as ethology have only diminished what seemed to be human characteristics: the use of tools and language are among the most striking examples. It is now established that certain species of birds and large primates habitually use tools (thanks in particular to the work of Jane Goodall on this subject) and the phenomenon has been observed in certain domestic animals as well. Language is no longer a characteristic of the human species since the discovery of the use of complex communication systems in marine mammals and other large mammals such as elephants. What is there that remains distinctly human, then? Some would answer that literature and art are human production *par excellence*. Glen A. Love explains the importance that literature (and art) must have if we accept this premise as valid:

> If the creation of literature is an important characteristic of the human species, it should be examined carefully and honestly to discover its influence upon human behavior and the natural environment, and to determine what role, if any, it plays in the welfare and survival of humanity, and what insight it offers into human relationships with other species and with the world around us. Is it an activity that adapts us better to life on Earth, or one that sometimes estranges us from life? From the unforgiving perspective of evolution and natural selection, does literature contribute more to our survival than it does to our extinction? (Love, in Murphy 15–16)

In regard to the ecological and social crises of the past decades (and, sadly, those still to come), it is easy to understand how important this question might prove. As Barbara Bennett reminds us in *Scheherazade's Daughters: The Importance of Storytelling in Ecofeminist Change*, Scheherazade's story is both the introduction and the cement of the Tales of a Thousand and One Nights. Bennett starts her book by reminding us of this story of which we all have a rough knowledge. We thought it worthwhile to briefly recall it here because it illustrates the role that literature may play.

A sultan, deceived by his wife, decrees that no woman can be faithful in love. For this reason, he takes a new wife every day, spends the wedding night with her, and has her executed the next day. When the kingdom begins to see the number of its young daughters diminish dangerously, Scheherazade, the grand vizier's daughter, draws up a plan. She begs her father to let her marry the sultan. The sultan initially refuses, not wanting to see his daughter put to death the day after her wedding. However, Scheherazade insists and adds a condition: that her younger sister, Dinerzade, be allowed to reside in her apartments on the wedding night. This is agreed upon, and Dinerzade wakes the young couple during the night, pretexting a nightmare, and asks her sister to tell her a story. The sister does so and keeps her audience in total suspense until dawn. She interrupts her story at a key moment in the narrative to prepare to be executed. Under the spell of curiosity, the sultan postpones the execution of his young wife until the following day so that he can find out the rest of the story. During one thousand and one nights, Scheherazade will thus captivate her husband with her storytelling, so much so that he will abandon his murderous habit and remain married to the grand vizier's daughter. It is thus literally through her ability to tell stories that the young wife changes the historical course of the kingdom.

Metaphorically, this tale is representative of the strength and consequences that a story can have. Bennett thus analyzes its foundation:

> It is a story about stories and the power they hold. It is a story about how stories can change people, even change worlds. We all acknowledge the ability of storytelling to make us laugh or cry, touch us in ways we did not know we could be touched, and connect us with worlds we would never see in our relatively limited sphere of living. Less is said, however, about the power of stories to change our minds, to alter our positions, to encourage us to action. (Bennett 2)

Some famous examples and the hindsight we now have show us what can happen when works deeply touch readers and scholars[1]. They also give us a glimpse of the importance that the study of literature has in our increasingly connected and abstract societies: taking the time to read, study and analyze literature allows us to nurture our imaginations. If anything, the past three years have shown how much society missed the natural world and contact with their fellow creatures, human and other-than-human alike; maybe more than ever before, has humankind then realized the urgent need for general re-enchantment. This desire to infuse life with a renewed sense of wonder has been visible, be it in the media, in literature and art, or in a popular "back-to-nature" movement. Meanwhile, the emergency of climate change has also been put on the political agenda as numerous countries worldwide finally acknowledged the concerns voiced by grassroot movements, activities, indigenous cultures, and ecocritics for the past decade. Politics have also started acknowledging the emergency of climate change. Literature, in that it allows a very intimate relationship for readers, thus has an important role to play in that it allows for the imagination or re-enchantment of other possible futures. Looking at ourselves through the eyes of others, human and non-human creatures, or through our relationships with them gives us new perspectives. For the past sixty years, what many books, whether they focus on animals, nature in general or environmental justice, have been demonstrating is a human need to reconnect with nature and, perhaps, to find in indigenous cultures, in landscapes, or in animals an answer to our ever-growing fears about ecology in contemporary societies. The natural world has been given a renewed role in literature: it helps us expand our vision by moving away from a focus on humans to re-enchant our relationship with the world.

As the reader will understand throughout the chapters to come, this re-enchantment takes place via a re-establishment of an affective bond expressed by the author and revealed by ecocritical and ecopoetical analysis, for as Bénédicte Meillon states in the introduction to *Lieux d'Enchantements*:

> As the American political scientist Jane Bennett points out in her study on the enchantment of modern life, the vision of a disenchanted world tends to hinder our emotional attachment to the world. Yet, as Bennett further demonstrates, the contemporary world, whether human or not, natural or artificial, still offers precious sources of enchantment; above all, experiencing moments of rapture remains essential to give meaning and ethical guidance to our being-in-the-world. (Meillon 4)

The images with affective resonance common to the works cited above as well as to those studied by the contributors in this book allow us to be more inclined to experience an empathic relationship with the other, human or non-human. As Moira Gatens explains in *Imaginary Bodies: Ethics, Power and Corporeality*, we cannot change our perception of things with a simple contradiction or rebuttal; affect is an essential ingredient of change. By first allowing themselves to feel enchanted by their personal reading and by sharing their analysis of how this re-enchantment is put to work, the contributors here « reintegrate human existence and the experience of the natural world along emotional and affective lines; humans thus become part of a community that includes their ecosystem instead of discrete entities who presume the non-human environment has only mechanical or pragmatic value. » (Magee 66)

We hope to show that the studies presented here, in addition to analyzing artistic processes that re-enchant the world, push us to renew our perception of it, to question the position of superior beings in which human beings have locked themselves. Although they deal with varied and sometimes distant subjects, what connects the present analyses is their capacity to renew, even reinvent, the way we look at the world and the way we tell human and natural history in an attempt to make it into a single interwoven narrative from which we could, perhaps, draw the energy to create a new world because

> With the Earth and its creatures in a state of desperate need, dwindling natural resources, political upheavals, and absent human and animal rights, the pertinent information a reader can glean from stories of both destruction and hope can make the difference between saving the world or choosing to let it fall further into chaos and decay. (Hogan xvii)

We, as editors, are proud to present a volume of highly diverse study subjects, ranging from graphic novels to films, from poems to Pope Francis's encyclical *Laudato Si*. Likewise, they encompass vast territories, whether real or imaginary: from North America to the Polynesian islands, from Europe to Japan, from India to 'Middle Earth.' Despite this variety, all converge into a sense of renewed wonder and weave a global worldwide narrative of interspecies respect. As their analyses engage a conversation, they unveil the paramount imprint of the natural world upon the imaginary. Discourses and stories thus connect: they echo each other and intertwine as weft and warp to give voice to new worlds. We contend that this polyphonic fabric of words and images braided into a meaningful entanglement of sensory experiences and intellectual reflection offers the reader a rare opportunity to immerse into the subtle network of reciprocity that links humankind to the other-than-human realm.

We have divided our volume into four parts, according to the main theme upheld by the contributors, as some elect to focus on the ecopoetics of specific landscape features while others adopt a broader perspective on a renewed being-to-the-world: We will first cast a postcolonial gaze upon nature, and analyze the close link indigenous literature develops between storytelling and storyweaving; We will then direct our attention on wild and reorganized gardens: where the poiesis of nature over the mind can fully be experimented; Thirdly, we will pinpoint on deceptive emptiness and lively deserts and how these apparent hostile environments can help reweave our sense of place; And finally, we will explore dwellings of enchantment and how the studies of these wondrous territories can help infuse a profound ecopoetics of reenchantment. Last but not least, we choose to complete the volume with a writer's corner to bridge the divide between academic scrutiny and artistic practice.

In our first section, we pay close attention to the entangled agencies of the human and the more-than-human realm on the contested territory of colonial settlements. From the many islands, rivers, and forests, Native voices rise in a surge of auto-representation and fully reinvest the richness of their cosmogonies, thus supplementing the vibrant descriptions of their land with a political subtext.

In the first chapter, Chloé Angué presents a highlighting analysis of the place of onirism in the writing of nature by Polynesian authors. Dwelling on Pierre Brunel and Véronique Gély's protocols, she fully embraces the distinctive sense of place that the Polynesian myths and literary images implement while setting the bases of a prolific post-colonial imaginary. Inspired by their love for the "mother land," Tahitian writers and thinkers subtly point out the source of their knowledge and inspiration, the island ecosystems, to underline the wide discrepancies imposed by colonialism through the notion of land ownership. Retrieving a sense of the sacred, modern Polynesian artists choose to reconcile antagonist frameworks into a telling syncretism of form and content. In this chapter, Angué engages in this revivified imaginary of the island to posit an everlasting bond between nature and the people who have actively inhabited it for centuries, passing on ancestral knowledge for it to be re-dreamed by each new generation. She aptly argues that the re-enchantment of the Earth as operated by Indigenous writers is con-substantial to a political statement reclaiming congruence in a stolen territory.

In the next chapter, Asis De further explores the meanders of island ecopoetics when applied to a contrastive cultural context: the Andaman Islands in India, such as depicted by Pankaj Sekhsaria's *The Last Wave*. Staging the struggle of two conservationists for the preservation of an endemic ecosphere, this Indian Anglophone novel nevertheless questions the naive assumptions of both characters regarding the assigned place of an Indian tribe confronted with encroaching modernity. De aptly argues that an ecological consciousness infusing fiction not only re-enchants the environment but also re-enchants the reader as the access to interpolated narratives gives way to an array of meaningful connections to the world. Tapping into material ecocriticism, De raises Sekhsaria's novel to the rank of a living text where natural and cultural stories engage in a conversation aiming at decentering the locus of enunciation, meanwhile casting a new light on the moral responsibility as well as the necessity to sustain distinctive habitats.

With Caroline Durand-Rous, we follow the water-driven initiatory journey of a contemporary young woman from the Cree nation along the tricky meanders of the rivers and lakes that shape the distinctive landscape of the Canadian Shield. Durand-Rous exposes how, in Joseph Boyden's novel *Through Black Spruce*, natural elements give essential meaning to the humans' apparently erratic wanderings by inscribing their deeds and accomplishments into the greater mythical narrative of creation. Caroline Durand-Rous thoroughly demonstrates how Annie, the protagonist, must experience a symbolic death leading to her being spiritually reborn, as she engages in a challenging quest to recover her missing sister. This relevant discussion highlights how the elemental plasticity of water reveals the magical value of the original landscape and connects tribal memories with personal memories, eventually leading the protagonists to self-reinvention. By means of a detailed analysis, drawing on literary critique and anthropology, Durand-Rous skillfully illustrates how the novel unfolds as a tale of self-empowerment since the ordeals encountered along the real and magical waters at work finally offer the characters congruence in a territory still bearing the scars of colonial history. Caroline Durand-Rous offers a detailed study of the game of correspondences lying at the core of this Native novel.

Concluding this section, Maxime Petit pays close attention to the way images word out the land and investigates how Western eurocentered documentaries have imposed a filmic syntax on the rendering of Native lands on screen that contemporary Native filmmakers enduringly contribute to deconstructing. As he reminds us in his introduction, nature undeniably occupies a central place in Native storytelling, whether in ethnographic documents meant to depict Native societies, or in autochthonous traditional myths and legends. However, both sources offer a highly contrasted vision of what land stands for. This cultural discrepancy is likewise incontestably present in documentary filmmaking, as Maxime Petit notices. In that regard, Petit's chapter closely examines Alanis Obomsawin's documentary about the Oka crisis entitled *Kanehsatake: 270 Years of Resistance*. Whereas the early Euro-American filmmakers' Bible-inspired vision of a pristine wilderness waiting to be tamed has long prevailed, Obomsawin's film firmly reinstates Native grounds as the depositary space of Indigenous knowledge and "survivance," to draw on Chippewa scholar and novelist Gerald Vizenor's concept. Petit's analysis reveals the tenuous distinction between storytelling and mapmaking in Native cosmovisions. Meanwhile, it gives insight into the existing Mohawk kinship to nature as the nation's fate is assessed through the preservation of the pines in the Quebec town of Oka, in terms of a sacred and cyclical continuity of the relationship linking a specific environment and the people inhabiting it.

The essays in the next section are also concerned with a distinctive way of inhabiting nature as they tackle the issue of co-viability, in other words, the extent of an acceptable intervention of humans upon their surroundings and, in return, the scope of nature's influence upon the formation of the human mind. By contriving gardens as spaces of entangled agencies, the novels, and the movie hereby question the assigned limits supposedly separating humans from the rest of the natural world.

In the first chapter, Stephen Greenfield examines the intertwined vegetal and narrative mazes that traverse *The Lord of the Rings*, thus performing an essential ecocritical reading of the novel. Indeed, he informs Tolkien's repeated use of the Christian symbolism of the labyrinth as a means to engage in a quest to restore balance and heal nature. Expanding on the notion of "eco-labyrinticity," the chapter attributes the convoluted structure as the path toward the re-enchantment of a degraded landscape where the hobbits are led through three essential liminal stages by their interactions with magical trees.

Catherine Hoffmann invites the reader to delve into narratorial ecology as she studies the interaction between textual economy and ecology in Dermot Healy's *Long Time No See*. Owing to the literary tradition of the pastoral and mindfully adopting the georgic mode, this Irish novel celebrates an acute sense of the land through the motif of the *hortus conclusus*, or walled garden. Hoffman's research exposes the literary devices through which the author allows the reworking of an enclosed space to transform into a condensed version of a wider territory of interactions. Due to the accuracy of the chosen vocabulary, and while eschewing literary ornamentation and focusing on verbs of action, Healy's prose offers the lifelike rendering of a thoroughly experienced countryside. Hoffmann's masterful demonstration emphasizes Healy's articulate writing of the subtle web of non-verbal communication with the other life forms as it smoothly weaves the warp of the description of everyday chores with the weft of the description of the enchanted surrounding nature.

The next chapter focuses on a threefold artistic reconstruction of wildness as David Latour explores Sean Penn's filming of Jon Krakauer's elaborated biography of Alexander McCandless from the latter's notebooks. Following McCandless's footsteps, *Into the Wild* portrays a highly subjective relationship with nature, where the latter proves appealing inasmuch as it stands as an antagonism to a rejected urban environment. Shooting the majestic American landscapes in bigger-than-life frameworks, Penn's camera provides a commentary on a doomed-to-fail personal quest based on an initial misunderstanding of wildness. David Latour scrutinizes the various filmic techniques employed by Penn to convey an emotional involvement with the main character as well as giving clues of his flawed subjective relationship with an idealized nature. He skillfully elaborates on McCandless's longing for fulfillment into a projection of wilderness first processed through Krakauer's words and further construed by Penn's lenses. Subsequently, the movie's climactic scene, the discovery of bus 102, and its surrounding area are shown as a clear echo to Thoreau's Walden Pond.

The third section focuses our attention on the incredible livelihood of so-called deserts. Far from complying with the assumed notion of barrenness, these environments, standing at the margins of human activities, call upon the visitor to get attuned to the profusion of beings and spirits animating the land, barely perceived but not far removed from the surface. By just willfully activating sentience, one can start acknowledging the material and spiritual vitality of these often-neglected places.

With Anne Cirella Urrutia's essay, we step into the fringes of urbanized environments where three graphic artists imagine a new being-to-the-world. Provided the reader relinquishes common assumptions such as the artificial dichotomy opposing cultural spaces to natural spaces, she will discover, even in the corners of disenchanted suburbanity, bright patches of re-enchanted wildness, as Cirella Urrutia astutely demonstrates. Drawing on Gaston Bachelard's notion of "felicitous homes," standing as reinvested and re-enchanted dwellings, and quoting Virilio's principle of dromology, or the fundamental role of the logic of speed in the human apprehension of space, Cirella Urrutia's analysis of two contemporary comic books, namely *Jeanne de la Zone* by Jacquet and Davodeau, and *Shenzhen* by Delisle, contributes to re-humanize cityscapes. Besides grounding the notion of "neighborhood" within the reality of a set of relationships between neighboring species (humans, pets, farm animals, vegetables...), she stresses the importance of this lively liminal space in constructing a new social identity within the margins. Through the graphic medium, both showing and telling, cartoonists Jacquet, Davodeau, and Delisle actively participate in raising an eco-consciousness in their young readers' minds.

In the next chapter, Peter Schulman invites us to decipher the artistic markers of a painful absence in contemporary landscapes. From the land that witnessed the American Civil War, the "acoustic shadows" still resonate in the collective unconscious. The seemingly empty battlefields amount to a rich palimpsestic land holding the multi-layered memory of a nation. Schulman contends that the deceptive void of present-day vacant lots hides fertile fields for the mind where geography firmly grounds distant history. Revealing the ghosts inhabiting these spaces, Southern artists such as photographer Mann and music band Granville Automatic give voice to the invisible specters, meanwhile performing a magical re-enchantment of places. Through the entanglement of the past and present perceptions of historical sites, they portray the ambivalent relationship humankind sustains with lived spaces.

In the last chapter, Adrian Tait proposes a thorough survey of British nature writing through the prism of road vagabondage. He thus demonstrates how, though initially endeavoring to roam empty and unpeopled dusty paths to observe a delusive static and passive natural world, the literary roamers eventually gain access to enlightenment through the immersive experience procured by stomping the ground and tuning one's corporeal rhythm to primitive natural rhythms. Tait's discerning study further underlines the steps leading the open road vagabonds from early naive wishful thinking to the actual recovery of a sense of wonder. Interestingly, although they engage in walking the British countryside to seek emptiness, thus construing nature as being to be devoid of the overwhelming amount of material objects contained by cities, the writers are soon confronted with an abundance of "animate things" to quote Jane Bennett. Looping back to the archetypal figure of the semi-god Pan, Tait addresses the underpinning sense of the sacred presiding over these personal encounters with non-human and more-than-human realms: a significant embodied experience of nature's wild and disruptive energies.

The last academic section of our volume focuses more specifically on the notion of an ecopoetics of re-enchantment through in-depth analyses of works ranging from Montbiot's *Feral,* Gretel Ehrlich to Pope Francis' encyclical *Laudato Si',* among others. Drawing on the interconnectedness of all things, this section further emphasizes the importance of a re-enchantment of our everyday lives and ordinary affects, essential tools in overcoming personal trauma or self-centeredness—evils our contemporary world has to face on a daily basis, and which have an impact on our ecological awareness and capacity for resilience and reactivity. Thus addressing the broad notion of an "alienation from place" and offering an analysis of how artists use an ecopoetics of re-enchantment to counter this woe, this last section offers to further rethink the human position within the whole of environmental creation, consequently dispelling "the illusion that we who speak and write are not part of nature, not part of each other" to quote Susan Griffin's article "Split Culture."[2]

Adrian Tait offers readings of New Nature writers Kathleen Jamie, Jay Griffiths, and George Monbiot's prose ecopoetics. He highlights how, resorting to different strategies and styles, the three writers take part in an effort "to re-wild—even re-enchant—our perspective on the earth." Tait shows how Jamie's ecopoetics takes issue with the term "nature"—"a problematic externalization of relationships that, in fact, constitute our very existence." He then zooms in on Monbiot's work on the notion of ferality. Finally, he turns to Griffiths' writing which at times embraces the viewpoint of indigenous communities and questions the opposition between nature and culture characterizing much Western thinking.

Leaping through time and space, the next chapter by Wes Berry explores notions of trauma and healing in Gretel Ehrlich's prose ecopoetics. Berry calls attention to the ways in which trauma can alienate one from both her body and the landscape she inhabits. Starting from memoirs that deal with the experience of trauma (Sue William Silverman, Terry Tempest Williams, or Philip Lee Williams), Berry then shifts his attention to Ehrlich's *A Match to the Heart*, sifting the text for signs of how "the body as bioregion" (Deborah Slicer) finds expression. Berry's investigation tackles generic issues, together with poetic, philosophical, and ecopsychological ones. As he demonstrates, such cross-disciplinary "works of nonfiction blend ecological science, knowledge of western medicine, and devotional language to show how particular dwellings are conducive to healing." Taking us along Ehrlich's restless journey as she suffers a serious case of post-traumatic alienation from place and body, Berry leads us in her tracks to discover the language of the landscape that co-composes a reenchanted ecopoetics of healing and belonging. As he argues, "employing some tricky poetic acrobatics in reversals of conventional landscape metaphors, Gretel Ehrlich in her ecological-medical memoir [...] explores how getting struck by lightning takes her on a journey onto the 'organscape' of her body—an enchanted dwelling intimately dependent on external landscapes for her wellbeing."

George Piggford's chapter then dwells on the evolutions of a Catholic worldview. His contribution openly espouses the theology of Teilhard de Chardin, Francis of Assisi, and, more recently, of Pope Francis—as exposed in his 2015 encyclical *Laudato Si'*—via a reading of Flannery O'Connor's short story "A View of the World." It gives a mythopoeic perspective onto the short story genre, which, in the wake of James Joyce's secular conception of art, has often been associated with secular epiphanies to be revealed by art—the fleeting moment of an existential revelation of some immanent meaning, truth, or radiance having become central to many short stories. Piggford offers here not a secular but a religious reading of the epiphany found in O'Connor's dark short story, grasped via exegesis of its mystical dimension and its potentially Christian imagery of the woods. This chapter stands out from the new materialist, ecopsychological, and sympoietic, approaches that prevail in this book on ecopoetics of reenchantment, as it dovetails with a (re) divinization of the world that some contributors to this volume may find contentious. Nevertheless, the chapter is important for presenting a view radically different from the other chapters. Piggford's reading of O'Connor's story meanwhile offers a form of reconciliation between the Christian theology it embraces and the ecofeminist spiritualities and myths it reaches out to. Moreover, it follows behind works such as John Baird Callicot's, bringing to the fore the dynamic evolution of our reading of myths, and the present potential of the Christian tradition when it comes to regenerating ecological ethics of care for the Earth. Such ethics are here derived from concepts of an "integral ecology," of divine "indwelling" and of a "eucharistic mysticism" that Piggford finds in Flannery O'Connor's ecopoetics. Piggford's contribution is welcome in this section as it indicates a healing incentive from within the Catholic church to counter the pathological alienation of humans from nature that has come from literal interpretations of the Old Testament— an influential, cultural phenomenon that has most famously been exposed by ecofeminists and by the ecocritic Lynn White Junior. Piggford self-consciously strays from the anthropocentric, patriarchal values that the Catholic church has often seemed to promote. Relying on Paula Gunn Allen's ecofeminist and indigenous theology, Piggford's chapter touches upon syncretic mythopoeia. In many ways, Piggford's analysis points to the avant-garde, ecofeminist strains already present in O'Connor's story. Despite the fundamental rift that still separates secular from religious ontologies and interpretations of stories, the different attitudes to the world here colliding over ecological concerns might pave new ways for what Paula Gunn Allen calls "walking in beauty" (Allen and Anderson 2001, xi—xii). It sparks new thoughts reaching across such divides so that, beyond our adherence to secular or religious views and discourses, to indigenous or European cultures, we may at least agree on cultivating "a habit of attention," and on treading the earth softly as we walk forward in the Anthropocene.

To conclude this section with yet another approach of the interlacing of the visible and the invisible in the flesh of the world, Keiko Takioto Miller loops back to phenomenological considerations derived from Heidegger and Merleau-Ponty, while focusing on the short haiku form. Haiku is here viewed as a quintessential form of ecopoetry. Like many in this volume, this last chapter carries syncretic resonances, oscillating between zen tenets and philosophy, references to Mother Earth, and indigenous worldviews. In its extreme shortness, the haiku studied here by Takioto Miller bears some resemblance to the short story genre, with its brevity and its implicit, poetic strategies of meaning. Focusing on the seventeenth-century Japanese poet Matsuo Basho, Takiato Miller contends that "truth shown in brevity is sufficient unto itself. In this sense," she goes on, "haiku came to serve as a transient literary vehicle, which offers its beholder to ride mindfully on the felt tension between nature and culture." Takiato Miller's language itself is ecopoetic, as she mindfully strives for an expressiveness that uses English—at times French—to word Japanese concepts and relate them to Western ones. It also shuttles back and forth between European and Asian metaphysics, between ancient thought-systems and contemporary ones, such as Tim Ingold's or David Abram's. Takiato Miller's contribution invites us to a meditative reading, as it threads scholarship with the creative writing of "an imaginative thought experiment [...] to illustrate the process of how language, as a dynamic nature-cultural phenomenon, may have emerged." It goes for a poetic and material approach of language as a corporeal activity taking place via our incorporation into the world—a body-mind embeddedness that remains at the heart of our humanity, despite "our ancestor's exponential distancing, or 'écartement,' from having formerly been immersed in nature." The language of haiku, she argues, emerges from a pre-reflexive experience of our dwelling within the world.

To complete the multifaceted approach developed in this book, we have made way for a "Writer's Corner" that offers poems by David Lloyd. These invite us to a direct, unmediated experience of ecopoetry that will resonate with many of the analyses collected in the preceding chapters. They come as precious gifts from an ecopoet who took part in the June 2016 Perpignan conference, where his work was read and discussed. They remind us of the necessity to make room for the writing and reading of poetry itself within our academic practices, in the midst of the distanced attitudes toward literature that many critics simultaneously strive for. They open the door to a moment of concrete re-enchantment and offer a corporeal, sensuous dwelling to temporarily put at rest our predominantly logos-driven, academic relationship to language and to the world.

Notes

[1] To name but a few, *Uncle Tom's Cabin, Black Beauty,* and *The Jungle* have had such an impact on their contemporary society that some claim; that they have changed the world.
[2] This and the following four paragraphs of our introduction were written by Bénédicte Meillon, as this last part and the writers' corner were originally meant to be included in the book *Dwellings of Enchantment: Writing and Reenchanting the Earth,* which she edited for Rowman and Littlefield. The book finally being over the word limit for R&L's ETAP series, Bénédicte Meillon had to trim down the volume she had initially put together. This last section, the corresponding chapters and the writer's corner were thus edited by her and transferred to this book, which is the third to stem from the June 2016 conference on Dwellings of Enchantment.

Works cited

Allen, Paula Gunn and Carolyn Dunn Anderson. *Hozho: Walking in Beauty: Short Stories by American Indian Writers.* New-York: McGraw-Hill, 2001, xi–xii.

Bennett, Barbara. *Scheherazade's Daughters: The Importance of Storytelling in Ecofeminist Change.* New York: Peter Lang Publishing, 2012.

Hogan, Linda. "Preface." *International Perspectives in Feminist Ecocriticism,* edited by Estok Gaard and Serpil Oppermann, New York: Routledge, 2013.

Love, Glen A. "Et in Arcadia Ego: Pastoral Theory Meets Ecocriticism." *Western American Literature,* Vol. 27, n° 3, 1992, pp. 196–197. As quoted in Murphy Patrick D. Farther Afield in the *Study of Nature Oriented Literature.* Charlottesville: University Press of Virginia, 2000, pp. 15–16.

Magee, Richard M. "Reintegrating Human and Nature." *Feminist Ecocriticism: Environment, Women, and Literature*, edited by Vakoch, Lanham: Lexington Books, 2012, pp. 65–75.

Meillon, Bénédicte and Margot Lauwers, eds. *Lieux d'enchantement : approches écocritiques et écopoét(h)iques des liens entre humains et non-humains.* Crossways Journal, n° 2 (1), 2018, p. 4.

Part I.
A Postcolonial Gaze upon Nature: Storytelling and Storyweaving

Chapter 1

The Polynesian Dream: Biblical and Ancestral Myths Re-enchanting the Postcolonial Imaginary of the Islands

Chloé Angué

University Paris Ouest Nanterre La Défense, France

Abstract: In *Mapping the Sacred*, Gareth Griffiths wrote: "there is a clear need to address, in the widest possible way [...] the many issues raised at the intersections of postcolonialism, geography and the sacred." In Polynesia, "the sacred" is not only based on pre-evangelical cultures; it also draws from Biblical sources and images; both, as well as their creolized forms, play an important part in contemporary literary works. I base this chapter on the conclusions of a broad study of the literary images of the Polynesian Islands and especially on how myths compose these representations: Western travellers created some of them and some, today, express how Polynesian writers see their own territory. My purpose is to survey the contemporary literary imaginary of the Polynesian islands, to show how these representations are re-enchanted through the rewriting of myths and cultural concepts.

Keywords: Polynesian imaginaries, biblical myths, Polynesian myths, dream, island, ocean

***

"What are the roles of myth when fiction and non-fiction draw from these other forms of discourse about the world? What impact does ecopoetics have on politics? And what is the place of oneirism in the writing of nature?" Raised during the 2016 international conference on ecopoetics in Perpignan, these questions deeply resonate with Polynesian postcolonial literature.

Located in the middle of the Pacific Ocean, Polynesia covers 14 million square kilometres, between New Zealand Aotearoa, Hawai'i, and Easter Island Rapa Nuit. It represents an immense triangle whose surface is larger than Europe. It includes seventeen territories like Samoa and French Polynesia, territories that are independent, in association with another state or sovereign.

In 1756, French scientist Charles de Brosses created the name "Polynésie" which based the identification of this territory on the plurality of islands it is composed of. The term was used again in 1832 by the explorer Jules-Sébastien César Dumont d'Urville, who distinguished this area from Melanesia and Micronesia based on more racial criteria than geographical: he immediately presented the Polynesian archipelagos as more civilized and more welcoming. Nowadays, this tri-partition is obviously challenged and with reason. Nevertheless, such a division enabled many anthropologists to reveal a common ground of lifestyles and cultures[1] current in Oriental Pacific islands. Of course, each archipelago has its own History depending on the eras when it was first populated, when the European explorers settled there and when it was then evangelized and colonized.

Europeans "discovered" New-Zealand in 1642 with Abel Tasman, a Dutch sailor. English explorers Samuel Wallis and James Cook, as well as French Louis Antoine de Bougainville, reached Tahiti and New Zealand between 1767 and 1769. In most islands, many Natives were killed or died from the consequences of these encounters. The explorers were soon followed by many missionaries: the London Missionary Society sent its first emissaries to Tahiti in March 1797 and to Samoa in 1830, while the Anglican Church Missionary Society settled in New Zealand in 1814. "Pagan" cults had to be rapidly forbidden, and the Bible was translated into vernacular languages which were written for the first time. Polynesian dialects were thus molded by the missionaries and shaped by Christian texts. After the missionaries came the settlers and officials of the colonial authorities. In 1840, most Māori tribe chiefs signed the Treaty of Waitangi, which marked the beginning of colonization, while from 1842 to 1901, France took possession of all Polynesian archipelagos, which were called French Polynesia in 1957. If New Zealand's statute evolved within the Common Wealth since the middle of the twentieth century, Hawaii and French Polynesia live under Washington's and Paris' administrations. Thus, except in independent Tonga and Western Samoa, Islanders of the Polynesian Triangle are not fully ruling their countries. According to Jean-Marc Moura, it is thus necessary to create a distinction between "postcolonial" literatures from countries that did not undergo a decolonization process, and "post-colonial" literatures from independent countries where artists describe the life that comes after this process.

In the afterword of *Mapping the Sacred, Religion, Geography and Postcolonial Literatures*, Gareth Griffiths wrote:

> Whatever the differences between the locations of the various spaces
> colonialism created and still creates—and they are clearly many and
> diverse—and, however powerfully these spaces are being overwritten
> and occluded by the emerging forces of a global system, there is a clear
> need to address, in the widest possible way [...] the many issues raised
> at the intersections of postcolonialism, geography and the sacred.
> (Griffiths 460)

In Polynesia, "the sacred" is not only based on pre-evangelical cultures; it
also draws from Biblical sources and images that play an important part in the
contemporary imagination, a part often studied by Frédéric Angleviel, Alain
Babadzan, Cleve Barlow, James Belich, Bronwyn Elsmore, Yannick Fer, Alistair
Fox, John Garrett, Georges-Goulven Le Cam, Bruno Saura, James Trevor...I
based this chapter on their work and the conclusions of a broad study of the
literary images of the Polynesian Islands and especially on how myths
compose these representations: Western travelers created some of them, and
some today express how Polynesian writers see their own territory. It also
leans on Pierre Brunel's and Véronique Gély's work on "mythocritique" and
"mythopoétique," on literary history, postcolonial methods, and most of all,
Polynesian syncretism and concepts in order to survey the contemporary
literary imaginary of the Polynesian islands. Its purpose is to show how these
representations are re-enchanted through the rewriting of myths and cultural
concepts.

Literary Representations of the Islands: Images Drawn from Ancient Polynesian Mythical Sources

Despite the long-term Western influences, and just as writers from many
other postcolonial areas, authors born in the Polynesian Triangle mostly
perceive their own territories as their ancestors did. Oral literatures[2] and other
cultural forms have kept alive many of these representations, which now
inhabit poetry, novels, theatre, and essays written by Islanders. In 1991,
Chantal Spitz published the first novel written in French by a Polynesian
author. Now translated into English, *L'Île des rêves écrasés*, *The Island of
Shattered Dreams*, tells the story of a three-generation family trying to care for
its homeland. As a father, a political activist, or as an artist, each family
member fights with his own strength to prevent the French government from
holding nuclear tests on the ancestral land, which becomes the obvious
metonymy of the whole region. Repeated several times in the novel, the
ceremonial burying of a child's placenta becomes a scene emblematic of the
connection between men and land. This connection ensures the preservation
of both entities:

This is the union of man with the earth into which he thrusts his roots, the union of the earth with man who makes his food spring forth from her belly. For every birth, a bountiful tree is planted in the earth. With this gesture Maevarua carries the ancient soul of his people into the future.[3] (Spitz trans by Jean Anderson 2007 24)

Chantal Spitz mingles plant and human images in order to emphasize the union of men and their land thanks to the symbol of the roots. She describes a traditional custom based on identity, cultural and postcolonial principles, a custom that shows how the Polynesians' conquest of and settling on this land, and how its transmission to their descendants still constitute the foundation of many myths of the origins that feed contemporary literatures. This custom relies on precolonial traditions as well as a practice linked to the Cultural Renewal movement born in the 1960s throughout Polynesia: burying the placenta of the new-born. For a long time, it remained "a family custom, private and discreet[4]" (Saura 2008 161), but it now inhabits the contemporary imaginary of all Polynesians and often appears in literary works where it becomes a symbol of a deep attachment to the family land as well as of nativeness. In French Polynesia, it partakes of "a true theology of the placenta[5]" (Saura 2008 161) predominantly theorized by Duro Raapoto and studied by Bruno Saura, who notices that it is primarily based on a Christian syncretism: "the celebration of the love for their Mā'ohi 'mother/maternal land' that bore her children, little worthy shoots[6], and preserves their placentas, marks of their origins, deep in herself[7]" (Saura 2008 161). Bruno Saura, of course, reminds us that the burying of the placental only became a sign of nativeness since colonization; before that, it was a mark of family or tribal identity.

Each child of Spitz's novel is associated with a tree:

Maevarua opens up the belly of the bountiful mother, places [his son Tematua's] placenta gently within, putting a young tumu 'uru on top of it, then replaces the soil. The [...] tumu 'uru will nourish him through his life as a man[8] (Spitz trans. by Jean Anderson 2007 24)

Called "breadfruit" in English, the *'uru* is one of the most nutritious fruit trees since it can prevent a whole family from starving. It represents the identity that Maevarua wishes for his son: a strong father who can provide for his family and be useful to his community. In the following chapters, Tematua reveals himself up to the task and chooses a tree for his own son.

Just like Chantal Spitz, the Tahitian writer who lives in Australia, Célestine Hitiura Vaite knows how important the *'uru* can be since she wrote in 2004 in *Frangipani*:

> The tree Materena prefers, she confides to her unborn daughter, is by far the breadfruit, because it is beautiful with its large green leaves; strong too, and what's more, it is a tree that feeds–always there for you when money is low. (Vaite 10)

The shade and the food this tree can offer are precious in Tahiti and Materena embodies the folk wisdom the narrator values. In this respect, the heroine reminds her daughter how symbolic the trees can be to the Tahitian people:

> She points out the trees planted to mark the day a child comes into the world, the day someone we love goes away, a day people will talk about in one hundred years (Vaite 10).

Materena thus highlights how trees can preserve the memory of a family, and can root the memory of a person into the earth. In 1978 in the Māori novel *Mutuwhenua*, another tree is planted to mark the birth of a child: it serves both a memory and a poetic function since Patricia Grace's heroine, Linda, chooses to bury her son's placenta into the earth under a new tree put into the ground next to the family home she has left:

> Later, although it was summer, I went to plant a tree, a ti kouka, beside the other one, and shaded from the sun's ferocity by the old one that stood behind, guarded by the one that stood before (Grace 152).

With its thick trunk and many edible leaves, this palm tree is planted next to an older one that was put into the ground when the child's grandfather was born. Continuity is maintained since Linda's father passes his first name to his grandson, who was born the day he died; his tree also protects the young one within its own shade. Besides, the child will grow up on the ancestral land since Linda's mother will take care of him just like she takes care of both trees.

In Polynesia, many myths associate men with plants: in some, men turn into plants, and in others, they mingle or grow up together. J.-L. Picard highlights the postcolonial range of these images:

> We can understand that the wandering sailor would want to 'naturalize' himself and connect to a land. Plants express the deepest possessions of the land. [...] Peoples searching for an identity that

would enable them to resist Westernization like stories that define them in terms of belonging. They finally become a *mā'ohi*, part of the *fenua*, the real soil of their island and, once turned natural, may claim an identity, an *iho*, that the Other, the foreigner, cannot claim as his. (Picard 178)

Because of the broad nature of his role, the guardian thus becomes an essential figure of Polynesian literatures: while caring for a piece of land inherited from his family, he keeps his ancestors alive, he watches over the relationship young people have with their ancestral land, where their placenta is buried. He also makes sure the environmental balance of the area is maintained. As a place of memories, land cannot be soiled. In the Māori tradition, in New Zealand Aotearoa, guardians are called *kaitiaki,* and their function is to attend to the *mauri*, the spiritual force residing in all natural beings.

The insular identity is indeed defined mainly by the environment. Referring to Mā'ohi (native from French Polynesia) traditions and the concepts developed by Tahitian thinkers Duro Raapoto and Henri Hiro, Chantal Spitz wrote in 2011 in the literary journal *Littérama'ohi*:

> The Ta'ata tumu claims his identity by stating the names of the places that compose the space of his community: mountain, river or spring, plants, meeting place, headland or bay. He is then Ta'ata 'ai'a, territory man. He is not Tahitian but 'Ta'ata Tahiti': Tahiti Man. He does not live in Tahiti. He is Tahiti.[9]

Following this idea, each Polynesian's connection with his land goes beyond the simple notion of ownership: it has more to do with mutual belonging; the land belongs to the people and the people to the land. This is what Bruno Saura describes in *La Société tahitienne au miroir d'Israël*:

> In Tahiti, the native land is called âi'a, the sustaining land, a word that also refers to 'kinship' in all the Polynesian languages. Man thus belongs to the land as he belongs to a family; he belongs to it much more than it properly belongs to him. (Saura 2004 221)[10]

Deeply linked to postcolonial theory, the relationship with the land has critical political stakes, and Gareth Griffiths describes this dimension in *Mapping the Sacred*:

Land, and its extensions into theories of the constructions of space and place, has emerged [...] as one of the most important recent sites for articulating contemporary cultural concerns. (Griffiths 445)

Thanks to many literary images conveyed by Polynesian languages, literatures from the Triangle show how people consider their lands, how they live, and how much of their spirituality is connected to the family and tribal space. The environment thus unites everything at stake in the notion of postcolonial sovereignty:

> in keeping their feet on the ground that they tread, we might say, the peoples subjected to colonization are enabled again to hold their heads up high. (Griffiths 445)

Written by Keri Hulme, Patricia Grace, or Witi Ihimaera, many novels retrace the media, political, or even physical struggle some young tribe members embark on in order to protect their land rights. In 2003, Witi Ihimaera published *Sky Dancer*, a novel in which the heroes are two sisters, Hoki and Bella. The younger quickly explains the purpose of her life:

> The only reason Manu Valley still exists is because Hoki and I are descended from the original protectors, the women priests who set up our system of guardianship. It's a family thing (Ihimaera 2003 39).

Ignored or discredited by everyone outside their valley, authorities included, the sisters are highly considered by the other heroes since they end up practically saving the world. In this story that draws on magical realism, Witi Ihimaera thus follows the contemporary tendency of ecological thought, which values each local action, each sign of commitment. In 2001, in the "Afterword" of *Mapping the Sacred*, Gareth Griffiths wrote:

> Indigenous attitudes to the land are so deeply imbued with ideas of the sacral that they have proved a powerful ally in the reassertion of the urgent need to preserve and nurture the material environment (Griffiths 446).

Indeed, Polynesian authors insist on the sacred nature of the guardians' task, which often explains the romantic commitment of the young heroes. The environment thus has an essential spiritual range which is due, on the one hand, to divine manifestations told by the Ancients' mythologies. The demiurgic god is not at the origins of such feats; they were accomplished by gods or demi-gods that appeared later like Rū and Tafa'i who pulled up most islands from the ocean in Tahitian stories and like Māui who fished out the North Island of New Zealand Aotearoa explaining why it is called Te Ika a Maui (Māui's Fish). Only after these exploits that modeled the land were men (like Tāne in New Zealand) created by the same kind of gods, mainly from the female principal Papa. On the other hand, Polynesian land is sacred because it is connected to the ancestors and the worship of their memory: "everywhere, place names marked the links of tūpuna [ancestors] with the land." (Parsonson 171) It is thus crucial for people to keep respecting and celebrating the land, to preserve the "values guaranteeing a healthy balance between the human, environmental, social and spiritual spheres[11]" (Smith 118). Of course, Polynesian peoples are far from being the only ones to regard land as a sacred place. Miriam Kahn relates such a vision to the Apache thought, quoting Martin Ball:

> For indigenous peoples, interaction with the land is always defined by conceptions of the sacred, the spiritual, and the power of the land and the beings that live within and on it. (Ball 11)

Literary Representations of the Islands: Images Drawn from Today's Complex Polynesian Societies

Polynesians thus consider the land as sacred based on pre-Evangelical concepts. However, European travelers and Christian missionaries imported into these islands the powerful myth of the Garden of Eden, which also influenced the perception of the land. Used as a poetic image when explorers and traveler writers "discovered" archipelagos like Tahiti and Hawaii or emphasized as an argument in favor of colonization in New Zealand, the Western myth of the Polynesian Eden is finally reactivated as a powerful touristic advertising tool.

  However, if many native writers address this Western literary myth as a symbol of the empires' discourse and fantasies, they also rewrite it in their own forms, for their own purpose. Because of the importance of Protestant and Evangelical Churches in the whole Triangle and because these Churches played significant roles in the preservation of native languages and customs, the Old Testament is essential in Polynesian contemporary imaginary where it finely and inextricably blends with ancient beliefs, traditions, and myths. Amongst others, the Eden episode and especially the image of a bountiful and fragile garden has become a major Polynesian literary motive. Based on the second Creation narrative in the Old Testament, rewritings often respect most of the images offered by the Biblical text:

But there went up a mist from the earth, and watered the whole face of the ground. [...] And the LORD God planted a garden eastward in Eden; and there he put the man whom he had formed. And out of the ground made the LORD God to grow every tree that is pleasant to the sight, and good for food; the tree of life also in the midst of the garden, and the tree of knowledge of good and evil. And a river went out of Eden to water the garden. (Gn 2 6–10)

In English, most authors refer to the King James translation unless their religion favors another one. Crucial motives remain the fresh water that ensures the fertility and diversity of the vegetation, as well as the food provided by the garden; the beauty of the scenery and, of course, the trees that symbolize morality and eternal life. A few verses further, "God took the man, and put him into the garden of Eden to dress it and to keep it" (Gn 2 15). Polynesian authors thus use the beginning of Genesis 2 as a metaphor for their islands' delicate ecological balance.

In French Polynesia, Henri Hiro was one the first poets to publish his texts and became famous for his written work and his major role on the cultural scene. A theological student before becoming an environment and politic activist, he explains in an interview given around 1978:

Their Eden, the Westerners are still chasing it. But as for the natural Eden, it really exists. It is here, all around. [...] Yes it still exists. I am not talking about buildings, roads and concrete. I am thinking about the way Polynesians behave, about what you can see in their eyes.[12] (Pambrun 2010 228)

Despite the simple phrasing, the argument is complex since Henri Hiro rejects the Western myth of the Polynesian Eden, which he considers a colonial fantasy. Instead, he values the Māʻohi version of the Eden myth, a syncretic version that relies on ancestral ideas inherited by contemporary Islanders. In the same way, contemporary Polynesia writers create numerous characters involved in some of the various Christian churches active in these archipelagoes because they constitute an important part of the insular imaginary and the complex representations of the sacred. Such a phenomenon already presides over the evolution of Polynesian Christianity ever since the evangelization led by European missionaries. Based on his study of the religious practices in the French Polynesian archipelago "les Australes," Alain Babadzan presents the "birth of a tradition" that now consists of "a state of absolute cultural compromise" (Babadzan 34). He first studied the different elements and concepts that favored the evangelization of the Polynesians. He then showed that Christian concepts introduced by the missionaries evolved alongside the Māʻohi concepts on which the missionaries based their teachings. At the end of *Naissance d'une tradition*, Alain Babadzan establishes a definition of the Polynesian syncretism that presupposes two systems in absolute contradiction named A and B:

> Syncretism will however work on what prevents one to mistake A for B: it will work on their difference, their incompatibility, because its goal is not only to maintain their global opposition but also to abolish it. Syncretism will recreate a *new unity* precisely from these contradictions so much so that A and B are reconciled in what one might call a formed compromise. In no way does this mean that elements from A and from B are integrated as such, 'in the raw', into the new system of representations that was born of contact. (Babadzan 177)

Often applied to French Polynesia, this model Babadzan established for the Australes is thus a set of representations and religious activities with contradictions that are neither denied nor hidden and with cultural or political ramifications that constitute a crucial part of today's Polynesian imaginary.

> Even if Polynesianity lost a lot of ground to acculturation, it still goes on asserting itself and resisting this eruption, just like the reed in the fable. A compromise was established about this definition of the cultural-self that tries to maintain the equal balance between the ideal (missionary) definitions of the pagan Polynesianity and the Christian Polynesianity through the respective denials of each of those two fictions; the new identity that was rebuilt on this basis since conversion both turns its back on paganism and refuses to go *beyond* what has to be done in order to dissociate itself from paganism, once the minimal concessions were made. (Babadzan 252)

Christianity in French Polynesia is thus a "Christianization of paganism" as well as a "paganization of Christianity." Far from being the result of a simple blending, it instead partakes in a creolization process. The literary rewriting of myths, as offered by Henri Hiro, comes within the scope of one of the movements that inhabit postcolonialism, a movement based on concepts of hybridity and cultural syncretism defined by Homi K. Bhabha in 1994 in *The Location of Culture*:

> the need to think beyond narratives of originary and initial subjectivities and to focus on those moments or processes that are produced in the articulation of cultural differences. (Bhabha 5)

Homi K. Bhabha adds further:

> These 'in-between' spaces provide the terrain for elaborating strategies of selfhood—singular or communal—that initiate new signs of identity, and innovative sites of collaboration, and contestation, in the act of defining the idea of society itself. (5)

In these "in-between" spaces, the Polynesian re-appropriation of the Biblical myths can develop as a subversive and founding quest for identity.

After years of fighting French nuclear testing in the Tuamotu, Henri Hiro settles back on the island of Huahine, in a small secluded valley described by Jean-Marc Pambrun in his biography of Henri Hiro:

> He takes care of the land and harvests the fruits of his labour, goes fishing every day. [...] He has thus reached the new life he had fought so much for. He is a Māʻohi, free and independent![13] (Pambrun 2010 419)

There, Henri Hiro gave life to the principles he believed in and to the wishes he described in 1990 in the poem "E aha atu ara?" ("What will happen?") written in Tahitian:

> Te here o to ù âià [...]
> E, ìa vai ā, e ìa vai noa atu ā!
> Ei para haamaitaì i to ù âià tumu,
> Ìa ruperupe, e ìa hotu te huāai,
> No to ù nei âià. (Hiro 62–3)

> Oh love of my country [...]
> May it live and water my native land
> So that can flower in their swarm
> The children of this ground
> Children of my country.[14]

Based on a classic symbol of fresh water as a life-giving principle that fertilizes mother Earth, a crucial symbol in the Polynesian imaginary that carries the memory of the migrations across the salty Ocean, the water metaphor is more political than psychoanalytical. It reveals how the poet feels physical and spiritual love for his land and hopes to see young Islanders preserve it. In New Zealand literature, a very interesting rewriting of the Eden image appears in most of Witi Ihimaera's novels. Located at the center of a fictitious village, the common-house named Rongopai is a place of celebration. Built in 1888 to honor a hero of the Māori resistance to the Imperial army, the house has painted inner panels that represent the many hopes of a generation:

> The dream was of a new, brave, world, the new Eden where the kowhaiwhai[15], [the drawings] was embellished with new colours, where painted spirals and floral patterns provided a panacea for war and a prayer for peace (Ihimaera 1996 191).

Witi Ihimaera then concludes this description from the 1986 novel *The Matriarch*:

> Ah yes, Rongopai was a fantasy as well as a real world. It conjured up an Eden where the spirit and the flesh were integrated, where creatures of light and creatures of darkness lived coincidentally with man in the one, single, universe (Ihimaera 1996 192–3).

Based on connection and harmony, the paintings create a syncretic vision of an idealistic future for New Zealand. However, in 2004 Witi Ihimaera minimized the unrealistic nature of the picture and presented these panels as "statements of Maori surviving within the colonial world" (Ihimaera 1974, 176). Indeed, Rongopai was built to celebrate the memory of one of the Māori prophets, Te Kooti, who led a sovereignty movement during the Land Wars of the 1860s. The religious symbol of Rongopai is thus a political one since land issues partake of the creation of the movements led by the Māori prophets, as the New Zealand historian Jean E. Rosenfeld explained it:

> all of the religious renewal movements of the Māori prophets were, in a fundamental sense, attempts to re-establish the vigorous 'world of light', te ao marama, by bridging the discontinuity between te ao tawhito, when land and people were connected, and te ao hou, when the people became alienated from the land. (Rosenfeld 37)

In order to distinguish the old world that was built on a form of balance between beings and environment from the modern world where beings were no longer connected to the land, Jean E. Rosenfeld uses the Māori concepts of *te ao mārama*[16] and *te ao tawhito*, the ancient world that can remind us of the Polynesian Eden painted by Māori and Tahitian writers. Just like in Henri Hiro's poetics, Eden is thus a political dream in Māori literatures, a myth meant to give hope to those still struggling for sovereignty on their own lands.

Dreaming the Island: A Political Statement

Thanks to such a complex imaginary—pre-Christian and biblical—insular writers create a new ideal pattern of what Polynesian archipelagoes may be. Since it is not only supposed to be the counter-model of today's societies, this pattern is not a utopia. It is rather a eu-topia, a place of happiness[17] (Fortunati 22). Poetics from the Triangle thus falls within the scope of many postcolonial literatures studied by Bill Ashcroft, Gareth Griffiths and Helen Tiffin, who wrote in *The Empire Writes Back*:

> Given that, for the environment no less than for human communities, a return to a pre-colonial primitive state is impossible, some post-colonial writers and critics have begun to explore the garden (and the Western myth of the Garden) as offering newly ambivalent versions of the trope of loss and possibility. The re-constituted and post-Biblical Garden thus becomes a space redolent of possibility for the human/ animal/environmental community. (Ashcroft, Griffiths, and Tiffin 214)

The title of Chantal Spitz's first novel is profoundly disenchanted: *The Island of Shattered Dreams*. However, the young hero, Tetiare, addresses her own pessimism and urges the Mā'ohi to do as well:

> Child, son of my people,
> I no longer know the dreams of our ancestors,
> Child, son of my people,
> Dream new dreams for your children,
> The new children of our people.[18] (Spitz trans. by J. Anderson 2007 138)

Even if most of the ancestral knowledge has been forgotten, the young woman believes that they can create new knowledge and forge new dreams without denying their Islander identity or dropping out of modernity's course. Selected in this poetic section by Chantal Spitz, the substantive "dream" is not isolated in Polynesian literatures where the word appears constantly. To express their vision of the future, authors from the Triangle use it while embracing both its idealistic and unrealistic dimensions. In his 1991 novel *Ola*, Samoan writer Albert Wendt insists on the spiritual loss the Polynesians have suffered since evangelization. Ola's father is a figure of the wise old man who regrets the past communion:

> Once all was a circle, a sacred circle, a unity of tree, bird, earth, fire, air, water, man, rock, atua[19], aitu[20]. All was blessed with mana. Together,

dreaming, giving meaning to one another [...] I know, yes, this person
knows, that he is what he has lost. (Wendt 1995 216)

The new apparition of the term "lost" discreetly reminds the reader of the
Fall and the biblical imaginary while the verb "to dream" is used to show that
the old world was a complex structure in which each element played a role in
maintaining a harmony that is now broken. A Māori professor of Education
and Indigenous studies, Linda Tuhiwai Smith, explains in *Decolonizing
Methodologies*:

> One of the strategies which indigenous peoples have employed
> effectively to bind people together politically is a strategy which asks
> that people imagine a future, that they rise above present day
> situations which are generally depressing, dream of a new dream and
> set a new vision. (Tuhiwai Smith 152)

This is the kind of strategy Henri Hiro, Chantal Spitz and Witi Ihimaera
develop in their literary creations, where dreaming the island to be is truly a
political statement. The latter thus build their stories on characters ready to
engage in political fights that are both individual—when they decide to enter
university, become a member of Parliament, or defend the rights of young gay
Māori—and collective since numerous heroes become leaders of cultural
renewal movements, of activist groups engaged in preserving the natural and
architectural heritage.

About the dream as a symbol of demanding hope more than of blind
idealism, the Tahitian researcher Stéphanie Ariirau-Richard then explains:

> The space of the dream seems inescapable in Polynesian literatures. This
> "tri-dimensional space" of the Polynesian writing (oneiric, geographic,
> and historical) is not really limited; it is not strict.[21] (Ariirau-Richard 94)

Indeed, it gives Polynesian artists a broad creating spectrum that stimulates
their political, literary, and poetic imagination. In 2003, the Mā'ohi
anthropologist and writer Jean-Marc Pambrun took part in a conference
celebrating the centenary of Paul Gauguin's death in Tahiti. On this occasion,
he urged his fellow citizens to get rid of the Western myth of the Polynesian
Eden, to go beyond this simplistic image in order to build with reason and
passion the world they should dream of as Islanders of the twenty-first
century:

In order to make it efficient, we have to match the collective dream with the reality of a people and consider our own lives like an ephemeral and yet glorious part of Nature.[22]

Just like Chantal Spitz, Jean-Marc Pambrun does not consider the future without mingling natural and cultural concerns: both need to evolve in harmony because of the deep link that unites the Polynesians described or dreamt here by Pambrun to their insular environment. In his representation, nature is indeed perceived through a complex imaginary that binds many myths—like the apparition of the world through the figure of Ta'aroa, the apparition of islands fished from the sea, or migration myths that set the Ancient's exploit into contemporary imaginary—and creates a sacralized relationship to the island and the ocean. Only a reader who would embrace this vision could understand this aspect of Polynesian literatures and, more generally, postcolonial literatures, as Gareth Griffiths explains:

In this way, we might both keep our feet on the ground and lift our heads from time to time to breathe a purer and transformed air in which the numinous forces of specific locations could have full play. (Griffiths 456)

Setting aside the pronoun "we" that seems to unite everyone in a blurry identity, Griffiths raises an important point made in 1986 by Chandra Talpade Mohanty, who studies feminism and also offers crucial methodological tools to postcolonial studies: writers from "specific locations" have their own concepts to describe the "numinous forces" that inhabit their imaginary.

These arguments are not against generalization as much as they are for careful, historically specific generalizations responsive to complex realities. (Talpade Mohanty 77)

In Polynesia, "complex realities" include a rich imaginary forged throughout the first migrations that led the Polynesians to the various archipelagoes they now inhabit but also the Biblical imaginary imported by the missionaries, its adaptations in each island and, of course, an immense number of ideas that travel around our globalized world.

Re-Enchanting the Present: Re-Imagining the Island

However, the eu-topian metaphor should not lead to believe that a model where land and its protection would be at the center of postcolonial claims model is only to be built in the future. It is to be found today since it represents a vision, a way to see the world and live in one's environment.

Many artists thus ask themselves about time and how to preserve and renew the link that connects them to their land. They also encourage anyone to re-enact symbolically the exploits of the gods or heroes who 'created' the Polynesian universe. The notion of creativity inspired by tradition but constantly renewed is thus crucial in their works. In 2003, Samoan writer Albert Wendt published his famous novel *The Mango's Kiss*, which tells the story of a three-generation family who struggles to find its way in a modern world. Despite the many challenges they are facing, the narrator explains:

> They knew already what the ideal life and society were; the aim was to maintain and balance that unity that their ancestors had created (Wendt 2003 200).

To maintain and balance the ancestral ways is actually to recreate a way of life, an economic system that would endanger neither the ecospheres nor the mutual exchanges with the environment. That is why the Ancients' economy based on measure and local activities is presented as a possible example. To Albert Wendt, each generation needs to both preserve and recreate its inheritance. Linked to the motive of the spiral that is a common representation of time in Polynesia, this double movement was already celebrated in 1994 by the great Tongan thinker Epeli Hau'ofa in his essay "Pasts to Remember," where he writes about the spiral:

> We could [...] formulate a benign philosophy that would help us pay greater reverence and respect to our natural environment than we do today. [...] We do not own the land, we only look after it. (Hau'ofa 2000 72)

Each Islander is a guardian who must ensure that his territory is neither forgotten nor sacrificed. Epeli Hau'ofa develops his thought when he presents the work he realized with the Oceania Centre for Arts and Culture that was created at the heart of the University of the Pacific, at the campus of Suva in Fiji. He explains what the ambition of the academic team and the students was:

> [...] to tie the arts to the most urgent need for protecting our oceanic environment: the sea and the islands. This should enable us to remain true to the tenets of our communities and to contribute significantly to the most important global environmental agenda: the protection of the ozone layer, the forests, and the oceans, for the continuity of life on earth. (Hau'ofa 2003 87)

Of course, this philosophy is to be applied to all Oceanian arts, for the department must be an inspiration to all artists and creators who care about their territory.

Linda Tuhiwai Smith shares this point of view and emphasizes what a rich model it could be for the postcolonial peoples who are struggling with their relationship to their environment and eventually a model to the Western countries who have forgotten how men need to be connected to their land through their culture:

> Indigenous peoples offer genuine alternatives to the current dominant form of development. Indigenous peoples have philosophies which connect humans to the environment and to each other and which generate principles for living a life which is sustainable, respectful and possible. (Tuhiwai Smith 105)

It is this same spiral movement based on circularity and progression that the Tahitian author Jean-Marc Pambrun depicts in 2010 in his opening speech for the tenth conference of the International Pacific Art Association. He argues that just like everyday life, artistic creation is deeply rooted in the Pacific Ocean and its islands:

> Today, we do not only have to preserve the objects of the past, but we also need to keep on creating them and investing them of the spirit of Ta'aroa.[23]

In Polynesian oral literatures, Ta'aroa is the god who organized the elements and the world as we know it. In 1928 Teuira Henry published stories collected by missionaries who interviewed Polynesians to preserve this cultural heritage. One of the most famous is the "Song of Creation," which begins with the presentation of Ta'aroa:

> O Ta'aroa te tupuna o te mau atua ato'a ; na'na te mau mea ato'a i hamani. Mai tahito a iuiu mai o Ta'aroa nui, Tahi-tumu.
>
> Na Ta'aroa iho Ta'aroa i tupua toivi noa ; oia iho to'na metua, aore to'na metua tane, aore metua vahine.
>
> Ta'aroa (The-unique-one) was the ancestor of all the gods; he made everything. From time immemorial was the great Ta'aroa, Tahi-tumu (The-origin). Ta'aroa developed himself in solitude; he was his own parent, having no father or mother. (Henry 336)

In this version, Ta'aroa uses the shell he appeared in to forge the world: Rumia is an image peculiar to this Tahitian story, and it strongly marks the artists' imaginary. Ta'aroa finally leaves his shell, and calls around, but he cannot find anyone. He goes back into Rumia and goes out again, determined to modify his environment:

> Ua rave ihora 'oia i taua pa'a hou no'na ra ei tumu nui no te ao nei ei papa fenua e ei repo no te fenua. E o taua pa'a o Rumia ra, i vetevete hia i mutaaiho ra, o to'na ia fare, te apu o te ra'i atua, o te rai piri ia, o te fa'aati i te ao i tupu ra.

> And he took his new shell for the great foundation of the world, for stratum rock and for soil for the world. And the shell, Rumia, that he opened first, became his house, the dome of the gods' sky, which was a confined sky, enclosing the world then forming. (Henry 337)

Ta'aroa does not create the world out of nothing: he uses everything he has in order to transform it into a place all living things can grow. Ta'aroa stands as the symbol of the "sacred" Gareth Griffiths described, the symbol of the primeval creation, of the first principle uniting all living things with their environment. Pambrun thus urges his fellow artists to seek a constantly renewed creativity, to re-enchant the present with the power of Ta'aroa, a power to create and recreate oneself and one's world.

In 2003, in the novel *The Mango's Kiss*, Albert Wendt explained how his Samoan characters perceive time:

> The concept of a time before the now and a time ahead of the now, of time moving in a one-dimensional way, was papalagi [white, foreign], he said. For them, time was everywhere, holding the Unity-that-is-All together; to change any part of it altered the whole; everything, including our dead, was in the ever-moving present, existing now. (Wendt 2003 200)

Wendt's hero confronts the Western perception of time that would be represented as a line to the vision of the archipelago's inhabitants that would be more global and include a form of continuity between each era. Māori writer Witi Ihimaera shared this point of view when he presented, somehow like an anthropologist, the international exhibit *Māori leurs trésors ont une âme* displayed in Paris in 2011: "Maori believe that we live within a continuum. So, within that continuum, there is no such thing as time passing" (Ihimaera 2011). He was already using this substantive in the novel *The*

Matriarch when he described "that eternal continuum known as the Creation" (Ihimaera 1996 193), mingling Māori and biblical concepts.

Contemporary writers thus largely base their work on a Polynesian vision of time. Their characters summon the past in the present or highlight a form of continuity that has many consequences on the narrative structure. This temporal 'continuum' is often represented with the symbol of the spiral, a mathematical form very present in nature as well as in Polynesian culture, especially in New Zealand Aotearoa. To Eva Rask Knudsen "the spiral is used to denote the independence—the power 'to rotate, to move'—as well as the interdependence of separate parts, or limbs." (Thornton 98–99) It somehow symbolizes changes in continuity. It distinguishes this vision from a Western symbolic time that would be linear but also from a circular or cyclic perception of time that was supposed to be how Polynesians considered time, according to European explorers and thinkers. If time evolves as a spiral, structures are repeated but not their contents. Albert Wendt describes in this respect the "ever-moving present" (Wendt 2003 452) that reveals the feeling of continuity created by a spiral time. To Samoan intellectual Caroline Sinavaiana-Gabbard this concept can easily be explained thanks to a simple universal law: "It's the idea that nothing is ever lost. Nothing is ever created or destroyed. We're just making it new. Sprucing up the boat of culture." (Sinavaiana-Gabbard 25)

In order to build the dream of tomorrow's Polynesian archipelagoes, writers follow the structural pattern of the spiral because the world they foresee is at the crossroads of preservation and renewal—circularity and progression, following the spiral movement—of their cultures and environment. In a paper devoted to "Polynesian paradises," the anthropologist John Connell wrote in 2003: "Islands and utopian visions are rarely simple phenomena; dreaming and displacement are eternal." (Connell 89)

In *Mythes et usages des mythes*, Bruno Saura explained: "the intimate connection, the carnal connection between men and land is nowhere expressed as obviously and explicitly as in myths" (Saura 2013). He thinks about the oral myths of the origins, be they myths about how the world appeared, was created, or organized, or myths about how Polynesians conquered their world after their fantastic maritime migrations. However, the concept could also include popular myths that have been created since the arrival of the missionaries, myths that now inhabit Polynesian considerations about their territories. Literary myths are thus extremely relevant when it comes to the study of the images of the environment. Indeed, a close reading of the rewriting techniques used by many Polynesian authors enables the reader to perceive how complex and rich Polynesian literatures are: in these literatures displacement leads to literary myths wavering between memories of pre-Christian traditions and biblical images. Through the poetic and political dream emerging from these images, writers from the Polynesian Triangle re-enchant their daily relationship to the environment; they re-enchant the contemporary imaginary of the insular territories.

Notes

[1] In this chapter, I understand "culture" according to the definition Bruno Saura's offered in *Tahiti Māʻohi, Culture, Identité, Religion et Nationalisme en Polynésie française* in 2008: "the entire ways of saying, ways of doing as well as the values of a human group—even of humanity—noticeable through actions (behavior, speech) and supports (outfits, tools, artistic creations…)." Of course, we do not forget that a culture is never homogeneous or rigid, especially when it is in contact with another one (cf. Saura 2008 23).

[2] In this chapter, we consider poetry, songs and all narrative forms (family stories, historical, mythological or even religious narratives) as part of an oral literature that constituted the core of pre-evangelical Polynesian civilizations. This literature takes part in the "oral tradition"—studied by Louis-Jean Calvet—of a territory where one did not pass on culture through writing and where, today, artists still choose alternative forms to preserve and reactivate this immaterial heritage. Oral literature still plays a major part in contemporary literatures which often questions postcolonial writers. In *Éloge de la Créolité* (*In Praise of Creolness*), Jean Bernabé, Patrick Chamoiseau and Raphaël Confiant wrote, for example: "After our traditional story-tellers, it was somehow silence: the dead-end. Elsewhere scribes (putting spoken words on paper) took over from epic poets, bards, griots, minstrels, troubadours and progressively gained their literary autonomy. Here, it was a breach, a gap, a deep gully between a written expression that wished to be modern and universal and traditional creole orality where a large part of our being lied dormant. This non-integration of oral tradition was one of the forms and dimensions of our alienation." In French Polynesia, most of the myths, legends and stories were recorded and transcribed by Marau Taaroa and Teuira Henry. In New Zealand, Elsdon Best and Alexander Wyclif Reed put in writing a major part of Māori oral traditions.

[3] « Union de l'homme à la terre dans laquelle il plonge ses racines, union de la terre à l'homme qui fait jaillir de son ventre la nourriture de l'homme. Pour chaque naissance d'homme, mise en terre d'arbre nourricier. Maevarua, par ce geste, perpétue l'âme millénaire de son peuple. » (Spitz 1991 33)

[4] My translation.

[5] My translation.

[6] Bruno Saura is quoting Raapoto's literal translation of the Tahitian word "māʻohi."

[7] My translation.

[8] « dépose délicatement [dans la terre] le placenta [de son fils Tematua] sur lequel il place un jeune tumu Ùru [qui] le nourrira en sa vie d'homme » (Spitz 1996 32—3).

[9] « Le Taʻata tumu affirme son identité en déclinant le nom des lieux de son espace communautaire : montagne, rivière ou source, plantes, place de réunion, pointe ou baie. Il est alors Taʻata ʻaiʻa homme territoire. Il n'est pas Tahitien mais "Taʻata Tahiti" : Homme Tahiti. Il n'habite pas Tahiti. Il est Tahiti. » (Spitz 2011 94). My translation.

[10] My translation.

[11] My translation.

[12] « Henri Hiro : Leur Éden, ils continuent toujours à courir après, alors que l'Éden naturel, il existe bien lui. Il est là, tout autour.
Les Nouvelles de Tahiti : Existe-t-il encore ?
Henri Hiro : Oui, oui. Je ne parle pas des bâtiments, des routes, du béton. Je pense au comportement des Polynésiens, à ce qu'on trouve dans le regard des Polynésiens. » My translation.

[13] « Il entretient sa terre, plante et récolte les fruits de son labeur, part à la pêche tous les jours. [...] Il a alors atteint la vie nouvelle pour laquelle il avait tant combattu. Il est Mā'ohi, libre et indépendant ! » My translation.

[14] « Oh, l'amour de mon pays, [...]
Qu'il vive et abreuve ma terre natale,
Pour que fleurissent en leur essaim
Les enfants de ce sol,
Enfants de mon pays ». My translation.

[15] "Painted scroll ornamentation commonly used on meeting house rafters" according to *Te Aka Dictionary*.

[16] "World of life and light, Earth, physical world," according to *Te Aka dictionary*. This expression comes from the Māori myth relating the apparition of the world.

[17] "Lieu du bonheur." The expression was used in French by Vita Fortunati about utopic islands in European literatures. It is not a Polynesian concept – as, of course, insular peoples do not think of the island as people living on a continent would.

[18] Enfant, fils de mon peuple,
Je ne sais plus les rêves de ceux de mon peuple,
Enfant, fils de mon peuple,
Rêve de nouveaux rêves pour tes enfants
Nouveaux enfants de notre peuple. (Spitz 1996 177)

[19] "God" according to the *Samoan Vocabulary*.

[20] "Ghost, spirit, daemon" according to the *Samoan Vocabulary*.

[21] My translation.

[22] « Il faut mettre le rêve collectif en adéquation avec l'existence d'un peuple pour qu'il soit efficace et considérer notre propre vie comme une parcelle éphémère, quoique glorieuse, de la Nature. » (Pambrun 2003 58) My translation.

[23] « Aujourd'hui, je dis aussi qu'il ne faut pas seulement conserver les objets du passé, mais qu'il faut continuer à les créer et les investir de l'esprit de Ta'aroa. » (Pambrun 2010) My translation.

Works Cited

Ariirau-Richard, Stéphanie. "La Révélation du Bambou noir." *Le Bambou noir*, Pambrun, Jean-Marc Tera'ituatini, Pape'ete: Le Motu, 2005, pp. 9–14.

Ashcroft, Bill, Gareth Griffiths, and Helen Tiffin. *The Empire Writes Back, Theory and Practice in Post-colonial Literatures* [1989, 2nd edition 2002]. London: Routledge, coll. "New Accents," 2005.

Babadzan, Alain. *Naissance d'une tradition, Changement culturel et Syncrétisme religieux aux Îles Australes (Polynésie française)*. Paris: ORSTOM, coll. "Travaux et Documents de l'ORSTOM," n° 154, 1982.

Ball, Martin. "People speaking silently to themselves: An examination of Keith Basso's philosophical speculations on 'sense of place' in Apache cultures." Quoted by Miriam Kahn in *Tahiti Beyond the Postcard*, Seattle: University of Washington Press, coll. "Culture, Place and Nature, Studies in Anthropology and Environment," 2011, p. 11.

Bhabha, Homi K. *The Location of Culture* [1994]. New York: Routledge, coll. "Classics," 2004.

Billington, Michael. *Samoan Vocabulary.* http://mike.bitrevision.com/samoan/, 2016. Accessed February 2019.

Church of England. *The Bible.* King James Version, translation into English, http://www.biblestudytools.com/kjv/, 1769, Accessed February 2019.

Connell, John. "Island Dreaming, the Contemplation of Polynesian Paradise." in *Îles rêvées, Territoires et Identités en crise dans le Pacifique insulaire*, edited by Dominique Guillaud, Christian Huetz de Lemps and Olivier Sevin, Paris: Presses de l'Université de Paris-Sorbonne, 2003, pp. 56–89.

Fortunati, Vita. "L'Imaginaire ambigu de l'île dans la tradition littéraire utopique." *Utopies insulaires*, Pape'ete: Bulletin de la Société des Études Océaniennes, 301, June 2004, pp. 21–35.

Grace, Patricia. *Mutuwhenua, the Moon Sleeps* [1978]. Rosedale: Penguin Books, 2010.

Griffiths, Gareth. "Afterword. Postcoloniality, Religion, Geography. Keeping our Feet on the Ground and our Heads up." *Mapping the Sacred, Religion, Geography and Postcolonial Literatures*, edited by Jamie S. Scott and Paul Simpson-Housley, Atlanta: Rodopi, 2001, pp. 445–461.

Hau'ofa, Epeli. "Pasts to Remember." *We Are the Ocean, Selected Works*, Honolulu: University of Hawai'i Press, 2000, pp. 60–79.

—. "Our Place Within, Foundation for a Creative Oceania." *We Are the Ocean, Selected Works*, Honolulu: University of Hawai'i Press, 2003, pp. 80–93.

Henry, Teuira. *Ancient Tahiti.* Based on material recorded by J.M. Orsmond, Honolulu: P. Bishop Museum, 1928.

Hiro, Henri. "E aha atu ra ? / Qu'en sera-t-il ?" *Hiro, Henri, Pehepehe i tā'u nūnaa, Message poétique* [1990], translated by the author and Alain Deviègre, Pape'ete: Haere Po, 2004, pp. 62–63.

Ihimaera, Witi. *Whanau.* Auckland: Heinemann, 1974.

—. *The Matriarch* [1986]. Auckland: Secker and Warburg New-Zealand, 1996.

—. *Sky Dancer.* Auckland: Penguin Books, 2003.

—. "Les Taonga." Video interview realized by Michel Viotte and posted on the website of the Musée du Quai Branly during the display of the international exhibit Maōri, *Leurs trésors ont une âme*, 2011.

Moorfield, John C. *Te Aka Māori-English, English-Māori Dictionary and Index* http://www.maoridictionary.co.nz/, 2011, Accessed February 2019.

Moura, Jean-Marc. "Postcolonialisme et Comparatisme." Posted on *Vox Poetica.* http://www.vox-poetica.org/sflgc/biblio/moura.html, 2006, Accessed February 2019.

Pambrun, Jean-Marc Tera'ituatini. "Triste sauvage." *Paul Gauguin, Héritage et Confrontation,* edited by Pineri, Riccardo, Pape'ete: Université de la Polynésie française, 2003, pp. 51–59.

—. *Henri Hiro, héros polynésien.* Biographie, Moorea: Puna Honu, 2010.

—. "Des esprits, des œuvres et des hommes." *L'Écriturien* (blog). http://terai tuatini.blogspot.fr/, 2010. Accessed February 2019.

Parsonson, Ann. "The Challenge to Mana Māori." *The Oxford History of New-Zealand* [1981], edited by Geoffrey W. Rice, Auckland: Oxford University Press, 1992, pp. 167–198.

Picard, Jean-Luc, Mā'ohi tumu et Hutu pāinu. *La Construction identitaire dans la littérature contemporaine de la Polynésie Française.* ftp://ftp.scd.univ-metz.fr/pub/Theses/2008/Picard.Jean_Luc.LMZ0817.pdf, Accessed February 2019.

Rask Knudsen, Eva. *The Circle and the Spiral, a Study of Australian Aboriginal and New Zealand Māori Literature.* Amsterdam & New York: Rodopi, coll. "Cross Cultures," 2004.

Rosenfeld, Jean E. *The Island Broken in Two Halves, Land and Renewal Movements among the Maori of New Zealand.* University Park: The Pennsylvania State University Press, 1999.

Saura, Bruno. *La Société tahitienne au miroir d'Israël, Un peuple en métaphore.* Paris: CNRS, coll. "CNRS ethnologie," 2004.

—. *Tahiti Mā'ohi, Culture, identité, religion et nationalisme en Polynésie française.* Pape'ete: Vent des Îles, 2008.

—. *Mythes et usages des mythes, Autochtonie et idéologie de la Terre Mère en Polynésie.* Paris-Louvain-Walpole: Peeters Publishers, coll. "Langues et Cultures du Pacifique," 2013.

Sinavaiana-Gabbard, Caroline. "Introduction: a Kind of Genealogy." *Alchemies of Distance, a Collection of Poetry,* Honolulu: Subpress/Tinfish/Institute of Pacific Studies, 2001, pp. 11–28.

Smith, Huhana. *Māori, leurs trésors ont une âme.* Paris: Musée du Quai Branly, Somogy éditions d'Art, 2011.

Spitz, Chantal T. *L'Île des rêves écrasés* [1991]. Pape'ete: Au Vent des Îles, 2003.

—. *Island of shattered dreams.* Translated by Jean Anderson, Wellington: Huia, 2007.

—. "Sommes-nous prêts à hériter de notre autochtonie ?" *Pape'ete, Autochtonie et Peuples autochtones, Littérama'ohi,* edited by Chantal T. Spitz, n° 19, Octobre 2011, pp. 94—98.

Thornton, Agathe. "Some reflections on traditional māori carving" [1989, Journal of the Polynesian Society]. *The Circle and the Spiral, a Study of Australian Aboriginal and New Zealand Māori Literature,* edited by Eva Rask Knudsen, Amsterdam & New York: Rodopi, coll. "Cross Cultures," 2004.

Talpade Mohanty, Chandra. "Under Western Eyes: Feminist Scholarship and Colonial Discourse." *Feminist Review,* n°30, Autumn 1988, pp.61–88.

Tuhiwai Smith, Linda. *Decolonizing Methodologies, Research and Indigenous Peoples.* Dunedin: Zed Books & University of Otago Press, 1999.

Vaite, Célestine Hitiura. *Frangipani, Love, Life, Families... Tahitian style!* [2004], London: Hutchinson, 2005.

Wendt, Albert. *Ola* [1991]. Honolulu: University of Hawai'i Press, 1995.

—. *The Mango's Kiss.* Auckland: Vintage, 2003.

Chapter 2

Toward an Island Ecopoetics: Reenchanting the Andaman Ecology and the Jarawa Tribal Reserve in Pankaj Sekhsaria's *The Last Wave*

Asis De

Mahishadal Raj College, India

Abstract: When literature becomes inspired by ecological imagination, it enlivens the bond between man and nature, and therefore, re-enchants the earth. The following essay considers an Indian island novel as a case study to explore the re-enchantment caused by ecological imbalance and the plight of a tribal community in the Andaman Islands in the post-Tsunami years. Pankaj Sekhsaria, an Indian scientist-conservationist, weaves his debut *The Last Wave* (2014) with a wealth of knowledge about the Jarawa community of the Andaman Islands alongside describing the story of Harish and Seema—fictional characters associated with conservationist activities. Tapping into material ecocriticism, this article focuses on Sekhsaria's depiction of two recent changes in the islands: imbalance in the natural biodiversity and the consequent behavioral change of the Jarawas. This essay shows how natural and cultural stories engage in a conversation aiming at decentering the locus of enunciation, meanwhile casting a new light on the moral responsibility to sustain distinctive habitats.

Keywords: Andaman Islands, island ecology, deforestation, "local born," Jarawa tribe

***

The critical practice of interpreting literary and cultural productions in terms of environment and ecology, as Cheryll Glotfelty posits in her exclusive 'Introduction' to *The Ecocriticism Reader*, "has one foot in literature and the other on land" (xix). The first professor of literature and environment in the academia of the United States, she also prioritizes the interconnection of literature and the locale it aesthetically represents: "literature does not float above the material world in some aesthetic ether, but, rather, plays a part in an immensely complex global system, in which energy, matter, *and ideas* interact" (xix; original emphasis). If we agree to the proposition that literature is the repository of ideas connecting place/s and people, nature and culture, the aesthetics of literature includes a representation of the enchanting physical world with its subtle aim to reenchant the reader. Literature is the aesthetic expression of human perceptions, a typically 'human' product that explores all possible relationships between the human and the non-human, biotic and the abiotic, and represents those relationships in infinite ways. Literary productions dealing with environmental consciousness as a *modus operandi*, concentrate on human responsibility in evaluating the fast-transforming relationship between the human and the surrounding environment on a bi-polar frame positioning the human as the 'us' and the environment as the 'other': the effect of reenchantment lies in the spirit of restoration and reformation. Ecological consciousness, which is subtly broader in scope than environmental consciousness, nourishes the effect of reenchantment by representing both the human and the non-human elements of the environment as "interdependent communities, integrated systems, and strong connections among constituent parts" (Glotfelty xx). Literary productions upholding ecological consciousness as *modus vivendi* draw inspiration from the ethical awareness of coexistence and justify the planet as a shared habitat. This chapter seeks to explore how island ecopoetics, a nascent feature of the Indian Anglophone literary landscape, effectively reenchants the readers by seeking ecological awareness of cohabitation in island locale with literary reference to the first Indian Anglophone 'island novel'—*The Last Wave* (2014) authored by Pankaj Sekhsaria. Sekhsaria's art of weaving words in representing the transforming world of the Andaman archipelago—the changes in the island ecosphere and in the cultural identity of the indigenous negrito-tribal community of the Jarawas by fast encroachment of modernity, makes one muse over the future of the paradisal island locale and the people inhabiting that space.

'Ecopoetics' as Ecological 'Poethics'

In response to the seemingly bewildering question 'What is ecopoetics?', people may suggest options like the making and discussing of the literature of wilderness, literature related to the environment, or maybe a literary discourse that advocates for environmental justice and demands a sustainable or greener planet. To Jonathan Skinner, the editor of the American journal of creative writing named *Ecopoetics*, the term 'ecopoetics' may be seen as a kind of 'poethics,' literary practice with a deep sense of ethical responsibility to the environmental locale, and more particularly, "as a form of site-specificity."[1] This 'site-specificity' of ecopoetics, the relation of any literary discourse with a particular locale, certainly makes greater sense when considering the diversity of environments. As a literary term gathering critical attention and impetus mainly from the second half of the previous century, 'ecopoetics' substantially adds to the ethical dimension of environmental humanities, critiquing the moral responsibility against man-made ecological disasters[2]. In this ethical context of ecopoetics, the famous statement of Rachel Carson makes clear sense: "Underlying all of these problems of introducing contamination into our world is the question of moral responsibility—responsibility not only to our own generation but to those of the future." (Carson 242) The inspiration behind any literary poetics, dwelling on environmental consciousness, arises out of either a deep love for nature or angst for the future of nature, and at times these two may be complementary. The angst for the future of nature or the surrounding environment is often causally related to the future of humankind, and the role of literature of place and environment in this context becomes crucial. In their book *Postcolonial Ecocriticism: Literature, Animals, Environment*, Graham Huggan, and Helen Tiffin justify the role of environmental literature in the postcolonial context as such: "The primary function of much of this literature has been that of global consciousness-raising in a wide variety of (post)colonial contexts in which the twin demands of social and environmental justice are conspicuously displayed" (Huggan and Tiffin 33). The role of literary ecopoetics in 'consciousness-raising' on the issue of 'justice' simultaneously reminds the writer of "public accountability" (Huggan and Tiffin 34). The issues of "moral responsibility" which Carson insists on, and "public accountability" in the words of Graham Huggan and Helen Tiffin, emphasize the ethical dimension of ecopoetics and its function in shaping a global consciousness across different environmental locales.

Contextualizing 'island ecopoetics' in Indian Anglophone Literature

When writing becomes inspired by ecological imagination, it enlivens the bond between man and nature at a particular locale. It simultaneously emphasizes the message of organic wholeness of life, which one may well find as reenchantment. 'Literature of place' is, in a way, a literature of consciousness that concentrates on the relationship between the human, other living organisms, and their shared habitat in a specific time and space. In the post-Tsunami years, this relationship between humans and the land they dwell in has earned sufficient academic attention in Asia and around the globe. In the Anglophone Indian literary landscape, fictional narratives like

Arundhati Roy's Booker winner *The God of Small Things*, Amitav Ghosh's *The Hungry Tide*, and Indra Sinha's *Animal's People* have dealt with environmental issues in their unique ways: the profound ecological issue of coexistence of certain Indian populations and their surrounding environments have been addressed alongside questioning the policies and politics of 'progress' and environmentalism in contemporary India. A relatively recent addition to this list, Pankaj Sekhsaria's *The Last Wave* (2014) is the first Indian Anglophone 'island novel,' which has given a wake-up call towards the change of ecological balance and the plight of a prehistoric negrito-tribal community known as the 'Jarawa' in the Andaman Islands.

The activist and conservationist Pankaj Sekhsaria weaves his debut novel with a wealth of knowledge about the Jarawa people and the wild denizens of the Andaman Islands while describing Harish and Seema's story, who are also associated with the conservationist activities like the author, on those islands. An environmental journalist himself, Sekhsaria has been researching and chronicling the island ecology and the people of the Andaman and Nicobar for more than two decades, and *The Last Wave* is a fictional rendering of an ecologist's anxiety over the complexities and subtleties of the fascinating island ecosphere, which entices the reader with a feeling of reenchantment. The effect of reenchantment becomes pervasive when the reader notices that geologically the Andaman archipelago is an extension of the Arakan Mountain range and is stretched between Cape Negrais of Myanmar and the Banda Arc of Indonesia, whereas all these islands and rocky outcrops are politically annexed to the Republic of India. The narrative further reenchants the reader effectively as it divides the 'human' factor into two—the settler and the indigenous, and then places them in a complex power relationship of conflict and taming in the island ecosphere of the Andaman Islands. In the 'Introduction' to *Ecocriticism and Indigenous Studies: Conversations from Earth to Cosmos*, American ecocritics Salma Monani and Joni Adamson find traditional indigenous knowledge of the environment as "cosmovision," which is both ethical and political by nature and opine that recognizing "Indigenous cosmovisions as participating in everyday and situated practices is to also comprehend them as dynamic epistemologies" (Monani and Adamson 8). In his book *Postcolonial Literary Geographies: Out of Place*, John Thieme observes that "the instinctive respect for the environment that has traditionally characterized the beliefs of the vast majority of Indigenous peoples offers a superior wisdom" though he simultaneously accepts the view that "practices that were once unquestioned in their cultures now find themselves in conflict with majoritarian national and global interests and any idea of putting the clock back to the imagined 'purity' of a pre-colonial past is an idealized fantasy" (Thieme 101). In the Indian context of the Andaman Island ecology and its relationship to the indigenous knowledge system of the negrito-tribal community of the Jarawas, Manish Chandi and Harry Andrews, in their article published in *The Jarawa Tribal Reserve Dossier* (UNESCO: 2010), posit: "It is the Jarawa that are in contact with the outside [...] and retain traditional knowledge systems of biodiversity. It is assumed that this knowledge is the basis for nature conservation in the Jarawa Reserve" (Chandi and Andrews 48). *The Last Wave* is quite pertinent in this discussion as the narrative concentrates on the debate arising out of the fissures and conflicts between the eco-ethnological conservation of the space for the indigenous Jarawas and the aggressive modernity and economic globalization transforming the island ecology steadily towards a future crisis.

An island locale is usually a more sensitive, tender, and vulnerable setting for the discussion of ecopoetics, as the threat of species extinction is highest on islands compared to the mainland. Loss of biodiversity due to invasive disturbances and unbridled socio-economic development of the standard of human life has a more pervasive effect on the living organisms on an island. Moreover, an island may be seen metaphorically as a real-life 'Garden of Eden' before the Lapse, with its pristine nature and peace. This 'Garden of Eden' formula may invade the mind of any reader of Sekhsaria's novel, as the cover page of *The Last Wave* holds the image of a Jarawa raising the right hand, probably in an 'Adam-like' gesture to pluck the 'forbidden fruit.' The cover page itself is a scientifically crafted visual emblem representing Sekhsaria's message of conservation of island ecology in the Andaman Islands. The bordering of green island space with turquoise blue rim explicitly indicates the coastline, the 'leafy' mangrove rainforest, its flora and fauna—images of a hornbill, a leatherback turtle, a crocodile, a fish and a wild pink flower (*Papilionanthe Teres*)—all contribute substantially to calibrate the conflict between the balance and imbalance of biodiversity in the island ecosphere.

Environmentalism in the Andaman Islands and the Jarawas

The Last Wave, subtitled by Sekhsaria as 'An Island Novel,' is divided into three Books, a 'Prologue' and an 'Epilogue': Book One is subdivided into ten chapters, Book Two into eleven and the Final Book is subdivided into three chapters. Before telling his tale, Pankaj introduces to his readers a one-page excerpt from '*A History of our Relations with the Andamanese*' written by M.V. Portman, the British officer in charge of the Andamanese in 1899 and a hand-illustrated map of the Andaman Islands with a title '*Around the Jarawa Reserve, 2004*'. These two pages at the beginning and a four-page chronology entitled '*The Jarawas: A Historical Sketch*' significantly concentrate on the center of Pankaj's attention: the Jarawas and their jungle, inseparably connected. When Madhusree Mukherjee, in a revealing review of the novel entitled 'Love in the Time of Development' observes—"...for Sekhsaria, the exquisite but fragile archipelago is the true protagonist" (Mukherjee 2), I slightly differ and like to opine that the 'human' interest is no less significant to Sekhsaria as he devotes more to the issue of the well being of the Jarawas— the indigenous tribe on these islands. Unless there are a human population and its interest, where is the relevance of *literary* discourse, and how one could emphasize the relation between the human and its habitat? If no 'human' perception is working over the place of dwelling, where lies the issue of either enchantment or re-enchantment?

However, the time frame of the narrative starts in 1998, primarily with the arrival of the 31-year-old Harish Kumar at the Andaman Islands in search of peace and meaning of life, after the failure of his disastrous marriage in Hyderabad. Later in the novel, Sekhsaria finds Harish as "the outsider, now in the heart of the ancient land of an ancient people" (Sekhsaria 2014 129). On his opposite, there is the 27-year-old Seema Chandran, who is a "local born" and has just returned home from Delhi to work on her Ph.D. dissertation on the "Andaman Local Born" people (Sekhsaria 2014 17). The term "local borns" stands for those people who are settled in the islands for at least over three generations and whose ancestors were brought as "deposits of the colonial project" (Sekhsaria 2014 22) in the 'penal settlement' of the Cellular Jail, set and maintained by the British people in Andaman. Here is a twist on the issue of ethnic identity, which Sekhsaria deals with in a crafty manner, as he makes Seema think of the Jarawas to be the "first born" (Sekhsaria 2014 23) people of the island living there from time immemorial and having the most authoritative right on the islands! Moreover, the issue of human intrusion from mainland India even after its political independence in 1947, the huge refugee influx from East Pakistan, and the gradual and steady expansion of those refugee settlements violating the biodiversity through ruthless deforestation accelerated the change of the island ecology in the Andaman and Nicobar Islands.

The economic transformation of the island society is so quick and gripping that Seema feels the rapid change after her absence of just a few years from Port Blair, the capital city of Andaman and Nicobar: "There was an increasing restlessness—more vehicles, more speed, more movement, more action, more desire and greater ambition [...] the shops bigger, the noises louder and the roads narrower. Garbage now accumulated on street corners and on the roads" (Sekhsaria 2014 33). The 1990s economy, inspired by globalization, has cast a thorough impact even on the architecture of the city:

> Old wooden Mountbatten Cinema was about to go and a steel and glass structure of a shopping mall was to come up in its place. The old wooden State Secretariat had gone too; everything was being replaced by

monsters of the modern age, concrete replacing timber with a rapidity
that would soon send termites out of business. (Sekhsaria 2014 33)

A fictional character, the old Krishna Raj, secretary of the Andaman Local
Borns' Association, reflects on the issue of human encroachment and tells
Seema anxiously: "It's like an incoming tide that keeps rising, a tide that now
refuses to turn back" (Sekhsaria 2014 36). Alongside depicting the changes in
the socio-cultural environment of the settler communities, of the rainforest,
and the surrounding sea, Sekhsaria takes up the issue of the 'indigenous': 'The
Jarawa' in chapter four. From the perspective of 'material ecocriticism' (Iovino
and Oppermann 2014), Pankaj Sekhsaria's *The Last Wave* becomes a narrative
that interprets "the way humans and their agentic partners intersect in the
making" of the island ecology, and the negrito-tribal community of the
Jarawas in the context of Andaman Islands could be seen as "living texts that
recount *naturalcultural* stories" (6; original emphasis).

One of the fictional characters in *The Last Wave*, Dr. David Baskaran—a
scientist of the Institute for Island Ecology, informs Harish about the "subtle
and complex aspects of the Jarawa," "the construction of the Andaman Trunk
Road through the heart of the Jarawa territory" (Sekhsaria 2014 38) and makes
him aware of their recent behavioral changes: "A paradigm shift appears to
have taken place in the outlook and perception of the Jarawas [...] The
enduring modern myth of the implacable junglee, the unfriendly inhabitant
of the deep dark forests, the hostile, violent Jarawa is shattered" (Sekhsaria
2014 38). By referring to the event of transporting an injured Jarawa teenager
to the Hospital in Port Blair for treatment, David argues that the Jarawas, who
were once considered to be "the fleeting shadows of the dark nights"
(Sekhsaria 2014 46), are becoming pacified by the 'careful' arrangement of the
island administration. The behavioral change, as David describes, was first
noticed after that Jarawa teenager's fast acquisition of the Hindi language
during his short stay in the hospital: "Main Tanumei. Tumhara naam kya?" [*"I
am Tanumei. What's your name?"*] (Sekhsaria 2014 49). After his recovery,
when this Jarawa boy Tanumei returns to the jungle, and re-emerges after a
month "with a group of young Jarawa boys like himself" (Sekhsaria 2014 51), it
becomes clear that things are changing fast[3]. After receiving all such bits of
knowledge about the Jarawas, Harish suddenly faces a first-hand experience
of seeing the Jarawas at the Uttara Jetty. He finds the attempt on the part of
the settlers to communicate with them in their unique but bizarre ways.
Chapter eight begins in a unique way—with a newspaper report dated
October 1, 2004, and published in a local newspaper named 'Island News,'
that reads 'Murderous Jarawas at it Again.' It is revealed by the news that
probably a different group of the Jarawas from a place called Tirur has made
the mischief of brutally murdering a policeman named Pillai[4]. Harish's casual

investigation further reveals that this policeman regularly visited the jungle in the name of duty but actually promoted poaching and sought sex with the tribal women. Vishvajit Pandya, an eminent Indian anthropologist long associated with the Andaman Islands and a research associate of Pankaj Sekhsaria, makes a crucial observation from his experience of fieldwork: "In many cases, poachers have lured Jarawas into procuring cells, venison, fish and other forest and sea produce in exchange for small portions of rice and other items of food and clothing. Outbreaks of hostility have been frequent whenever the relations of exchange/exploitation have come under strain" (Pandya 206). Pandya embarks on this issue of illegal poaching and exploitation more elaborately in his book *In the Forest: Visual and Material Worlds of Andamanese History (1858–2006)*, where his experience asserts the point that in the post-Tsunami period, the Jarawas have become more consciousness of their rights and territoriality: "The AAJVS staff accompanying me expressed the view that in these changing times the Jarawas seemed to have begun to realize that the reserve territory belonged to them and no one else [...] Jarawas were frequently apprehending poachers of foreign origin and handing them over to the police camps nearby"[5] (Pandya 289). The element of reenchantment here, the most remarkable change in the behavioral pattern of the Jarawas is their interaction with the police personnel and the sentries of the forest outposts, as they have already realized their liminality, the bordered space of the Jarawa Tribal Reserve. In Sekhsaria's novel *The Last Wave*, the fictional character of Uncle Pame, the old man working as the attendant of the researchers at the Institute for Island Ecology for years, tells Harish: "Things have changed all around the Jarawa, but in many ways the Jarawa have remained the same" (Sekhsaria 2014 164).

Jarawa Tribal Reserve as the Space of the 'Exotic'

Jarawa Tribal Reserve (JTR), the forest space designated for the Jarawas under the Andaman and Nicobar Islands Protection of Aboriginal Tribes Regulation (1956), came into existence in 1957. Stretched between the Middle and South Andaman and spread over almost 1000 square kilometers, this rainforest-clad, sea and mangrove-encircled landmass with its primitive negrito-tribal inhabitants ('*erem-taga*': forest dwellers) reenchants the explorers and readers historically, anthropologically, politically and ecologically from the late 19th century till date. In the 'Introductory Note' of *The Jarawa Tribal Reserve Dossier* (UNESCO: 2010), the editors Pankaj Sekhsaria and Vishvajit Pandya observe this Tribal Reserve as a "contested" space with an exclusive ecosphere: "a space that ecologists see as a critically important repository of the islands' biological diversity [...] home to a host of critically endangered and endemic species of plants and animals including the Andaman wild pig, the saltwater crocodile and the Andaman day gecko" (Sekhsaria and Pandya 7). In his novel *The Last Wave*, Sekhsaria depicts the Jarawa Tribal Reserve as the "lifeline for the islands" (Sekhsaria 2014 211), which is fast being transformed with depleting forest, encroaching settlers and poachers, pacified and culturally modernizing Jarawas and the rather indifferent state authorities. The role of the state authorities, as Vishvajit Pandya in his book *In the Forest: Visual and Material Worlds of Andamanese History* (1858–2006) observes, could be compared with the British colonizers: "Like the British colonial administration the Indian government however seemingly lost interest in undertaking any sustained investigations into the cultural conditions of the Jarawa hunters and gatherers and began to regard them more as a 'problem' and perhaps a nuisance in the path of progress" (Pandya 267). The mission of pacifying the hostility of the Jarawas by establishing friendly contact along the west coast of the Jarawa Tribal Reserve was first taken by the Andaman and Nicobar Administration in 1974. In 1988-89, the construction work of the Andaman Trunk Road (NH 223) partially through the Tribal Reserve in the South and Middle Andaman became complete. This construction of Andaman Trunk Road (ATR) through the Jarawa Tribal Reserve, itself proof of encroachment of the state, is the point of contention between the state and several forums of activists, anthropologists, and environmental scientists. Samir Acharya, the secretary of the Society for Andaman & Nicobar Ecology, observes in his article entitled 'Andaman Trunk Road and the Jarawa situation' in *The Jarawa Tribal Reserve Dossier*: "The Andaman Trunk Road has marginalised the Jarawas like nothing else, admits the Master Plan for Tribal Development" (Acharya 74).

The Last Wave, Pankaj's island novel, effectively reenchants the reader on the contradictory role of the state that permits the construction of the highway through the Tribal Reserve on the point of setting communication for the 'civilized' islanders and for the promotion of tourism to earn more revenue. Promoting tourism through the Jarawa Tribal Reserve and the sight of passing buses and vehicles packed with curious tourists looking for wandering Jarawas alongside the Andaman Trunk Road is a practice of showcasing the 'exotic' in their 'natural' environment. The image of the 'primitive' Jarawa by the roadside may draw more tourists and earn more revenue for the state, but this extension of the contact-zone between the tribals and the non-tribals also damages the insularity of the tribal cultural space, and the purpose of securing a Tribal Reserve becomes meaningless. Moreover, the highway through the forest space of the Tribal Reserve makes the ecosphere of the rainforest more vulnerable in the hands of poachers, timber-contractors and intruders who enter the Jarawa Tribal Reserve to plunder the forest resources. In 2002, the Supreme Court of India ordered the closure of those parts of the Road that runs through the Tribal Reserve to prevent further conflicts between the settlers and the Jarawas. Though that order has not yet been implemented even today. In this context, it is amazing to note a relationship between the title of the novel—*The Last Wave,* and the sub-title of chapter nine—'The Last Hope,' as the word 'last' is significantly revealing here. Mainly focusing on a night-time expedition of crocodile hunt in the creeks along the coast of Jarawa Tribal Reserve, this chapter summarily concludes with the sentence: "The Jarawa Reserve was indeed the last hope" (Sekhsaria 2014 103). To save the crocodiles and the island ecology, the ferocity of the tribal Jarawas was the only threat to the invading settlers and the only way to block the human encroachment as the "wave of humans and their settlements had penetrated deeper and deeper, trashing the forests as David often said, and destroying prime croc habitat" (Sekhsaria 2014 103).

Pankaj's reference to the "fancy sounding Andaman Canopy Lifting Shelterwood System"[6] (Sekhsaria 2014 185) in chapter sixteen (significantly subtitled 'Flower Power') of *The Last Wave,* is another example of the indifference of the state in securing the forest space of the Jarawa Tribal Reserve. The scientific evidence of the ecological imbalance due to massive timber extraction in the Jarawa Tribal Reserve is the blossom of a wild pink flower known as *Papilionanthe Teres* (in short, PT). Dr. Sreekumar Kutty, the fictional character of a botanist who has been working on these islands for years, tells Harish that "the evergreen forest here is slowly changing... it's becoming dryer, more brown, and with that, the associated forms of small plants and animals are also changing, even disappearing" (Sekhsaria 2014 185). The botanist further explains to Harish that an "important ecological characteristic" of this orchid-like flower is that it "needs to receive direct sunlight to bloom," which is why this flower "can be called an ecological indicator" (Sekhsaria 2014 187). He also informs Harish that as he was going to the northern Andaman Islands, he "noticed the flower all along the Andaman Trunk Road from Port Blair right up to Mayabundar" (Sekhsaria 2014 187), and more particularly in those forests "where I was seeing PT now, had seen extensive timber extraction over the years" (Sekhsaria 2014 188). In reply to Harish's exclamation—"maximum orchids in the extracted forests, and almost none in the unlogged forests?" Dr. Kutty asserts emphatically, "Not a single in the original, undisturbed forests" (Sekhsaria 2014 188). He challenges the logic behind the government project of the 'Andaman Canopy Lifting Shelterwood System,' probably addressing some imagined policymakers before him: "They wanted scientific evidence. Here it was" (Sekhsaria 2014 188). The beautiful pink flowers of that orchid, blooming in millions together and "swaying gently," may induce the eyes with temporary comfort, but the botanist Dr. Kutty finds the scene "very beautiful, but it's like an offering at a funeral," as the blooming of *Papilionanthe Teres* means, "the entire hydrology of the area changes" (Sekhsaria 2014 189). With an air of total resignation, Dr. Kutty sighs: "We have to be thankful to the Jarawas for the last remaining forest—there is no doubt about that. I know how the settlers here used to fear the Jarawas. But *that was then* [...] There cannot be much hope. This is only the beginning [...] And the Jarawa Reserve? [...] The Jarawas have no sense of this boundary" (Sekhsaria 2014 199; my emphasis). Dr. Kutty's conviction about the forthcoming ecological catastrophe is not any fanciful imagination. With the change of time ("that was then"), the future of the Jarawa Tribal Reserve is becoming more uncertain as the Jarawas do not have any sense of the boundary. They only have the sense of the boundary that nature has made encircling them—the boundary of the sea. It is the intruders, the settlers, who attempt to impose a boundary to restrict them even in their own land. The survival of the Andaman Rainforest and the survival of the Jarawas are complementarily connected as it is the Jarawas who have conserved most of the rainforest of the Tribal Reserve, simply by not allowing settlers to trespass.

'Local Born' Settlers, Politics of Civilization and the Future of Andaman Ecology

Discussion of Andaman ecology and the debate over the forest space inhabited by the Jarawas can never be complete without understanding the stand of the "local born" settlers and the political scenario under their control. In the second chapter of the narrative, the fictional character Seema Chandran, a "local born" of Port Blair, joins the Institute for Island Ecology on her research assignment. The pristine wilderness of the surrounding environment, the enchanting beauty of the evergreen forested hillocks, and the encircling turquoise sea have made the Andaman archipelago a paradise to travelers, but Pankaj shows that the "local born" people of the islands are all so happy with their association with the island ecology: "Coral, fish, turtles, dolphins, jellyfish — these were a regular part of their privileged lives as residents of the islands [...] in one of the world's richest and most pristine ocean waters" (Sekhsaria 2014 120). Book Two of *The Last Wave* begins with more research activities and assignments. A survey-trip to Constance Bay and Port Campbell proves to be useful for Seema, as she feels very delighted by the sight of a dolphin and the coral reef inside the turquoise water of the sea. One evening in Port Campbell, a hotspot in the land of the Jarawas, while resting on the boat, all the five members of the research party became "*mesmerised as they listened to the ancient rhythm*" of the Jarawas coming from the coastline forest:

> Riding the darkness and the silence, announcing the takeover of the advancing night, rising from somewhere deep in the surrounding dark forests, came the high-pitched, *haunting yodel of the Jarawa*. It wasn't loud, but it was clear, with the mysterious quality of *a very real dream*. (Sekhsaria 2014 129; my emphases)

Sekhsaria's narration takes the reader into a world of utterly mystic enchantment—"a very real dream." The literal becomes visual. The "haunting yodel of the Jarawa" may be considered as a warning against the encroachment of the civil society, deforestation, and devastation of the island's ecology.

The politician character in *The Last Wave*, Samaresh Basu, proposes something abstract before the Chief Conservator of Forest Mr. Yadav, Justice Singh, Harish, Seema, and David, that may sound absurd but not altogether unexpected from a politician, who always insists on material developments: "They live a very miserable life in the forest, sir— no home, no proper food— moving around from one place to another, digging roots, hunting, fishing. Sir, *we need to civilize them*" (Sekhsaria 2014 214–15; my emphasis). Basu's utterance takes the reader to the well-known phrase coined by Rudyard Kipling in his poem—'the White Man's burden.' The civil society in independent India takes the 'white man''s role and voluntarily wants to act as the 'emissary of light' to find another parallel coinage in Joseph Conrad's *Heart of Darkness*. In his narrative, Pankaj expresses his angst as an environmentalist writer, as he shows the arrival of reports from different corners of the island that the Jarawas are learning Indian languages like Hindi or Bangla, using metal-made utensils (supplied by the administration), using plastic bags and even wearing some garments, too. However, who can/would measure whether these people are progressing or regressing? The colonial myth of the 'white man's burden' has now been borne by 'responsible' Indian politicians and policy-makers in the name of development, in the name of the "future," and thus negating all sorts of 'moral responsibility' of mankind could well be counted as the most pressing danger before us which has been repeatedly emphasized by Rachel Carson, and which I have already mentioned at the very beginning of this chapter. As the fictional character of the politician Basu asks—"For 300 Jarawas, should we be denied *the opportunity to make our lives and the future of our children secure*?" (Sekhsaria 2014 216; my emphasis), one can notice the difference between Carson's notion of "future," which involves the entire mankind, and Basu's "future," which includes only the settlers and tactfully excludes the indigenous Jarawas. The inclusion of the indigenous in the mainstream Indian population is just a plea towards removing the obstacles in harvesting the profits from the island's natural resources by excluding the "first borns" of the island.

The narrator's reflection could be cited as expressive of the angst of Harish: "The fate of the Jarawa, as far as he could see, had been sealed […] the original people were on their way to becoming the had-beens" (Sekhsaria 2014 236). With the economic and ecological changes in the islands, everything pristine and indigenous change, and something sadly leads to extinction. Harish starts pondering over the 'fairness' of this change, the slow but definitive transformation of an ethnic tribe in these islands, and their gradual move towards oblivion:

> How could this world *negotiate fairly* with the Jarawa? That was the question and therein lay the challenge [...] The other original islanders, the Onge and the Great Andamanese, who had cohabited these forests with the Jarawas, had all but gone. The Jarawa were now being dragged down the same path. There was the evidence and the weight of history—the Jarawa would be pushed down *the road to annihilation.* (Sekhsaria 2014 237; my emphases)

The phrase "road to annihilation" probably metaphorically aims at the newly built Andaman Trunk Road through the Jarawa Tribal Reserve, as Harish tells Seema later: "The road is the most important vector, bringing in all kinds of influences upon the Jarawa from the outside world" (Sekhsaria 2014 241). Nevertheless, it should not appear to be such a simple imagistic association only, as the issue of annihilation is certainly a bigger one. Pankaj's clear binary of the tormentor ('annihilator') and the victim ('annihilated') on the issue of power and survival is a distressing alarm that seriously troubles the consciousness of the reader with "the immensity of this responsibility" (Sekhsaria 2014 238).

The word 'responsibility' in any literary discourse of ecopoetics holds the essence of arguments on both sides. When Seema refers to the inconveniences and discomfort that would arise due to the closure of the Andaman Trunk Road only for the sake of the Jarawas, Harish insists on the moral and ethical responsibilities of the civil society on the ground of the extinction of a vulnerable tribe living inside the forest. Power allows for ruling, but it is the responsibility of knowledge that promotes protection. When Seema reacts to Harish's argument as "too dramatic" (Sekhsaria 2014 244), which more or less every environmentalist faces very often, Harish cuts short by insisting on the issue of "choice that has to be made" quite immediately: "It is the convenience of one against the survival of the other. It is not an easy choice, but that is what it is" (Sekhsaria 2014 244). Book Two ends with all these questions behind, and meanwhile, Harish and Seema come close to each other as there grows an emotional attachment, and they board a ship named *MV Chowra* to the Great Nicobar Island to see the Giant leatherback turtle just before the day of Christmas in 2004.

The Epiphanic 'Epilogue' and Reenchantment

The reason behind mentioning the date precisely is to emphasize the issue of island ecology. Sekhsaria subtitles the second chapter of the final Book as '26

December 2004,' which the well-informed reader could easily associate with the last terrific ecological disaster in the Andaman and Nicobar Islands: the last deadliest Tsunami in the Indian Ocean. In the rather pleasant chapter entitled 'Nesting Turtles,' the idyllic 'Garden of Eden' setting of the island mesmerizes the reader with its beauty and eternal peace, and Pankaj remains quite successful in re-enchanting the island locale: "This was the eternal play of land and ocean, nature's rhythm of the sun, the moon, the stars, the oceans, the land, earth, life" (Sekhsaria 2014 254). The night of 25th December had been an "exceptional night" as "Harish and Seema had spent the entire night walking up and down the beach looking, spending time with each of the turtles that had come ashore to nest" (Sekhsaria 2014 258). The daybreak of the next day arrives with an earthquake: "It took her a moment to realise that it was an earthquake they were experiencing. Even as she gathered her wits, the rumbling quickly turned into a violent shake" (Sekhsaria 2014 258).

The cinematic presentation of the giant wave of the Tsunami in chapter 23 is so meticulous, as if narrated by an eyewitness. Pankaj uses every word after careful selection, and the semantic impact of the narration on the reader is simply massive:

> It was a strange sight indeed. There was a greyish haze on the early morning horizon and the sea had withdrawn into the distance [...] in the distance the water was beginning to rise [...] a wall of dark, grey, angry water [...] The wall of water, even as it kept building up, started to move— towards them [...] an irate, petulant sea [...] coming back." (Sekhsaria 2014 260–61)

After two successive giant watery walls which had already emptied them out of energy, the third massive wave washes them apart, and the reader feels mesmerized: "The big, grey-brown mass of water thundered in with uncompromising power, scooping up Harish and Seema and sending them swirling into the vast, now empty, waterscape beyond." (Sekhsaria 2014 265) Seema remains missing after the wave returns; Harish is narrowly saved and transported to the hospital. After he partially recovers and comes to know about Seema's fate, Harish feels as if "he was drowning, in a hopeless surge" (Sekhsaria 2014 277) of deep mourning. The 'Epilogue' brings consolation as well as the answer, as a Jarawa man named Erema approaches Harish's bedside in the hospital, introduces himself, and then asks him in Hindi about Seema, thus making it clear that the so-called 'junglee' had noticed them together and realized the nature of their relation. This Jarawa man Erema informs Harish in broken Hindi and English that his daughter has been washed out—"Mera ladki washout" ["*My daughter has been washed out*"], and his son is down with high fever—"Mera ladka, garam bukhar" ["*My son is suffering from high fever*"], and thus makes Harish feel "a moment of unexpected liberation" (Sekhsaria 2014 281). Harish keeps on pondering— "How could he compare his loss to that of Erema's, the loss of his family, his way of life, his people?" (Sekhsaria 2014 281)

This epiphanic moment brings the ultimate realization with which Sekhsaria wraps his tale: "Now, as a grieving Erema sat beside him on his hospital bed, Harish knew he had found the answer. There was nowhere Erema could go. There was nowhere anymore, he was himself going [...] He would stay—at these crossroads, in these islands. So, he hoped, would Erema's people" (Sekhsaria 2014 282). The narrative ends, leaving infinite reverberations related to one's place in the grand scheme of existence. As the setting of The Last Wave, the islands, pristine human dwellings of enchantment, have been enlivened by Pankaj's humane treatment and these small dots of land in the Indian Ocean on the map of the world become places reenchanted by both loss and hope. As there is life, so there are progressive and regressive changes, and as there is love, so there is hope for the future.

Notes

[1] In a reflective commentary on ecopoetics, Jonathan Skinner makes the observation that the function of ecopoetics is "to shift the focus from themes to topoi, tropes and entropologies, to institutional critique of "green" discourse itself, and to an array of practices converging on the oikos, the planet earth that is the only home our species currently knows."

[2] The use of pesticides in farming, the establishment of river-dams, intensive deforestation worldwide, and probably the atomic disaster of the Manhattan Project in the Second World War epitomized these regular ecological disasters.

[3] This fictional reference is based upon a real incident, where an injured Jarawa boy named Enmey was taken to the G.B. Pant Hospital in Port Blair in 1997, and after his recovery, he was sent back to his forest home in Middle Andaman. For details, please see Pankaj Sekhsaria's collection of essays entitled *Islands in Flux* (2017), p. 59.

[4] This fictional event of Pillai's murder is based on a real incident in Tirur in 1992. To me, Sekhsaria is probably purposive in using a real-life event of 1992 as a fictional happening in *The Last Wave* and quite particular in putting that event in 2004, the year which is important for two reasons: 2004 is the year of adopting the 'Jarawa Policy,' by the Andaman and Nicobar Administration along with re-notifying an expansion of the area of Jarawa Tribal Reserve to about 1000 sq. kilometers; it is again, the year of Tsunami (26 December 2004), the most severe geological disaster in the Indian Ocean region in the first decade of this century.

[5] AAJVS (*Andaman Adim Jan Jati Vikas Samiti* [Andaman Primitive Tribal Welfare Association]) is a state agency funded and controlled by the Government of India in the Union territory of Andaman Islands. It was established in the post-Nehruvian era, by the Prime Minister Mrs. Indira Gandhi with the objective of the "welfare" of aboriginal and indigenous communities designated as 'Primitives,' vulnerable and therefore, required to be 'protected.'

⁶ 'Andaman Canopy Lifting Shelterwood System' is a process of regenerating the rainforest of the Andaman Islands even after havoc timber extraction. This process, approved by the forest department as 'scientific,' was introduced in the Andaman ecosphere before the Indian Independence in 1947. Even after the Independence, the forest department of the Government of India continued timber extraction to feed the need of industry in the name of this 'scientific' process. Modern research has shown that 'Canopy Lifting System' converts the evergreen forest into deciduous forests and alters the entire floral composition, encouraging other botanical species' growth. (Please see Report of the Project for Formulating a Land Evaluation Survey of Andaman and Nicobar Islands, by Satish and Shanthi Nair, Department of Environment, Government of India, 1983). In *The Last Wave*, the reference to this report has been mentioned (Sekhsaria 2014 184).

Works Cited

Acharya, Samir. "Andaman Trunk Road and the Jarawa situation." *The Jarawa Tribal Reserve Dossier: Cultural & biological diversities in the Andaman Islands*, Pankaj Sekhsaria and Vishvajit Pandya (Eds.), Paris: UNESCO, 2010, pp. 72–76.

Carson, Rachel. *Lost Woods: The Discovered Writing of Rachel Carson*. Edited with an 'Introduction' by Linda Lear. Boston: Beacon Press, 1998.

Chandi, Manish and Harry Andrews. "The Jarawa Tribal Reserve: the 'last' Andaman forest." *The Jarawa Tribal Reserve Dossier: Cultural & biological diversities in the Andaman Islands*, edited by Pankaj Sekhsaria and Vishvajit Pandya, Paris: UNESCO, 2010, pp. 43–53.

Glotfelty, Cheryll. "Introduction: Literary Studies in an Age of Environmental Crisis." *The Ecocriticism Reader: Landmarks in Literary Ecology*, edited by Cheryll Glotfelty and Harold Fromm, Athens and London: The University of Georgia Press, 1996, xv–xxxvii.

Huggan, Graham and Helen Tiffin. *Postcolonial Ecocriticism: Literature, Animals, Environment*. London & New York: Routledge (First Indian Reprint), 2010.

Iovino, Serenella and Serpil Oppermann, eds. *Material Ecocriticism*. Bloomington and Indianapolis: Indiana University Press, 2014.

Monani, Salma and Joni Adamson. "Introduction." *Ecocriticism and Indigenous Studies: Conversations from Earth to Cosmos*, New York and London: Routledge, 2017.

Mukherjee, Madhusree. "Love in the Time of Development." himalmag.com, 1–6, doi: https://www.academia.edu/25108290/The_Last_Wave_-_Review_ Himal, 2016.

Pandya, Vishvajit. "In pursuit of fireflies: the poetics and politics of 'lightscapes' in the Jarawa forests." *New Histories of the Andaman Islands: Landscape, Place and Identity in the Bay of Bengal, 1790-2012*, edited by Clare Anderson, Madhumita Mazumdar and Vishvajit Pandya, Delhi: Cambridge University Press, 2016, pp. 201–227.

—. *In the Forest: Visual and Material Worlds of Andamanese History* (1858– 2006). Lanham/ Boulder/ New York: University Press of America, 2009.

Sekhsaria, Pankaj. *The Last Wave: An Island Novel*. Noida/London/New York: Harper Collins, 2014.

—. *Islands in Flux: The Andaman and Nicobar Story*. Noida/London/New York: Harper Litmus, 2017.

Skinner, Jonathan. "What is Eco-Poetics?" eco-poetry.org. doi: http://www.eco-poetry.org/what-is-eco-poetics-.html

Thieme, John. *Postcolonial Literary Geographies: Out of Place*. London: Palgrave Macmillan, 2016.

Chapter 3

Flowing with the Stream: Real and Magical Waters in Joseph Boyden's *Through Black Spruce*

Caroline Durand-Rous

OIKOS-CRESEM, University of Perpignan, France

Abstract: North American writer Joseph Boyden sets his second novel on several Native American contested landscapes where the environment undergoes the consequences of economical and political tensions between communities. However, far from being a pessimistic pamphlet denouncing the lack of sovereignty of the first nations over their land, *Through Black Spruce* displays an interesting literary plea for individual self-reinvention. Infused with myth, nature challenges its inhabitants' expectations and questions their place in reality, thus participating in the main character's personal quest for closure.

Drawing on Gaston Bachelard's works on the imagination of matter and Helen May Dennis's study of the Homing-in paradigm in Native American literature, this chapter aims to study how the permanence of water, declined in its different states throughout the novel, offers guidance to the main character towards a reinvented sense of self on postcolonial land and subsequently grounds her whole community into a reenchanted and congruous environment.

Keywords: contested landscapes, self-reinvention, totemism, reciprocity, water, ecopoetics, Native American literature, myth, postcolonial literature, environmental justice

***

Can the 'disenchanted' land of the reserves, a land bearing the stigmata of broken promises and false hope, be re-enchanted by literature? In contemporary novels, Native writers make a clear connection between racial and environmental injustice. Likewise, they highlight the necessity of healing the land, in other words reenchanting it, to heal the individuals belonging to the land. How does this re-enchantment process reconcile the novel's Western genre with the specificities of non-Western thought?

In her keynote address at the June 2016 ecopoetics conference held in Perpignan on "Dwellings of Enchantment[1]," Joni Adamson referred to the space-time continuum used by Native writers as a prominent feature of their literature. Indeed, in many indigenous novels from North America, characterization and narrative strategies draw as much on oral traditions as on immediate contemporaneity. Thus, much Native writing challenges the boundaries between realms that Western thinking holds as separate: between ancestors and their descendants, between the human and the nonhuman, between territories thousands of miles apart and yet linked by a common mythical and mystical history. In her 1986 introduction, Laguna Pueblo literary critique Paula Gunn Allen already asserted the importance of the creative flux at the core of this indigenous worldview, for it relies on the acknowledgment that nature is animated by spirit:

> American Indian thought is essentially mystical and psychic in nature. Its distinguishing characteristic is a kind of magicalness—not the childish sort described by Astrov, but rather an enduring sense of the fluidity and malleability, or creative flux, of things. This is a reasonable attitude in its own context, derived logically from the central assumptions that characterize tribal thought. The tribal person perceives things not as inert, but as viable and alive, and he or she knows that living things are subject to processes of growth and change as a necessary component of their aliveness. Since all that exists is alive and since all that is alive must grow and change, all existence can be manipulated under certain conditions and according to certain laws. These conditions and laws, called 'ritual' or 'magic' in the West, are known to American Indians variously. The Sioux refer to them as 'walking in a sacred manner,' the Navajo as 'standing in the center of the world,' and the Pomo as 'having a tradition.' (Gunn Allen 1986 2)

This distinctive worldview permeates contemporary Native literature, revealing itself through the many 'magical' and eerie occurrences that disrupt the conventional realistic linearity of the narrative: "In magical realist texts, ontological disruption serves the purpose of political and cultural disruption: magic is often given as a cultural corrective, requiring readers to scrutinize accepted realistic conventions of causality, materiality, motivation" (Zamora and Faris 3). Scholars do not always agree on the notion of "magical realism" to designate Native literature. Bo Schöler, for instance, prefers the use of "mythical realism." Native writers undeniably use magic as a tool of critical thinking to introduce alternative discourses to the dominant voice. However, magic cannot be reduced to an artificial literary device, for it is constituent of a complex system of belief. In March 2018, when asked the question: "Do you believe in magic?" by French journalist François Busnuel, Ojibway novelist Louise Erdrich answered: "I don't know if it's magic. I only know that it's another form of reality. The question is not to believe or not in magic. I know these things actually happen." In Native American worldviews, different simultaneous realities overlap and interact, giving way to magical events.

Joni Adamson articulates one aspect of the mythical or magical realism as she chooses to refer to Native American worldviews as 'cosmovisions' explaining that they are directly linked to current cosmopolitical movements seeking environmental justice along with social justice: "Cosmovisions are laying the foundation for cosmopolitics that are thousand of years in the making" (Adamson 6'30). Forming part of these endeavors, literary cosmovisions offer animalistic figures meant to be integrated as thought experiments: they act as boundary crossers thanks to their potential transformative powers inherited from the 'Dreamworld.' They are shapeshifters and, to that respect, offer mediation between the different strata of reality: "Contemporary indigenous writers weave the characteristics of anthropomorphic animals, androgynous and monstrous human figures from the oral tradition into their indigenous characters" (Adamson 5'10). These liminal beings abound in Ojibway Louise Erdrich's novels as well as in Chickasaw Linda Hogan's. This chapter focuses on the novel *Through Black Spruce*, part of a trilogy by Joseph Boyden, a Canadian writer claiming mixed Scottish, Irish, and Métis ancestry[2]. I argue that his postcolonial ecopoetics has actively contributed to modeling the element of water into a thought experiment by rewriting and reinventing totemism. In his novels, the multidimensional nature of water often opens the doors of perception, giving the protagonists access to a panel of renewed versions of themselves while grounding the characters into contested landscapes. In their introduction to the *Studies in American Indian Literatures* "Water is Life: Ecologies of Writing and Indigeneity" special issue, scholars Christina Boyles and Hilary E. Wyss note that "[w]ater inherently is linked with both sovereignty and climate change" (Boyles and Weiss 5). They explain that "water forms and re-forms the land, bringing structure and change to our ways of life" (Boyles and Wyss 5). This elemental plasticity is a key feature found in Joseph Boyden's novels. Thanks to it, water reveals the Native characters' inner disparities and challenges their assumptions. Doing so compels them to confront the intricacies of their hybrid identities as postcolonial subjects in between two cultures.

Through Black Spruce comes second in the trilogy while forming part of a five-novel cycle, two of which are still to be written. The three novels issued so far display a similar narrative structure, alternating several characters' first-person interior monologues. They are related by a close genealogy tying different generations of the same family together[3]. The first novel, *Three Day Road*, narrates Xavier Bird's return home after fighting during World War I. The novel starts with the reunion of two main characters, both Canadian Crees, Xavier, and his aunt Niska on the train platform. It unfolds as they make their three-day canoe journey back to Moosonee in northern Ontario. During this travel, which parallels the three-day journey of the newly deceased souls to the realm of the dead in Cree cultures[4], Xavier and Niska go back in time to retrieve memories about the combat zone (Xavier) and the end of her tribal bush life (Niska). In *Three Day Road*, water acts as an essential channel toward healing: it literally carries both characters on their way back to the Ancestors' land and metaphorically frees their voices by allowing them to put their personal ordeals into words, the stream of words embracing the pace of the river. Boyden's third novel, *The Orenda*, takes place in 1640 in an unspecified location in the Canadian outback. Three characters, Snow Falls, a young Iroquois girl, Christophe, a French missionary, and Bird, a fierce Huron warrior who abducted them, each tell their versions of the gruesome events that eventually led to the entanglement of their destinies. The three characters travel along the net of rivers flooding the land and, they do so, weave close ties between cultures which thereon start to share a common and yet contested history, thus prefiguring future Canada and announcing its enduring social inequities between the First Nations and the descendants of European colonists. In this novel, water operates as both a geographical link between people and a battlefield, absorbing the blood shed in the name of conquest and keeping the memory of past struggles.

As for *Through Black Spruce*, it is set nowadays in Moosonee, northern Ontario, a faraway city situated on the James Bay shore. The story adopts the perspectives of two homodiegetic narrators: Will Bird, Xavier's son, and Annie, his niece. At the novel's beginning, Will is in a coma after a brutal attack. In his mind, he speaks to his nieces, Annie and Suzanne. He then evokes past tragedies, explains what deed constrained him to fly up north into the bush, and what ordeals he thereafter met before being able to rebuild his sense of self. Meanwhile, urged by the hospital nurses to talk to the unconscious man, Annie begins to narrate the hardships she faced when she went down south looking for Suzanne, her missing sister who had left for the cities of Toronto, Montreal, and New York City to become a model. Her meaningful trip will not allow her to find Suzanne, who will reappear at the novel's end without giving any explanation. However, Annie's travel from one city to the next gradually evolves into an initiatory journey and eventually brings her closure. Thus,

Will's and Annie's narratives similarly give their accounts of past events without answering each other directly. Nevertheless, the act of storytelling, because it takes place once the protagonists have regained their familiar landscape, in other words, reserve grounds, makes their analogous trials significant and fully relevant. The intermingling narratives make sense of what happened and what is still to come by inscribing the characters' destinies into heroic cycles.

The unromanticized landscape described in the novel shows the crude reality of an isolated city affected by unemployment, poverty, alcoholism, and drugs. Likewise, the depiction of the bush, a remote flat marshland with a harsh climate, reveals its inherent roughness. At the same time, Joseph Boyden depicts its fragility owing to the aggressions of Western consumerism as when Will notices plastic refuse thrown back on the Bay James shore after a storm. In the novel, men and nature are subjected to similar pressure; environmental injustice mirrors social injustice as, to borrow Joni Adamson's expression, all *earth beings* undergo the same lack of consideration.

Water completely shapes the novel's territory: the Moose River, which links Moosonee to the island of Moose Factory; a myriad of streams and the multitude of lakes cover the outback, and heavy snow seasonally covers the scenery. It forms part of the Canadian Shield hydrographic basin, a vast region spreading from the Dakotas to the Atlantic Ocean and from Indiana to the Arctic Ocean. Among others, it encompasses the sources of two major North American rivers, namely the St Lawrence and the Mississippi, as well as the five Great Lakes. Home of the Algonquin nations, this once unified linguistic and cultural territory was split into two separate countries. The land thus contains the history of intersecting forms of violence: not only colonial forces thus severed the historical link between the Native populations, but also, they restricted these peoples' movements by assigning them specific reserve land away from coveted natural resources. Furthermore, authorities created a distinctive legal status belittling Autochthons as wards. The situation resulted in what Paula Gunn Allen referred to as the "Separation Trauma," a literary trope permeating Native fiction that she defines in such terms:

> Consider the use of the experience of enslavement in works by black writers. [...] For us, the whole issue of enslavement is part of the issue of conquest and colonization. In that context, it becomes a theme that shows frequently in Native writers' stories about jail, boarding school, war, and abduction. In all of these stories, the underlying theme is about forced separation, signifying the loss of self and the loss of personal meaning. (Gunn Allen 1989 8)

However, far from being a pessimistic pamphlet denouncing the lack of Native sovereignty, Boyden's novel offers a compelling plea for individual self-reinvention. Indeed, having accomplished their water-driven initiatory journeys (delving into the darkest depths as well as being washed away by the fastest streams), Annie and Will's renewed glance over the familiar landscape re-infuses the latter with myth, re-enchanting and reinvesting places with a long-lost, symbolical meaning.

In their introduction to the collection of essays entitled *Sounding the Depths: Water as Metaphor in North American Literature*, Gayle Wurst and Christine Raguet-Bouvart note the prominence of a doubleness of water in North American literature. Quoting 18th-century French-American writer St Jean de Crèvecoeur, they observe his water metaphors: "[Rushing water] is a horizontal image, one of the violent collision between *surfaces*, but the inherent doubleness of water metaphors also makes them an excellent vehicle for figurative exploration of *depth*" (Wurst and Raguet-Bouvart 2). Later on, Bernadette Rigal-Cellard explores the use of water symbolism by Ojibway writer Louise Erdrich, setting her novel on the same territory: the Canadian shield. Bernadette Rigal-Cellard then states: "In a land ridden with overflowing rivers and lakes, and covered half the year in lethal snow and ice, the symbolism of water cannot but be polysemous, implying death and excruciating suffering just as often as life and happiness" (Rigal-Cellard 1998 167). Undeniably, the intersecting tales in *Through Black Spruce* also draw on polysemous and ambiguous water images to challenge the characters' perceptions and bring them to face their inner turmoils.

In this chapter, I intend to address the different functions held by water in the novel: I will first explore the notion of whitewater, a water in motion providing a means of travel. Then I will analyze the images used by the characters of pure water as transformative water. Finally, I will study the dense and malleable totemic water that helps characters achieve self-reconciliation. By doing so, I will show how establishing a dialog with the elements of an ambivalent nature allows the Native characters of the novel to reinvent their identity.

Whitewater: Water in Motion

Even though Boyden sets his plot on contemporary ground, the novel regularly refers to traditional practices such as hunting, trapping, and fishing, albeit performed with modern tools. Indeed, the narrators make significant allusions to water acting as a useful commodity and still playing a central role in the characters' subsistence. Water has long been essential to the inhabitants of this faraway land. It was a means of travel, a surface sometimes liquid, sometimes frozen which served as roads to indigenous people, as well as a means of subsistence, a depth where to fish and harvest wild rice in the good season, and trap animals during wintertime. In *Through Black Spruce*, Annie daily rides her skidoo on the Moose River back and forth to the hospital where Will lies. Likewise, throughout the novel, Will and his friend Dorothy visit each other, borrowing the river taxis. Further on, Will flies away to the outback thanks to his hydroplane, hopping from rivers to lakes.

Meanwhile, Annie and Will regularly use the ancestral knowledge of hunting, especially of beaver trapping, to catch some meat and sell the furs to the store. Accomplishing this gesture, they acknowledge the cultural value of having such skills and also acknowledge the ritual value of hunting and trapping. For instance, Annie asserts this immemorial technique as proof of the common cultural inheritance of the Great Canadian shield Algonquin tribes. She is also grateful for the first catch given: "Just as you always taught me, our first gift from the water is a kit" (Boyden 2010 323). Through its diverse uses, water contributes to ground and legitimate the main characters in a specific *hic et nunc* encompassing every human/non-human interaction that has occurred on the land.

French anthropologist Emmanuel Désveaux, who lived many years among the Big Trout band, the farthest north residing band of the Ojibway nation, notices that the Indians living on this territory have developed unusual mental cartography where streams, rivers, and lakes prevail. He also observes that their spatial awareness defies our western cartography logic, granting the same river or lake several names according to the specific features of their different parts. Hence, their mental projection of space proceeds from punctual locations subservient to hunting and fishing necessities: "A significant homology exists between the Indians' representation of the hydrographic network and their general apprehension of space. This homology reveals the primacy of dots over lines" (Désveaux 26). The Algonquin nations do not rely on mapped roads but instead, picture dots that they can connect according to their traveling needs. Every dot is thus reinvested, generation after generation, by each visitor who adds the memory of a miraculous catch, an unsatisfactory hunting, an unexpected storm, or desperately thin ice even at the core of winter. Indeed, Algonquin geography consists, first of all, of a lived and fully experienced geography, in places time and time again strode upon, and indeed not the Western fantasy of a *terra incognita* that the white settlers developed when entering the Canadian bush.

Emmanuel Désveaux adds: "From a certain point of view, this perpetual rediscovery of the territory, though not quite being one, amounts to its reappropriation" (Désveaux 43). Paralleling Linda Hogan's *Solar Storms* initiatory journey on water for which three women rely on the older one's youth memories to find their way back to the ancestors' land[5], Boyden's protagonists comply with this Native figuration of a lived geography where places are cyclically re-engaged with each new experience and each new memory, and where imagination links the meaningful spots according to the traveling needs. Will flies his hydroplane from Moosonee to Atimiski island, where he hides. He then flies to Fort Albany on the Ghost river and back to Moosonee. Likewise, Annie leaves Moosonee to settle momentarily in three cities of water; in other words, cities situated on a river or a lake and comprising an island in their territory. She goes to Toronto on Lake Superior, then Montreal on the St Lawrence, and lastly to New York City on the Hudson River. Her many travels along the equilateral triangle thus formed are never narrated, for only the adventures experienced on those three points that define the triangle, mirror images of the initial city, prove relevant. "This city like Montreal times ten, like Moose Factory times a million, the island of Manhattan surrounded by rivers. I can't escape the rivers. I'm not meant to escape islands, either, apparently" (Boyden 2010 224).

At the beginning of her journey in Toronto, as she is looking for her sister, Annie is led to homeless Indians who have settled by the river. She is told to "Head toward the water" (Boyden 2010 78) to reach them. Their chief, a trickster figure who drinks Perrier out of bottles wrapped in brown paper bags, assigns her a protector in the person of Gordon, a mute urban Ojibway who cannot put into words the trauma he has suffered. Old Man then commands her to comply with her mission. A double water, both surface of displacement and depth of experience, thus compels Annie to achieve a quest from which she cannot withdraw as she clearly phrases it: "All I want is to go home, but something in me believes him when he tells me I don't have a home anymore till I travel further" (Boyden 2010 102). Each and every city that Annie explores belongs to the long-lost Algonquin territory. Each and every one of them reflects the deceitful image of another possible version of her life as she steps into her sister's shoes and becomes a model.

In "Native American Novels: Homing-In," William Bevis, having studied the Native American Renaissance novels, posited a recurrent literary trope in which damaged Indian characters needed to regain reserve ground in order to heal. In his article, Bevis opposed this *Homing-In* paradigm to the *Bildungsroman* structure in which the Western hero leaves home for faraway places in search of personal accomplishments[6]. However, most recent Native fictions sustain a more complicated and ambivalent relation to home. In Louise Erdrich's *Tracks*, the protagonists already live on the reserve, and they remain on it with the notable exception of Fleur leaving for the city by the end of the last chapter. In her other novel *Shadow Tag*, the characters stay in the city from the beginning to the end. In David Treuer's novels, also an Ojibway writer, either the characters do not leave the reserve and evolve in this closed world (*Little*), or the anti-hero departs to the city without regret at the beginning of the story and will not set foot on reserve ground again (*The Translation of Dr. Apelles*), or still one of the main characters, Simon, intends to perform some sort of *Homing-In* in order to put himself back together, but fails and has no other solution than going back to the city (*The Hiawatha*). Scholar Padraig Kirwan has compared Treuer's different narrative structures. He observes:

> Simon's dislocation, although reflecting many similarities to the difficulties experienced by Tayo [in *Ceremony* by Leslie Marmon Silko] and Abel [in *House Made of Dawn* by Scott Momaday], is a very different narrative arc to those found earlier in Native American novels. For him [...] the archetypal association between traditional home and the recovered self is far too insufficient to carry the family story or bring [him] "respite." (Kirwan 11)

In her book, *Native American Literature: Towards a Spatialized Reading*, critic Helen May Dennis thus quotes Native novelist Louis Owens: "Today [...] Euroamerica remains involved in an unceasing ideological struggle to confine Native Americans within an essentialized territory defined by the authoritative utterance 'Indian.' Native Americans, however, continue to resist this ideology of containment and to insist upon the freedom to reimagine themselves within a fluid, always shifting frontier space" (Owens 27). Later on, Helen May Dennis underlines the active process of imaginative synthesis that hustles narratives by decentering the archetype of *Home*.

In Boyden's novels, the characters' motion adopts the dynamics of an upward spiral that allows readers to rediscover Moosonee with each new generation. They are born and bred on the ancestors' land; they leave this cherished territory for faraway places that reveal, through an array of similarities, the magical value of the original landscape; then, they come back home to narrate their journey and, through this storytelling, they symbolically regenerate their sense of place. Water connects their personal memories and projects the protagonists into a movement of self-reinvention: "Though water expresses a great spectrum of meanings, the most prominent one associates it with individual memory, tribal memory and home" (Rigal-Cellard 1998 166). This element contains the first memories and adds to them the successive memories of new events lived on the initial territory as well on the analogous territories. It operates through the many moments of contemplation of surfaces that act as many meditative pauses which absorb the recollection of the many experienced ordeals. Moreover, thanks to its inherent plasticity, water, pervading the narratives in all its phases, enables displacement and evolution, hence reenchanting familiar landscapes by casting a new light on them as when, after a three-day storm, Will can eventually open his door:

When I emerged, the world was a different place […] This town, my
world, was frozen so still it looked like a photograph, the photograph of
what this town wished it could be […] Roofs of houses overhung with
wind-carved drifts, the ratty yards, the litter of broken bicycles and
dolls and children's missing running shoes, all under dazzling white.
The once dusty road, pothole ridden and washboarded, was now a
glittering diamond of ice stretching into the sun. (Boyden 2010 345)

Snow has embossed a new geography. By subsuming the city into the
immaculate bush, it offers Will a last motionless journey through which he
discovers a symbiosis of both environments that synthesizes every landscape
he has experimented with during his getaway.

Pure Water: Ablutions and Transformations

Through displacement and territory reappropriation, the characters
acknowledge the spiritual capital of a landscape infused with myth. While
proceeding to mental cartography, the members of the Ojibway tribe studied
by Emmanuel Désveaux do not merely figure landmarks on a commodity
territory. They endorse the existence of an ambivalent reality: each creek, each
part of the river is relevant to their imagination because they are both real and
magical, both a means of subsistence ruled by seasons and a mythical place
where one can interact with ancestors. In *Through Black Spruce*, Will and
Annie are given access to a parallel reality. Guided by water and confronted
with an array of visions and supranatural apparitions that challenge their
perception of reality, they are granted the opportunity to re-establish an
ancestral link to mythical times.

   In Montreal, where she quenches her tremendous thirst with bottled water,
Annie enters a trance of hybrid nature mixing both traditional rituals and
western drugs. Lost in a hype night-club, her senses, awakened by Ecstasy, are
captured by the haunting rhythm of synthesized Indian chanting. A
"fulgurance" then strikes her: so far from home, she has reached the Great
Primeval Ocean, the breeding ground of humankind: "People flow around me,
the sweat of their arms the salt of the ocean. Oh my god! That makes perfect
sense. We once came from the ocean, and we are mostly water. I am in an
ocean of people" (Boyden 2010 147). A few pages later, she reaffirms this
common origin ("We crawled out of the ocean millions of years ago. Humans
are mostly water" Boyden 2010 150) and concludes: "This is why I live by a
river." Everything brings her back to a liquid universal home. She then starts
to deconstruct her identity, playing with common stereotypes and alternately
adopting distinctive status referring to her plural origins: a French woman, an
Indian princess, and the fake naivety of a bush girl. By doing so, she gradually

recovers her Native language. She makes use of it to mock her discussion partners: "I begin speaking Cree in earnest now, the words at first awkward and chosen poorly, telling Soleil that her hair is green, she has small tits, that she is too skinny and needs to eat more moose meat. Oohs and aahs come from Soleil, and then from the ones around her" (Boyden 2010 262). Thus, the Great Primeval Ocean also echoes the flood of the Algonquin myth of origins and its ambivalent water, both destructive and re-creative. According to the legend, a terrible flood submerged the first version of the world and left the animals previously created afloat. Willing to reconstruct what had been lost, they begged Sky Woman to come and live with them. Big Turtle lent its back to welcome the goddess and her future babies. Muskrat dived into deep waters to retrieve a handful of dirt. Sky Woman then breathed life on the dirt, and the universe was created anew on Turtle Island, the Americas[7]: a world on fragile balance, floating on an endless ocean.

This powerful mythical water resurfaces in the numerous ablution scenes of the novel as a transformative water that reveals inner personalities through an anamorphosis process. Throughout the novel, water, associated with mirrors, and its metaphorical extensions, disrupts the protagonists' perception of selves. More than once, Annie splashes her face, and the image sent back by the mirror shows Suzanne's face: "[I] am startled by Suzanne's face staring at me from the mirror, water dripping off the sharp cheekbones" (Boyden 2010 37). This scene is the first transformation narrated in the novel and, in the meantime, the last to occur according to chronology. In contrast, at the beginning of her journey, when in Toronto, and while feeling lonely and irrelevant, Annie does not recognize her sister's face in a magazine ad: "[...] a woman with black hair tied back, splashing water across her face that shimmers in tiny droplets" (Boyden 2010 83). The magazine's glossy pages represent a figurative mirror surface that blurs limits and alters reality, thus revealing the instability of the characters' essences.

In Montreal, before immersing herself in her sister's life, Annie takes a hot shower to wash away her bush girl identity. Lost in the steam, she catches glimpses of her reflection in the mirror, but the situation proves reversed: her reflection looks at her and judges her through her "devil eye." Her attention remains polarized by this other self, and she keeps addressing the mirror while talking to Gordon: "I see Gordon staring up at me in the mirror. "I'm going out." I say to my reflection" (Boyden 2010 124). Progressively, mirror reflections become more real to Annie than the world surrounding her. Meanwhile, she undergoes an actual physical transformation: she loses weight, wears elaborate make-up, is dressed in trendy clothes, and learns to walk on the catwalk. At first, fascinated by the image of her evolving appearance, she is seized by vertigo, after taking drugs, at the exact middle of the novel.

Suzanne was here. She slept in this bed, and wore this shirt that I now wear, high across my bust.

> "I recognize you!" Violet says. She doesn't seem to care that I feel like I'm going to drown now [...] She leads me to the mirror and hovers right behind.
>
> I take a breath and open my eyes. I can't quite believe what stares back. I see the long black hair first, then the tall, thin body. The high cheekbones. Then I see the bright eyes. What has happened?
>
> I can see you, sister. I see you, Suzanne. (Boyden 2010 204)

Having first engaged in self-effacement, then endorsed an alien, and yet, so close identity, Annie finally accepts to move on and is reborn to herself. At the end of this painful journey, feeling at peace, she contemplates the Hudson River and feels ready to go back to Moosonee: "It's been a long way to New York City, and I'm ready to head home, paddle with the current for a while" (Boyden 2010 328).

This process is made possible by the intrinsic virtues of magical transformative water, for it possesses "an active and substantial purity," to borrow Gaston Bachelard's terms. In that regard, it is analogous to baptismal water: "Water is truly a transient element, the essential ontological metamorphosis between fire and earth. Beings committed to water are trapped in vertigo. They die every minute, for a part of their substance flows steadily away" (Bachelard 164). Indeed, whereas Annie experiences this metamorphosis vertigo by becoming her sister, Will is eager to immerse in the *Fountain of Youth* to retrieve a previous version of himself: "If I ever came back, I would come back reborn" (Boyden 2010, 181). At the beginning of his narrative, he admits to having become a mere shadow of his former self. He lost his wife and sons to a fire and turned to alcohol: "I've always been the bush man in this town. I've been the hunter, the trapper, the feeder of mouths. A thing passed on from father to son, and I was the one in possession of it. But it was slipping from me" (Boyden 2010 61). His physical and social decline then mirrors his community's, for Moosonee is subjected to domination by a gang of drug dealers. One day, Will retaliates, shooting one of them. He subsequently initiates a twofold self-reconstruction process by walking into his father's footsteps: first through action (he shoots a man, he hides in the bush, and survives thanks to traditional hunting and trapping), second in the flesh (like his father who lost a leg, Will suffers physically as well: his left leg is injured, he becomes emaciated and grows his hair).

Then, at the exact middle of the novel, he too experiences an epiphany: he drinks alcohol and enters a trance that makes him realize his metamorphosis: "I lay down on my blanket, stared down at my long body and really admired it for the first time. My gut was all but gone [...] [My arms] were as roped with muscle as when I was twenty-one [...] I felt something I'd not in a long time. I felt young and useful again. I felt powerful" (Boyden 2010, 212). Exhilarated, he undresses and immerses himself in the lake, confronting death: "The water pulled me, and I didn't fight it. My lungs ached and my chest began to pulse and spasm, wanting to suck in air. But if I opened my mouth now, I would fill with water and drown" (Boyden 2010 212). As he receives the vision of Suzanne's face, he finds the strength to get out of the water. Like Annie, he has experienced a mock death by drowning and is subsequently reborn thanks to Suzanne's apparition. He then enters a process of symbolic return to the earth: he covers himself with mud to become, according to his own terms, "invisible" and follows a stream leading to the skeleton of a beached whale. He enters this open-air cathedral and lies down, finally at peace. After this mystical experience, Will prepares for his return to civilization.

Totemic Water and Self-Reconciliation

The combination of the different waters appearing in the novel leads to the materialization of a porous frontier zone between different realities (the familiar territory transposed into other places), different times (the various stages of life), and between the world of the missing (whether dead or just absent) and the living. Lakes and islands seen from above become eyes witnessing Will and Annie's life path, whereas Will, staring at the lake's surface, catches a glimpse of his deceased wife. In her thesis directed by David Treuer, academic Jennifer Miller thus defined the purpose of such water frontier zones as found in many Native American novels: "The boundaries that appear in these texts serve as physical representations of interstitial spaces, thus functioning not as barriers or sites of separation, but as spaces of movement and coming together that facilitate the entry of the fantastic into the text" (Miller 16). This liminal space, allowing an area of negotiation between the contradictory elements of self and other, is characteristic of totemic water intervening as a catalyst providing energy for change. In *The Ritual Process: Structure and Anti*-Structure, Victor Turner analyzes liminality as the transient phase taking place in rites of passage, a "betwixt and between" state in which neophytes experiment with the coexistence of antagonist identities:

> The attributes of liminality or liminal *personae* ("threshold people") are necessarily ambiguous since this condition and these persons elude or slip through the network of classifications that normally locate

states and positions in cultural space. Liminal entities are neither here
nor there; they are betwixt and between the positions assigned and
arranged by law, custom, convention, and ceremonial. (Turner 95).

Water's substantial plasticity allows for this ontological ambiguity to take
shape. It represents a fluid space of exchanges between realities that enables
the protagonists to make complex alliances with totemic powers.

In *Through Black Spruce*, Will is under the influence of a deadly totem, the
Mauser his father acquired during the war and whose voice convinces him to
retaliate against his assailants. In the meantime, he develops a special
relationship with an old bear, the incarnation of a benevolent tutelar spirit.
Nonetheless, both influences on Will cannot be reduced merely to a
conflicting binary opposition of good to evil, for the combined energy of this
triangular relation replaces, at its core, necessary violence. Indeed, sometimes
after the whale cathedral episode, a polar bear, the combinatorial variant of
the familiar old bear, attacks Will's camp, and the latter's survival is only
insured by his use of the Mauser on the beast. Later on, to achieve his rite of
passage, Will attains the Ghost River, a place haunted by the memory of a fur-
trading post thus peopled by the ghosts of Indians as well as of the first white
settlers: "The abandoned settlement lay just the hill and in a grown-over
clearing. Fort Albany Cree called it *chipayak e ishi ihtacik*, whispered it was
full of ghosts, and they are the ones, I guess, who gave this river its name."
(Boyden 2010 295). There, reality is reversed. A supranatural storm makes the
river run sideways. Seen through a pane of glass Will dug out of the ruins, the
world seems distorted: his hand suddenly looks like a claw, branches turn into
black serpents, and the river becomes a lava flow. Unnerved by the
permeating ambivalence thus revealed, Will breaks the glass and finally feels
ready to go back to Moosonee after completing his rite of passage.

Many other contemporary Native fictions, among which are Louise Erdrich
and David Treuer's novels, make use of this hybrid totemism to challenge the
characters' certitudes and bring them to redefine their identity. In each of
these novels, deep and furious water, whether an untamed river or a
bottomless lake, asserts itself as an interface to mythical times, performing as
the only substance where totems can be born and, in turn, annihilated.
Indeed, all literary representations of totemic water retain, in their nature, a
part of the primal totemic water as portrayed in the Ojibway myth of the first
totems. According to this myth, six supranatural and anthropomorphic beings
were born out of the ocean. They decided to go and live with humans to teach
them essential knowledge. However, due to their magical origin, they had to
control their incommensurable power; otherwise, their sacredness could kill
mortals. One of them, in particular, needed to keep a blindfold and was

forbidden to lay eyes on humans. Unfortunately, he disobeyed, and his glance struck a man who died instantly. The other five beings condemned him to dive back into the ocean, the only substance potent enough to contain sacred powers. The five remaining beings became the first five totems of the Ojibway clans: crane, catfish, loon, bear, and marten[8]. Thanks to its fundamental ability to shapeshift from solid to liquid, from liquid to gas, and back again, water materializes an open door to the invisible realm. In *Through Black Spruce*, it pervades the characters' reality using all its possible physical states and re-infuses totemic magic in their environment.

Boyden's novel begins with Will's description of the *Dreamworld*, a world made entirely of water in all its forms, which has enveloped him completely since he fell into a coma: "The snow's deep here, nieces. I'm tired, but I have to keep walking. I'm so tired, but I've got to get up or I'll freeze to death. Talking to you, it keeps me warm" (Boyden 2010 5). If cold water (snow and ice) predominates, another warm water, a river stream of voices, pushes him onward. He feels attracted to it but fears its power and dreads drowning in its strong current. At the end of the novel, as he stands dangerously at the edge of the liminal zone, Will grows bolder: "Now that I am beside this river, I finally understand how I've gotten here. I can put it into words. Just under the current, I hear the babbling of voices. They are the voices of my family and of my friends. They are excited. They are happy. I'm warm again here, even if the right side of my face stills feels frozen. The river's sound is pleasant, and the sun through the spruce makes me sleepy" (Boyden 2010 382).

The novel makes use of the duality of totemic water: on the one hand, real water soaking the territory with its magic, and on the other hand, the figurative flow of water that carries both protagonists' narratives. It forms waves of emotions that are said to "wash over" the characters. It also manifests through the liberated speeches that make sense of past ordeals, "heal with words" and consequently restore cosmogony. When she returns, Annie states: "The world really did shift on its axis during my time down south" (Boyden 2010 367). Back in town, Will notices that the world has finally become "complete," that Moosonee has turned into "the perfect place." Thanks to the stream of language, the protagonists achieve the reconciliation of the fragments of a shattered identity. The novel ends with the happy picture of a reconstituted clan comprising family members (Will, his sister Lisette and his nieces Annie and Suzanne), white and Indian friends (Gregor and Joe), new lovers (Gordon and Dorothy), and the departed: "A cool wind blows off the bay, and waves splash against my canoe. The sun shines on the salt water all around me. My lost one, my two lost ones, walk closer" (Boyden 2010 404). Their gathering on Xavier's winter hunting camp on the Bay James shore, near the mouth of the Moose River, then mirrors the many family reunions Will and

Annie had participated to on that very spot when Xavier was still alive. The novel concludes on a note of hope, Will asserting: "I'll be fine" (Boyden 2010 404) as every member of the reconstituted clan reaches out to help him stand on the beach. His use of the modal *will* leaves no doubt as to the result of his personal rite of passage: although physically impaired, Will has reconquered an active sense of self. The dense and malleable material of totemic water thus enables Will and his relatives to reinvest a hybrid identity, reinvent the notion of the clan and operate the reappropriation of their vernacular territory by attaching a new shared memory to it.

Conclusion

Joseph Boyden's reenchantment of the land dwells on what Huggins calls a "literary water ecolog[y]" (Huggins 54). Boyden infuses this element with magic and symbolism to guide his characters toward closure. Resisting the Western stereotype of an untouched wilderness—the only one worth preserving according to mainstream thinking—the novelist urges us to reinvest in a lived and inhabited nature, an ever-changing land that forms part of the great circle of life, for, as Leslie Marmon Silko so rightly explained: "Those who claim to love and protect the Mother Earth have to love all of her, even the places that are no longer pristine" (Silko 1991 95).

I would like to conclude this chapter by quoting Bernadette Rigal-Cellard again "The protagonists [of Native American novels] must learn to decipher the signs that surround them and engage into a semiology of day-to-day life, for it duplicates the semiology of the spiritual world that governs and controls us" (Rigal-Cellard 2004 254). Indeed, the many waters of *Through Black Spruce* form a complex network of connections between the visible and invisible realms. Reversing polarities and upsetting the perception of reality, they act as a hall of mirrors, eventually unveiling the underlying magic of the landscape. While deciphering those many signs, the characters sustain a reciprocal relationship with their environment: their renewed glance over familiar grounds re-enchants the territory, which, in turn, sustains their initiatory journeys. Because they willfully enter this dynamic process, Annie and Will, and through them their whole clan, redefine a new way of being in the world, making it the sum of a multiplicity of complementary potentialities and overcoming exclusive propositional logic: being Indian or white, being defeated or victorious, maintaining a traditional way of life or integrating mainstream society. As Joni Adamson so accurately notices in *American Indian Literature, Environmental Justice, and Ecocriticism: The Middle Place*, when she analyzes the actions of Louise Erdrich's boundary crosser character, Nanapush: "Struggling for alternative visions of the world then requires a knowledge not only of the vernacular landscape but of the official one as well.

Moving intelligently and cautiously between two landscapes, Nanapush opens both to the possibility of reinterpretation and re-signification, and finds tools to create new ceremonies and new knowledges in both places" (Adamson 2001 111). Like Angel, the main character in *Solar Storms*, who sheds her skin to discover a renewed version of herself, the protagonists in *Through Black Spruce*, Annie et Will, are ritually reborn after unmasking inner selves that were previously hidden under inadequate corporeal shells. Thanks to the water element, the novel gives the characters access to multifaceted landscapes where they feel embedded and regain confidence in their ability to make sense of any new context. In that regard, Boyden offers a remarkable illustration of Gerald Vizenor's *Survivance* concept: "Survivance is an active sense of presence, the continuance of native stories, not a mere reaction, or a survival name. Native survivance stories are renunciations of dominance, tragedy and victimry" (Vizenor vii). Having developed a privileged bond with real and magical waters, Boyden's protagonists give a clear rebuttal to the *vanishing Indian* stereotype. Being neither victims, nor super-heroes, but only profoundly human, Boyden's Indians are in the place, still in the place, and clearly decided to endure.

Notes

[1] Joni Adamson's keynote address can be accessed in its entirety at http://ecopoetics perpignan.com/watch-videos-keynotes-writers-and-academics/

[2] Joseph Boyden's claims are at the core of ongoing controversy as many people contest the veracity of his Native identity. The issue has divided the aboriginal community as Native writers, journalists, and artists have vigorously taken a side on the matter. For instance, Salish novelist Lee Maracle supports Boyden, pointing out a destabilization attempt. She argues that the proof-based colonial system—compelling individuals to show official documents assessing the tribal enrollment of their ancestors—is a doomed process that deprives Indian nations of valuable members. Other prominent figures, such as Nooksack journalist Robert Jago, have denounced the opportunistic maneuver of a "Wannabe" Indian who has falsified his identity. Despite the boiling debate over his ancestry, Boyden's writing still falls in the category of Native studies. Displaying a complex entanglement of culturally informed patterns and subtle work on narrative structures, his novels deserve to be analyzed within the specific framework of postcolonial studies.

[3] By doing so, Joseph Boyden clearly adopts the narrative patterns used early on by Ojibway novelist Louise Erdrich. Throughout her 16 novels, she developed a complex web of interconnected families going back and forth between the epoch of first contacts and contemporary times. Often complementary and sometimes contradictory, the many personal narratives construed by the author offer access to a multifaceted reality of the 'Native American experience.'

[4] In Cree cultures, the wake lasts for three days and three nights, during which friends and relatives take turns telling stories to the deceased. Crees believe that, during that wake, the soul of the deceased accomplishes a journey to the afterlife where he or she is welcome by the Ancestors. While articulating the main events occurring in the life of the loved one and recalling Creation stories, mourners ensure him or her a safe passage to the realm of the dead. Likewise, they heal their own sorrow.

[5] In "Writing a Way Home: Magical Realism, Liminality, and the Building of a Biotic *Communitas* in Linda Hogan's *Solar Storm* and *People of the Whale*," Bénédicte Meillon appropriately labels this movement "a return to the οἶκος through ecopoetic, magical realist prose" (Meillon 207). To heal and eventually find closure, the three women need to connect to this "liminal geograph[y] in between land and water, providing contact zones in postcolonial situations" (Meillon 208). Immersing in this highly symbolic landscape enables Native characters to challenge assigned representations for the many metamorphoses of water contribute, as we shall see later on, to grant access to a renewed being in the world. Telling and retelling the water-driven journeys through the prism of the Ancestors' stories, assesses the place of the Native characters in the set of connections linking the human world and the nonhuman world: "Essentially, albeit ruled by mystery and spirituality, [Linda Hogan's] magical realist fiction in many ways proves coherent with an ecological understanding of the world" (Meillon 210). Joseph Boyden's novels comply with this narrative discourse.

[6] In "Native American Novels: Homing-In," William Bevis compares the narrative structures of D'Arcy McNickles' *The Surrounded* (1936) and *Wind from an Enemy Sky* (1978), Scott Momaday's *House Made of Dawn* (1966), Leslie Marmon Silko's *Ceremony* (1977), James Welch's *Winter in the Blood* (1974) and *The Death of Jim Loney* (1979). He is then able to determine a common pattern that brings the characters back to the land of their ancestors: "All six novels present a Western "self" seeking to transfer energy to a tribal context" (Bevis 1987 618).

[7] Basil Johnston gives a more comprehensive account of this myth of origins in *The Manitous: The Spiritual World of the Ojibways* (xv).

[8] The five initial totems evolve into a plurality of other totemic species. The full account of the myth and its development is found in W. W. Warren's *History of the Ojibways* (43).

Works cited

Adamson, Joni. *American Indian Literature, Environmental Justice, and Ecocriticism: The Middle Place*. Tucson: The University of Arizona Press, 2001.

Bachelard, Gaston. *L'eau et les rêves : essai sur l'imagination de la matière*. Paris: Le Livre de poche, 2012.

Bevis, William. "Native American Novels: Homing In." *Recovering the Word: Essays on Native American Literature*. Edited by Brian Swann and Arnold Krupat, Berkeley: University of California Press, 1987.

Boyden, Joseph. *Three Day Road*. London: Penguin Books, 2006.

—. *Through Black Spruce*. London: Phoenix Paperback, 2010.

—. *The Orenda*. London: Oneworld Book, 2014.

Boyles, Christina and Hilary E. Wyss. "Water is Life: Ecologies of Writing and Indigeneity." *Studies in American Indian Literatures*, Vol. 30, n° 3-4, Fall-Winter 2018, pp. 1–-9.

Dennis, Helen May. *Native American Literature: Towards a Spatialized Reading*. Oxon: Routledge, 2007.

Désveaux, Emmanuel. *Sous le signe de l'ours : mythes et temporalité chez les Ojibwas septentrionaux*. Paris: Maison des sciences et de l'homme, 1988.

Erdrich, Louise. *Tracks*. New York: Harper and Row, 1988.

—. *Shadow Tag*. New York: Harper Perennial, 2010.

Gunn Allen, Paula. *The Sacred Hoop: Recovering the Feminine in American Indian Traditions*. Boston: Beacon Press, 1986.

—. *Spider Woman's Granddaughters*. Boston: Beacon Press, 1989.

Hogan, Linda. *Solar Storms*. New York: Scribner Paperback, 1997.

Huggins, William. "Pipelines, Mines, and Dams: Indigenous Literary Water Ecologies and the Fight for a Sustainable Future." *Canadian Review of Comparative Literature / Revue canadienne de littérature comparée*, vol.44, n°1, March 2017, pp. 53–66. Project Muse. Accessed 7 Sept. 2018.

Johnston, Basil. *The Manitous: The Spiritual World of the Ojibways*. Saint Paul: Minnesota Historical Society Press, 2002.

Kirwan, Padraig. "Remapping Place and Narrative in Native American Literature: David Treuer's The Hiawatha." *American Indian Culture and Research Journal*, n°31 (2), 2007.

Meillon, Bénédicte. "Writing a Way Home: Magical Realism, Liminality, and the Building of a Biotic Communitas in Linda Hogan's *Solar Storms* and *People of the Whale*." *Dwellings of Enchantment: Writing and Reenchanting the Earth*, Lanham: Rowan & Littlefield, 2020.

Miller, Jennifer. *From Water Margins to Borderlands: Boundaries and the Fantastic in Fantasy, Native American, and Asian American Literatures*. Ph.D. Dissertation. Minneapolis: University of Minnesota, 2009.

Momaday, Scott. *House Made of Dawn*. New York: Harper Perennial, 2010.

Owen, Louis. *Mixedblood Messages: Literature, Film, Family, Place*. Norman: University of Oklahoma Press, 2001.

Rigal-Cellard, Bernadette. "Pebbles, Lakes, Floods and Beads: Chippewa Water Metaphors in Louise Erdrich's Tracks and Love Medicine." *Sounding the Depths: Water as Metaphor in North American Literature*, Liège: Liège Language and Literature, 1998.

—. *Le mythe et la plume, la littérature indienne contemporaine*. Monaco: Les éditions du rocher.

Silko, Leslie Marmon. 1986. *Ceremony*. New York: Penguin Books, 2004.

—. *Yellow Woman and the Beauty of the Spirit*. Toronto: Simon and Schuster, 1991.

Treuer, David. *Little*. New York: Picador USA, 1997.

—. *The Hiawatha*. New York: Picador USA, 1999.

—. *The Translation of Dr. Apelles*. New York: Vintage Contemporaries, 2006.

Turner, Victor. *The Ritual Process: Structure and Anti-Structure*. New York: Cornell Paperbacks, 1977.

Vizenor, Gerald. *Manifest Manners: Narratives on Postindian Survivance*. Lincoln: University of Nebraska Press, 1999.

Warren, William Whipple. *History of the Ojibways*. Saint Paul: Minnesota Historical Society Press, 2009.

Wurst, Gayle and Christine Raguet-Bouvart. *Sounding the Depths: Water as Metaphor in North American Literature*. Liège: Liège Language and Literature, 1998.

Zamora, Lois and Wendy Faris. *Magical Realism: Theory, History, Community*. Durham: Duke University Press, 1995.

Chapter 4

Worlds of Stories: Narrating Native American Land in Documentary Film

Maxime Petit

University of Toulouse 1 Capitole, France

Abstract: This paper investigates the way Native American land is narrated in documentary films, from early ethnographic films such as *In the Land of the Head Hunters* (Edwards S. Curtis, 1914) or *Nanook of the North* (Robert Flaherty, 1922), to the 1993 documentary about the Oka Crisis *Kanehsatake: 270 Years of Resistance* by Alanis Obomsawin. It first focuses on the way early films by Western documentarians offered romanticized depictions of Native lands and emphasized their pristine character, thereby implying that Native lands were available for appropriation and commodification. The second part of the paper explores how Native documentaries may offer a vision of the land that both goes against the grain of early ethnographic films and seeks to reinstate traditional conceptions of the land through the use of oral traditions. The analysis of Obomsawin's film reveals the tenuous distinction between stories and maps in Native conceptions of the world, and provides insight into the way documentary films can take part in the process of re-appropriating Native land.

Keywords: Native American land, ethnographic film, Edward S. Curtis, Robert Flahery, Native American documentary film, Alanis Obomsawin, Native American oral traditions, Oka Crisis

***

Even though Native American cinema was popularized through a number of feature films that met with considerable critical acclaim in North America and Europe, documentaries hold a special place in the larger corpus of Native films, a specificity which is perhaps best exemplified by the number of documentary films produced compared to that of feature films.[1] In assessing the specificity of Native documentary, Leuthold surmises that it constitutes a specific genre "distinct from non-native documentary film" because of "the concerns of contemporary native documentarians" which he lists as follows:

> a shared understanding and valuation of nature; a concern for communicating the indigenous understanding of history; legal and moral issues related to land; ideas about native spirituality; and an attempt to create a strong sense of collective identity within native communities. (Leuthold 1997b 74)

While he does not establish a clear hierarchy between these concerns, the relationship with the land and the natural world is often seen as the cornerstone of Native identity, the aspect from which all others stem. Thus, the importance of nature in Native documentary is linked to specific balanced conceptions of the world. This focus may also provide Native filmmakers with an opportunity to offer corrective responses to the overwhelming place that nature holds in traditional non-Native documentaries about Native Americans. Indeed, for Houston Wood, a common characteristic of Indigenous-made films is that they generally share not so much "content but rather a similar relationship to the dominant cinematic traditions that they, to various degrees, oppose" (Wood 2).[2]

This essay attempts to investigate nature's central place in documentaries related to Indigenous people, from early ethnographic films to recent documentaries by Native filmmakers. The first part focuses on representations of Indigenous land in the films of Edward S. Curtis and Robert Flaherty as well as on the culturally-biased and commercial background that both informed their modes of representation and imposed preconceived narratives upon Indigenous land. The second part explores how Native documentaries may offer a vision of the land that both goes against the grain of early ethnographic films and seeks to put Indigenous-centric conceptions of the land center stage by focusing on different narrative modes and cartographic discourses derived from oral traditions. To address this question, I focus on Alanis Obomsawin's iconic 1993 documentary about the Oka Crisis *Kanehsatake: 270 Years of Resistance*.

This choice was motivated by two main reasons. The first one lies in the fact that the film has often been seen as a document more than as a documentary. That the film is an invaluable account of the events that took place in Oka in the summer of 1990 is undeniable, but reducing it to this dimension only is problematic as it implies, on the one hand, a reductive vision of the work of an artist who masters the medium she works with and, on the other hand, a somewhat naive belief in the supposed objectivity of the documentarian which Obomsawin herself does not claim.[3] The second reason is that analyses of *Kanehsatake* often tend to focus on its socio-political aspect and overlook the links between this question and specific conceptions of the land informed by traditional Indigenous beliefs and oral traditions. Indeed, the film also highlights the spiritual roots of the conflict so as to both undermine dominant discourses on Native land and engage Native communities in the process of reasserting both their specific relationship with the natural world and their land rights.

Native American Land and Early Documentaries

It is commonly acknowledged that the origins of documentary filmmaking lie in early ethnographic films such as Curtis's 1914 film *In the land of the Head Hunters* and Flaherty's 1922 hit *Nanook of the North*. The term "documentary" was coined by documentarian and theoretician John Grierson in a 1926 review of Flaherty's *Moana* written for *The New York Sun*. He borrowed the word from the Lumière brothers, who in the 1890s made a number of "documentaires" which "were in essence travelogues" (Hayward 90). Thus, the genre is historically linked to the exploration of foreign and, more often than not, Indigenous lands. Consequently, many early ethnographic films' titles or subtitles mention a geographical area and stress a close relationship between the land and its inhabitants. Titles and subtitles such as *In the Land of the Head Hunters: A Drama of Primitive Life on the Shores of the North Pacific* and *Nanook of the North: A Story of Life and Love in the Actual Arctic* establish a sense of belonging to a specific area which unfolds on two distinct levels: while the title vaguely situates the setting of the film, the subtitle emphasizes a precisely identifiable or authentic area as if to balance fantasy with precise geographical or topographical knowledge.[4]

This relationship, however, was perceived through the filter of a romanticized view of the land. The prologue of the book version of Curtis's *In the Land of the Head-Hunters* is a telling example of this tendency. The text opens with a lengthy description of Kwakiutl land—the Queen Charlotte Strait on the coast of British Columbia—emphasizing a pristine and hostile natural environment. The land is described as a place where "a somber gloomy forest meets a forbidding sea" and where trees are "gnarled, twisted, and low-bent" due to "the angry ocean winds." The description relies on a plethora of adjectives that highlight the dramatic hostility of the landscape. The surf is described as "ever-beating" and "roaring," the cliffs as "worn," the waves as "dashing" and the peaks as "rugged." The winters are depicted as "long" and "gloomy" with their fair share of "wild, lashing winds and ceaseless rains" (Curtis 1). The area seems to be deprived of "song birds [...] as if these forests were too vast and gloomy for their liking" (Curtis 2). In keeping with a kind of environmental determinism, the adjective "gloomy," abundantly used to describe the land, is further applied to its inhabitants, a people "whose character seems in harmony with their gloomy, forbidding homeland." The forests and mountains, however, abound with game while the sea "fairly teems with life" and "the sands and rocks abound with shell-fish," providing potential food for the natives. In a particularly colorful passage, the sea-depths become a fantastically abundant land "so covered with plants and sea anemones, that to look into the crystal depths is to glance into fairyland" (Curtis 5). This kind of depiction of Indigenous land as both a land of plenty and a howling wilderness was essentially inherited from early Bible-inspired descriptions of the North American continent.[5]

Such visions were, of course, deeply rooted in the belief in a "vanishing race" soon to be overwhelmed by progress and the taming of the forces of nature by Euro-Americans.[6] Ethnographic filmmakers thus offered a distorted vision of Native people, which erased all traces of adaptation to technology. As Rony states, such filmmakers were akin to "taxidermists" in their efforts to record "archetypal moments" in which truth had to be reshaped so as to fit the Western fantasy of the "authentic first man" (Rony 102–3). Curtis and Flaherty famously indulged in anachronistic scenes which mirror this tendency. *In the Land of the Head Hunters*, for example, features a scene in which an old man is trying to ignite tinder with two pieces of wood at a time when Kwakiutl people commonly used matches. The end of Curtis's description of Kwakiutl land and character in the book's prologue illustrates the same quest for archetypal moments: "Such was the country, thus lived the people, when the white man first touched these shores" (Curtis 6). Flaherty similarly portrayed Nanook hunting seal with a spear when the use of rifles was well-established in Nunavik or trying to bite a gramophone while visiting a trading post when such devices were not unknown to Inuk people.[7]

It is no coincidence that early landmark ethnographic films such as Flaherty's were often at least partly funded by corporate sponsors who had an interest in the exploration and exploitation of the land and wished "to associate their image with his romantic vision" (Aufderheide 20).[8] *Nanook*, for example, was financially backed by Révillon Frères, a French fur trading company whose name appeared both in the opening credits and on the original promotional poster. The film offered a convenient advertisement for the company and legitimized its activities in Nunavut by presenting them as economically beneficial for Inuk people. In enclosing Indigenous peoples in a narrative of inevitable destruction, ethnographic films promoted their sponsors' products and justified the appropriation of Indigenous land for commercial purposes.

The dramatization of the original material was often emphasized in titles and subtitles as well as in the promotional material for the films through references to those narrative genres that were most likely to attract spectators. The above-mentioned subtitle of *In the Land of the Head Hunters* labeled the film as "a drama of primitive life" while the original poster and a 1915 brochure advertising a screening of the film at Carnegie Hall presented it as an "Indian Epic Drama of the Northern Sea" and specified "Entire Drama Enacted by Primitive Indians," thereby emphasizing the dramatic dimension of the film.[9] A similar marketing technique was used to present *Nanook* as "a story of life and love." While the term "story" enticingly highlighted narration and the dramatization of the original footage, the notions of "life and love" insisted on the supposed universality of a plot that was actually typical of Western cultural productions.[10]

Native American Documentary Film and Oral Traditions

The work of Native documentarians, Leuthold contends, contrasts with the narrative structures of early ethnographic films insofar as they "tell the histories of survivors," "of historical continuity" and the "weight of history" on contemporary lives (Leuthold 1997a 730). Leuthold's word choice is not incidental, as a number of scholars and filmmakers have noted a continuum linking oral traditions and documentaries. Tuscarora scholar Richard Hill, for instance, goes so far as to state that documentaries "have replaced oral tradition" (in Leuthold 1997a 730). Navajo scholar and documentary filmmaker Beverly Singer notes that film has the capacity to restore the enduring continuity of oral traditions:

> Our films and videos are helping to reconnect us with very old relationships and traditions. Native American filmmaking transmits beliefs and feelings that help revive storytelling and restore the old foundation. (Singer 2)

From this perspective, Indigenous media constitute powerful acts of resistance that "contribute to the maintenance and autonomy of native cultures" rather than disrupt traditional cultural productions (Beattie 64).[11]

The study of the relationship between documentaries and oral traditions is particularly relevant to understand the specific place nature holds in Native documentary as Native oral stories are grounded in specific landscapes to which they confer spiritual significance. Conversely, in the traditional belief systems of Native people, precise and intimate knowledge of the landscape informs spirituality.[12] Oral traditions, of course, are not just about spirituality. In many ways, they have practical uses. "Mythic tales linked to specific places contained morals and teachings that enabled people to live as true human beings," Colin Calloway writes (7). Abenaki writer Joseph Bruchac similarly notes that experience and oral traditions were the ways Native people acquired the knowledge that "enabled them to blend into the land" (Bruchac ix-x). For example, stories can contain teachings on how to hunt and fish or information about the use of medicinal plants. They also provide powerful representations of the land similar to Western printed maps. Pre-contact maps, Nabokov notes, were more likely to be transmitted orally than "committed to paper" (Nabokov 246). Native oral traditions often contain precise geographical details that ground the community in a specific landscape but also function as mnemonic tools to identify locations or itineraries, thus blurring the boundary between "stories" and "maps."[13]

Oral traditions are even more important in the case of Alanis Obomsawin's work since, as Lewis notes, it "was an essential part of her childhood as well as the first place she found success as an artist."[14] Her reliance on storytelling techniques and the influence of oral traditions on her work have been noted by several critics and scholars.[15] Saulteaux artist and critic Robert Houle, for example, calls Obomsawin "a storyteller who makes films" (Houle 204, my translation). Aspects of her films that suggest the influence of traditional storytelling include but are not limited to: her use of the voiceover to guide viewers through the film, her habit of telling stories (including shorter narrative sequences focusing on remote historical events which are embedded in the wider narrative) and of letting the people she interviews tell their own stories, the calm rhythm she adopts when narrating her stories along with occasional pauses and silences which invite a form of dialogic interaction with the viewers/listeners.[16]

Inhabiting Kanehsatake

Interestingly enough, *Kanehsatake* opens with a map and Obomsawin's voice introducing the geographical context of the film: "The story you will see takes place near Montreal," a statement which literally presents the film as a "visual story" focusing on a specific geographical area (0:15). The next shot shows a golf course seen from what appears to be a dark spot in a forest. However, as the narrative voice explains the reasons that led to the Oka crisis, the camera slowly zooms out to reveal tree trunks and tombstones, and the spectator is drawn into the heart of the matter: the pines and the burial ground on the land of the Mohawks. The following shot shows a board nailed onto a tree trunk reading "MOHAWK TERRITORY." As the filmmaker narrates the events that led to the Oka crisis, a long tracking shot shows a vast extent of land already occupied by the golf course, which takes on a particularly invasive dimension and becomes a potent symbol of the commodification of the land. Meanwhile, the narrator relates the progressive appropriation of the commons by the town of Oka, the damage done to the land, and the dispossession of the

Mohawks. Obomsawin also emphasizes the use of the land made by the Mohawks and explains that people from Kanehsatake complained in the 1930s because "the cattle were being chased away with golf sticks and there was nothing for the animals to eat," implying that this was no "idle land" contrary to the argument often used to support the appropriation of Indian land (1:20). This is further evidenced throughout the film by a variety of occasional shots featuring cows or hens. The theme is common to a number of Indigenous documentaries and contravenes early ethnographic films' depictions of Indigenous land as pristine wildlife sanctuaries: Indigenous people do use the land, and its protection is a matter of physical and spiritual survival.

The film's opening, which ends with a low-angle shot of the pines, points at another central element in Obomsawin's and other Native filmmakers' approach to filming the land. The ethnographic film tradition generally emphasizes Indigenous people's relationship with the land through grandiose and spectacular images of the natural world verging on the sublime. This mode of representation is grounded in those early ethnographic films that emphasized man's struggle against nature. Spectacular shots of the natural world, such as the sea-towering cliffs in Curtis's film or the vast windswept expanses of snow in *Nanook*, conveyed a sense of nature's beauty and its intrinsic harshness. Such images were meant to both inspire wonder and curiosity and trigger the kind of "terror" that Edmund Burke cast as "the ruling principle of the sublime" (58). Conversely, Native filmmakers tend to avoid majestic shots of nature and favor average landscapes over picturesque locations. "Spirituality, Chris Eyre explains, is about the day to day, hanging in there" (in Fielding 8). Similarly, Obomsawin shows the spiritual significance attached to the land using images of the land, which, even though they are sometimes technically complex, feature non-spectacular elements of the natural world.

As the movie unfolds, Mohawk leader Ellen Gabriel describes the arrival of the SWAT team at the roadblock blocking access to the golf course. She explains that the women in the group decided to go to the front "because it's our obligation to do that, to protect the land, to protect our mother" (3:02). The theme is further echoed in *Rocks at Whisky Trench*, one of Obomsawin's subsequent films about the Oka Crisis in which Selma Karioniakatste Delisle can be heard stating: "Women are the title holders to the land and we will never give that up" (1:17:51). This emphasizes the sacredness of the land and the relationship that unites the Mohawks and the pines, but it also hints at the part played by women in the preservation of the traditional order of the world in Iroquois culture.[17]

Communality and Continuity in the Pines

Following the death of Corporal Lemay, the crisis intensifies, and the film offers another low-angle shot of the pines. It is accompanied by Obomsawin's statement that "the first stand is made in the pines by the Longhouse people" (6:55). This refers to the traditionalists of the Kanehsatake Longhouse and establishes a distinction between the Longhouse, the Band Council, and the Warriors.[18] However, the filmmaker stresses that "the Mohawks now present a united front in spite of tensions among different factions in Kanehsatake" (7:00).[19] This counters the Canadian government's emphasis on factionalism to both explain the Oka Crisis and the failure of peaceful negotiations and discredit the Mohawk Warriors (Kalant 156-9).[20] Moreover, the phrase "Longhouse people" brings to mind the term "Haudenosaunee," which does not refer to the Mohawks only but to the Iroquois Confederacy as a whole and gives more weight to the struggle. Obomsawin further mentions that "Warriors from other communities come to support their brothers and sisters," referring to supporters from the Iroquois reservations of Akwesasne and Kahnawake (7:06). The notions of sisterhood and brotherhood thus reactivate the ties that united the Iroquois Confederacy and potentially extend them to other Native people across the Americas as Obomsawin shows that delegations from Indigenous communities from Canada, the United States, and Mexico have come to Oka to show their support for the Mohawks. As the camera pans across the pines in a circular motion, it becomes obvious that it is placed behind an embankment in what seems to be a pit in the ground. The shot poetically conveys the idea that the pines constitute a haven that must be protected. However, if we keep in mind Obomsawin's habit of working, as Lewis notes, as much as she can "from within," another level of interpretation can be formulated (Lewis 144).[21] Indeed, it recalls two foundational Iroquois oral stories.

The first one is the Iroquois creation story which posits that before the world as we know it existed, there was a place in the sky where a man and a pregnant woman lived. There was also a great tree which was eventually uprooted, creating a hole in the ground. Skywoman came too close to the hole and fell through it. She was rescued by birds which carried her and brought her down toward the vast extent of water that stretched below the sky. She finally landed on a giant turtle's back, and animals started bringing earth from the bottom of the ocean to create a safe tract of land on the turtle's back for Skywoman to have a place to stand. This tract of land became the Earth, which is how the world was created. Thus, the hole created by the tree serves as a symbol of the creation of the world.[22]

The second story is about the creation of the Iroquois Confederacy, the Great Peace established between the five Iroquois tribes sometime between 1450 and 1600. The legend of the founding of the Confederacy revolves around the figure of Dekanawida, a prophet who wanted to put an end to a crippling state of warfare among the five tribes. As the legend goes, he uprooted the tallest pine tree at Onondaga, the center of the Confederacy, and buried underneath it the weapons of war that symbolically divided the five nations. The tree was then planted anew to ensure that peace would last (Hewitt 141).

These events are not just myths that occurred in ancient times. As scholars have noted, Iroquois conceptions of time rely much on a "preoccupation with continuity and discontinuity" and a concern for maintaining continuity (McElwain 274). Consequently, as Michelle Raheja suggests, the creation of the world is more than just a foundational moment:

> While this originary event occurred in time immemorial, it can also be imagined to recur every time a child is born, as it moves from the space prior to its earthly existence ("Sky World"), travels through the birth canal (the abyss through which the Woman Who Fell from the Sky moves), and brings its own special gifts in the form of metaphoric seeds to this world. (Raheja 172)

The founding of the Iroquois Confederacy can similarly be seen as an event that had to recur and be reenacted in order to maintain peace, stability, and prosperity. Williams notes that Iroquois time "arose out of the Deganawidah epic, which taught that the organization of their confederated league had brought order and stability out of a time of intense chaos, crises, suffering" and that "maintaining the league as an institution devoted to sustaining and renewing the Great Peace" would prevent a return to chaos (Williams 176). This story was thus reenacted long after the original event occurred, with trees, and pines in particular, acting as powerful symbols of "life, status and authority" (Fenton 297). Seneca anthropologist Arthur Parker noticed that trees were potent peace symbols that informed many aspects of Iroquois culture and history. In dealing with other Native tribes or Euro-American colonists, the Iroquois would sometimes uproot a tree "to afford a cavity in which to bury all weapons of war." The tree would then be "replanted as a memorial" (Arthur Parker 608–9).[23]

In the film, the land is thus perceived through a filter of enduring continuity with these origin stories. These references inform the mapping of the land, stress the spiritual dimension attached to it, and reaffirm the traditional conception of nature based on balance rather than antagonism. The recurring image of protesters bearing the flag of the Iroquois Confederacy, in which the central piece represents the great tree of peace, further echoes the continuity with tradition and the function of the tree of peace as a place of communal gathering. As the conflict drags on, the statement that "the people are determined to protect the pines" displaces ever so slightly the original bone of contention between the Mohawks and the local authorities. The pines become a metonymy for the land itself (18:36). Midway through the film, as the situation worsens. The negotiations end, Mohawk negotiator Minnie Garrow can be heard declaring to an assembly of journalists:

> We are native people to this land. We're not trying to take your land or anybody else's property. [...] We were here to protect our burial grounds and the pines from a nine-hole golf course. (45:42)

Once again, this statement shows the importance of the continuity of Iroquois traditions in the face of impending danger. However, it also hints at the discrepancy between Native and Euro-American conceptions of land and place. As Leuthold stresses, conflicts over land stem from different views of nature: while Euro-Americans "often perceive conflicts over land in legal terms," Native attachment to the land includes but is not limited to the notion of physical ownership (Leuthold 2001 60–1). For example, an interview with a warrior nicknamed Wizard establishes a link between global damage to the environment and the fate of the Mohawks and, thus, stresses the sense of kinship with the natural world:

> The fish is dying, the air is dying, the plants are dying, the animals are dying. We're not too far behind them as the Mohawk Nation. (51:36)

Threats to the natural environment are further emphasized in a scene in which a flare shot by the Canadian army sets fire to bushes in the woods, endangering the pines. If the Iroquois conception of the world is recalled through numerous shots of the sky above the pines at various moments of the day, the circling helicopters represent the danger that continuity might be broken. The enduring force of tradition is also illustrated in a scene in which medicine man Loran Thompson is shown teaching children the Mohawk names of various trees within the zone besieged by the Canadian Army. It exemplifies how Native American traditional ways of "living *with*, not just *on*" the land, as Bruchac puts it, are still meaningful and constitutive for the community (Bruchac ix; emphasis in the original). Once again, however, continuity is threatened by the noise of the helicopters, which covers Thompson's voice and forces the children to cover their ears.

Obomsawin's film offers compelling examples of how Native documentaries may convey a conception of nature which is both inherited from Native traditions and adapted to the cinematic medium and documentary genre. It also resonates as a reaction to the romantic descriptions of Indigenous lands and their inhabitants in ethnographic films in the sense that it emphasizes a balanced relationship with nature rather than a longing for a pristine wilderness. Her refusal to bask in nostalgia also implies that the land and the relationship with the land are never completely lost. The final scene of *Kanehsatake*, which opens on a march commemorating the one-year anniversary of the events at Oka, introduces a cyclicality that highlights the enduring spirit of resistance prevailing among the Mohawks. As the march proceeds, a male voiceover reads a speech delivered in 1869 by Mohawk Chief Joseph Onasakenrat to confront the Sulpician priests who first appropriated the Mohawks' land:

> This land is ours—ours as a heritage given to us as sacred legacy. It is the place where our fathers lie; beneath those trees our mothers sang our lullaby, and you would dare to take it from us and leave us wanderers at the mercy of fate? (1:56:15)

The passage echoes a historical segment occurring earlier in the film, which relates the dispossession of the Mohawks from Jacques Cartier's second voyage to Canada onwards. The recurrence of the speech at the end of the film introduces a sense of cyclicality and reasserts continuity despite the status quo regarding the unresolved land dispute.

Reclaiming the Land Through Film

In Obomsawin's films, the discourse on nature and Indigenous relationships with the land unfolds on different levels. While some references are obvious, because they are made through interviews or explicit mentions, others are less easily identifiable. Wood's statement about Native feature films is also true of the documentary:

> In many instances, outsiders will not even recognize when significant Indigenous scenes are being shown. Panning across a particular landscape [...] for instance may seem to mainstream audiences as yet another stereotypical establishment shot or an attempt to show the beauties or harshness of nature. These same shots may be seen by Indigenous people as images of their ancestors, or as invocations of spirits or gods, or as wordless retelling of historical events. (Woods 95)

However, Obomsawin's films do not target an exclusively Native audience. Instead, they constitute places where Indigenous people can gather and express themselves, but also where various communities can interact, confront different understandings of the land and ultimately, reinvent ways of coexisting peacefully.[24]

Obomsawin's films exemplify the significant part that the work of Native documentarians can play in the task of remembering and reminding the spiritual meaning attached to the land. In other words, they reactivate Native cartographic discourses thanks to a reliance on oral traditions that convey a sense of nature's sacredness. As Victor Masayesva Jr. puts it, there is a sense of the sacred at the heart of Native art:

> We want to start participating and developing an Indian aesthetic. And there is such a thing as an Indian aesthetic, and it begins in the sacred. (in Leuthold 1994 48)

This process is a highly political endeavor rooted in a quest for "visual sovereignty" that implies the overturning of stereotypes and the creation of "self-generated representations of Native American identity," but also the re-appropriation of the land from a Native perspective (Raheja 128).[25] As Louis Owens once stated, "mapping is, of course, an intensely political enterprise, an essential step toward appropriation and possession" (in Vizenor 170). The appropriation of the continent by Euro-American settlers was partly carried out through the imposition of a Western cartographic discourse upon Native land. We can, however, surmise that the opposite—the superimposition of Native cartographic discourses on lands occupied by Euro-Americans—could act as a way of retaking the land. As Leslie Silko writes: "The Indian with a camera is an omen of a time in the future that all Euro-Americans unconsciously dread: the time when the indigenous people of the Americas will retake their land" (Silko 178).

Notes

[1] *Smoke Signals* (1998) by Cheyenne/Arapaho director Chris Eyre and *Atanarjuat: The Fast Runner* (2001) by Inuk filmmaker Zacharias Kunuk are two examples of Native American feature films that put Native cinema in the limelight.

[2] Chris Eyre's *Smoke Signals* (1998) and *Skins* (2002) are obvious examples of Native productions tackling the representation of Native people in westerns. Documentaries such as *Imagining Indians* (1992) by Hopi filmmaker Victor Masayesva Jr. and *Reel Injun* (2009) by Cree filmmaker Neil Diamond explicitly target the representation of Native people in mainstream cinema.

[3] Worth and Adair's book *Through Navajo Eyes* based on their experiment with Navajo youngsters with no prior experience in filmmaking, represents an early acknowledgment of the value of subjectivity in Native American documentary. Although the Navajo Film Project has been criticized on various grounds and the so-called "bio-documentary" has remained somehow marginal, Worth and Adair have set a strong precedent for showing how film reflects "the view and values of the maker" (26). See also Leuthold 1997b, 74-5. Drawing on documentary film theoreticians Jay Ruby and Bill Nichols, Leuthold signals a shift from "previous assumptions that the author remains objective

in documentary making" to a focus on authorship and the subjectivity this entails (2001 56). Obomsawin herself has acknowledged that she might not be completely objective. She declared in a 1989 interview: "I may not be objective but that does not bother me too much. The duration of a film is limited and I give this time to my people" (in Laprévotte *et al.* 167, my translation). For more on subjectivity in Obomsawin's films, see Loft; Laprévotte *et al.* 182.

[4] Some of Flaherty's later films offer further examples of this emphasis on lands. One of his 1926 film *Moana*'s subtitles, *A Romance of the South Seas* situates the main character within a specific geographical context. *Man of Aran* (1934) is reminiscent of *Nanook of the North* and its use of the conjunction "of." Despite being set off the west coast of Ireland, the film has much in common with *Nanook*'s display of human beings struggling to survive under extreme conditions.

[5] For more on nature as a wilderness in colonial and early American literature, see Nash, 23-43.

[6] See Ginsburg, 95.

[7] For more on these aspects, see Calder-Marshall, 95-7; Heider, 22-3; Geiger, 54-6; Gidley, 241; Beattie, 32-3.

[8] Flaherty's own background reflects this aspect. As a child and young adult, he went with his father, a mining engineer, on prospecting expeditions in various parts of Canada and occasionally lived in mining camps. He was later trained as a prospector and mining engineer and worked for several mining companies (Rotha 7-28). See also Geiger, 52-4.

[9] The World Film Corporation that financially supported Curtis's film specialized in theatrical films. The original poster and the Carnegie Hall brochure can be accessed on the website dedicated to the newly restored copy of the film: https://www.curtisfilm.rutgers.edu/. Accessed October 1st, 2016. Kathryn Bunn-Marcuse calls *In the Land of the Head Hunters* "an exotic Hollywood melodrama" (Bunn-Marcuse 306).

[10] Flaherty famously described his approach to ethnographic truth as inevitably entangled with lies: "Sometimes you have to lie. One often has to distort a thing to catch its true spirit" (in Calder-Marshall 97). Geiger notes that *Nanook* relies on a dual system of identification and differentiation as it "posits primitive figures that are in key ways 'like us'" and yet "also unlike us: 'noble savages' who exist at close quarters with nature's rhythms" (Geiger 56).

[11] Singer further states that in the same way that storytellers "have the power to heal the spirit," "one of the reasons for making films is to heal the ruptures of the past" (Singer 3).

[12] Chickasaw writer Linda Hogan reflects on this reciprocal relationship in *Dwellings*: "Sometimes beliefs are inventions of the mind. Sometimes they are inventions of the land" (85).

[13] In her essay "Interior and Exterior Landscapes," Leslie Silko analyzes a Pueblo hunting story that "might also serve as a map" (32), thus implying that stories and lands are complementary entities that mutually inform each other. She writes of a Pueblo oral story about Laguna sheepherders who were killed and robbed of their sheep "in an area known as Swahnee" identifiable by a "high, dark mesa." She concludes by stating that "the high, dark mesa and the story of the two lost Laguna herders became inextricably linked" in a reciprocal fashion: "Thus the continuity and accuracy of the oral narratives are reinforced by the landscape—and the Pueblo interpretation of that landscape is *maintained*" (34-35; emphasis in the original).

[14] Obomsawin was raised on the Abenaki reservation of Odanak in Southern Quebec, and was deeply influenced by storytellers such as Théophile Panadis. She later became a professional singer-songwriter and storyteller and performed at various festivals around the world before she started working for the National Film Board of Canada in 1967 (Lewis 58-69; Caruso §3-4).

[15] Roche states that Obomsawin favors words, voices, and stories over images: "her films are first and foremost oral accounts in the present tense" (Laprévotte et al. 165). Caruso notes Obomsawin's use of "unique 'Native-view' methods of storytelling in the Oka documentaries" (§8). See also Loft, §3.

[16] See Houle 207; Lewis 64-6. Obomsawin describes films as "a tool to make conversations happen" (in Andrew Parker §9).

[17] Traditional Iroquois societies were matrilineal, which accounts for the prominent place of women in political and social life. As "progenitors of the Nation" and cultivators of the land, they were considered to be the owners of the land (Baskin 43-44). For more on the role of women in Iroquois societies, see Tooker, 109-24. Obomsawin's portrayal of women activists playing an active role behind the barricades in the Oka films contrasts with the general perception of the situation. During the crisis, several Canadian officials and the mainstream media indulged in gendered representations of the people behind the barricades, stressing the hyper-masculinity of the dangerous Mohawk Warriors while consigning women to more traditionally-ascribed roles such as managing food supplies or looking after children (Kalant 158-9; Valaskakis 39). For more on gender in Obomsawin's films, see Freeman, 187-212; Lewis, 70-87.

[18] Factionalism has long been an important socio-political trait of Kanehsatake. The emergence of these factions was based on political and religious factors and led to a complex network of divisions and alliances that have evolved according to the political situation. By 1990, two main factions existed: the Band Council, the official governing body imposed by the Indian act of 1876 and the Longhouse, which advocated a return to the traditional spiritual and political institutions of the Mohawks and rejected the idea that the Mohawks were Canadian citizens or that they should abide by the rules set by the Indian affairs at Ottawa. The Warriors mostly came from other Iroquois reservations and ideologically differed from the other two factions. For more on Iroquois factionalism and the Oka Crisis see Redhead, 134-137; Kalant, 157-9; Valaskakis, 35-65.

[19] In analyzing the work of several Native women filmmakers, Lewis notes that they generally tend to downplay "divisive issues that might weaken resolve against the perceived greater enemy: government neglect of Native rights and white ignorance about Native people" (84).

[20] Other observers or actors of the Crisis have similarly emphasized unity despite ideological differences during the Oka crisis (Kalant 129-61; Valaskakis 63). In her films and later interviews, Obomsawin also insisted on divisions between government and local officials and army officials regarding the handling of the Crisis (see Andrew Parker, §17).

[21] See also Andrews, §4.

[22] For other versions of the Iroquois creation story, see, among others, Baskin, 43; Armstrong and Chafe, 515-531; Bruchac, 5-9.

[23] The tree of peace was a ubiquitous trope in Iroquois diplomacy. Records of encounters between Iroquois people and Euro-American colonists feature extensive use of the tree as a symbol of peace in Iroquois oratory.

[24] See Houle, 207; Lewis, 88-121; Laprévotte et al. 168.

²⁵ Raheja defines "visual sovereignty" as "a practice that takes a holistic approach to the process of creating moving images, and that locates Indigenous cinema in a particular historical and social context while privileging tribal sovereignty" (193).

Works Cited

Filmography

Curtis, Edward S. *In the Land of the Head Hunters*. DVD. Harrington Park, NJ: Milestone Film & Video, 2015.

Flaherty, Robert. *Nanook of the North*. DVD. New York: Criterion, 1999.

Obomsawin, Alanis. *270 Years of Resistance: The Collection*. DVD box set. Montréal: National Film Board of Canada, 2008.

Bibliography

Andrews, Mallory. "Voice(s) of the People: An Interview with Alanis Obomsawin." *cléo* 2, 2014. http://cleojournal.com/2014/08/21/voices-of-the-people-an-interview-with-alanis-obomsawin-2/. Accessed October 10ᵗʰ 2016.

Armstrong, John, and Wallace Chafe. "Seneca Creation Story." *Voices from Four Directions: Contemporary Translations of the Native Literatures of North America*, edited by Brian Swann, Lincoln: University of Nebraska Press, 2004, pp. 515-31.

Aufderheide, Patricia. *Documentary Film: A Very Short Introduction*. Oxford and New York: Oxford University Press, 2007.

Baskin, Cyndy. "Women in Iroquois Society." *Canadian Woman Studies/Les Cahiers de la Femme* n°4, 1982, pp. 42–46.

Beattie, Keith. *Documentary Screens: Non-Fiction Film and Television*. Basingstoke & New York: Palgrave Macmillan, 2004.

Bruchac, Joseph. *Native American Stories*. Golden, CO: Fulcrum, 1991.

Bunn-Marcuse, Kathryn. "Kwakwaka'wakw on film." *Walking a Tightrope: Aboriginal People and Their Representations*, edited by Ute Lischke and David T. McNab, Waterloo, ON: Wilfrid Laurier University Press, 2005, pp. 305–334.

Burke, Edmund. *A Philosophical Enquiry into the Origin of Our Ideas of the Beautiful and the Sublime*. edited by J. T. Bolton, Notre Dame, IN: University of Notre Dame Press, 1968.

Calder-Marshall, Arthur. *The Innocent Eye: The Life of Robert J. Flaherty*. New York: Harcourt, Brace and World, 1966.

Calloway, Colin G. *One Vast Winter Count: The Native American West before Lewis and Clark*. Lincoln: University of Nebraska Press, 2003.

Caruso, Donna Laurent. "Abenaki Filmmaker Earns Luminaria Award." *Indian Country Today*, January 1, 2008.

Curtis, Edward S. *In the Land of the Head-Hunters*. Yonkers-on-Hudson, New York: World Book Company, 1915.

Fenton, William N. "This Island, the World on the Turtle's Back." *The Journal of American Folklore*, n°75, 1962, pp. 283–300.

Fielding, Julien R. "Native American Religion and Film: Interviews with Chris Eyre and Sherman Alexie." *Journal of Religion and Film* 7, 2003. http://www.unomaha.edu/jrf/Vol7No1/nativefilm.htm. Accessed October 9th 2016.

Freeman, Barbara M. *Beyond Bylines: Media Workers and Women's Rights in Canada.* Waterloo, ON: Wilfrid Laurier, 2011.

Geiger, Jeffrey. *American Documentary Film: Projecting the Nation.* Edinburgh: Edinburgh University Press, 2011.

Gidley, Mick. *Edward S. Curtis and the North American Indian, Incorporated.* Cambridge: Cambridge University Press, 2000.

Ginsburg, Faye. "Indigenous Media: Faustian Contract or Global Village?" *Cultural Anthropology,* n°6, 1991, pp. 92–112.

Hayward, Susan. *Cinema Studies: The Key Concepts.* Second edition. London and New York: Routledge, 2000.

Heider, Karl G. *Ethnographic Film.* Revised edition. Austin: University of Texas Press, 2006 (1976).

Hewitt, J. N. B. "Legend of the Founding of the Iroquois League." *American Anthropologist,* n° 5, 1892, pp. 131–48.

Hogan, Linda. *Dwellings: A Spiritual History of the Living World.* New York: Norton, 2007 (1995).

Houle, Robert. "Alanis Obomsawin." *Terre, Esprit, Pouvoir: Les Premières Nations au Musée des Beaux-Arts du Canada,* edited by Dian Nemiroff, Robert Houle Charlotte Townsend-Gault, Ottawa: Musée des Beaux-Arts du Canada, 1992.

Kalant, Amelia. *National Identity and the Conflict at Oka: Native Belonging and Myths of Postcolonial Nationhood in Canada.* New York and London: Routledge, 2004.

Laprévotte, Gilles, and Thierry Roche. *Indian's Song: Des Indiens d'Hollywood au Cinéma des Indiens.* Crisnée et Amiens, France: Yellow Now and the Festival International du Film d'Amiens, 2010.

Leuthold, Steven. "An Indigenous Aesthetic? Two Noted Videographers: George Burdeau and Victor Masayesva." *Wicazo Sa Review,* n°10, 1994, pp. 40-51.

—. "Historical Representation in Native American Documentary." *Ethnohistory,* n°44, 1997a, pp. 727–39.

—. "Native American Documentary: An Emerging Genre?" *Film Criticism,* n° 22, 1997b, pp. 74–90.

—. *Indigenous Aesthetic: Native Art, Media and Identity.* Austin: University of Texas Press, 1998.

—. "Rhetorical Dimensions of Native American Documentary." *Wicazo Sa Review,* n°16, 2001, pp. 55–73.

Lewis, Randolph. *Alanis Obomsawin: The Vision of A Native Filmmaker.* Lincoln: University of Nebraska Press, 2006.

Loft, Steve. "Sovereignty, Subjectivity, and Social Action: The Films of Alanis Obomsawin." 2001. http://ggavma.canadacouncil.ca/htmlfixed/Archives/2001/2001-06-e.html. Accessed: September 20th 2016.

McElwain, Thomas. "Seneca Iroquois Concepts of Time." *Canadian Journal of Native Studies,* n°7, 1987, pp. 267–77.

Nabokov, Peter. "Orientations from Their Side: Dimensions of Native American Cartographic Discourse." In *Cartographic Encounters: Perspectives on Native American Mapmaking and Map Use*, edited by G. Malcolm Lewis, Chicago: The University of Chicago Press, 1998, pp. 241–69.

Nash, Roderick Frazier. *Wilderness and the American Mind*. 4th edition. New Haven, CT: Yale University Press, 2014 (1967).

Parker, Arthur C. "Certain Iroquois Tree Myths and Symbols." *American Anthropologist*, n°14, 1912, pp. 608–20.

Parker, Andrew. "Resistance and Resilience: A Talk with Alanis Obomsawin." *Toronto Film Scene*, November 1, 2015.

Raheja, Michelle H. *Reservation Reelism: Redfacing, Visual Sovereignty, and Representations of Native Americans in Film*. Lincoln: University of Nebraska Press, 2010.

Redhead, Robin. *Exercising Human Rights: Gender, Agency and Practice*. New York: Routledge, 2014.

Rony, Fatimah Tobing. *The Third Eye: Race, Cinema, and Ethnographic Spectacle*. Durham, NC: Duke University Press, 1996.

Rotha, Paul. *Robert J. Flaherty: A Biography*. Edited by Jay Ruby. Philadelphia: University of Pennsylvania Press, 1983.

Silko, Leslie Marmon. *Yellow Woman and A Beauty of the Spirit: Essays on Native American Life Today*. New York: Simon & Schuster, 1996.

Singer, Beverly R. *Wiping the War Paint Off the Lens: Native American Film and Video*. Minneapolis: University of Minnesota Press, 2001.

Tooker, Elizabeth. "Women in Iroquois Society." *Extending the Rafters: Interdisciplinary Approaches to Iroquoian Studies*, edited by Michael K. Foster, Jack Campisi and Marianne Mithun, Albany: State University of New York Press, 1984, pp. 109–124.

Valaskakis, Gail Guthrie. *Indian Country: Essays on Contemporary Native Culture*. Waterloo, ON: Wilfrid Laurier University Press, 2005.

Vizenor, Gerald. *Fugitive Poses: Native American Indian Scenes of Absence and Presence*. Lincoln: University of Nebraska Press, 1998.

Williams, Robert A. *Linking Arms Together: American Indian Treaty Visions of Law and Peace, 1600-1800*. New York and London: Routledge, 1999 (1997).

Wood, Houston. *Native Features: Indigenous Films From Around the World*. New York: Continuum, 2008.

Worth, Sol and John Adair. *Through Navajo Eyes: An Exploration in Film Communication and Anthropology*. Bloomington: Indiana University Press, 1975.

Part II.
Wild and Reorganized Gardens: The Poesis of Nature over Mind

Chapter 5

The Ecological Christian Labyrinth and the Significance of Trees in *The Lord of the Rings*

Stephen Greenfield

University of Wolverhampton, UK

Abstract: From its origins as a spiral unicursal design in pre-historic cave art onwards, the labyrinth has been used as a means of representing ecological structure. In the Middle Ages, the unicursal labyrinth was assimilated by the Roman Catholic Church as a symbol of Christian cosmology. The characteristic unicursal, revolving circuits were identified as reflecting sacred design and the natural authentic order. Labyrinthine structure was incorporated and embedded into the design of Christian philosophy, literature and music.

This paper offers a reading of *The Lord of the Rings* that identifies an eco-labyrinthine narrative thread that draws together Norse representations of the World Tree while enveloping this imagery within a Christian labyrinthine framework. The importance of the tree as an ecological motif in *The Lord of the Rings* extends its narrative reach beyond a short-term quest for survival to the long-term ecological sustainability of the mythical Middle-earth.

Keywords: Labyrinths, ecology, narrative structure, Tolkien, trees

***

This reading of *The Lord of the Rings* is mediated through the text's structural relationship with an eco-labyrinthine paradigm. Rachel McCoppin has previously championed a structural ecological exegesis of heroic quest literature in *The Hero's Quest and the Cycles of Nature: An Ecological Interpretation of World Mythology* (2016). McCoppin assesses the extent to which various hero myths represent the subjugation and reconciliation of the hero figure to the natural cycle of growth, maturity, and mortality. McCoppin's method of mapping the journey toward quest heroism to the botanical cycle primarily appears to apply to ancient mythology and pre-industrial agrarian societies.

As a twentieth-century text, *Rings* was composed when the debate over ecology and authenticity had become more complex. Darwinian notions of ecology disrupted the idea of the fixed cycle of nature and introduced the idea of an evolving and dynamic ecology. The latter encouraged a secular approach to ecology, albeit one Darwin was reluctant to endorse fully. Darwin famously retained an affection for the notion of the 'entangled bank,' which allowed for the possibility of a providential force and posited the equilibrium model of a balanced ecology. Alternative models of ecology direct divergent approaches to how we approach ecocriticism. Cyclical and iterative models continue to vie with dynamic and evolving ecological perspectives, while confusion accounts for inconsistencies in application.

As a paradoxical dichotomy, the labyrinth encompasses the same structural tensions as the term 'ecology.' In its original pictorial form the unicursal labyrinth design represents a regular series of concentric loops that gravitate inwards towards, or revolve around, a fixed central point. Against this, the multicursal labyrinth, also referred to as a maze, eschews regularity in favor of dynamism, choice, uncertain progress, and the possibility of error or dead-ends.

The labyrinth paradigm provides a model to explore *Rings*'s structural architecture. Claude Levi Strauss described mythology as working through symbolism to replicate fundamental structures or laws. At the core of his approach resides the identification of binary opposites that together create meaning, Roland Barthes raises the idea of a text having "a sort of instinct of preservation in narrative which…always chooses the outcome which makes the story 'go on'" (Barthes 1988 139). Noting that such an obvious element is 'hardly studied at all' Barthes refers to the structure as having "uniquely in view the 'salvation' of the narrative and not this or that character in it" (Barthes 1988 140), which by analogy might be extended to the preservation of ecological sustainability as the stage on which narrative activity takes place. Ultimately, Barthes argues that we should not regard authorial intent as necessary to prove because as "we free the work from the constraints of intention, we rediscover the mythological trembling of meanings" (Barthes 1987 77). Barthes encourages the search for signs that lead to the inference of structure by causing 'a second language – that is to say a coherence of signs – to float above the first language of the work' (Barthes 1987 80). For Barthes, the key to identifying structural architecture is locating the centrality of an image that stands for the entirety of the structure/meaning as "in the work 'everywhere' and 'always'" (Barthes 1987 83) and not tied to the quantitative frequency of symbolism.

Rings fundamentally focuses on an existential threat characterized by a fall from an authentic state of harmony. The cause of disharmony resides within the seductive nature of corrupting power. Signs of the fallen nature of Middle-earth abound in the discontinuities, divisions, and struggles between races/tribes, rejection of duty and selfish appropriation of transformative power, destruction of the environment, and genetic deviations creating inauthentic lifeforms bent entirely on evil. The heroism of Frodo and his companions resides in the rejection of personal power, self-sacrifice, and surrender to the greater good. The quest journey winds its way across Middle-earth as a rite of passage toward enlightenment. Separate from the quest to destroy the illicit, eponymous ring of power, we find adjacent adventures that deal with ecological disharmony in Middle-earth. Once the ring quest has been settled, the hobbits, having completed a rite of passage, return equipped to use the lessons learned to heal their own homeland.

Tolkien and Mythology

J.R.R. Tolkien's invention of his fictional world of Middle-earth spans three major pieces of work. The first book, *The Hobbit,* is unashamedly a children's story, originally written for his own offspring. The posthumously published *The Silmarillion,* which set out the cosmology behind the stories, was compiled by his son, Christopher, from drafts that Tolkien was developing before and after the publication of the epic *Rings,* which bridges the gap between children's fiction and Tolkien's grander cosmology. Tolkien wrote that *Rings* was "the best, of the entire cycle, (which) concludes the whole business," and in which "Hardly a word in its 600,000 or more has been unconsidered. And the placing, size, style and contribution to the whole of all the features, incidents and chapters has (sic) been laboriously pondered." (Tolkien 1981 159–60).

Rings accords with the author's treatise *On Fairy Stories* in which he describes the faerie form as ascending to myth, which in turn he saw as consonant with articulating religious truth. Karen Armstrong defines mythology as stories through which humanity exercises the imagination to identify our place within a wider pattern, which provides individual life with meaning, and enables "us to live more intensely within (the world)." (Armstrong, 3).

Tolkien's blending of Christian and pre-Christian influences proceeds from his understanding of mythology, most cogently set out in his role in the conversion of his friend C.S. Lewis. Tolkien challenged Lewis's premise that the Christian story, while compelling, was only a fictitious myth. Tolkien responded by defending mythology, in general, as the medium through which fragments of immanent truth emerge. Tolkien accepted the Christian story itself as being a myth, but a myth that is literally true and actually happened.

The perfection of Christian myth accounts for Tolkien's unease with Arthurian mythology, which adds an addendum to Christian mythology. In correspondence, Tolkien admits a desire to produce a mythology for England (Tolkien 1981 144) informed by his admiration of historical, pre-Christian Northern European mythology while remaining true to his Roman Catholic faith (Tolkien 1981 172). As a consequence, the narrative intent for *Rings* was more serious than had been the case with *The Hobbit*. One aspect of this was to set out a myth that might validate the broader Northern European mythological tradition by covertly accounting for it in a way that would assimilate it within the span of Christian mythology. Tolkien privately wrote of his literal belief in the Biblical fall and how all mythology reflects the same underlying sense of environmental loss. *Rings* also reflects Tolkien's understanding of the "Faerie" form as a heightened way of perceiving the environment through an elevated consciousness that re-enchants nature.

The ecological reference point in Christian myth resides in the depiction of humanity's original home of Eden as a state of ecological harmony with nature. Adam and Eve's taking of the forbidden fruit of the tree of knowledge symbolizes the rape of nature. It accounts for expulsion from an enchanted, harmonious environment to exile in a disharmonious, disenchanted world. Following the fall, humanity employs knowledge to attain mastery over nature. Redemption consequently requires the rediscovery of enchantment alongside the relinquishing of human power over nature.

In weaving these influences into his world of Middle-Earth, Tolkien adds a sense of depth beneath the surface quest to destroy the illicit power of the ring. Cryptically, Tolkien confessed that "the struggle between darkness and light [...] is for me just a particular phase of history, one example of its pattern, perhaps, but not The Pattern" (Tolkien 1981 121). Likewise, while an immediate threat to the existence of an ecologically diverse Middle-earth, the ring represents a single strand in a deeper, structural, ecological malaise.

The Christian Labyrinth

The rationale for this reading resides in the applicability of encountering the text as a Christian labyrinth. Penelope Reed Doob coined the term "labyrinthicity" to account for "metaphors and texts that function like labyrinths even though they may not be identified as such" (Reed Doob, 2). Doob's study, *The Idea of the Labyrinth from Classical Antiquity through the Middle Ages*, identifies that Christian labyrinthine architecture historically structures narrative within philosophy and literature as an organizing feature pregnant with cosmological significance.

Developing the idea of "eco-labyrinthicity" as a means of reading narrative structure as illustrative of a divine ecological order recalls the origins of the pictorial single-circuit labyrinth in pre-history, where the symbol in cave art has been interpreted as representing the womb of nature. (McCaffery 113). Hermann Kern meanwhile describes the labyrinth as the site of initiation rites that represent rebirth. (Kern 30–31).

The adoption of the labyrinth in its unicursal form by Christianity was used to articulate the one true path that forms a route to the divine. As such, the labyrinth was a cipher. It was aligned with ideas about cosmological architecture, replicated pictorially for ritual purposes to direct Easter celebrations in Christian places of worship. At its height, it consciously informed the compositional structure of devotional music and literature. The unicursal labyrinth represented the holistic system of creation incorporating the course of the planets and reflecting the cyclical renewal and rebirth of nature and the life and resurrection of Christ. Symbolically it was embossed with the cross.

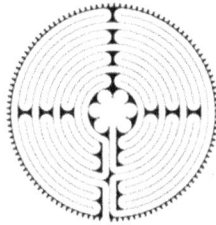

Figure 5.1.

The unicursal Christian labyrinth delineates a convoluted path that continuously doubles back on itself, revisiting almost the same point while moving inexorably closer to its illuminative centre. Repetition by stages is a key feature of the labyrinthine design. The recurring themes build knowledge and understanding incrementally.

The Ecological Christian Labyrinth and the Significance of the Tree in Rings

A labyrinthine reading of *Rings* encompasses and reinterprets the familiar and established tropes of Northern European mythology within its folds. The unveiling of the tree at its narrative center, to represent ecology, reflects Tolkien's affinity with trees, while the overarching architecture encloses the quest within a Christian frame.

Rings' revolving labyrinthine narrative returns to the figure of the supernatural tree in three significant episodes, conveying a broader ecological theme to the narrative that develops ecological consciousness. The labyrinth as a path to Christian enlightenment itself involves a three-stage process. Progress proceeds through: <u>purgation</u>, through undertaking to walk the circuit as a substitute for a penitential journey or pilgrimage; <u>illumination</u>, where a central point is reached and essential knowledge imparted; leading to a final, ultimate, stage of; <u>union</u>, where the individual integrates divine labyrinthine knowledge on return to their ordinary lives, to live authentically in communion with the divine (Artress 28–30).

Three symbolic manifestations of the tree are encountered at the beginning, middle, and end of *Rings*. These manifestations reprise the location and function of the three roots of The World Tree, Yggdrasil, in Norse mythology. Gertrude Jobes describes how Yggdrasil "grows out of past, lives in the present, and reaches toward the future" (Jobes 1706) to identify the ecological sustainability in the cosmological Norse world. The World Tree's three roots represent separate spheres of consciousness through which to perceive nature. The first root resides in the enchanted underworld of Niflheim, the second in Midgard, the world of men, while the third joins the tree to the heavenly cosmos of Asgard. Mirroring the Norse myth, *Rings* locates mythological trees within a Faerie underworld, in the fictitious narrative reality of Middle-earth, and lastly, as a means of expressing divine sanction and the sacred nature of ecology.

Purgation

The three roots of Yggdrasil are variously embedded at the foot, middle, and crown of the tree. In depictions, the root at the foot of the World Tree is embedded in the fog-realm of Niflheim; the "underworld of misty darkness [...] (the) Northern abode of those who died of old age or disease" (Jobes 1169). Here, a well supplies the rivers that flow at the beginning of the world. In the martial world of the Vikings, Niflheim is a negative site, broadly equivalent to hell.

In *Rings*, the mythological tree is first encountered in a threatening, if misunderstood, Faerie underworld. In the chapter entitled The Old Forest, four hobbit companions, diminutive half-human figures who are entrusted with the quest to destroy the ring of power, seek to elude pursuit by passing through the Forest. Their decision to enter this environment is formed out of necessity and in the face of misgivings due to its mysterious and threatening reputation.

The Old Forest geographically lies at the very edge of the hobbits' homeland of the Shire, and mythically at the edge of their consciousness. The journey through the Forest comprises a rite of passage. The entry point to the Forest is sharply demarcated, highlighting liminal allusions to crossing a threshold into another world. The hobbits arrive at a boundary hedge and literally descend into the earth via a secret underground passage. Their entry marks a hiatus in the plot, abruptly separating the hobbits from the focus on the single issue of the ring of power. They will later re-emerge, re-born, out of the earth to rejoin the quest. As such, the environment symbolizes a return to the ecological womb, recalling interpretations of the pre-historic labyrinth.

Initially, the hobbits attempt to orient themselves in relation to a site near the Forest's edge where trees, felled in the past by fellow hobbits, had been burned. This destruction was directed in response to the encroachment of trees into hobbit 'territory,' indicative of ecological tensions separate from the quest. From this point, it becomes clear that the Forest will henceforth guide the hobbits' footsteps. Essentially a unicursal route is formed by the Forest flora that dictates their direction of progress. The consciousness and antipathy of the trees toward the hobbits appears through the agency they are granted to let branches fall in the hobbits' path or to trip them with their roots. Eventually, the path leads to a treeless hill, which the hobbits ascend in winding circuits. This feature makes an allusion to the turf labyrinth, commonly attested to as being particular to the landscape and mythology of England (Matthews 67). The hobbits' weary journey to the summit of the hill here serves to recall the Christian penitential function of navigating cathedral labyrinths on the knees in an arduous cycle to approach a point of illumination (Wright 47). The hill provides an elevated position from which to briefly re-orientate their selves before re-entering the Forest.

From the hilltop, the hobbit entrusted with mapping their route points out the direction in which they need to aim. It is also made clear that they need to avoid "The Withywindle valley […] said to be the queerest part of the whole wood–the centre from which all the queerness comes, as it were" (Tolkien 1992 128). Yet, this engagement with the heart of the Forest is inescapable as, once more, the trees conspire to dictate a unicursal passage toward the riverbank at the bottom of the valley.

The parallels to the fog-realm of Niflheim are pronounced at the riverbank as everything becomes hazy. Three of the four hobbit companions are lulled into an unnatural sleep next to a tree. Referred to as Old Man Willow, this tree represents the rotting-heart of the Old Forest (Tolkien 1992 145). The unconscious hobbits' sleep is rudely broken as the Willow tree tips the ring bearer, Frodo, into the river and holds him down with a root. Here submersion suggests a further example of purgation, consonant with the Christian practice of baptism to cleanse sin. Simultaneously boles in the tree open to partly consume two of Frodo's companions. They are held in a vice-like grip, with only their lower bodies extruding.

Some critics have identified the malevolence of the tree at this point as providing the first instance of villainy in the text (Campbell 269). However, this appears flawed. Rather, Tolkien's representation of the Willow seems to recall his earlier treatise entitled *On Fairy Stories*. Here Tolkien rejected criticism that Faerie represented pure escapism from reality. Tolkien likened escape through Faerie to articulating a desire to break free from an artificial cultural prison and return home. He continued by linking "real Escape, and what are often its companions, Disgust, Anger, Condemnation, and Revolt" (Tolkien 2008 376) and noting that "Escapism has another and even wickeder face: Reaction" (Tolkien 2008 377).

The hobbits' own escape from their predicament is brought about by the timely appearance of a character called Tom Bombadil, who fulfills the role of *genius loci* or nature spirit. Bombadil presents a striking figure. His dancing gait is aligned with a predilection to communicate in recursive songs echoing the cyclical music and dance that are features of the Easter ritual as enacted in cathedrals in medieval times, which imitate pagan forms of celebration (Wright 138–9).

In freeing the hobbits, the nature spirit refrains from meeting out retribution against the tree for attempted hobbitcide. This is in marked contrast to the treatment reserved for 'evil' or 'corrupted' characters elsewhere in *Rings*. In most other instances, representatives of 'evil' are summarily dealt with, while the demise of those revealed as corrupted is similarly, subsequently assured. In this context, the Willow Tree's actions are partly legitimized, or at least reflect the author's empathy with them.

Bombadil aids the hobbits' rite of passage in teaching them lessons that diminish the importance of the ring. The ring holds no power to make Bombadil invisible, unlike all others who wear it; on the contrary, Bombadil makes the ring disappear. It highlights that in The Old Forest the immediate threat to ecology resides in the expansion of the Shire.

Finally, Bombadil secures the hobbits' release from the Faerie underworld, symbolically effected by raising them out of the earth of a prehistoric burial chamber. In addition to Faerie's role in expanding their consciousness, the hobbits are re-clothed and partially physically equipped by the spoils from the barrow. They emerge at the furthest border of Faerie from their home, prepared to return to Middle-earth and the ring quest.

Illumination

The second explanation of ecology through the medium of the mythological tree appears at the next point, where the narrative splits from directly focusing on the ring quest. The company of the ring is split up as Frodo takes the ring to its doom in the east. Meanwhile, two of the hobbits seek shelter beneath the eaves of Fangorn forest.

While The Old Forest represents faerie, Fangorn stands adjacent to the tower of Orthanc, the abode of the corrupted wizard Saruman, and theoretically within the human realm of Rohan (Wynne 575) congruent to the location of the Norse World Tree's second root in Midgard, "also called Manna-heim (home of man)" (Jobes 1100).

Within the surrounding forest dwells its eponymous hero, Fangorn, or colloquially "Treebeard" (Tolkien 1992 578), the eldest of a kind of supernatural tree known as an ent. The ents are described as holding responsibility over the forest as tree-shepherds. Treebeard makes the hobbits his wards while deliberating on whether the time has finally come to take action against Saruman. While granting them the power of speech, Tolkien retains the Ents' integrity as trees by conferring on them their own language unintelligible to outsiders. However, in a concession to the continuation of the narrative, they are also endowed with the ability to communicate in "the common speech." In "On Fairy Stories," Tolkien sanctioned "The magical understanding by men of the proper languages of birds and beasts and trees" (Tolkien 2008 328), which encompasses humanity's desire "to hold communion with other living things" (Tolkien 2008 326). The long-winded language of the Ents is a useful means of illuminating the temporal difference in how trees engage with the world according to their nature and recalls the circuitous nature of the unicursal labyrinth.

Once stirred to action, Tolkien alters the temporal frame within which the trees of Fangorn Forest physically act. In doing so, he depicts the trees as conscious and re-enchants them to articulate that they are living entities that do things rather than inanimate objects that have things done to them. Their destruction of the wizard's fortress is described as being accomplished according to their nature through accelerated time. The text describes how "It was like watching the work of great tree-roots in a hundred years, all packed into a few moments" (Tolkien 1992 590).

Eco-Linguist Arran Stibbe has argued that a primary factor in developing a deep ecological consciousness of the life of non-human lifeforms is to present them as active agents. As "sentient beings actively engaged in living their lives" (Stibbe 2006 73). Stibbe argues that to represent lifeforms in ways that recognize their lives as intrinsically valuable, irrespective of humanity, it is nevertheless necessary to highlight aspects of their life that provoke human empathy with them as individuals rather than as a faceless species.

As part of this illuminative process, Tolkien graphically describes the horror of the nature of attacks on trees and of the destruction of individual trees in just such personal terms. Drawing attention to their individuality participates in re-enchanting trees, highlighting that each tree is unique and irreplaceable. Quickbeam gave a cry: "the tree-killer, the tree-killer!" Quickbeam is a gentle creature, but he hates Saruman all the more fiercely for that [...] his people suffered cruelly from orc-axes [...] "Several of the Ents got scorched and blistered. One of them, Beechbone I think he was called, a very tall handsome Ent, got caught in a spray of liquid fire and burned like a torch: a horrible sight" (Tolkien 1992 591).

When the Ents are finally roused, a number of parallels are found with the Norse mythological model of the World Tree. The battle for Orthanc parallels the downfall of the gods at Ragnarok. Prefiguring Ragnarok, the World Tree, Yggdrasil, shudders in anticipation. Snorri Sturluson's *Prose Edda* describes how: "Heimdall blows loud/his horn raised aloft,/Odin speaks/with Mimir'shead;/Yggdrasil trembles,/old outspreading ash,/and groans/as the giant gets free" (Sturluson 88). A literal definition of the name Heimdall is "heaven defender" (Jobes 743). Heimdall held unceasing vigil as "the watchman of Asgard" (Jobes 743.) Heimdall is also attributed as "a guardian of flocks" (Jobes 743), drawing parallels with Tolkien's Ent as a tree-shepherd. Jobes identifies Heimdall's counterpart "In medieval schemes (as) [...] Saint Peter, who keeps the door of heaven" (Jobes 743).

The battle for Orthanc is preceded by the hobbits' account of having gone "to Entmoot, a gathering of Ents [...] it lasted all that day and the next [...] in the third day of their moot, the Ents suddenly blew up. The Forest had felt as tense as if a thunderstorm was brewing inside it [...] like a music of horns and drums" (Tolkien 1992 587–8). Echoing Heimdall, the Ents' attack features a pre-apocalyptic blast as "A great hoom, hom rang out like a deep-throated horn in the woods and seemed to echo from the trees" (Tolkien 1992 500–1) and as "Night fell and there was silence: nothing was to be heard save a faint quiver of the earth beneath the feet of the Ents" (Tolkien 1992 508).

During the Ent assault on the otherwise impregnable tower, the valley is flooded. The submersion of Orthanc by water mirrors the aftermath of Ragnarok, but inverts it. The Norse Armageddon depicts the destruction of the world of the gods and its mythology. In *Rings,* the trees prevail and save the natural, enchanted world from Saruman's reduction of nature to disenchanted material prized only for its utility.

As a final additional corollary to Norse myth, in the Viking sagas, Midgard is joined to Asgard, the abode of gods, by "Bifrost, the Rainbow bridge" (Jobes 1100). In the wake of the Ents' victory, the flooded valley creates its own "great rainbow" (Tolkien 1992 595), a parallel suggesting restoring a bridge, however temporary, to heaven.

Treebeard's assistance at Orthanc does not necessarily endorse the confederation ranged against the wizard, which includes humans. "I don't know about sides. I go my own way; but your way may go along with mine for a while" (Tolkien 1992 487). This marked independence reminds the reader that the tree is not a resource at the service of humans or their mythological counterparts. In addition, Treebeard provides a significant and tangible motif for altering ecological consciousness. We may find moss-covered trees on our own woodland walks, which bring to mind the Ent and bring about a re-enchantment of nature.

Union

Still, in Northern mythology, the third root of the World Tree establishes a link from the underworld, and the world of experience, to the heavenly realm and divinity. Located in Asgard, the abode of deities, the root is preserved from decay in a place of judgment and destiny. In Norse mythology, the preservers of the tree are the Norns, a triumvirate of goddesses presiding over fate.

Union with the divine is the third and final stage of the labyrinthine Christian journey. Artress describes how 'Union begins as we leave the center of the labyrinth, following the same path back out that brought us in ... integrating the insights ... gained' (Artress 30). We find union in the narrative in the advent of re-enchanted relationships with nature that represent a renewal partnership. The third manifestation of the tree is invoked after the ring has been destroyed. The narrative now continues in order to illustrate ongoing challenges framed within an ecological dimension.

The character Aragorn is set to fulfill the prophecy of the return of the King of Gondor. Tolkien is explicit that the ring quest brings to an end one age of Middle-earth and ushers in another, the age of man (Tolkien 1992 1007). This age is, however, still subject to divine mythological sanction. The White Tree of Gondor has withered, and as fated in the omnipresent references to prophecy, it will only flourish again on the return of the rightful king. As the putative new King, Aragorn is troubled by the tree's condition, its link with his right to rule, and the state of his kingdom.

The wizard Gandalf, who has already assumed a position of spiritual elevation by having symbolically passed the abyss of death and returned to life, advises Aragorn. He directs Aragorn to look in the wilderness for a sign. There Aragorn finds a sapling of the original tree of Gondor. Aragorn's joy is apparent, and the significance of the symbolic health of the tree is articulated through the King and the Wizard's pronounced use of high-blown, biblical language. "Lo! Here is a scion of the Eldest of Trees!" cries Aragorn. To which the wizard adds the rejoinder: "Verily this is a sapling of the line of Nimloth the fair" before going on to give its line of descent from its precursor in the heavenly realm. The tree's flowering is the foundation that legitimizes Aragorn's status as returning king. Aragorn's continued legitimacy, and that of his line, remains linked to the tree as Gandalf instructs Aragorn to plant the seeds when the tree produces fruit to make sure that it does not die out. Gandalf notes that the tree comes from a longer line of descent than Aragorn, thus inferring that the human, even in the age of man, should not assume precedence over the tree. This point softens Tolkien's representation of the young tree willingly relinquishing the soil to enable Aragorn to transplant it. Aragorn perceives the subsequent thriving and blossoming of the tree as a sign that the time is ripe for his marriage to the Elf Princess, Arwen.

The representation of union with the divine as the culmination of the labyrinthine Christian pilgrimage is twofold. Firstly, the pilgrim reaches the central point of union through perseverance and faith in pursuing an arduous journey. Secondly, the experience is meant to be transformative and instructive. The labyrinthine pilgrim retraces their steps to re-emerge and employ the reflective lessons and changes effected by the experience. In *Rings*, the post-labyrinthine hobbits repeat the sacred ecological renewal process in the Shire's pseudo-English land. The symbol of renewal mirrors Gondor in the founding of a sacred tree that amalgamates societal and ecological health. The mode of renewal in the Shire also features re-enchanted nature as the hobbit Sam plants an Elven tree as the focal point to replace the most auspicious of the lost native trees. As a gardener, Sam reminds us of the possibility of new beginnings and reprises humanity's original role as steward/gardener of Eden in the Biblical myth of the fall.

Conclusion

Re-enchantment of nature in fantasy literature particularly resonates with young adult readers. Alun Morgan writes of how "environmental education and education for sustainable development … see such mythic re-enchantment of the world as the precursor to developing deep affection for, and ethic of care and reverence towards, the environment" (Morgan 150–151).

Rings has traditionally been popular among young adult readers. Noting the orientation of its labyrinthine structure raises questions about the narrative world's internal consistency and where tensions arise between unicursal/equilibrium models of ecology and multicursal/evolutionary ecology. Labyrinthine architecture highlights repetition and is suited to didacticism. As Perry Nodelman observed, "One of the clichés of educational thought is that we learn actions or thought processes by repeating them and being thus imprinted by them" (Nodelman 233). The repetitive circuits of the labyrinth return us to adjacent themes, while the use of the tree as a significant ecological symbol suggests a ubiquity that might transcend the text and reach beyond into the real world of the reader.

Indeed, there is evidence of the effect of Tolkien's mythology on the real world of environmental or ecological activism. Andy Letcher's article for the journal Folklore entitled "The Scouring of The Shire: Fairies, Trolls and Pixies in Eco-Protest Culture" overtly references the point in the epic where Tolkien's hobbits return to their homeland equipped to right the environmental wrongs carried out in their absence. Letcher's account of the 1990's eco-protest culture in Britain characterized eco-protestors as engaging and personally identifying with "fairy mythology" as an inspiration in a variety of ways, including as a living myth (Letcher 147–161). The book's continued success reflects a need for re-enchantment in the modern age. In its recycling of mythology, firmly framed within religious architecture, the text suggests that the values it espouses are timeless.

The unicursal labyrinthine rite of passage that the reader vicariously follows draws together separate examples of trees as signifiers within a unified whole. Both unicursal and multicursal labyrinths produce disorientation and confusion as their overall structure remains invisible from within. The unicursal labyrinth's horizons are limited by its regular turns, while the multicursal maze introduces elements of choice and suggests that there is no overall design but rather an evolving future subject to constant transformation.

This chapter has focused on one aspect of Rings's structural unicursal ecological imperative. My wider study of eco-labyrinthicity in *Rings* identified binary oppositions whereby multicursal labyrinthine mazes manifest evil and form the focus of ecological deterioration and a mortal threat to central virtuous characters and the quest. The Eco-labyrinthine scheme also provided a model against which to assess the ecological sensibilities and behavior of character groups. Most notably, this facilitated a new critical ecological reassessment of Tolkien's elves, typically accepted at face value as ecologically virtuous.

Works Cited

Armstrong, Karen. *A Short History of Myth*. Edinburgh: Canongate Books Ltd, 2006.

Artress, Lauren. *Walking a Sacred Path: Rediscovering the Labyrinth as a Spiritual Tool*. New York: Riverhead Books, 1995.

Barthes, Roland. *Criticism and Truth*, edited and translated by Katherine Pilcher Keuneman, London: The Athlone Press, 1987.

—. *The Semiotic Challenge*, translated by Richard Howard, Oxford: Basil Blackwell Limited, 1988.

Campbell, Liam. *The Ecological Augury in the Works of JRR Tolkien.* Zurich: Walking Tree Publishers, 2011.

Greenfield, Stephen Richard. *Ecological Labyrinths and Myths of the Fall: an earth-centred approach to The Lord of the Rings and His Dark Materials.* PhD Thesis, University of Wolverhampton, 2021.

Jobes, Gertrude. *Dictionary of Mythology Folklore and Symbols, Part 1.* New York: The Scarecrow Press Inc, 1962.

Kern, Hermann. Through *the Labyrinth: Designs and Meanings over 5000 Years,* edited by Robert Ferre, New York: Prestel, 2000.

Letcher, Andy. "The Scouring of The Shire: Fairies, trolls and pixies in eco-protest culture." *Folklore,* n°112 (2), 2001.

Levi Strauss, Claude. *Myth and Meaning.* London: Routledge Classics, 2001.

Matthews, W.H. *Mazes and Labyrinths.* Marston Gate: Forgotten Books, 2008.

McCaffery, Steve. "To Lose One's Way (for snails and nomads): The Radical Labyrinths of Constant and Arakawa and Gins." *Interfaces,* n°21–22, 2003, pp.113–144.

McCoppin, Rachel. *The Hero's Quest and the Cycles of Nature: An Ecological Interpretation of World Mythology.* Jefferson: McFarland & Company Inc, 2016.

Morgan, Alun. "*The Lord of the Rings* – a *mythos* applicable in unsustainable times?" *Experiencing Environment and Place through Children's Literature,* edited by Amy Cutter-Mackenzie, Phillip G.Payne and Alan Reid, Abingdon: Routledge, 2014, pp.145–161.

Nodelman, Perry. The Hidden *Adult: Defining Children's Literature.* Baltimore: The John Hopkins University Press, 2008.

Reed Doob, Penelope. *The Idea of the Labyrinth from Classical Antiquity through the Middle Ages.* Ithaca and London: Cornell University Press, 1992.

Stibbe, Arran. "Deep Ecology and Language: The Curtailed Journey of the Atlantic Salmon." *Society and Animals,* 14 (1), 2006.

Sturluson, Snorri. *The Prose Edda of Snorri Sturluson: Tales from Norse Mythology* translated by Jean I Young. Berkeley: University of California Press, 1992.

Tolkien, J.R.R. 'On Fairy Stories' in *J.R.R. Tolkien: Tales from the Perilous Realm.* London: Harper Collins, 2008.

—. *The Letters of J.R.R. Tolkie.,* Edited by Humphrey Carpenter, London: Harper Collins Publishers, 1981.

—. *The Lord of the Rings.* London: Harper Collins, 1992.

Wright, Craig. *The Maze and the Warrior.* Cambridge:Harvard University Press, 2001.

Wynne, Hilary. "Rohan." in *J.R.R. Tolkien Encyclopedia: Scholarship and Critical Assessment,* edited by Michael D.C. Drout, Abingdon: Routledge, 2007.

Chapter 6

At Ground Level: Narratorial Ecology and Economy in Dermot Healy's *Long Time, No See* (2011)

Catherine Hoffmann

University of Le Havre, France

Abstract: Narrated at ground level by its protagonist, Philip Feeney aka Psyche, *Long Time, No See,* Dermot Healy's last novel, combines loving observation of a rural environment, physical engagement with it, and quiet expression of elegiac feeling.

In his narrative, Psyche records a short transitory period in 2006 when, after leaving school, he was doing a variety of odd manual jobs.

This essay studies the interweaving of narratorial ecology—i.e., the imaginative treatment of the relationship between the protagonist-narrator and his habitat—and a textual economy, informed by biocentrism, involving an egalitarian treatment of humble story material and stylistic sobriety.

In *Long Time, No See,* Healy achieved an idiosyncratic form of Irish pastoral, free from nostalgia, of the Georgic rather than Arcadian mode, although the novel revisits some components of this tradition: the garden Psyche is making for his mother evokes an Edenic motif while, as in Arcadia, death is present in the form of story events and unsettling *memento mori.*

Keywords: death, *memento mori,* garden, *hortus conclusus,* habitat, North West Ireland, human plant, narratorial ecology, narratorial economy, pastoral, Arcadia, georgics, physical, environment, stylistic sobriety

***

No crash, no drama
That was how life happened.
No mad hooves galloping in the sky,
But the weak, washy way of true tragedy.
A sick horse nosing around the meadow for a clean place to die.

(Patrick Kavanagh, *The Great Hunger*, 1942)

Taken out of context, and provided we substitute the present for the past and a sick cow for the sick horse of Kavanagh's verse, the quotation reads like a condensed version of both the unspectacular story-world and narrative of the Irish novelist and poet Dermot Healy's last novel, *Long Time, No See* (2011).[1] Yet, although Healy is often regarded as "the heir to Patrick Kavanagh" (Seamus Heaney),[2] his last novel and volume of poems, *A Fool's Errand* (2010), stand in sharp contrast to Kavanagh's long poem. While *The Great Hunger* is a bitter anti-pastoral,[3] emphasizing its protagonist's frustration and the drying up of his desire and emotion, "*Long Time, No See* is a quiet hymn to the troubled ecstasy of life on the Atlantic seaboard and a celebration of the whole gift of existence" (Hopper 227). In his ultimate works,[4] Dermot Healy, who died suddenly in 2014, combines loving observation of the environment, physical engagement with it, and sober expression of elegiac feeling, not for a lost world, but for dead friends, relatives, or animals.

The homodiegetic narrator, Philip Feeney aka Mister Psyche, records from an unspecified position in time and space, a short transitory period in August–September 2006, when, after his School Leaving Certificate, he was doing a variety of odd jobs: looking after a sick cow and an aging relative, building a garden wall, clearing the beach after storms, collecting lobsters from the pots, helping to bale hay and to cut a donkey's hooves. His world— the townland of Ballintra, a small rural territory on the coast of North West Ireland—is, in spite of its wild weather and raging sea, a hospitable microcosm, a global local world, shared peacefully by local people and "strangers" from Eastern Europe, domestic and wild animals and plants.[5]

The central concern of this essay is to examine how these diegetic components, together with the narrative and stylistic economy of the novel, give textual shape to an active ethical way of dwelling in the physical world, the habitat in which the "human plant" is rooted and with which it interacts. The imaginative treatment of the relationship between the human protagonist and his environment is termed here "narratorial ecology," a concept seeking to take into account the narrative features conveying a vivid sense of this interaction. Although there are many affinities between the ecopoetry of Healy's *A Fool's Errand* and *Long Time, No See*, prose fiction relies on specific means to express the same vision. Thus, the voice and perspective are no longer the aging poet's but those of a young character-narrator. The novel also offers the scope and generic context for the transformation of a place into a story-world, while the development of the sequence of actions and events emphasizes Psyche's dynamic, concrete experience of living in this world.

The analysis of the interaction between textual economy and ecology will involve a related discussion of the novel's idiosyncratic relation to the literary tradition of the pastoral and to the motif of the garden. I will, in particular, contend that, while primarily heir to the georgic, or work and days, tradition, *Long Time, No See* also, perhaps surprisingly, revisits some Arcadian topoi.

It will be observed that, throughout this essay, the neutral expression "the physical environment" or the more metaphorical one "Mister Psyche's habitat," in keeping with the image of the human plant, are used in preference to "nature" or "the natural world," which would require clarification, given the polysemy of the concept of nature, and the incompatible ideological uses to which it has been put, as shown by Kate Soper in *What Is Nature? Culture, Politics and the Non-Human* (1995).[6] Besides, the words "nature" and "natural" do not seem to be part of the narrator's and characters' vocabulary. The novel, in fact, defies conceptualization of these terms since Mister Psyche, the character-narrator, inhabits a world without hierarchy or clear categorical boundaries between human and non-human, nature and culture, wild and domesticated, so that, in his narrative, wildlife coexists with gardens, meadows, fields, domestic animals and cultivated plants, and permanent physical human interaction with the environment.

"The tangible and the mysterious": The "human plant" in its Habitat

The image of the human plant is borrowed from the French writer Julien Gracq who used it first in a radio broadcast, "Les yeux bien ouverts" (1954), and later in a lecture at the École Normale Supérieure, "Pourquoi la littérature respire mal" (1960). In both cases, he expressed dissatisfaction with the stifling atmosphere of French novels of the period. In the radio broadcast, he deplored what he called "le côté *fleur coupée* du roman psychologique à la française" (Gracq 1989 844)—the "cut flower" aspect of the French psychological novel—and went on to state that his interest lay in the human plant, a conception he developed in the lecture:

> What strikes me when reading those stifling novels which keep out fresh air and the outside world [...] is a deliberate and systematic exclusion: the exclusion of a kind of marriage of inclination as much as of necessity, yet a trusting and indissoluble marriage sealed every minute daily between man and the world which bears him, a marriage at the root of what I have called the *human plant*. (Gracq 1989 878–9, my translation)[7]

As if echoing Gracq, Seamus Heaney also uses the marriage metaphor in his reflections on the sense of place, which in its "richest manifestation" involves a "feeling, assenting, equable marriage between the geographical country and the country of the mind" (Heaney 132). It is the kind of marriage that Healy's novel celebrates, not through mystical or philosophical commentary, but in the narrator's minute recording of action and motion in the townland of Ballintra, his participation in private and social rituals, and his observation of the world, both "tangible and mysterious" (Healy 1996 240), which constitutes his habitat. As a character, Psyche lives in direct, intimate contact with his surroundings, and since the narrative is filtered through the perspective of the narrated-I rather than the narrating-I, it conveys an immediate experience of life at ground and sea level, whether of Psyche "coated in straw" (367) after baling hay, "swimming in mud" (323), slipping on seaweed or making his way "through piles of small blue mussels blown ashore at Shell Corner" (51). Landscape, with its pictorial overtones and the panoramic vision which conditions its existence, is not applicable here as an aesthetic category. Though there are some moments when Psyche looks out to sea, so do the hare and the heron: "I sat in against the wall and looked out to sea" (51); "Out the rocks the hare was now sitting by his friend the heron looking out to sea." (425) Such static observation, therefore, is not a human privilege, and the identical vocabulary used in the narrative emphasizes the similarity of attitude between the human protagonist and the animals. Most of the time, however, Psyche is actively engaged through work and motion in a physical world itself in constant flux, under the combined action of wind, rain, the sea, and human agency.

At the diegetic level, the characters make no or little difference in their considerate attention to and care for humans and animals alike, whether, as in Psyche's case, they look after an aging relative or a sick cow:

> Myself and Da carried water in a tall milk can into the North meadow. We poured a few drops onto the lips of a sick cow. Then filled the stone basin. Lying on her stomach with her hooves to the side she looked off into the distance. He patted her down.
>
> I like that animal.
> The cow continued to stare ahead.
> He stared into her eyes.
> Get better soon, he said. (52)

The same kind of egalitarian treatment characterizes the narrative in its accurate recording of the movements and attitudes of humans, animals— characters in their own right—and even plants, and its descriptions of friendly interaction between humans and animals, such as the scene where Psyche observes a robin perched on Joejoe, his great-uncle's boot:

> I stood and watched. The bird looked my way, then turned to him. It lifted one claw and looked at it, scattered its wings, closed them and brushed its breast with its beak. Then it looked off to the left as if remembering something, bowed quickly, hopped onto his knee, fidgeted, then back again to the toe of his boot. Good man, said Joejoe smiling. (54)

The most memorable instance is the episode of the stray donkey with bad hooves:

> a stray ass came out of the forest and followed me. He'd step up and bite at my sleeve. He had huge deep eyes and his hooves were bad. They were long and painful [...] I spent a long time looking into his eyes. I turned back to the house with him at my side. He liked to put his chin nearly, but not quite, on my shoulder, then he'd tug at my elbow.

> Settle son, I said to him as he butted me quietly. He bubbled his upper lip. (74)

Not only does this passage registers with painstaking precision the nonverbal means of communication used by the animal, but it also manages, with its spare grammatical economy and avoidance of expression of feeling, to convey Psyche's immediate awareness of the donkey's pain, which will duly lead to action, hoof-cutting in this case.

To be absolutely accurate, one should, however, note that some animals—of the shellfish persuasion in particular—are excluded from this egalitarian and affectionate treatment at the diegetic as well as the narrative level and are only mentioned as foodstuff freely available in the sea or on the shore.

The world inhabited by Psyche, his friends, and relatives is both a densely material and contemporary one and one that is full of wonders. This is reflected in the absence of textual boundaries between the most mundane aspects of Psyche's story-world and its mysteries. There is no need for re-enchantment here since contact with enchanted phenomena or beings such as ghosts and fairies is integral to Psyche's everyday experience. The hare, for instance, goes and sits on the rocks by the sea because it is enchanted, says Joejoe. The donkey with bad hooves appears out of nowhere, does not seem to belong to anyone, and later vanishes into the woods (81), soon to be replaced by a deer:

At the edge of the woods a deer stood. I had seen him very few times in my life. At first I took him to be the donkey but then he materialised into a deer. He looked at us a long time then turned away as if he had grown tired at looking at us humans. (81)

In such passages, the narrative moves seamlessly from the realist observation of flesh-and-blood animals to the fairy-tale atmosphere of enchanted woods and their shape-shifting inhabitants.

A Record of Work and Days: Mister Psyche's Democratic Georgics

In the quietly celebratory mode of its narratorial ecology, *Long Time, No See* manifestly stands apart from Irish anti-pastoral as exemplified in Kavanagh's *The Great Hunger* and, more recently, in Paul Lynch's novel *The Black Snow* (2014). At the same time, it exhibits none of the nostalgia for a lost culture that Oona Frawley regards, for historical reasons, as a defining feature of Irish pastoral:

So intimate are nature and nostalgia as themes [...] that Irish literature's use of nature is characterized by a continual heightening over time of the nostalgia present in the traditional pastoral mode derived from Theocritus and Virgil, resulting in what I will call the nostalgic mode, or, more simply, Irish pastoral. (Frawley 4)

Terry Eagleton's view that "Nature in Ireland is too stubbornly social and material a category, [...] for it to be distanced, stylized" as "an object of aesthetic perception" (Eagleton 7-8) is much nearer the mark in the present case. Similarly, Michael Cronin's observation about Healy's *A Fool's Errand* applies just as well to his novel:

Healy's concern with the "actual place" is not to pinpoint historical loss in the plaintive Come-all-ye of the elegiac mode but to show how the particularity of place [...] sustains solidarities of feeling and understanding without, on the one hand, falling for the blandishments of messianic universalism or on the other, surrendering to the exclusivist pieties of blood and soil. (Cronin 395)

As already mentioned, much textual space is devoted to narrating the manual work that Psyche was doing in the transitory period after leaving school and before entering adulthood. Many of the tasks performed are habitual: collecting lobsters, feeding animals, and looking after the sick cow. Some are occasional: baling hay, cutting the donkey's hooves, clearing the beach after a storm, and helping to dig graves. However, building a garden wall, the job occupying Psyche for most of the narrated period, involves a long process. The curved wall in the making will shield a garden that does not yet exist (242) but will eventually be an offering to his mother, Geraldine. While the physical work required by the wall and, later, the garden itself is very concrete, the garden as a motif suggests the interweaving of an Arcadian topos with the prevailing georgic mode of the novel.

The material process involves recycling stones from a ruined building—possibly the remains of a monastery—and, later, shifting fertile topsoil—"good Protestant earth" (321)—from an Anglo-Irish estate to Geraldine's "Catholic" garden. Recycling, in this case, implies a spatial as well as a temporal transaction: as observed earlier, nothing in Psyche's world is ever static and stones and soil are on the move, whether this is caused by human action as in this case, or by elemental forces, for instance when a storm "dragged down the boulder clay and uncovered [an] ancient stone wall" (51) The making of the new garden also means recycling history into the future. In *Long Time, No See*, history is neither dead matter nor a narrative of the past: it is a geological formation of evolving layers of materials or objects which may, at any time, return to the surface. Even the know-how of the original builder is transferred to the making of the new wall: "I was trying to repeat the pattern of the old stone work in the new wall." (242)

Geraldine's garden is, in some ways (its surrounding wall, its two intersecting paths running from corner to corner, the flowers which will grow in its fertile soil) reminiscent of the Marian or monastic *hortus conclusus*,[8] its Edenic echoes in keeping with the prelapsarian atmosphere of the novel. Yet, if the garden is to be a small paradise, an oasis, or miniature Arcadia, in the rough salt and rain-drenched world of North West Ireland, this will not materialize until the following spring and summer: it involves, therefore, looking forward to the fruits of human labor, not backward to a mythical world forever lost. The making of the garden is indeed primarily a very physical undertaking, the various stages of which are carefully traced by the narrative. In this respect, it forms an integral part of the georgic mode. In addition to its literal meaning, it is also possible to read Psyche's wall building for the garden as an allegory of his egalitarian story-telling: "No stone should be proud; and stand out from the rest. It is the small stone that no one sees gives all the balance" (242). In this allegorical reading, the same principles apply to Psyche's narrative in the selection of story components, the balance between them, and the general economy of the text. As Dermot McCarthy puts it, in an analysis linking the artistic and ecological dimensions of the novel:

> The building of the walled garden is cognate with the telling of the
> story. The search for, selection, and laying of the right stones in the
> right order and leaving them to 'settle,' is a precise metaphor for
> Healy's art and enterprise, the work of words grounded in the labour of
> being-in-the-world. (McCarthy 318)

Throughout *Long Time, No See*, the choice of narratable material reflects
what Jacques Rancière sees as the all-embracing democracy of the humble
world of work and days (Rancière 25–26). The narrator's role is restricted to
that of a recorder of conversations and of "the banal events of those days,"
which, perhaps, to paraphrase Healy's memoir *The Bend for Home* (Healy
1996, 288), he would otherwise not recall. The narrating-I refrains from
judgments, comments, and explanations and eschews any superiority given
by hindsight and function in an attitude to the story material which parallels
the position of the narrated-I in relation to his environment and closely
interweaves narratorial economy and ecology. This narrative unobtrusiveness
originates in Healy's decision to "leave out all motives" as he said in an
interview with the *Observer*, so that the reader has "the suggestion of what
happened rather than it being spelt out." (O'Hagan 2011) The extensive use of
dialogue largely contributes to the limitation of the narrator's role and
discursive presence and also means that Psyche, the character's voice is only
one among others. In the hoof-cutting scene, for instance, Psyche, who says
little while he assists Tom Feeney aka the Blackbird, does not answer Miss
Jilly's question, "Why did you bury the parts of the hooves" (84) after she has
seen him bury the nail filings. The answer "[b]ecause […] they would stick in
the throat of a dog and choke him." (84) is given by the Blackbird. Psyche's
sense of responsibility towards animals is once more corroborated in the
physical action he performs, not in verbal self-expression of his ecological
awareness, while the economy of the Blackbird's explanation leaves out moral
or sentimental considerations, its force arising from the combination of its
concreteness and the suggestive power of its alliterations.

Deceptive Simplicity

In keeping with the egalitarian narrative treatment of the diegetic material and
with Healy's leaving out all motives, the text is characterized grammatically by a
scarcity of subordination and causal links. As in Psyche's dry-stone wall-
building, what prevails instead is juxtaposition and coordination. Here, for
instance, is an extract from the chapter in which Psyche, his father, and two
Russian sailors work together on cleaning Miss Jilly's chimney:

> I laid out a large black roll of plastic in front of the grate, took the
> stones off the mantelpiece, and the orange man slowly let the plastic

bags down and a shower of soot fell out of the grate onto the plastic. I took the box out of the grate. It was full to the brim with the debris of nests, dead birds and soot. The lads rolled the plastic sheet into a balloon, then we carried the box and the plastic outside, and emptied them into the cement bags [...] (230)

Grammatical and stylistic minimalism renders the men's concentration on the sequence of tasks, the only brief, descriptive sentence relating to the concrete result of the work done.

As the previous examples show, utterances in the narrator's discourse are almost exclusively in the form of statements of facts, even when reporting dreams or hallucinations, with the corollary that modality hardly figures in the grammar of the text. While adjectives and adverbs are used sparingly, short verbs of physical action and motion, generally Anglo-Saxon in origin, prepositions, and particles abound, contributing to a rhythmic quality of the text which, to quote Healy, "gives you the jump in the feet" (O'Hagan 2011):

[Da] spun the digger round, saw us and slowly rose the bucket high up in the air, then swung round and dug up a pile of clay and held it aloft waiting. Myself and Desmond jumped out and Gary backed the lorry in and took the first load, and after the second Da jumped down out of the digger. (319)

Such stylistic sobriety is indeed intended to convey the sounds and rhythms of the vernacular of North West Ireland: "When I was writing," Healy told Sean O'Hagan in the *Observer* interview already quoted, "I was trying to let the dialogue kick in the way it is spoken where the novel is set, which is just out of Sligo a bit on the verge of Donegal. In a way, I was trying to stay out of it and let the reader take over and run with it." (O'Hagan 2011) Since there is little stylistic difference between the narrator's and characters' diction, the novel offers a harmonious soundscape of stylized vernacular. Words are carefully chosen and grouped to form sound and rhythmic patterns, sometimes amounting to micro ecopoems often of the alliterative kind as in "The dying buachalawns[9] were bunched up in dry stacks of brown" (307) or the following passage: "The rushes were bent and swishing. Montbretia was swaying its lucifers, and here and there were the last of a few harebells and the torn ends of what was once the wild woodbine." (367)

The accuracy of the vocabulary referring to plants and animals, such as the lucifers of the montbretia, in the previous quotation or the reference to the choir of starlings (242) may be read as a mark of consideration for the non-human inhabitants of Psyche's world, while also forming in the narrative text fragments of fauna and flora of the Irish North West. In the case of the observation of animals, the narrator, however, as he does in his vignettes of human attitudes or gestures, occasionally delights in humorous analogies: "a starling like a gent on a street corner was whistling at the ladies" (307–8), while the hare "strolled into the ditch like a person entering a shop" (211). These anthropomorphic comparisons, testifying to Psyche's acute observation of the inhabitants of his microcosm, do not reintroduce anthropocentrism in disguise but partake of the novel's global abolition of hierarchies by emphasizing similarities between the physical attitudes or movements of humans and animals in everyday life, while the use of "like" maintains a distance between the humorous verbal vignettes and the realities of animal action.

Certainly, these linguistic and stylistic features of the novel reveal Healy's "fondness for words" (Healy 1996 57), their effect on the imagination and the senses surpassing the effect of their referent in the physical world. In his memoir, *The Bend for Home*, Healy recalls this discovery when, as an adolescent, he wrote an essay on rain, plagiarised from a book by Charles Lamb: "I can still remember the liquid feel of those words for rain. How the beads were blown against a windowpane, and glistened there, and ran. The words for rain were better than the rain itself. I wanted to type up words." (Healy 1996 57)

For our greatest delight, that is what he did in later life, inviting the reader to share in the wonders of text and world.

Conclusion: Et in Ballintra Ego

This ecopoetic discussion of *Long Time, No See* would be incomplete and even somewhat misleading if it did not include the elegiac dimension of the novel, which connects it to the melancholic strain of classical Arcadia, although, as stated earlier, it is entirely free from traditional pastoral's nostalgia for a lost or disappearing idealized world. In Ballintra, as in the Poussin paintings *The Arcadian Shepherds,*[10] death, in its least spectacular, most inescapable form, is present in the form of story events, happening within the short diegetic time span: the death of the sick cow is followed by the successive deaths of the two old men, the Blackbird and his friend Joejoe, Psyche's great-uncle. Another, more violent death, which took place a year before the narrated period, haunts Psyche and his narrative: the death in a car crash of Mickey, Psyche's best friend. The narrative is punctuated by private silent rituals of grief and by the practical actions that death requires in the present: digging graves or calling the Dead Animal Removal Service. Shared mortality reinforces the connection between the human and animal inhabitants of Psyche's world, while the deliberate avoidance of physically violent events and narrative complexities, in contrast to Healy's earlier novels, enhances the unspectacular sadness of ordinary quiet deaths: "Next morning at eight the Animal Removal wagon arrived and drove into the meadow and hoisted the cow into the back as Da and myself watched. He whacked my shoulder and looked away, then at the gate he paid the driver" (335).

The elegiac mode in *Long Time, No See* also expresses itself in the form of strange, unsettling still lifes: textual *memento mori*, such as a forlorn jacket and a pair of shoes, to be found not in some bucolic grove but on the seashore after a storm:

> The shoes were placed well back from the floods. No one was out swimming. No boats, only a wreck. Myself and the buoy and the shoes. A tidy man. I sat down and looked out at the water and then I looked at the shoes. Around size 9. I didn't know him. He was a stranger to me. One quick step and away. A man about to take a leap.
>
> They were sad shoes.
>
> Next day, as with the coat, the shoes were still there. And the day after. The leather turning white and the toes rising. (407)

And yet, even in this *memento mori* with its corpselike shoes and its flitting moment of pathetic fallacy, Psyche's narrative remains firmly anchored in the concreteness of life, and it is unlikely that size 9 shoes, however sad, ever found their way into Arcadia.

It is fitting that Psyche should have discovered the jacket and shoes on the shore: like empty shells, the humble vestiges of an anonymous life seem to belong by right to this liminal space, a site of transaction between sea and land, past and present, reality and legend, life and death, a place which is also Joejoe's habitat and the destination of the narrator's daily walks. In a world that is both densely material and full of signs and wonders, the eerie presence of the jacket and shoes foreshadows impending loss: Joejoe's death a few pages later. In the novel's last chapters, the garden's Edenic enclosed space with its promise of fruitfulness recedes from the textual foreground. The narrative ends with Psyche's walk from the village pub back to Joejoe's cottage for the wake of his dead great-uncle, and its closing sentence offers a condensed version of the world inhabited by the characters: its smells and feel, its small wildernesses and cultivated patches, its communal rituals. With its capital letter and potential for polysemy, the last word of the novel, rather than induce the sense of an ending, stimulates the reader into complete wakefulness and renewed attention to the text and the world it so vividly evokes:

"I said good night, and went out and took the Bog road, and started the walk, with the torch, through the smell of dung, back down through the cut fields, past the rushes and whins and grey shuffling reeds, to the Wake." (438)

Notes

[1] Dermot Healy (1947-2014) was a poet, short story writer, playwright, and novelist. His novels include *A Goat's Song* (1994), generally regarded by his fellow writers and by critics as his masterpiece, *Sudden Times* (1999), and *Long Time, No See* (2011). He is also the author of a much-praised memoir, *The Bend for Home* (1996). Six collections of his poems were published between 1992 and 2015. Healy's writing displays both a vivid sense of place—whether the area near the border with Northern Ireland or the North-West coast—a keen sensitivity to myth, legend, and liminal states, and an acute ear for the vernacular. Held in high regard by other writers, including Seamus Heaney, Aidan Higgins, Annie Proulx, and Patrick McCabe, his work has not received the international academic and critical attention it deserves. To address this neglect, Keith Hopper and Neil Murphy edited a collection of observations and essays on Dermot Healy – some of them referred to in this essay – entitled *Writing the Sky* and published in 2016.

[2] Heaney's interview in the documentary film on Dermot Healy, *The Writing in the Sky*, RTÉ, 2011, 5'53'. Also quoted in Garry Keane 2016 154.

[3] Anti-pastoral acts as a corrective to the idealization of the pastoral by "exposing the distance between reality and the pastoral convention when that distance is so conspicuous as to undermine the ability of the convention to be accepted as such." (Gifford 128) Terry Gifford goes on to analyze Kavanagh's poem as "an example of an anti-pastoral text that bitterly attacks a form of cultural pastoral that leads to emotional alienation." (128)

[4] The novel and the volume of poems have so much in common that Dermot McCarthy considers that "*Long Time, No See* is one half of a diptych, the other half being *A Fool's Errand* (2010), the long poem written during the same period." (McCarthy 316)

[5] On Mister Psyche's world, see Hoffmann 2016.

[6] The glossary of *The Green Studies Reader*, for instance, defines nature as "the physical, non-human environment, including wildlife and wilderness, flora and fauna, and so on; but also the 'essence' of anything, including humanity, in which case it is often spelled with a capital N and should be used with caution." (Coupe 303) The anthology contains a number of texts on the debate between realist and culturalist conceptions of nature/"nature" (see for instance the extracts from Terry Gifford's "The Social Construction of Nature" and from Jonathan Bate's *Romantic Ecology: Wordsworth and the Environmental Tradition*). See also Greg Garrard's remark that "[t]he challenge for ecocritics is to keep one eye on the ways in which 'nature' is always in some ways culturally constructed, and the other on the fact that nature really exists, both the object and, albeit distantly, the origin of our discourse." (Garrard 10)

[7] « [...] à lire ces romans étouffants d'où l'air libre et le monde extérieur sont exclus [...] ce qui me frappe, c'est une exclusion délibérée et systématique. L'exclusion de cette espèce de mariage, mariage d'inclination autant que de nécessité, mariage tout de même confiant, indissoluble qui se scelle chaque jour et à chaque minute entre l'homme et le monde qui le porte, et qui fonde ce que j'ai appelé pour ma part la *plante humaine*. »

[8] The walled garden, or *hortus conclusus*, appears in the "Song of Songs" as a metaphor for the bride's chastity, an image which, in late Medieval European painting, became an allegory of the Immaculate Conception and purity of Mary. The Marian *hortus conclusus* also derives from monastic gardens, inspired by literary or visual representations of Eden, which they materialized within their walls, for instance, in their intersecting paths symbolizing the four rivers of Paradise. The monks carefully tended and cultivated the monastic gardens for fruit, vegetables, and medicinal plants. The enclosure of the monastic and Marian *hortus conclusus* marks the boundary between profane and sacred space and, in the case of the monastic garden, between wild and cultivated nature. In the same way, the garden that Psyche builds as a gift for his mother forms an oasis of fertile ground demarcated and protected from its raw and often chaotic environment. It is the only instance in a novel where boundaries are otherwise blurred or abolished in a clearly and deliberately circumscribed space, a miniature reconstruction of Eden.

[9] From the Irish 'buachalàn' meaning ragwort.

[10] Two paintings by Poussin are titled *The Arcadian Shepherds*: the Chatsworth version c. 1629-30 and the Louvre version c. 1638-40.

Works Cited

Coupe, Laurence, ed. *The Green Studies Reader. From Romanticism to Ecocriticism.* London: Routledge, 2000.

Cronin, Michael. "Banished Misfortunes?: Dermot Healy and the Rise of the Posthuman." *Writing the Sky: Observations and Essays on Dermot Healy*, edited by Neil Murphy and Keith Hopper, Victoria, TX: Dalkey archive Press, 2016, pp. 382–98.

Eagleton, Terry. *Heathcliff and the Great Hunger. Studies in Irish Culture.* London: Verso, 1995.

Frawley, Oona. *Irish Pastoral. Nostalgia and Twentieth-Century Irish Literature.* Dublin: Irish Academy Press, 2005.

Garrard, Greg. *Ecocriticism.* 2nd edition. London: Routledge, 2012.

Gifford, Terry. *Pastoral.* London: Routledge, 1999.

Gracq, Julien. "Les yeux bien ouverts." (1954). *Préférences, Oeuvres Complètes* vol.1., Paris: Gallimard (La Pléiade), 1989, pp. 843–56.

—. "Pourquoi la literature respire mal." (1960). *Préférences. Oeuvres Complètes* vol.1, Paris: Gallimard (La Pléiade), 1989, pp. 857–81.

Healy, Dermot. *Long Time No See.* London: Faber and Faber, 2011.

—. *A Fool's Errand.* Oldcastle (Co. Meath): The Gallery Press, 2010.

—. *The Bend for Home.* London: The Harvill Press, 1996.

Heaney, Seamus. "The Sense of Place." *Preoccupations: Selected Prose 1968-1978*, London: Faber and Faber, 1980, pp. 131–49.

Hoffmann, Catherine. "Mister Psyche's Microcosmos." *Writing the Sky: Observations and Essays on Dermot Healy*, edited by Neil Murphy and Keith Hopper, Victoria, TX: Dalkey Archive Press, 2016, pp. 331–48.

Hopper, Keith. "'The Passionate Transitory': Dermot Healy and the Sense of Place." In *Writing the Sky: Observations and Essays on Dermot Healy*, edited by Neil Murphy and Keith Hopper, Victoria, TX: Dalkey Archive Press, 2016, pp. 210–30.

Kavanagh, Patrick. *The Great Hunger.* Poemhunter.com. 2016. http://www.poemhunter.com/poem/the-great-hunger. Consulted on 11 May 2016.

Keane, Garry. *The Writing in the Sky* (documentary on Dermot Healy). Ireland: RTÉ. 54 mins, 2011.

—. "At the End of the Day." *Writing the Sky: Observations and Essays on Dermot Healy,* edited by Neil Murphy and Keith Hopper, Victoria, TX: Dalkey Archive Press, 2016, pp. 148–54.

Lynch, Paul. *The Black Snow.* London: Quercus, 2014.

McCarthy, Dermot. "Psyche's Garden: The Labour of Mourning and the Growth of the Self in Long Time, No See." *Writing the Sky: Observations and Essays on Dermot Healy,* edited by Neil Murphy and Keith Hopper, Victoria, TX: Dalkey Archive Press, 2016, pp. 314–30.

O'Hagan, Sean. "Dermot Healy: 'I try to stay out of it and let the reader take over'." (Interview with Dermot Healy). *The Observer,* April 3 2011. http://www.theguardian.com/books/2011/apr/03/dermot-healy-interview-long-time. Consulted on 18 June 2014.

Rancière, Jacques. *Le fil perdu. Essais sur la fiction moderne.* Paris: La Fabrique, 2014.

Soper, Kate. *What Is Nature? Culture, Politics and the non-Human.* Oxford: Blackwell, 1995.

Chapter 7

Sean Penn's *Into the Wild* or Filming Nature with/and Passion

David Latour

REMELICE - University of Orléans, France

Abstract: Inspired by the true life story of young Christopher McCandless, Sean Penn's *Into the Wild* (2006) portrays an idealistic character who refuses to play by the rules of reality and who seeks refuge into wild nature through the powerful power of imagination. His romantic passion for nature drives him away from the material contingencies of life, whether social or environmental, for he dreams of Alaska as the place where he will finally be able to be himself. As he considers the wild as an extension of his subjectivity, and is blinded by his fascination for classic nature writers, he wishes to assert his individuality through choices that will lead him to a fateful and lonely end. Caught up in his pride, his symbolic salvation will ultimately come from a transcendent communion with the divine in nature.

Keywords: environmental films, *Into the Wild*, nature, passion, romanticism

***

"If we admit that human life can be ruled by reason, the possibility of life is destroyed," claims the hero of Sean Penn's *Into the Wild*, an environmental movie in which the idea of passion is central. The film is a biographical adventure movie written and directed by Penn, who brought the story of Christopher J. McCandless (played by Emile Hirsch) to the screen in 2006. It is dedicated to his memory and is based upon Jon Krakauer's biography and travel essay *Into the Wild* (1996); it reconstructs the last two years of the life of the hero via flashbacks. Penn's challenge was to provide images where Krakauer's words prevailed in conveying both the sublime and tragic life story of the hero. The filming of nature holds a central place in the movie as the hero is an American 20th-century character filmed through the prism of 21st-century environmental issues. Wild nature is filmed with passion as the idea that it is in danger and might be lost forever has become more and more of a reality in our century.

Life should be a journey filled with surprises, according to McCandless, whose definition of passion is grit and dedication. Passion is at the heart of a fulfilling life, the kind of existence the hero of the movie wants to lead in the wild. Here, passion is seen as the driving force behind one's life and deeds. More generally speaking, passion is defined as an intense, unreasonable, and wild state of mind. According to the *Oxford Dictionary*, it's "a strong or uncontrollable emotion" such as "a state or outburst of strong emotion" or "intense sexual love." It's a psychological and emotional state which can often correlate with love. Philosophically and morally, two movements prevail in defining passion. On the one hand, it denotes suffering (from the Latin "*patior*," to suffer) as it refers to what someone or something undergoes, what they are a slave to in a state of passivity as opposed to action. For 17th and 18th-century philosophers such as Descartes and Kant, wisdom needs to dominate our passions for us to be free and autonomous individuals; as for Spinoza, knowing our passions can help us free ourselves. On the other hand, romantic philosophers such as Hegel hold that passion is a positive force that fuels our actions and makes us assert ourselves in the world.

In light of these different meanings, I intend to inquire into Sean Penn's depiction and filming of nature and the relationship of the main character to nature until his fateful death by comparing and contrasting it with other environmental fiction or non-fiction films. I wish to show how the movie comes to create such passionate emotions with regard to nature through the prism of the main character's passions. I will first deal with the passionate relationship between the film and the viewer. Then, I will investigate Christopher McCandless's/Alexander Supertramp's passion for Thoreau. Finally, I will examine the question of nature depicted as something irresistibly attractive.

The Driving Forces of a Nostalgic Rebel

A Romantic against 20th Century Social Conformity

Into the Wild is characterized by a sense of nostalgia for 18th-century romantic values at a time when non-fiction environmental films such as Davis Guggenheim's *Inconvenient Truth* (2006) and Nadia and Leila Conners' *The 11th Hour* (2007) endeavored to tell humanity about its responsibility towards the natural environment. These documentaries attempt to raise public awareness of global warming and its dire consequences, such as the greenhouse effect and the melting of glaciers, and to warn it about the radical changes that will have to be made to face ecological emergencies. Yet, Penn's

2006 film does not incorporate a sense of ecological urgency in its plot; nature seems eternal and untouchable. The movie depicts an American 20th-century character as a passionate hero who aims to express the emotions of his own tortured soul and advocate the cult of his personal self by exploring wild nature. In the movie, the hero refuses to become a productive member of society for "careers are a twentieth-century invention" (1:49)[1] as he tells Ron Franz whom he meets at the Market/post office in Salton City, California. He is infused with the definition that Hegel gives of passion in his *Lectures on the Philosophy of World History.* "I use it here to denote any human activity which is governed by particular interests (...); men dedicate the entire energy of their will and character to attaining such ends, and will sacrifice other possible ends and indeed all other things to this object." (Hegel 71) The philosopher concludes that "nothing great has been accomplished in the world without passion." (Hegel 72) Passion is necessary because it is the creative energy of the will and the ultimate force toward a focus. Penn's character seems out of touch with the environmental concerns of the 21st-century reality that characterizes the film industry during the movie's shooting. One explanation for this is given by director of photography Eric Gautier who recalls in an interview transcribed in *AFCinéma* that McCandless' adolescent idealism "resonates with many things from (Penn's) childhood. His father, in particular, used to take him to the desert, to the bush, on long trips." (Péron) The movie seems estranged to its time of creation. The impetuosity of youth took over when filming nature as an object of passion from the hero's point of view.

Into the Wild is structured as a *Bildungsroman* depicting the intellectual and moral education of McCandless. Five chapters compose the movie: "My own birth," "Adolescence," "Manhood," "Family," and "Getting Wisdom," which all represent the steps of his inner quest and personal evolution. For about two years before eventually settling down in Alaska, the hero lives a nomadic life, mostly as a "leather tramp" (27), to quote Jan, journeying across the country on foot, hitchhiking, and jumping on freight trains. This reveals a strong personality trait in him. His sister Karine recalls his innate temperament that "Chris had always been driven, had always been an adventurer." (1:02) His taste for adventure makes him an American contemporary *Wilhelm Meister.* The various steps of his journey are symbolized by a leather belt he fashions with Ron. First, he inscribes his initials C.J.M. and a No-U-turn sign; then, he engraves a dozen other pictures representing the various places he has been to until the letter "N" that stands for going "North" to Alaska. These natural landscapes reflect the quest for meaning of the hero who has a taste for imagination and the unknown into the wild. To him, settling down in Alaska epitomizes "(t)he climactic battle to kill the false being within and victoriously conclude the spiritual revolution." (12) At his camp in California, he urges Ron to do the same: "You should make a radical change in your lifestyle. I mean, the core of man's spirit comes with new experiences." (1:55) A quiet life of habits is moribund; life should be impetuous to be worth living according to Penn's hero. His passion is a positive force that makes him search for new adventures.

The movie also incorporates elements of a road movie where the hero is a nomad in a world of abundance. *Into the Wild* doesn't convey that social and ecological solidarity should be preserved; it advocates individualistic values. This stands in striking contrast to another road movie of the same period, John Hillcoat's post-apocalyptic film *The Road* (2009), which depicts a world where material comfort has disappeared, and nomadism is both a punishment and a vital necessity to survive as the remaining inhabitants of the earth have begun resorting to cannibalism. Hillcoat's 2009 adaptation of McCarthy's novel pictures an earth that is no longer a home to humanity, as neither nature nor society can provide for its basic needs. Penn's movie, on the other hand, shows a character who has access to wealth and profusion and who has willfully opted for a nomadic life as he tells Ron: "I have a college education. I'm not destitute. I'm living like this by choice." (1:49–1:50) McCandless is a rebel craving for an exhilarating life and, in so doing, wanting to cut himself loose from any family or social ties. His adventure begins with the lonesome hopeful figure of the hero secretly leaving Atlanta, driving his Datsun B210 West as the sun rises. The audience watches him inaugurate his stay in Alaska two years later by engraving a wooden board inspired by the lyrics of Roger Miller's "King of the Road," revealing his untamable spirit: "Two years he walks the earth. No phone, no pool, no pets, no cigarettes, ultimate freedom. An extremist. An aesthetic voyager whose home is the road." (11) Moreover, the audience witnesses McCandless making radical decisions such as giving all his college funds to Oxfam America and eventually setting the remaining of his cash on fire. When in California, he laments to Jan that money "makes (him) precautious." (28) He wants to remain a vagabond with no strings attached to anyone or anything. Penn's character feels very far away from the planes flying up in the immense blue sky in various directions throughout the movie – out of touch with society and with 2006 environmental awareness.

As a true romantic, the hero believes he can become a new character of his own. Penn builds his individuality by filming McCandless to create a new identity for himself to erase his past, family, and social origins. Meaning to forge a new self, he writes, "Alexander Supertramp was here July 1990" (23) in red lipstick on the restroom mirror of a bar in Arizona. The name "Supertramp" represents bravery, whereas "McCandless" stands for pusillanimity. This latter has always been scared of water, and the scenes shot in Colorado in chapter 2 exemplify the courage he musters to overcome this fear. The hero challenges himself to face his biggest fear and decides to peddle down the Colorado River by himself. The camera films him staring at the torrent—petrified by fear. Determined to overcome his dread, he measures himself against the raging waters of the rapids with no training whatsoever and no life jacket or helmet. Making it alive and still full of adrenaline, he raises his fists in a sign of triumph and shouts: "I am Supertramp!" (55), thus implying that Supertramp has succeeded where McCandless would have failed. This scene conveys how irreconcilable McCandless and Supertramp are and how his choices cannot be undone. As his voice echoes through the Canyon, the film shows a hero driven by positive passions that fuel his actions and his need to cut himself off from society and start afresh.

Wild Hopes for Self-Exploration in Walden

A positive driving force behind the hero's actions, namely hope, also fuels his passion with boundless expectations for what a more natural life could be. The wild he wants to reach is never represented as endangered or damaged. On the contrary, it is envisioned as a pristine and enchanting area full of endless possibilities that is protected from any sort of human intervention. This conception is reminiscent of the heroine's state of mind in Jean-Marc Vallée's *Wild* (2014), in which unprepared Cheryl Strayed goes on a 1,100 miles hike on the Pacific Crest Trail. Her adventure in the wild is, first and foremost, a journey of self-discovery and healing that she assumes only nature can provide. Penn places his film under the aegis of verses from Lord Byron's *Childe Harold's Pilgrimage*, emphasizing that McCandless' romantic appeal for nature is stronger than his contempt for humankind:

> There is a pleasure in the pathless woods,
> There is a rapture on the lonely shore,
> There is society, where none intrudes,
> By the deep sea, and music in its roar:
> I love not man the less, but Nature more.
> (Canto iv 178)

These opening lines insist on his passion-driven quest for a wild nature that is, in fact, very much unclear to him. When talking to Wayne in a bar in Carthage, he specifies that he is not going to the city of Alaska where there are stores, but to "Alaska, Alaska." (44) He shares with him his wildest dreams: "I'm gonna be all the way out there (…), just on my own. Ya know, no fucking watch, no map, no axe, no nothing, no nothing. Just be out there, just be out there in it. Ya know, big mountains, the rivers, sky, game… just be out there in it, ya know, in the wild." (44) He only has vague notions of what his life could be like and emphasizes the immediacy and thoughtlessness of his outlook: "You're just livin', man. You're just there in that moment, in that special place in time." (44–45) The object of his enthusiasm is as vague as his passion is ardent. His love for nature is so wild that it makes him blind to the very nature of his affection. Wild nature seems timeless and untouchable.

Penn's filming reflects the hero's attraction to the wilderness of Alaska, which he conceives as a blank slate, a white page on which his future can be written. McCandless' passionate idealism and thirst for self-exploration are fueled by the need to start anew in unknown landscapes. This is exemplified at the very beginning of the movie by the image of the white snow-blanketed Alaskan landscapes he discovers for the first time. As William Cronon remarks in *Uncommon Ground* about wilderness: "As we gaze into the mirror it holds up for us, we too easily imagine that what we behold is Nature when in fact we see the reflection of our own unexamined longings and desires." (Cronon 69–70) Nature is the product of his imagination; it is what he needs it to be, a representation of his expectations. Into the Alaskan wild, one retreats from civilization to experience freedom and non-conformity in solitude. Alaska, being known as the "last frontier state," is the last frontier of the US northward and within himself as well. McCandless has come all this way to meet the challenge of Alaska, which becomes a metaphor for his inner search. Alaska exemplifies this process particularly well, as it is untamed and far away from human civilization. According to Scott Slovic, the Alaskan wilderness is "the place many Americans take to be the home of more-than-human reality." (Slovic 375) In Alaska, nature cannot be wilder and further from our daily human condition. At the beginning of his stay, he engraves the following words on a wooden board and reads to himself that he "walks alone upon the land to become lost in the wild" (12–13). Penn's character is willing to start from scratch and needs to get lost in order to find himself. At week three in Alaska, he can't find game and the rice stocks are getting scarce, the audience hears him talking to himself: "Strong, you can do anything, you can go anywhere. Money, power, is an illusion. It's up here. You can be here, me and you." (39) He wants to will his way through these hardships. Alaska requires the bravery and moral strength the hero yearns for; it is perceived as a place where humanity cannot cheat with pretense because it is nakedly facing itself.

The Power of Imagination over Reason

Illusions of Imagination

Emile Hirsch plays a young hero who doesn't quite fathom how much more powerful than humanity's wild nature is, mainly because he is inspired by classic fiction. He has fallen victim to his own passion, which stands for a state of passivity and enslavement to the body according to the classical philosophical tradition. Descartes defines it in a letter to the Princess

Elisabeth of Bohemia as resulting from the action of the body on the mind, so "one can generally call passions all the thoughts that are excited in the soul (…) without the concurrence of its will (…). For everything that is not an action is a passion." (Descartes 118) Similarly, according to Kant, passion is a sickness of the soul that prevents us from being free and leads to servitude. It is a state that subordinates all of our other desires and emotions. Hence, passions are destructive and prevent us from reaching high moral grounds. In his *Anthropology from a Pragmatic Point of View*, Kant explains that "passion is regarded as a sickness that comes from swallowing poison, or a deformity which requires an inner or an outer physician of the soul" (Kant 150–-151). McCandless' idealistic passion for nature is destructive, for it will keep him blind and will cause his death.

His passion for the wild stems first and foremost from literature and philosophy books, namely from the tradition of nature writing and not at all from hands-on experience. Since College, the hero has shown reverence towards authors such as Thoreau and London, but also Stegner, Tolstoy, Gogol, and Pasternak, whose works are so precious to him that he buries them like cherished treasures in Colorado and then digs them up to bring them to Alaska. Through his reading, McCandless' passion is fueled by the philosophical search for simplicity and truth. In this quest for wisdom and introspection, he desires to live by himself and restricts his belongings to the bare minimum. He refuses to let his parents buy him a new car for having graduated from Emory University, Atlanta. He exclaims, mirroring Thoreau's call in *Walden* for "Simplicity, simplicity, simplicity!" (Thoreau 395): "I don't want anything. Things, things, things, things" (19). Besides, once in Alaska, upon finding bus 142 at the beginning of the movie, he notes down in his journal that he is "starting Walden" (39), making it his home in the wilderness. McCandless expects that attempting to live a life by Thoreauvian precepts will enable him to reach higher ethical truths. As Jan is trying to have a conversation with him about his parents, he paraphrases Thoreau in *Walden* from memory. He responds: "Rather than love, than money, than fairness, give me truth" (28), tellingly insisting on the notion of justice, as the original quotation goes: "Rather than love, than money, than fame, give me truth" (Thoreau 585). Revisiting his mentor's thoughts, "fairness" replaces "fame," showing he considers the ethics of living a righteous life as valuable above all. From a philosophical standpoint, he places the quest for truth at the heart of his life, and it is in the wild that he intends to find true virtue.

The hero has gross misconceptions about what it takes to live in the Alaskan wilderness. He hasn't read or watched any contemporary source that would have provided him with vital information. Instead, having been stimulated by reading *The Call of the Wild* and *White Fang*, Mc Candless fosters a passion for

London and appears to be blinded by his own romantic imagination. He tells Rainey at the hippy camp that "Jack London is King!" (1:28), for he too hears this Alaskan call, but he does not comprehend all that it entails being answered in safe conditions. London is a very practical-oriented writer, and this fact seems to have gone widely unnoticed by the hero who has not prepared enough for his journey and who only wishes to reach his destination with the strict minimum in the Alaskan wild. Krakauer's point of view on the matter is that "London's fervent condemnation of capitalist society, his glorification of the primordial world, his championing of the great unwashed —all of it mirrored McCandless passion." (Krakauer 44) London had spent several months in the Yukon where part of *The Call of the Wild* is set. This gave him vital knowledge of what struggling for survival in the wild means, a fundamental fact that McCandless ignored. His passionate feelings towards Thoreau and London seem delusional since they only make him foster a vision of nature that is quite far from its complex material reality. The actual nature of the wild thus remains shrined in mystery.

And yet, McCandless does not remain completely passive in his love for nature and literature, for he aspires to eventually become a nature writer. In a bar in Carthage, he explains to Wayne: "Maybe when I get back I can write a book about my travels" (45). The final words on his journey should be his. By the end of the movie, Karine comments upon her brother's endeavor: "Chris was writing his story, and it had to be Chris who would tell it." (2:11) The hero never has the opportunity to reach this point and his dream of writing nature never becomes real. His journal remains a draft he never gets the chance to elaborate on and account for his most intimate thoughts on his brand-new relationship with the natural environment. Indeed, his journal entries are mostly lists of things to do and revolve almost exclusively around food, the weather, and his physical condition. Still, Penn does not portray a frustrated nature writer but a character that lives in the moment and, to some extent, remains a victim of his passionate impulses. He does not have the opportunity to take action and leave a testimony of his adventure to humanity, probably believing that writing, taking pictures, or filming would have killed the spontaneity of his approach. He enters the world of nature writing and nature filming as a romantic hero whose life and experience provide material for future books and movies.

A Passion of Grief in the Last Frontier

Penn's filming debunks an over-romanticized and idealized vision of nature inherited from the hero's deceptive imagination and sense of self. It is reminiscent of what happens to the heroine of *Wild* and the hero of Danny Boyle's *127 Hours* (2010). Both become victims of nature as Cheryl Strayed loses one of her boots and ends up without water for an entire day before meetings potential rapists, and mountaineer Aron Ralston gets his arm stuck in a slot canyon and eventually has to cut it loose to survive. In Penn's movie, after four months in Alaska, the hero is getting ready to go back to civilization. With new hopes for the future, he says goodbye to the verdant wild, but when he arrives where he had planted the hat Jan had knitted for him, he realizes he can no longer cross the Teklanika River because the melted glaciers have turned the ice canal into an abundant and wide river. He tries to cross it anyway but almost gets swept away. Forced to turn back, he returns to the bus under heavy rain and writes down in his journal: "Rained in – lonely, scared" (1:47). He understands he may die defeated by the place in which he had initially sought freedom and life. Contrary to what McCandless had anticipated, Alaskan nature is no friendly place for someone who does not have a realistic clue as to what it precisely takes to survive in it. One's subsistence entirely depends upon one's environment, as McCandless bitterly learns.

Perfection can be a dangerous thing to aspire to. McCandless's search for a better place in the wild leads him to delusions and untimely death. Incapable of finding any more game, he finds inspiration in a quotation from *Doctor Zhivago*, which reads: "For a moment, she re-discovered the purpose of her life. She was here on earth to grasp the meaning of its wild enchantment and to call each thing by its right name" (1:59), and decides to play the naturalist apprentice. He identifies and picks up various fruits, herbs, and berries with the help of the *Tanaina Plantlore*. In this scene, the viewers share the hero's field of vision, who is trying to recognize the Alaskan plants' names, frantically going from bush to bush barefoot on his knees while reading aloud the name of the different species. In the following scene, the hero is woken up by the sunlight; he is exhausted, extremely pale, dehydrated, nauseous, and even skinnier. He has dark circles around his eyes, cannot drink, and can barely stand up because of something he ate. Penn has chosen to inspire himself from the earliest but quickly discarded theory of how McCandless actually died, according to Krakauer's nonfiction account. Rereading the *Tanaina Plantlore*, the hero realizes he got confused between "wild sweet pea," which is inedible, poisonous, and deadly—the word "poisonous" jumps off the page at him—and "wild potato Alaska carrot." As he is agonizing, he tries to make himself vomit, in vain, and, a few days later, comes to an excruciating realization that he writes in his journal: "I have literally become trapped in the Wild." (2:05). McCandless proves incapable of bridging the gap between natural objects as described by written words categorizing nature and the shape under which they appear in the physical world. This tragic episode depicts the agony of a young passionate hero who believed that knowing nature from books, whether through literature, philosophy, or natural sciences, would be enough to survive.

His infatuation with the image he has created of Thoreau also leads him to his downfall. Thoreau's work is most inspirational to the hero. However, McCandless' mistake is only to acknowledge the aspects of Thoreau's writing that have been qualified as "pastoral," ignoring aspects that concern the dark and hostile character of the wild towards humankind. He tries to relive *Walden* but has not foreseen that he will also relive an episode close to *The Maine Woods*. This is exemplified by a scene in chapter 3, in which the hero is hunting a moose, killing it as it screams, and gutting it in a bloody and vivid scene, the sound of the knife slashing the skin, giving it a vibrant intensity. Then, he tries to prepare the meat by removing the moose's head and heart to smoke the meat following the advice of a friend of Wayne's; but the body soon gets covered in flies and larvae. Although he had been told to hurry up so as to avoid a fly infestation, guilt-ridden McCandless, who had a moment of weakness during the skinning of the animal, took the time to wash his hands, clean his face and take some time off to breathe, showing how challenging the killing of the moose is for him. After finding out that the body of the moose is rotting and infested with worms, the audience sees him record his failure in his diary: "Wish I'd never shot the moose" (1:25). He also describes this event through tears as "(o)ne of the biggest tragedies of (his) life." (1:25–1:26) While the wolves and eagles are eating the remains of the animal, the voice-over reads from Thoreau's *The Maine Woods*: "There was clearly felt the presence of a force not bound to be kind to man. It was a place of heathenism and superstitious rites" (Thoreau 645) (1:26). The intensity of the death of an innocent animal is a great source of mental and moral distress that he had not anticipated. His fervent search for a passionate existence in the wild is driven by a blinding passion for nature he hoped to belong to, but the wilderness is no tamable nature. The Alaskan wilderness is no hospitable Walden and contrasts sharply to the hero's preconceived ideas.

Paradoxical Passions for the Wild

Hubris and the Possibility of Reconciliation

Sean Penn's filming creates a proud character that refuses to play by the rules and often challenges the audience to impose his own principles. It leads the hero to adopt an attitude of defiance of artistic norms and provoke the traditional rules of filmmaking by asserting his overconfidence to the point that, on several occasions, he even plays with the viewers and stares back at them as though he is trying to play with them. His breaking the fourth wall conveys a sense of hubris since his behavior is fueled with pride and excessiveness. In chapter 2, for instance, he is pulling a face at the camera after eating an apple, having a conversation with it as if it were a person: "I'm Supertramp and you're Super Apple" (37); his face is filmed from a slightly low angle-shot to enhance the comic effect of the scene as he seems to be mocking the audience, talking to himself through the apple. Regarding this scene, in which he plays smart with the audience and tells the apple "You are the apple of my eye, ha!" (37), Pierre Floquet comments in "*Into the Wild*: la Nature, ce n'est pas du cinéma!" that "he breaks the diegetic charm and unveils the gap prevailing between his very personal vision on the one hand and the way others look at his condition within the state of Nature, on the other hand." (Floquet par. 17) His sense of self and the way he considers nature is stronger than anyone else's judgment. Penn's filming technique reflects on the notion of point of view, conflicting the audience's with the protagonist's. The hero proudly tells the spectators that his viewpoint is the only one that matters and that the audience will have to adopt it if they want to follow him.

The way to deal with one's passion for nature can be challenged. For instance, naturalist and film-maker David Attenborough went from compiling 60 years of work in his *Passion Projects* (2016) to filming projects that take into account the hard facts of the Anthropocene, such as *Extinction: The Facts* (2020) or *A Life of our Planet* (2020). The cold, rational reality of climate change has tinted his passion. In Penn's movie, reason and knowledge could have educated the hero's passionate temper. They would have provided him with a more informed point of view on his ability to overcome the Alaskan wilderness. As Spinoza proposes in *Ethics*: "An emotion, which is a passion, ceases to be a passion, as soon as we form a clear and distinct idea thereof." (Spinoza 213); the corollary follows: "An emotion therefore becomes more under our control, and the mind is less passive in respect to it, in proportion as it is more known to us." (Spinoza 214) Knowing our passions can educate the imaginary representation of the world that is fed by passions. By the same token, listening to others' advice may have spared the hero's life. He could have been enlightened on the dangers awaiting him on his journey in many instances. Rainey tries to temper his optimism for a life on the road and informs him on the beach in California that "(a)ll is not well on the hippie front." (31) His friend Wayne also warns him twice against his Alaskan endeavor telling him that is "a mistake!" (46), and forbidding him: "Remember Alex, no Alaska 'till spring!" (49) Triggering an effect of dramatic irony in the audience, McCandless tells Ron—a grandfather figure to him—who is worried about his situation as a nomadic youth: "I think I've got my head on my shoulders pretty good." (1:49) The hero stays deaf to all these obvious signs that Penn has shown the spectators who cannot but feel helpless in the view of the devastation caused by McCandless' fervent passion.

By week nine on the bus, the hero has eventually reconciled himself with his family and society at large. His reckless quest for a passionate life is over. Still, he does not know that this epiphany will come too late. As the hero's voice reads from Tolstoy's *Family Happiness*, the spectators read the page from his point of view: "I think I have found what is needed for happiness. A quiet, secluded life in the country, with the possibility of being useful to people" (1:42). The word "people" jumps from the page expressing the hero's realization that he needs a family to be fulfilled. By the end of the movie, as tears are running down his face because he knows he has poisoned himself, he writes a sentence echoing back to this quotation into his copy of *Doctor Zhivago*: "Happiness only real when shared." (2:11–2:12) He was unhappy and is now ready to interact with humankind – but it's too late. His death is nevertheless not a bitter one, for he leaves in peace. As his life is coming to a close, he leaves an epitaph on a piece of cardboard signed with his birth name as if to show he has reconciled himself with his past identity: "I have had a happy life and thank the Lord. Goodbye and may God bless all!" (2:13) while he repeats the quotation from *Doctor Zhivago* twice, "call each thing by its right name" (2:13). He has no regrets as he has been able to reconcile his passion for a reckless life of adventure in the wild and his longing for a quiet social life. Nature is where he has found his innermost self; it is where his dreams and hopes come true.

Centrifugal Romantic Forces and Transcendent Natural Phenomena

The hero's point of view on nature is a horizontal extension of himself. There is a paradox between nature as a development of the hero's subjective passionate nature and wild nature as a dominant and dangerous force. This tension between McCandless' interiority and the powerful elements of the landscape seems at first transcended by his subjectivity. Although the scenery pictured in Penn's film is undoubtedly stunning, natural American landscapes are not filmed only to provide a beautiful backcloth to the story. They provide an actual viewpoint on the world, that of the hero's who is irresistibly attracted to a wild nature he desires ardently, for it represents a chance to clean himself off of society's impurity, release his most inner and primal needs, and give way to his emotions. In chapter 3, for example, the hero climbs to the top of a mountain to try and appropriate his environment. On the mountaintop, the camera rotates around him at a 360° angle three times, offering a panoramic view. With this shot, the audience sees the sky and the snow-covered mountains of Alaska from his point of view. He puts his arms in a cross and breathes deeply, taking in the majesty of the landscapes. The scene merges into a shot of him running freely like a wild animal at the feet of the mountains. This scene is both about appropriating the wild and drastically changing perspective on the world as it offers a bird's eye view of the surroundings and makes the spectators see things from the hero's perspective; he is at the center of his own life, and so are we.

Settings do not so much provide a background to the diegesis as they provide a narratological system that connects the audience and the movie together through the viewpoint of the hero. Hence, space is not simply a location but a *locus* that situates the viewers' point of view. The film moves from the interiority of the hero's passion, the driving force behind his endeavors, to the object of his intense desire for the wild. Penn's filming defines nature as a space for the imagination in which and which both the hero and the audience can project strong emotions. André Gardies' conception of the cinematographic narrative provides a theoretical framework through which to rethink settings in general and the organization of space in particular in the movie. Hence, the movie is organized as a centrifuge narrative in which "the hero progresses, going through concentric spaces from the center to the furthest periphery" (Gaudin 26) writes Antoine Gaudin rephrasing Gardies in *L'Espace cinématographique*. Spectators can understand the movie's concrete topographical setting, and these settings also reinforce the abstract representation that the audience builds up with the movie. Penn's filming of natural landscapes conveys the hero's longing for natural elements as a rejuvenating quest. The wild does not just transcend and leads us to a better life; it also dominates us and rules life on Earth.

Nature is not pictured as endangered but as a danger to pride men and women who defy its magnitude. Penn's artistic vision seems to be a symbolic act of resistance against what would soon be called the Age of the Anthropocene. The director seems to be telling the audience about the wild more than what McCandless can comprehend, as these landscapes also stand for his future tomb. The hero's romantic conception of wilderness as an expression of his individuality clashes with its sublime, transcendent, and ultimately vertical character. Thanks to images of wide open spaces, nature is understood as a superior entity dominating humanity's insignificant earthly condition. The film provides the audience with a vivid example of one of these landscapes and their unequaled force through images of the Grand Canyon of Arizona and the Colorado River that are so immense that McCandless' existence seems meaningless in comparison. About the work of director of photography Eric Gauthier, Bertrand Pleven writes in "*Into the wild*": "The splendid photography (…) creates landscapes that are too wide for man." (Pleven par. 7) The sceneries are beautifully filmed but also convey a sense of threat and infinite dominance over humanity.

The tension between the conception of the wild as a horizontal extension of his subjectivity and the vertical force of the sublimity of nature finds a resolution of some sort in the presence of the divine. This is exemplified when the hero challenges Ron to get off the tailgate of his pick-up truck and climb up a steep hill in the desert to see the beautiful vista of the desert. McCandless is thrilled and calls out: "God, are you watching this right now?" (1:57) Ron has adopted the hero's point of view to see life in a new light. When back at the feet of the hill, he tells Ron: "God's placed (the joy of life) all around us. It's in everything. (…). People just have to change the way they look at those things." (1:57) At that moment, they look up at the clouds that split and make way for the sun, a rainbow appears as if God was answering back with a manifestation of His presence. This scene parallels the very end of the movie when the hero is trembling, lying down, dying, and hallucinating on bus 142. The spectators see McCandless staring into the sun; a rainbow appears through the clouds. The picture gets deformed as they see and hear him scream. He asks his family: "What if you saw me running into your arms... Would you see then...what I see now?" (2:14) He takes his last breath, the drumbeats of his heart intensifying. Through his hallucinations, the hero is transitioning into death in a state of confident ecstasy that is both blissful and sad. Looking up at the sky, he cries for the last time, and a cloud obscures the sky. The light shines again onto his lifeless face and eyes, conveying a feeling of deep serenity. He has reached wisdom, and things could not have happened any other way; he lived and died with passion in his heart. There is redemption in nature, after all.

Conclusion

To conclude, *Into the Wild* reflects romantic and idealist values inherited from the 18th century that show passion in a positive light. It is filmed as McCandless' *Bildungsroman* and seems at first impermeable to contemporary environmental issues. In this road movie, his individualistic take on life is that to experience life to the fullest; one should commit oneself to adventure and be forever unafraid of danger. Thus, the hero has high hopes for a life in a wild environment that he conceives as untouched by humankind; it is a blank slate onto which he can project a representation of himself. His passion for nature blindfolds McCandless. This unreasonable lack of control comes from his fascination for classical nature writers, whom he misunderstands. His passion for the mysterious wild could have allowed him to become a nature writer. However, he never got this chance, as if the wild could only be spontaneously experienced and never set on paper. His life in the Alaskan wild eventually leads him to great suffering and delusions as his endeavors as a naturalist, and a hunter teach him. The hero's conception of himself as having a special bond to nature is characterized by a sense of hubris. Reason and knowledge may have made him moderate his impulses, but the impetuosity of his youth made him discard all warnings. The movie creates a paradox between the hero's conception of nature as a horizontal extension of his subjectivity and the vertical strength of the sublimity of the landscapes. The only moment when he realizes this verticality is on his deathbed as God manifests Himself in the sky as the hero is taking his last breath and has achieved his goal of experiencing the wild to the fullest. Penn's wild nature remains a shrine that can welcome the wildest passions, but for how long?

Notes

[1] Numbers between parentheses refer to the hours and minutes in the movie.

Works Cited

Cronon, William. "The Trouble with Wilderness." *Uncommon Ground: Rethinking the Human Place in Nature*, edited by William Cronon, New York: W. W. Norton & Company, Inc. 1995.

Descartes, René. *The Correspondence between Princess Elisabeth of Bohemia and René Descartes*. Chicago: The U of Chicago P, 2007.

Floquet, Pierre. "Into the Wild: la Nature, ce n'est pas du cinéma !" *Mise au point 4* (2012). Cahiers de l'association française des enseignants et chercheurs en cinéma et audiovisuel. Association française des enseignants et chercheurs en cinéma et audiovisuel, April 18, 2012. Accessed November 15 2016, http://map.revues.org/786.

Gaudin, Antoine. *L'Espace cinématographique. Esthétique et dramaturgie*. Paris: Armand Colin, 2015.

Hegel, Georg Wilhelm Friedrich. *Lectures on the Philosophy of World History, Introduction: Reason in History*. Cambridge: Cambridge UP, 1984.

Into the Wild. Directed by Sean Penn, Paramount Vantage, 2008.

Kant, Immanuel. *Anthropology from a Pragmatic Point of View*. Cambridge: Cambridge UP, 2006.

Krakauer, Jon. *Into the Wild*. New York: Anchor Books, 1997.

Péron, Clémentine. "Entretien Avec Eric Gautier, Directeur De La Photographie d''Into The Wild' De Sean Penn." AFCinéma, May 3, 2010. Accessed November 15 2016, http://www.afcinema.com/Entretien-avec-Eric-Gautier-directeur-de-la-photographie-d-Into-the-Wild-de-Sean-Penn.html.

Pleven, Bertrand. "Into the wild," *Géographie et cultures 69* (2009). Accessed November 15, 2016, http://gc.revues.org/3627.

Slovic, Scott. "The spirit of these rocks and water." *A New Literary History of America*, edited by Greil Marcus and Werner Sollors, Cambridge: Harvard University Press, 2009, pp. 371-375.

Spinoza, Benedict de. *Ethics*. London: Penguin Classics, 2005.

Thoreau, Henry David. *A Week on the Concord and Merrimack Rivers, Walden or Life in the Woods, The Maine Woods, Cape Cod*. Edited by Robert F. Sayre, New York: The Library of America, 1985.

Part III.
Deceptive Emptiness and Lively Deserts: Reweaving our Sense of Place

Chapter 8

Re-enchanting the City in Graphic Novels: Walking Past and Future (Sub) Urban Spaces in Davodeau & Jacquet's *Jeanne de la zone* (2008) and Delisle's *Shenzhen: A Travelogue from China* (2006)

Anne Cirella-Urrutia

Huston-Tillotson University, USA

Abstract: Davodeau and Jacquet's *Jeanne de la* zone (2014) and Delisle's *Shenzhen* (2006) are infused with Virilio's principle of dromology as the "science (or logic) of speed"; a means of apprehending speed and its pivotal– and potentially destructive–role in contemporary global society (Virilio 440). Applying Virilio's principle to two graphic novels, I demonstrate how resistance to speed has consistently been eroded, and the physical world adapted, in order to satisfy the urge to move further and faster, consistent with the speed of modern urban life and the interaction of man within the city. I examine how human components in these two graphic novels fare in the face of the relentless urbanization. In looking at the consequences of this acceleration of speed, I contend that the accelerated pace of construction of the urban space described by Delisle's recent trip to Shenzhen, China, contrasts with Davodeau and Jacquet's suburban space of the 1902 *Zone*.

Keywords: city; zone; suburb; space; speed; dromology; graphic; re-enchantment; *bande dessinée*; youth; comics; French; Quebecois; ecocriticism

***

There is a link between children's literature, *bande dessinée* (literally drawn strip), and the city as a modern living space. Children's literature and graphic novels are often preoccupied with questions of size and stature as they relate to space, what French philosopher Gaston Bachelard defines as "the perspective of size" (Bachelard 150). In recent years, the overlapping of ecocriticism and geocriticism has gained popularity in Europe with a critical focus on the "spatial turn." In the United States, Robert T. Tally has done tremendous work in assembling and discussing critical perspectives on spatiality, such as the writer as a map-maker, the literature of the city and urban space, and the concepts of literary geography, cartography, and geocriticism. Tally has also contributed to introducing major theorists of spatiality, including Michel Foucault, David Harvey, Edward Soja, Erich Auerbach, Georg Lukács, and Fredric Jameson.[1] In France, Bertand Westphall, a specialist in geocriticism at the Université de Limoges, has long advocated a "geocentered" approach to literature and its affinities with geography, architecture, and urban studies.[2] Although the community of French ecocritics has grown internationally, overall, the movement itself has been slow to survey the terrain of urban environments in children's literature and graphic novels.[3] I wish to extend this critical lens onto two graphic novels in French as new sites that foster an urban ecological discourse partaking in the re-enchantment of two urban places. On the one hand, the erased 1902 *Zone* of Paris is revived by French comic writer Étienne Davodeau and historical archivist Frédérique Jacquet in the form of a graphic novel targeting 8–12 years old children and the creation of a female protagonist as the mapmaker who grew up in this area. The graphic novel combines archival photographs and a collage of fictional/poetic texts arranged in a lexical dictionary that describes this place's activities and linguistic specificity and contributes to its re-enchantment.[4] On the other, Quebecois comic author Guy Delisle emphasizes the pace of development of a Chinese mega-city in the form of an autobiographical *bande dessinée*. Delisle creates a personal map with unconventional graphic panels reflecting on his personality while trying to immerse himself into the Chinese spatial-temporal and cultural differences.

Both Davodeau and Jacquet's *Jeanne de la* zone (2008) and Delisle's *Shenzhen* (2006)[5] are infused with Paul Virilio's principle of dromology as the "science (or logic) of speed"; a means of apprehending speed and its pivotal– and potentially destructive–role in a contemporary global society (Virilio 440).[6] Applying Virilio's idea to the analysis of these two graphic works, I demonstrate how resistance to speed has consistently been eroded, and the physical world adapted in order to satisfy the urge to move further and faster, consistent with the speed of modern urban life and the interaction of man within the city. Specifically, I examine how human components of the environment fare in the face of relentless urbanization. In looking at the consequences of this acceleration of speed in both works, I contend that the accelerated pace of construction of the urban space described by Delisle's recent trip to Shenzhen, China, contrasts with Davodeau and Jacquet's graphic representation of the suburban space of the 1902 *Zone*. While both works do re-enchant urban landscapes, they do so in different rhythms, reflected in each author's personal cartography. On the one hand, Davodeau and Jacquet stress the importance of developing their readers a sense of place, following female protagonist Jeanne's slow-paced journey. On the other, Delisle remaps his physical journey to China, highlighting the many cultural challenges Shenzhen presents to the westerner, distorting sizes of objects and frames, losing himself in time and space.

Both graphic novels portray cityscapes that have emerged and transformed or have been erased and the way humans strive to live in them. My reading of both works' space/speed relationship will also depart from the premises developed by American ecocritics Michael Bennett and David Teague, and by French sociologist Henri Lefebvre. Social ecocriticism, Bennett argues, "makes room for the urban, suburban, small-town, rural, and wild spaces that fill the physical and cultural landscape of the United States, West and East, and its literature" (Bennet and Teague 41).[7] For Lefebvre, to understand and correctly read the city as a process is to understand the political, creative, and humane potential of its inhabitants: "Lefebvre poses questions about the role space plays in our lives, from the conceptualization of the world to cities and rural environments, and the homes we live in" (Lefebvre 3). Both graphic works' graphic and narrative quality informs us of urban ecological pressing matters in two different geographical contexts and times: France and China. This commitment to the urban environment noted in the graphic medium raises a major question: How does it effectively present sociological and ecological changes to children? My essay investigates how the medium has captured urban space and how particular environmental questions are thrown up by the urban spaces displayed.

Walking the everyday *Zone*: Emotional Ec(h)ography in *Jeanne de la zone*

Children's literature and graphic novels have displayed many fictional and real landscapes and have addressed ecological messages to the youth.[8] Whose past, whose memory are we trying to preserve, memories of what places? Historian and archivist Frédérique Jacquet, a specialist in the Paris Zone, explains her graphic project in tandem with Davodeau: "It is a lively and intimate vision, the space of Jeanne's memory, what will then remain of childhood. [...] The shacks—because they are the shacks, well maintained, and not a slum—impacted the suburbs, even if there is nothing left today, except the beltway."[9] Jeanne's story begins in 1900 before the *Zone* was erased and replaced by a *boulevard périphérique* or *périf*.[10] Indeed, Paris's infamous *Zone* (a no man's land) is not a well-defined place.[11] This quality makes it a paradox as the *Zone* was neither a suburb (a *banlieue*) nor a town: it is peripheral not only to the capital's core but to the area that is generally at the urban periphery itself. The *Zone* has been constituted as a *hinterland* (the German term for "land behind"); the opening to the *banlieue* of the northeast at *porte d'Aubervilliers* Jeanne's father Baptiste crosses at both *porte de la Chapelle* and *porte de Clignancourt*.[12] As soon as space is observed or physically experienced (by being walked through, for instance), space becomes invested by Jeanne's embodied subjectivity and pace.[13]

Part 1 is entitled "Jeanne." It is the major section that spans from Jeanne's birth to her school years and her graduation from middle school. This section is narrated by Jeanne's own daughter as an act of memory. Within the limits of Jeanne's house, the everyday has become a project associated with social status, cultural capital, and, mostly, the careful management of memory and spatial turn. The association of the house with nostalgia, in particular, represents a denial of what Henri Lefebvre, in his *Critique of Everyday Life*, sees as the repetitiveness and 'residuality' of the everyday; "the way in which people's ordinary lives lag behind the more dramatic transformations of industry, technology and business" (Lefebvre 192). Part 2, entitled "le monde de Jeanne" (Jeanne's world), abounds with indexed references about the *Zonards'* everyday life, black and white photographs, and literary excerpts by French authors who dealt with it. This section summarizes and augments Part 1 with useful information pertaining to it. Part 3, entitled "la fille de Jeanne" (Jeanne's daughter), is the shortest one. It is set in 2007 when Camille and her grandmother (Jeanne's daughter) are caught in the traffic jam of Paris's loop or *périf* near *Porte de la Chapelle;* "a procession of gleaming sheets, with thousands of paper lanterns, progresses in spurts" (Davodeau and Jacquet 91).[14] This section takes place in today's 18th *arrondissement* suburban *Saint-Ouen*, a quiet suburb with *HLM* buildings,[15] where Camille's grandparents live in a "brick cottage with a backyard. Trees, flowers and a vegetable garden" (Davodeau and Jacquet 94).[16] The layout of the graphic novel engages young readers to frame the ideas of their present, their past, and their future.

Indeed the replica of real-world places such as the *Zone* is evidenced in the opening page, which reflects that space (both narrative and graphic) consisting of a black and white panoramic view of the *Zone* with, in its core, Baptiste's house and vegetable garden "across from the wall that encircles Paris" (Davodeau and Jacquet 11).[17] Through activities as varied as urban gardening and the everyday appropriation of disused land by immigrants (Baptiste is a *chiffonnier* or a rag-and-bone man), as seen on page 17, the *Zone* displays alternative forms of difference within Paris's suburban space where Baptiste "has built their home without asking anything to anyone. This is the way things work in the *Zone*, in the shack neighborhood" (Davodeau and Jacquet 12).[18] Two pairs of passers-by are compared: one pair inside the fence of the *Zone* and the other outside of it, along the *fortif* wall that separates it from the center of Paris. In this way, young readers can sense the living conditions of people within the *Zone;* the slums all around the outskirts have become a liminal space. As with all binaries, the Paris/Zone dichotomy conceals as much as it reveals of Paris's urban environment; the social and cultural differences between an elite block of Paris's *porte d'Aubervilliers* as suggested by the image. Nonetheless, it suggests that the *Zone,* for all its misery, is a peaceful place where speed has decelerated. It has become one place of social bonding and mutual aid with safe playgrounds for children near the *fortif* wall. From this vertical viewpoint, Jeanne's father, Baptiste, built his home "with all kinds of abandoned construction materials: from thick boards, light boards, stems of metal, tiles of plaster, a door frame, shutters, some corrugated zinc, a fireplace, some sheet metal, and even asphalted cardboard sheets" (Davodeau and Jacquet 12).[19] As the gaze moves away from above the ground level and toward the confined *Zone,* the cityscape changes into a gloomy panoramic view consisting of "several sheds glued to each other, somewhat in disarray. A tangle of barracks, of shacks and shelters" (Davodeau and Jacquet 12).[20]

Figure 8.1. © Davodeau & Jacquet, *Jeanne de la zone,* p.20.

This intimate space, Jeanne's home,[21] evolves into an expansive spatiality embodied by the *Zone* itself, reflecting Gaston Bachelard's idea in his essay *The Poetics of Space* that "it is through their 'immensity' that these two kinds of space—the space intimacy and world space—blend [...] In this coexistentialism every object invested with intimate space becomes the center of all space" (Bachelard 203). How is this Bachelardian in/out space represented in *Jeanne de la zone?* Bachelard suggests that space begins with the home, which, when broadly conceived, is the fundamental space of the human imagination: "all really inhabited space bears the essence of the notion of home" (Bachelard 5). Indeed, the story begins within the privacy of Jeanne's 1902 home (inside her mother's bedroom), where a cluster of friends welcomes Jeanne into the world. The midwife's objection regarding going to her neighborhood indicates its unsafety: "the Zone, nobody goes there! We are too scared of it" (Davodeau and Jacquet 14).[22] In *The Practices of Everyday Life* (1984), Michel De Certeau conceptualizes the nexus of power, representation, and everyday life. His chapter "Walking in the City" explores the use of urban space as an example of the ways in which consumers, as *bricoleurs*, actively re-use culture and "reappropriate the space organized by techniques of sociocultural production" (De Certeau xiv). De Certeau stresses the manipulative nature of acts of reading as "silent productions" that insert the reader's world, histories, pleasures, and body into the author/designer/administrator's place of the city or the written text: "words become the outlet or product of silent histories. The readable transforms itself into the memorable" and contribute to the re-enchantment of the *Zone*. (De Certeau xxi). His assertion that "space is a practiced space" in light of one particular set of practices that convert one peripheral space, such as the *Zone*, into a central one is compelling. Readers perceive this intimate world through Jeanne's daily life as she walks from her home to other spaces inside or outside the liminal space of her *Zone*: "to get out of her neighborhood, Jeanne takes a path that zigzags between the shacks, the trailers, and the garden sheds. In *la zone*, there are no real streets" (Davodeau and Jacquet 20).[23] This also applies to public spaces caught between the suburb and the city Jeanne crosses outside the *Zone*, and that signal acceleration and technology:

> At the entrance of the city, Jeanne crosses the corner of the factories. First, she passes in front of the factory of chemicals beside the gut-dressing factory; and then in front of the factory of presses, the factory of the pyrites, the soap factory Sapic, the factory of manures, [...], in front of the factory of matches. Jeanne recognizes it with its chimney made of bricks which springs, immense towards the sky. On Haie-Coq Street, workmen rush to the call of the sirens. On foot or with bicycles (Davodeau and Jacquet 20).[24]

Particularly relevant to the analysis of space (and concurrent to Bachelard's in/out house dichotomy) is Marc Augé's principle of synesthesia in his philosophical essay *L'impossible voyage*. This principle is of utmost importance in the poly-sensory description of Jeanne's space as one erased suburb, namely, in the ways, these sensory ties complement Davodeau's graphic and poetic space. Augé asserts regarding the sensitive and material existence of the city space that it is "landscape, sky, shadows and lighting, movement; it is smells, odors varying with the seasons and the situation, places and activities–the smell of gasoline or motor oil [...] it is noise, din, uproar or silence [...] This material dimension plays its role" (Augé 150–51). Throughout the many places Jeanne crosses on foot, she is exposed to an array of smells and sounds, either comforting or frightening (or both), that trigger her senses. Unknown sounds occur within the area of the factories as the full-picture image Jeanne suggests standing fully erect at the foot of a gray wall, her face facing the wall in a frozen attitude: "What happens behind the walls? The noise that escapes from it breaks her ears. A never-ending crash [...] and often she blocks her nose too" (Davodeau and Jacquet 22–24).[25] Opposing loud noises and malodorous smells associated with male workers and factories, Jeanne takes her readers to the laundress Rosalie where smells become very sensual, soothing, and feminine: "the air is sweet, scented with lavender" (Davodeau and Jacquet 24).[26] Sounds consist of high-pitched voices of female workers who "talk loudly, mock and guffaw" (Davodeau and Jacquet 25).[27] Urban landscape seems to be "gendered." Concurring with this poly-sensory space, the school is the other place that reflects Jeanne's intimate secret space in her imaginary, conveying a range of smells and sounds. As a *zonière*, her poly-sensory experiences are made of the "smell of cabbage, bleach and chalk dust. A secret smell that brings pleasure. A smell that Jeanne sniffs in the hollow of the pages a bit secretly" (Davodeau and Jacquet 26).[28] These smells are fused to more sounds experienced at lunchtime, such as "a noise that flays the ears. The clinking of spoons on iron plates resonates up to the beams of the schoolyard" (Davodeau and Jacquet 27).[29]

This poly-sensory world is best echoed in part 2, entitled "Le monde de Jeanne" which lists an enumeration of terminology alphabetically, referring to the plants, the objects, the activities, the long-gone professions, the housing, the literature, and the many archival photographs that attest its richness. For example, French novelist Eugène Dabit describes the Zone's unique architectural qualities of the suburb in his own *Faubourgs de Paris* as such: "built with bits and pieces but always rich in embellishments and small architectural findings" (Davodeau and Jacquet 79).[30] Dabit's own description concurs in making the fictional *Zone* illustrated by Davodeau, a place of re-enchantment: "I was contemplating the pansies, the wallflowers, the daisies that I had only seen at the florist's" (Davodeau and Jacquet 77).[31]

Walking as Map-Making: Perambulations in *Shenzhen*

For Michel De Certeau, the exploration of a city text generated by acts of walking produces a particular kind of urban embodied subject: the pedestrian or the voyager-voyeur. The pedestrian subject reads/writes the city as an everyday user of place, producing space–writing the actual city–in the process.

Walking is framed as a personified form of experiencing urban space—a productive yet relatively unconscious reading/writing of the city (De Certeau xxi).[32] The kind of reading/writing undertaken by Delisle when he claims: "I analyze and comment on things I see [...] I'm both narrator and spectator" (Delisle 83). This results in the form of a graphic *bricolage* and enunciation that partakes in the re-enchantment of Shenzhen in the act of drawing. Delisle recounts his solo trips on assignment to oversee his French company Dupuis Animation's outsourcing studios in mainland China. In his comic travelogue, Delisle acts as if the pedestrian inhabits both the space of his graphic novel and that of the eponymous Southern Chinese Special Economic Zone (SEZ). In their study entitled *Comics and the City*, Ahrens, and Meteling assert that "comics do not demand the contemplative as well as the fixed gaze of the classic central perspective. Instead, they demand the loose and moving gaze of the urban *flâneur*" (Ahrens and Meteling 7). This contention is reflected in Delisle's first principle based on his own "loose and moving gaze" and the analogy between bicycle riding and sequence building. This principle relates to the creation of comics, especially when Delisle fills up a page or a frame: form mirrors content when Delisle represents the Chinese conception of occupying space. Delisle's first principle, "An empty space may be filled at any time," resonates with his assessment of the Chinese's way of riding a bicycle which epitomizes the density of the Chinese population as well as cultural norms regarding public space (Delisle 72). Delisle-as-narrator's comment that in order to succeed in riding a bicycle, "you have to first put aside all culturally ingrained politeness" (Delisle 73/1) is not a neutral statement and constitutes the foundation for the second principle of urban Chinese bicycle riding: "Nobody else matters" (Delisle 73/1). This second principle offers an interesting, object-effacing spin on Virilio's concept of dromology where "inanimate objects exhume themselves from the horizon" (Virilio 440). Such is the case when Delisle states: "The visual effect is disturbing since we're all stationary but moving forward. I get the strange impression that the street itself is moving. It's like the world is spinning under our wheels without managing to pull us along" (Delisle 74/2) in the caption beneath the image of cyclists appropriately filling the square frame. Providing further support of the parallel between urban and comic space, this text itself fills an empty space, sitting as it does alongside the framed (words), "first principle," yet contained by no visible frame itself, and therefore occupying a blank (textual) space.

Virilio's principle of dromology is reflected in both the graphic novel and the actual Special Economic Zone (SEZ) as the pace of construction of Shenzhen (the city) and of *Shenzhen* (the graphic novel) demonstrate. Virilio's essay entitled Speed and Politics contends that "cities galvanize both human and non-human metabolisms, channeling them, amplifying them into centers, domesticating them, concentrating them into centers, domesticating them into suburbs" (Virilio 11). Yet speed, associated with modernity, may entail carelessness and correspond inversely with deceleration and therefore waste. Delisle's graphic layout is prompt and consistent with the speed of postmodern urban life in Shenzhen "a dream city for many in China" (Delisle 46). Equally, Delisle highlights many public spaces of everyday life—what Marc Augé labels the "non-places" such as motorways, subways, commuting trains and office parks, which encourage functional, transient behavior, and produce a peculiar mix of alienation.[33] Delisle-the-narrator's gaze includes the presence of vehicles that exemplify technological speed, such as airplanes, high-speed trains ranging from French TGVs to Japanese bullet trains to the Shenzhen Express, which Delisle takes "after racing against the clock through Cantonese traffic" (Delisle 45/11).

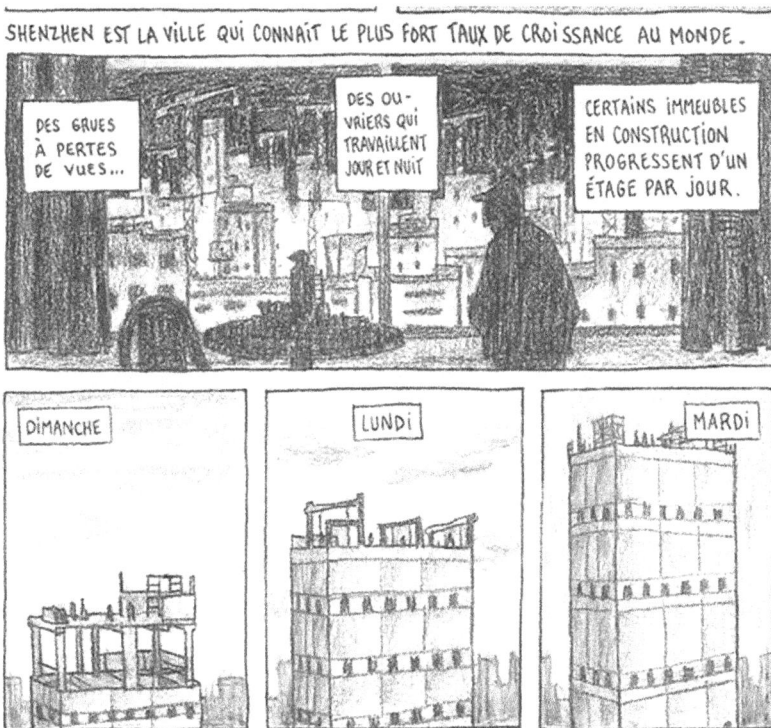

Figure 8.2. © Guy Delisle, *Shenzhen* (L'Association, 2000), p. 64.

China's rapid entry into globalization drives construction in the SEZ. The caption "Shenzhen is the fastest growing city in the world" occupies the area between the borders: a liminal white space crammed with two square panels in the top third of page 64 and the bandeau in the middle third of the page. More captions contained in rectangular frames with typical black-on-white text punctuate the middle bandeau with curtains pulled to either side of the panel: "Cranes as far as the eye can see" [...] "Workers laboring day and night" [...] "Some buildings go up at the rate of one floor a day" (Delisle 64/3). In the lower third of the same page, three separate panels are labeled simply "Sunday," "Monday," and "Tuesday," with the words aligned under the caption of the middle panel. The illustration shows a huge building growing one story per day (and per image), thus emphasizing the fast-paced construction of this city.

Indeed, the recent creation of Shenzhen and its resulting uniformity goes back only a few decades. It is populated by mere buildings which are functional rather than aesthetically appealing:

> Shenzhen [...] has transformed from a fishing community of 30,000 to a sprawling industrial and financial megacity, with a population that by some estimates exceeds 12 million. Described by Chinese officials as a miracle, Shenzhen has some of China's biggest skyscrapers and shopping malls, with a new subway and other constructions proceeding so quickly that there is no room to put all the excavation waste.[34]

People and buildings densely occupy the former fishing village, as frames, images, and words crowd the pages of the graphic novel. Many times across the novel, a single panel occupies a full page image with a dark background highlighting buildings either finished or with cranes shaded in gray, foregrounding the process of construction and as displayed successively in pages 5, 21, 37, 53, 69, 85, 101 & 133.

In *Système de la bande dessinée*, a French expert on comics Thierry Groensteen states that a *bédéiste* often begins by laying out the panels on a page in a grid-like fashion and then proceeds to fill them in (Groensteen 51). Groensteen justly notes that "architectural metaphors are frequently used to describe its [the strip's] place in the general economy of the page. Indeed, the page resembles a house that has several stories" (Groensteen 69).[35] Buildings were erected on the once sparsely populated land and housed migrant workers who moved to Deng's Shenzhen to work there. Similarly, "constructions" such as panels and bubbles fill the pages of Delisle's comic book *Shenzhen*. The construction of buildings in Shenzhen as one suburban space, which is a recurring theme in the narrative, parallels the construction of the graphic novel. Angularity rather than circularity and other forms of curve-linearity typify the construction of Shenzhen and Delisle's graphic novel. The frames are mostly quadrilaterals, with some non-outlined panels seated between or next to such angular frames as on pages 44/2, 42/1, 42/9, 43/4, and 52/5.

Buildings tend to be boxy high-rises. Roofs of otherwise boxy, nondescript skyscrapers are at times non-angular, especially when space at the peak of a skyscraper would not be used and so "wasted." For instance, page 30 displays the roof of a tall building at the far left of the first panel: its shape is concave, in a pagoda-like fashion. The "gigantic buildings like convention centers" featured in the middle bandeau image are also structurally curved (Delisle 39). Their uselessness is even more compelling as they sit "in the middle of nowhere [...] without a surrounding city" as Delisle heads north across from Shenzhen "sealed off by an electric fence guarded day and night by soldiers in watchtowers." (Delisle 38)

Paralleling the population of the pages of *Shenzhen*, the rapid increase in the number of Shenzhen's inhabitants has resulted in population density. Delisle not only homogenizes the Chinese by crowding them (and himself) into a single page but also represents population density through techniques such as the proliferation of speech bubbles as well as the reduction of panel size. As exemplified by the full-page image of a crowd of Chinese people (this image is also the cover art of the English hardcover edition) on page 37, the collective undermines the individual reflecting density. Delisle intentionally draws Chinese people with analogous features, accessories, and clothing such as round eyeglasses and business suits. Ironically, Delisle-the-animator, who stands toward the panel's upper left corner, almost blends in. *Shenzhen* symbolizes the paradox of China's simultaneous fast/slow motion in the age of globalization. The accelerated pace of construction of the urban space of the actual Shenzhen and the fast-paced consumption encouraged by the layout of the bande dessinée form contrast Delisle's perceptions and graphic representations of temporal deceleration (and even cessation) as a result of his sense of alienation and boredom.[36] Shenzhen's uniformity and lack of deep history render it monotonous for Delisle, whose own representation of the SEZ yet attests to the richness of contemporary graphic novels. The only architectural sites Delisle depicts located in Shenzhen and which depart in shape from boxy non-descriptiveness are the miniatures of monuments such as the Eiffel Tower, the Leaning Tower of Pisa, and the Pyramids of Egypt on page 61. Paradoxically, these miniatures of monuments are confined within the limits of the "Windows of the World" theme park, the city's only tourist attraction.

Shenzhen typifies the feat of Delisle's endeavors: concerted efforts are more fruitful than speed. The time lapse between, on the one hand, Delisle's stint and recording of daily experiences in December 1997 and his published graphic novel in 2000 is fairly short. The absence of chapter divisions encourages readers to move uninterruptedly throughout the text. The inclusion of *bandeau* and single-page panels accelerates the reading process. Delisle plays with the notion of the frame by inserting many contour(less) panels and captions lined up above, beneath, or in between frames on pages 94 and 144, and where words and images may extend beyond the frames. Finally, Shenzhen's location in southern China, close to Hong Kong, stresses the blurring of boundaries between spaces. Whereas Shenzhen is so new that it has little, if any, architectural and cultural richness, Delisle combines the new with the old effectively and creates a complex graphic work that epitomizes an architectural model for the graphic novel. Ultimately, *Shenzhen* breaks out of the box formally, unlike the architecturally non-descript SEZ of Shenzhen. Delisle's unconventional graphics are dissonant with Shenzhen's architectural homogeneity. Drawing outside the box resonates more with Chinese postmodern urban spaces such as Shanghai or Beijing, as well as postmodern urban architectural innovation in cities across the globe. Like the contemporary graphic novel, such metropolises tend to start from the paradigm of angular uniform spaces (such as typical skyscrapers) and even populate their spaces with those primarily. Similarly, *Shenzhen* departs from that base for variety and innovation. Regardless of whether elements of contemporary graphic novels boom in shape and form with urban structures of a particular metropolis, cityscapes provide a compelling paradigm for constructing the contemporary (eco)graphic novel and re-enchantment of less-known mega-cities.

Geo-graphisms: Navigating Past and Future Cities in Graphic Novels

Over the past decades, urban ecocriticism has developed discourses to analyze new spaces. As such, it offers suggestions for a re-conceptualization of ecocriticism that targets a new category of readers: children and young adults. The overlapping of ecocriticism and geocriticism enables a very productive and open engagement in the light of contemporary environmental challenges graphic novelists and urban archivists attempt to address to today's young global citizens. Furthermore, graphic novels have unique abilities to capture urban space because of their hybrid nature, consisting of words, pictures, and sequences. The specific way these two instances display urban transformations and speeds makes them useful pedagogical tools conveying powerful ecological messages in a time of environmental crisis. When the interaction between history and memory is translated into the built environment, a sense of history is embedded in the collective memory that locates us in time and space. Davodeau and Jacquet do tremendous work instilling an eco-consciousness regarding changing urban landscapes such as the *Zone*. In re-enchanting these landscapes, they can have an invigorating impact on children's sense of place. Jacquet, who is an archivist and specialist in Paris suburbs, has complemented Davodeau's graphic novel with an illustrated and poetic mini encyclopedia in part 2. The collage of photographic and poetic excerpts drawn from a collection of authors who wrote about the *Zone* is powerful in the re-enchantment of this erased section of the city. Bachelard's in-house/out-house dichotomy has proved to be very useful in discussing the graphic novel's structure as part of the collection named "L'histoire sensible." The intimate space of Jeanne is mostly captured through Jeanne's daily itineraries as a map-maker.

My reading of the urban landscape in these two graphic novelistic works does not limit itself to categorizing works according to the country versus city paradigm. Instead, I have attempted to highlight the representation of rhythms, emotions, urban relationships, spatial perspectives, senses of movement, and identity formation according to each fictional narrator. In both examples of peri-urban zones, human life uniquely adapts to its environment, performing numerous activities with a focus on 'ordinary' spaces experienced by both Jeanne and Delisle-the-animator. Both graphic novels re-enchant places that have either disappeared or are greatly developing to encourage a less repressed, more cheerful way for readers to engage with old and new geographies of the world. My analysis addressed new perspectives of representations of both the domestic and public spheres. Daily mobility is represented in both graphic works in the act of walking, reflecting spatial practices that differ from one point in history to another, and geographically. Both works immerse us in urban realities beyond what children and young adults may learn in geography textbooks. Davodeau and Jacquet, and Delisle, while re-enchanting cityscapes, develop within the medium a discourse that is of utmost urgency: helping young people recognize how directly their environment contributes to shaping their identity and their sense of place.

Notes

[1] On this subject, see Robert T. Tally, Jr., Christine M. Battista, and Bertrand Westphall.

[2] Because it also correlates to philosophical concepts developed initially by such philosophers as F. Deleuze and F. Guattari, environmental literary studies have come to be associated with a body of critical works in ecocriticism devoted to the study of urban ecology in contemporary capitalist culture. I recommend on this subject Nathalie Blanc, N. Blanc, T. Pughes and D. Chartier, and C. Younes.

[3] The city has captured the mind of French and Francophone children's authors, illustrators, and graphic novelists as mapmakers since the 1980s. I recommend on this subject Isabelle Papieau, Jörn Ahrens, and Arno Meteling.

[4] See also Kerry H. Whiteside, I. Delanoy's, Douglas L. Boudreau, and Marnie L. Sullivan, and Stéphanie Posthumus.

[5] I use the 2006 English translation of the graphic novel in my analysis. See Guy Delisle's *Shenzhen: A Travelogue from China.*

6 Virilio noted that the speed at which something happens may change its essential nature, and that which moves with speed quickly comes to dominate that which is slower. That is the case of the *zone* of Paris, which has been erased and replaced with a loop highway, as both Davodeau and Jacquet demonstrate in their work.

7 This collection of essays presents the ecological component often missing from cultural analyses of the city and the urban perspective often lacking in environmental approaches to contemporary culture.

8 On children's literature and ecocriticism, I highly recommend Kenneth B. Kidd, Esther Lasó y Léon, and Nathalie Prince, and Sébastian Thiltges.

9 My translation of "Je voulais montrer des séquences fortes qui vont forger la vie de Jeanne ensuite. C'est une vision intime et vivante, l'espace du souvenir de Jeanne, ce qui restera ensuite de l'enfance. [...] Les bicoques—parce que ce sont bien des bicoques, bien entretenues, et non un bidonville—ont marqué la banlieue, même s'il n'en reste rien aujourd'hui, si ce n'est le périph." https://www.auracan.com/Indiscre tions/indis.php?actu=207.

10 In 1914 about 200, 000 people are settled in the Zone. By 1926, more than 40,000 *zoniers* occupy an area of 125 meters wide, non-constructible, surrounding the wall of Paris called "enceinte de Thiers." On the topic of urban geography, see Andrew Newman.

11 The area is best described as a space along the fortified military wall built by Adolphe Thiers (1797-1877), also nicknamed *fortifs* of Paris. The fortification was a belt of some 24.5 miles long, with 52 gates called *portes*. The bastioned "enceinte de Thiers" was demolished between 1919 and 1929. See Eric Hazan, Claire Le Thomas, Hans Christian Adam, and Jean-Louis Cohen and André Lortie.

12 The *périphérique* highway was built between 1956 and 1973 and follows the inner border of the erased *Zone*. See Laurence Boccara, J. Merriman, and Mickaël Guiho.

13 Tracing the interweaving of urban space in graphic novels, analyzing the relationship of the child to her environment, and studying the role of real spaces are paramount to many scholars who advocate the spatial turn in children's literature as part of its multicultural bent. See in particular Jean Perrot.

14 My translation of "une procession de tôles rutilantes, aux mille lampions, progresse par à-coup."

15 *HLM* is the acronym of *Habitation à Loyer Modéré* ("rent-controlled housing"), a form of public housing in France. The *HLM* system was created in 1950 in response to France's postwar housing crisis in France and the Paris region. HLM (initially HBM or habitation à bon marché) offered a modern alternative to both *bidonvilles* and many deteriorating areas such as the *zone*.

16 My translation of "un pavillon de briques avec sur l'arrière un jardin. Des arbres, des fleurs et un coin potager."

17 My translation of "face à la muraille qui ceinture Paris."

18 My translation of "a édifié leur demeure sans rien demander à personne. C'est comme ça sur la zone des fortifs, dans le quartier des bicoques."

19 My translation of "toutes sortes de matériaux de construction abandonnés : des planches épaisses, des planches légères, des tiges de fer, des carreaux de plâtre, un cadre de porte, des volets, du zinc ondulé, une cheminée, de la tôle et même des plaques de carton bitumé."

20 My translation of "plusieurs cabanes collées les unes aux autres, un peu dans le désordre. Un enchevêtrement de baraques, de cabanons et d'appentis."

[21] See on this topic, James Adams, "Troubled Spaces: Domestic Space in Graphic Novels" In Our *House: The Representation of Domestic Space in Modern Culture.*

[22] My translation of "La Zone, personne n'y va ! On en a bien trop peur !"

[23] My translation of "pour sortir de son quartier, Jeanne emprunte une sente de terre qui zigzague entre les baraques, les roulottes et les cabanons de jardin. Sur la Zone, il n'y a pas de vraies rues."

[24] My translation of "A l'entrée de la ville, Jeanne traverse le coin des usines. Elle passe d'abord devant l'usine de produits chimiques à côté de la boyauderie ; et puis devant la fabrique de présure, l'usine des pyrites, la savonnerie Sapic, l'usine des engrais, [...], devant la manufacture d'allumettes. Jeanne la reconnaît à sa cheminée de briques qui s'élance, immense vers le ciel. Rue de la Haie-Coq, les ouvriers se pressent à l'appel des sirènes. À pied ou à vélo."

[25] My translation of "Que se passe-t-il derrière les murs ? Le bruit qui s'en échappe casse les oreilles. Un fracas sans fin [...] Et souvent aussi elle se bouche le nez."

[26] My translation of "l'air est doux, parfumé à la lavande."

[27] My translation of "parlent fort, se moquent et s'esclaffent."

[28] My translation of "une odeur de choux, d'eau de Javel, d'encre et de poussière de craie. Une odeur secrète qui fait plaisir. Une odeur que Jeanne renifle au creux des pages un peu en cachette."

[29] My translation of "un bruit qui écorche les oreilles. Le cliquetis des cuillères sur les assiettes de fer résonne jusqu'aux poutrelles du préau."

[30] My translation of "faites de bric et de broc mais toujours riches en embellissements et petites trouvailles architecturales" Eugène Dabit, *Faubourgs de Paris* (Paris: Gallimard, 1990).

[31] My translation of "Je contemplais les pensées, les giroflées, les reines-marguerites, que je n'avais vues que chez le fleuriste."

[32] Michel de Certeau affirms that itineraries allow the point of view to be located at ground level. I recommend reading, in particular, the chapter "Walking in the City," 91–110.

[33] On this topic, see Marc Augé.

[34] See Gladstone.

[35] My translation of "Pour décrire sa place [celle de la bande dessinée] dans l'économie générale de la planche, on recourt assez spontanément à une métaphore architecturale. La planche, en effet, ressemble à une maison qui compterait plusieurs étages."

[36] See on the theme of boredom in comics, Greice Schneider.

Works Cited

Adam, Hans Christian. *Paris Eugène Atget 1857-1927*. London, Los Angeles, Paris, Madrid: Taschen, 2008.

Adams, James. "Troubled Spaces: Domestic Space in Graphic Novels." *Our House; The Representation of Domestic Space in Modern Culture*, edited by Gerry Smith and Jo Croft, Amsterdam, New York: Rodopi, 2006, pp. 161–74.

Ahrens, Jörn, and Arno Meteling. *Comics and the City: Urban Space in Print, Picture and Sequence*. New York, NY : Continuum, 2010.

Augé, Marc. *L'impossible voyage. Le tourisme et ses images*. Paris: Rivages, 1997.

—. *Non-Places: Introduction to Anthropology of Supermodernity*. Translated by John Howe, London: Verso, 1995 (orig. published in 1992).

—. *Non-lieux : Introduction à une anthropologie de la surmodernité*. Paris: Editions du Seuil, 1992.

Bachelard, Gaston. *The Poetics of Space*. Translated by Maria Jolas, Boston: Beacon Press, 1994 (orig. published in 1958).

—. *La poétique de l'espace*. Paris: PUF, Quadrige, 2004.

Barthélémy, Lambert. *Imagination(s) environnementale(s), Raison Publique*. No. 17, Hiver 2012.

Bennett, Michael, and David W. Teague. *The Nature of Cities Ecocriticism and Urban Environments*. Tucson, AZ: The University of Arizona Press, 1999.

Blanc, Nathalie. *Les nouvelles esthétiques urbaines*. Paris: Armand Colin, 2012.

Blanc, Nathalie, Thomas Pughe, and Denis Chartier. "Littérature & écologie : vers une écopoétique." *Écologie & politique*, n°36, 2008, pp.15–28.

Boccara, Laurence. "Les portes de Paris changent de visage." *Les Échos*, October 26, 2006. Consulted on 5/17/2016. http://www.lesechos.fr/26/10/2006/Les Echos/19781-138-ECH_les-portes-de-paris-changent-de-visage.htm.

Boudreau, Douglas L., and Marnie L. Sullivan. *Ecocritical Approaches to Literature in French*. Lanham, Boulder, New York, London: Lexington Books, 2016.

Cohen, Jean-Louis, and André Lortie. *Des fortifs au périf ; Paris, les seuils de la ville*. Paris : Picard/Edition du Pavillon de l'Arsenal, 1991.

Dabit, Eugène. *Faubourgs de Paris*. Paris: Gallimard, 1990 (orig. published in 1933).

Dacheux, Eric. *Bande dessinée et lien social*. Paris : CNRS éditions, 2014.

Davodeau, Étienne, and Frédérique Jacquet. *Jeanne de la zone*. Ivry-sur-Seine : Les Éditions de l'Atelier, 2014. First edition 2008.

De Certeau, Michel. *The Practices of Everyday Life*. Translated by S. F. Rendall, Berkeley: University of California Press, 1984.

Delisle, Guy. *Shenzhen*. Paris: L'Association, 2000.

—. *Shenzhen: A Travelogue from China*. Translated by Helge Dascher, Montreal: Drawn and Quarterly Books, 2006.

Dobrin, Sidney, and Kenneth Kidd. *Wild Things: Children's Culture and Ecocriticism*. Detroit: Wayne State University Press, 2004.

Gladstone, Rick. "Shenzhen: The City Where China's Transformation Began." *New York Times*, December 21, 2015. http://www.nytimes.com/2015/12/22/world/asia/shenzhen-site-of-landslide-embodies-chinas-rapid-growth.html?_r=1

Guiho, Mickaël. « Avant le périph' : les fortifs et la Zone » April 25 2013. https://franciliensdemain.wordpress.com/2013/04/25/avant-le-periph-les-fortifs-et-la-zone/

Groensteen, Thierry. *Système de la bande dessinée*. Paris : Presses Universitaires de France, 1999.

—. *The System of Comics*. Translated by Bart Beaty and Nick Nguyen, Jackson: University of Mississippi Press, 2007.

Hazan, Eric. *The Invention of Paris*. London: Verso, 2010, pp. 222-23.

Lasó y Léon, Esther. "La literatura infantil y juvenil: El nacimiento de una conciencia medioambiental." *Ecocríticas: Literatura y medio ambiente*, edited by C. Flys Junquera, J. M. Marrero Henriquez, and J. Barella Vigal, Madrid: Iberoamericana, 2010, pp. 340–367.

Lefebvre, Henri. *Rhythmanalysis: Space, Time and Everyday Life*. London, New Delhi, New York, Sydney: Bloomsbury, 2015.

—. *Critique of Everyday Life, Volume 1: Introduction*. Translated by John Moore, London : Verso, 1991.

Le Thomas, Claire. "L'album Zonier d'Eugène Atget." *Histoire par l'image*, consulted on 11 May 2016. http://www.histoire-image.org/etudes/album-zonier-eugene-atget?i=838

Merriman, John. *Aux marges de la ville. Faubourgs et banlieues en France, 1815-1870*. Paris: Seuil, 1994.

Newman, Andrew. *Landscape of Discontent: Urban Sustainability in Immigrant Paris*. Minneapolis, London : University of Minnesota Press, 2015.

Papieau, Isabelle. *La Banlieue de Paris dans la bande dessinée*. Paris: L'Harmattan, 2001.

Paquot, Thierry, and Chris Younes. *Philosophie de l'environnement et milieux urbains*. Paris: Éditions La Découverte, 2010.

Perrot, Jean. *L'Europe, un rêve graphique ?* Paris: L'Harmattan, 2002.

Persels, Jeff. *The Environment in French and Francophone Literature and Film*. Volume XXXIX, New York, Amsterdam: Editions Rodopi, 2012.

Posthumus, Stéphanie. "Penser l'imagination environnementale française sous le signe de la différence." *Imagination(s) environnementale(s)*, edited by L. Barthélémy, Rennes: Presses Universitaires de Rennes, 2012, pp. 15-31.

Prince, Nathalie, and Sébastian Thiltges. *Éco-graphies: écologie et littératures pour la jeunesse*. Rennes: Presses universitaires de Rennes, 2018.

Smith, Gerry, and Jo Croft. *Our House: The Representation of Domestic Space in Modern Culture*. Amsterdam, New York: Rodopi, 2006.

Schneider, Greice. *What Happens When Nothing Happens: Boredom and Everyday Life in Contemporary Comics*. Leuven: Leuven University Press, 2016.

Tally, Robert T. Jr. *Spatiality*. London, New York: Routledge, 2013.

Tally, Robert T. Jr., and Christine M. Battista. *Ecocriticism and Geocriticism: Overlapping Territories in Environmental and Spatial Literary Studies*. New York: Palgrave Macmillan, 2016.

Virilio, Paul. "The Overexposed City." *The Blackwell City Reader*, edited by G. Bridge and S. Watson, Oxford: Blackwell Publishing, 2002.

—. *Speed and Politics: An Essay on Dromology*. Translated by Mark Polizzotti, Los Angeles: Columbia University Press, 2006 (orig. published in French in 1977).

Westphall, Bertrand. *La géocritique. Réel, fiction, espace*. Paris: Éditions de Minuit, 2007.

Westphall, Bertrand. *Geocriticism: Real and Fictional Spaces*. Translated by R. T. Tally, Jr., New York: Palgrave Macmillan, 2011.

Whiteside, Kerry. *Divided Natures: French Contributions to Political Ecology*. Cambridge, MA: MIT, 2002.

Younes, Chris. "L'écosophie urbaine comme corythme." *Théories et pratiques écologiques : de l'écologie urbaine à l'imagination environnementale*, edited by A. Milon, and M. Antonioli, Paris: Presses universitaires Paris 10, 2014, pp. 31-38.

Chapter 9

"Acoustic Shadows": Civil War Spaces in Contemporary Works

Peter Schulman

Old Dominion University, USA

Abstract: While preservationists have fought legal battles to protect many American Civil War battle sites from uncontrolled construction, the photographer Sally Mann and the folk group Granville Automatic have also championed historical sites but also overlooked spaces connecting the past to twenty-first-century landscapes. This chapter will examine their artistic efforts to both honor the ghosts of the Civil War and underline the meaning of the spaces they inhabited. By giving voice to stories that have been long forgotten and by valorizing spaces that are under constant threat of physical and spiritual oblivion, Mann and Granville combat the "acoustic shadows" caused by modern obstructions as well as time itself and bring attention to what Pierre Nora would call "places of memory" that can dwell deep in the soil but are often seemingly invisible, usurped or trampled upon.

Keywords: American Civil War spaces; Acoustic Shadows, Sally Mann, Granville Automatic

***

Acoustic Shadows

"During the American Civil War," Mark Slouka explains, "observers noted a curious fact: the sounds of a battle, clearly distinguishable at ten miles, could be utterly inaudible at two. These weird wrinkles in the landscape were called 'acoustic shadows'" (Soukla 89). There were many instances, for example, when General Ulysses S. Grant could not hear the sounds from nearby enemy cannons because of wind drift or, conversely, would see the burst of lights emerging from a battle but not hear any sound. For documentary filmmaker Ken Burns, for example, "acoustic shadows" can be seen not only as a metaphor for the continuing relevance of the Civil War in contemporary

America but as a metaphor for the idea that "the further we get from those four horrible years in our national existence—when paradoxically, in order to become one we tore ourselves in two—the more central and defining that war becomes" (Burns *Times*). In recent political discourse in America, there has been much political action against the nefarious usage of the confederate flag as an insidious symbol of Southern racism, yet, both in the North and in the South, there have been other struggles to protect Civil War battlefields from urban development and sprawl which threaten to destroy historical and collective memory along with old buildings or memorial statues. The corporate giant Walmart infamously wanted to open a superstore on the Gettysburg battlefield, the site of one of the war's bloodiest and most decisive battles. Similarly, slot machine parlors and gambling casinos were also proposed on other significant battle sites.

While political activists and historical preservationists have fought legal battles to protect many sites from uncontrolled construction, a handful of poets, artists, and musical groups have also written wistfully not only of the disappearance of historical sites with a capital H but smaller, seemingly insignificant quotidian wreckage that threatens the everyday "magic" connecting the past to twenty-first-century landscapes. The photographer Sally Mann, for example, has taken haunting pictures of desolate but beautiful patches of greenery where destructive Civil War skirmishes once took place. The contemporary folk musical group Granville Automatic (their name refers to a nineteenth-century typewriter) has also been especially on the vanguard of contemporary artistic efforts to both honor the ghosts of the Civil War and underline the meaning of the spaces they inhabited. They record their videos on the melancholic sites that they write about, such as "Salem Church" (a spot that has been under constant threat of destruction), where a soldier once deserted his unit to be with his family in North Carolina, or "Goodnight House" where a Kentucky doctor once struggled to save soldiers' lives on both sides of the war but is now a parking lot. As Jeff Martin writes in his *Washington Times* review of Granville Automatic's latest album, *An Army Without Music*: "Music is one way the stories of the war can be told and re-told, even if many of the battlefields in Atlanta, Nashville, and other cities are now buried by neighborhoods and business districts" (Martin). Although they are not "nature songwriters" *per se*, Granville Automatic's lyrics are infused with the beauty of fields and prairies, spots of grass and trees amidst ruthless bulldozers and cranes. By giving voice to old civil war stories that have been long forgotten and by valorizing spaces that are under constant threat of physical and spiritual oblivion, Granville Automatic combats the "acoustic shadows" of modern obstructions and brings attention to what Pierre Nora would call *lieux de mémoires* or "places of memory" that can dwell deep in the soil but are often overlooked, usurped or trampled upon.

"For Southerners, memory is most often an act of will," Sally Mann writes in her preface to her book of photography, *Mother Land: Recent Landscapes of Georgia and Virginia*, "and once we conjure it, we are unashamed to overlay it with sentiment. Our history of defeat and loss sets us apart from other Americans, and because of it, we embrace the Proustian concept that the only true paradise is a lost paradise."[1] Similarly, Shelby Foote, a historian of the South known for his lyrical civil war historical novels and his comments in Ken Burns' landmark 1990 PBS documentary, *The Civil War* (Burns PBS), also writes of a thanatosian mixture of death and romanticism he sees as inherent in most Southern writings:

> I remembered what my father had said about the South bearing within itself the seeds of defeat [...] we were sick from an old malady, he said: incurable romanticism and misplaced chivalry [...] too much Walter Scott and Dumas read too seriously. We were in love with the past, he said; in love with death. (Burns PBS)

Can the same be said for Mann's photos or the haunting lyrics of Granville Automatic's songs? They are all fascinated with ghosts, ghosts of a collective American memory of the civil war, or individual ghosts who inhabit spaces they cherish but that have been neglected or forgotten. Mann, in fact, was born in Stonewall Jackson's house, and as she conjectures: "It is easily feasible that the great paladin, Robert E. Lee, rode across these same pastures" (Mann 1997 1). In a catalog to an exhibit at the University of Kentucky Art Museum titled *A Place Not Forgotten: Landscapes of the South*, Jesse Poesch notes that even in the early days, southern artists and writers imbued their work with an eighteenth-century aesthetic of ruins that had already enriched their work with romantic notions of melancholy within landscapes. As Poesch remarks in discussing a description of the Falls of Towaliga in Georgia by a writer at the time, "the writer evoked images of a 'ruin of a lofty bridge' and of a 'dilapidated mill' suggesting that even this newly established area had a certain antiquity" (*A Place Not Forgotten* 13), just as the south was beginning to transform itself into an economic powerhouse.

J.C. Richards, writing to entice visitors to Georgia in 1842, had, indeed, also written of the South's changes with an almost giddy excitement:

> The majestic steam packet now gallantly rides lord of the stream, which so lately yielded to naught but the wild man's paddle. The imperious and trackless desert of yesterday, is today, intersected in its length and breadth, by railroads and canals, those mighty engines of advancement of human intelligence and happiness. (*A Place Not Forgotten* 13)

Would Richards have been equally charmed by the contemporary southern landscape? Guy Davenport, for example, is quick to answer that he would surely not:

> Where there used to be cotton fields and fields of corn and sugar cane, there now sprawl windowless German fiberglass factories and Japanese manufacturers of Styrofoam. The small towns and medium-sized towns have rotted from lack of parking space. The shopping mall with shoddier goods than any Main Street merchant would have dared offer rings all southern cities. (*A Place Not Forgotten* 45)

Similarly, contemporary southern novelist Bobbie Ann Mason recounts that the Kentucky farm she grew up in has basically vanished:

> The landscape is still changing. On the highway, not far from our farm, are a tobacco-rehandling outfit, a John Deere business and a chicken hatchery. The little frozen custard stand, fallen to other uses and then to ruin, stood there until fairly recently but the motel disappeared long ago. In its place is a collection of grim little buildings. (*A Place Not Forgotten* 55)

The Erasure of Memory

While the destruction of a bucolic past has been bemoaned by many a southern writer, just as everyday history-filled buildings have been demolished and replaced by steely high rises and glassy towers, one would think that historical landmarks would be able to withstand the onslaught of urban expansion. Yet, in such cities as Norfolk, Virginia, for example, where large patches of historical streets were bull-dozed in favor of rebarbative 1970s eye-sores, or, as recently as in 2007, for hotel projects that never materialized[2], commemorative memorials to Civil War dead sprinkle an ever-shrinking historical space. As Granville Automatic has documented in their song about the Glorieta Pass in New Mexico, the site of a gigantic Confederate defeat and, by definition, a lauded Union victory, there are no memorials to those who fought there, just "a State highway now abruptly cuts through the middle of the battleground" (Granville Automatic track 2) As they describe it in the song: "Santa Fe is round the corner I can see it now/This land is ours and I'll be sure that I can hear the sound/ of Glorieta/ and I believe in the fight/ride on down to New Mexico/Turn your back to the sun and the one's you love."[3] For Granville Automatic and Mann, bronze statues might very well be perceived as soulless and emotionless, and although in Richmond, Virginia, for example, there is a Monument Avenue lined with monuments to Confederate leaders, it is the land itself that is replete with memories and ghosts longing to be heard. Even historical battlefields such as Antietam, chronicled by famous Civil War photographer Alexander Gardner in 1862, who showed how stacked it was with endless corpses, have fallen into disrepair to the point where charitable organizations led by The Civil War Trust are forced to buy up large parcels of land before commercial interests get their hands on them. That is why The Civil War Trust's monthly magazine for its members is called *Hallowed Ground*.[4] For preservationist organizations such as The Civil War Trust, the land has sacred qualities even though it is under constant threat of unsentimental development projects. Writing about notions of disappearance in urban settings such as Hong Kong in *The Culture and the Politics of Disappearance*, Akbar Abbas points to a new way of confronting vanishing spaces in terms of *dis-appearance* "in a specific sense (imagine the term as hyphenated) in that it gives us a reality that is not so much hidden as purloined, a reality that is overlooked because it is looked at in the old familiar way" (Abbas 25). Abbas identifies the speed with which contemporary societies do away with markers of spatial memory as a type of *déjà-disparu*:

> the feeling that what is new and unique about the situation is always already gone, and we are left holding a handful of clichés, or a cluster of memories of what has never been. It is as if the speed of current events is producing a radical desynchronization: the generation of more and more images to the point of visual saturation going together with a general regression of viewing, an inability to read what is given to view. (Abbas 26)

Mann entitles her book of Virginian and Georgian photographs *Mother Land* in a manner that suggests that she took looks upon the spaces she inhabits in a non-routine way encouraged by Abbas as the land she photographs is filled with invisible specters that demand to be interpreted and listened to amidst a noisy world of vapid over-stimulation. As Mann understands the Southern fixation with loss and memory, it is not a phenomenon of nostalgia or "looking back" that interests her, but rather a simultaneous cohabitation of the past and the present transformed into artwork: "But we know that love emerges from this loss, becomes memory, and that memory becomes art" (Mann 1997 5).

The Artist as Medium

Mann and Granville Automatic are able to connect with forgotten voices as though they were "mediums"—not only in the sense of their art (the camera for Mann; music for Granville) but in the manner spiritualists supernaturally communicate with the dead. As Jennifer Blessing and Nat Trotman describe it in their introduction to an exhibit Mann participated in called *Haunted*, at the Guggenheim Museum in New York in 2010:

> Reproductive mediums and performance are defined structurally by the layered temporality they present: they viscerally refer to past and prior acts that are perceived in the present in such a way as to bring the past into the present, to metaphorically bring the dead back to life and to suspend the viewer or audience between history and the immediate. It is because of this quality that photography, like performance, has been seen from its inception to have a kind of magic power, if not to transcend death then to constantly remind us, as a *memento mori*, of the inexorable passage of time. (Blessing and Trotman 11)

For Granville Automatic and Mann, symbols such as the discovered camera lens of a civil war photographer or the Granville Automatic itself, a 19th-century typewriter, act as portals that channel lost voices from the past towards the present. Just as Roland Barthes admired how looking at a photograph of Napoleon's brother gave him what Mann calls "the fantastic possibility of looking through the same eyes that looked at the Emperor,"[5] (Mann 1997 6) in *Camera Lucida*, Mann was fortunate enough to have discovered a trove of 10 000 glass negatives taken around her town by a returning civil war veteran and photographer, Michael Miley. Although Miley became famous for his portraits of Robert E. Lee after the war, Mann found thousands of quotidian and ordinary portraits of average people. Miley had only photographed historical figures after the war. As she explains: "Instead, interspersed with the thousands of nameless portraits, there were images of familiar places, unchanged in a century. Among them were easily recognizable images of our river and cliffs taken amidst fumes of ether and collodion" (Mann 1997 6). Mann then "cleaned, sheathed and printed all those negatives, slipping," as she says "indistinguishably between the centuries" (6). She would photograph the same landscapes such as her own empty but pastoral contemporary photo of the Antietam battle site in 2001 and other "mother-land" photos with what Lisa Saltzman has called "the uncanny experience of oscillating between past and present [...]. It could be said that Mann summoned the spirit of those archival photographs, if not their actual subjects" (Saltzman 131).

Similar to Steven Soderbergh's 2006 film set in 1945 Berlin, *The Good German*, which Soderbergh shot with 1940's director Michael Curtiz's actual lenses in order to accurately recreate, if not give life to that era, Mann not only used antique lenses but experimented with a "wet collodion process to produce her black and white silver nitrate prints" (Saltzman 131). The absence of any modern indices or even of human life in her photos, with their emphasis on shadows and nature, brings a haunting, disorienting sensation to her pieces which she describes in terms of "an oneiric warp [that] embraces time and memory and become the still point at which they intersect" (Mann 1997 6). As always, she writes, "that stillness brings longing and a dizzying time–traveling spiral into the radical light of the American south" (6). If Barthes admits that he "wanted to explore photography not as a question (theme) but as a wound" (Barthes 1), Mann also describes *Mother-Land* in terms of a particularly southern condition:

> Living in the South means traveling in that peculiar, imperishable war which, with perfect indifference both nourishes and wounds us. To identify a person as a Southerner is always to suggest not only that her history is inescapable and profoundly formative but that it is also paralyzingly present. Southerners live at the nexus between myth and reality where that peculiar amalgam of sorrow, humility, honor, loyalty, graciousness and renegade defiance plays out against a backdrop of profligate, physical beauty. (Mann 1997 6)

In another of Sally Mann's books, an eerie set of untitled black and white spectral faces shown at the Gagosian Gallery in New York in 2006 that resemble the famous "noyée de la Seine" (the drowned girl from the Seine, discovered in the late 1880s but popularized in the early 1900s), she quotes Sophocles as an epigraph, "Man is but breath and shadow" (Gagosian epigraph), which could also apply to Granville Automatic's aesthetic which favors heroic unknown individuals over famous historical ones and even gives a narrative voice to those who literally cannot speak such as horses, houses, and wraiths. Each of these elements are witness to historical actions and yet champions what it means to be simply human. As Granville Automatic's Elizabeth Elkins has remarked: "Every second of battle in the American Civil War was filled with stories, many of which have gone untold" (Martin). They seek to rediscover traces of memory as though they were particles strewn about the ruins they visit. "Lanterns at Horseshoe Ridge," for example, is written from the point of view of a ghost, a legendary woman "dressed in white who haunts the Chickamauga battlefield in Tennessee." Although Interstate 29 runs through it now, "once wives, daughters and mothers," as Granville describes it, "spent the night searching the fields by lamplight hoping to find their loved ones" (Granville Automatic track 7). "When the order came to charge," the ghost asks, "did you think of me/ And I don't know if you're dead or I'm dreaming/ And here I am wandering all alone/By lantern light searching for my own." As Martin explains: "The band's goal is to capture the immense emotional imprints the war left not only on soldiers but their loved ones" (Martin). "Chantilly Grace" is written from a sideboard's point of view, in a mansion the widow Cornelia Lee Turberville Stuart had owned along with an attached farm. Since Stuart shared the same last name as the famous rebel commander Jeb Stuart, her house was often ransacked or commandeered by Federal troops. As Granville understands it:

> By the Fall of 1862, the house was deserted and dilapidated, personal family pages were scattered about and all the furniture was reportedly removed except for a mahogany sideboard that was too heavy to lift. As the house continued to change hands throughout the war, the sideboard sat and watched the soldiers pass. The song is told from its perspective. Today not much of Chantilly's war history has survived. Only a small house from the Chantilly farm remains, just across a shopping center. (Granville Automatic track 3)

The Presence of Ghosts

Granville's interactions with ghosts are not dissimilar to crime fiction writer James Lee Burke's description of his detective, Dave Robicheaux's conversations with Confederate general John Bell Hood who appears and disappears with his men in the Lousiana-set novel *In the Electric Mist with Confederate Dead*. The ghosts of the Confederate soldiers become visible to Robicheaux in order to warn him of the evils of the contemporary Louisiana underworld that surrounds him but also to give weight to a traumatic historical past that had been ignored, if not obliterated by those who now inhabit that land. The general too speaks of acoustic shadows as a symbol, if not a warning for generations that can hear the sound waves a hundred years later: *"You've never heard that sound, the electric snap before?"* He asks Robicheaux as they speak about different wars (the Vietnam war for Robicheaux), *"'Then you know it's the innocent about whom we need to be most concerned,'* he exhorts" (Burke 321). At one point, Robicheaux accidentally drives through the ruins of what was once a sugar planter's home before it had been horrifically ravaged during the war:

> In 1863 General Banks's federal troops had dragged the piano outside and smashed it apart in the coulee, then as an after-thought had torched the slave quarters and the second story of the planter's home. The roof and cypress timbers had collapsed inside the brick shell, the cisterns and outbuildings had decayed into humus, the smithy's forge was an orange smear in the damp earth, and vandals had knocked down most of the stone markers in the family cemetery, and, looking for gold and silver coins, had pried up the flagstones in the fireplaces. (Burke 200–201)

At the end of Burke's novel, the Confederate general asks Robicheaux to pose with his men in a war photograph which he describes as a type of prism with which he can "look down the long serpentine corridor of amber light again and see thousands of troops advancing on distant fields [...] and a collective sound that's like no other in the world rises in the wind and blows across the drenched land" (432); and later, as the apparitions disappear again, he sees them as pure refraction, "the light arcing over them as bright and heated and refractive as a glass of whisky held up to the sun" (433). Burke describes this refractive light so well through the acoustic shadows that bring the soldiers' lament to Robicheaux through time and that Granville captures in their own songs. Despite all their ghostly imagery, Granville Automatic also underlines the resilience of memory through empathy and kindness, as they write:

> I could tell you of strong men just looking on down
> How the ghosts of them wander this ground
> I've seen some things no man should ever have to see
> Just listen to me because Time don't erase
> The way that the heart feels when everything changes
> Surrounded by strangers but all alone
> She says that no one knows what she's been through
> Believe me Cornelia I do Chantilly grace
> I hold on and I keep every memory
> All the fire of the world can't burn them away (Granville Automatic track 3)

The Chantilly house is actually not far from the behemoth Dulles Airport near Washington, DC, which overdetermines the notion that many of the vibrant historical spaces evoked by Granville are laden with sparks of souls that are increasingly eclipsed by what Marc Augé has labeled "non-places"— nondescript homogenous spaces such as airports, malls, and chain stores. If Abbas tells us to re-orient how we look at things that seem to evaporate before our very eyes, Granville urges us to listen to the stories hidden between unsuspecting walls and bricks. This is why the notion of "home," similar to Mann's "mother land," anchors Granville's songs which try to combat the opposite of a home-land, that is to say, physical erasure and antiseptic commercial spaces. "Goodnight House," for example, a song that is set in Perryville, Kentucky, in 1862, describes a barn where a town doctor was called upon to work all night to save wounded soldiers while Mr. Goodnight played the fiddle and administered whisky to dull their pain: "So play me home and I'll let go/ of those goodnight dreams," the doctor requests, "Now John is here with the whisky/from a little town in Tennessee/ Bet he wishes he could disappear/ behind the fiddle's melody" (Granville Automatic track 4). He may have wished to disappear, but, as most of the battlefield land where the house once stood, Granville observes, "much of the landscape that was the battlefield at Perryville is rapidly sold off to developers each year" (Granville Automatic track 4). Similarly, "Rose of Sharon," set in Mansfield, Louisiana, in 1864, describes the keepsake a soldier leaves his family. "He is last seen sitting under an old oak tree," Granville explains, but "the Mansfield site is now mostly destroyed by lignite mining operations" (Granville Automatic track 8).

In Search of Keepsakes

Two exhibits, "Photography and the American Civil War," in 2013 at the Metropolitan Museum of Art, and the Brooklyn Historical Society's 2015 "The Civil War Remembered in Photos and Letters of Brooklyn Soldiers," both focused not only on photos of the war dead but the soldiers' attempts to be remembered by their loved ones while they were away through lockets, stones, jewelry, and letters or anything that could be used as a memento. The exhibits echo the "Rose of Sharon" soldier who writes: "Looking at you through the letters I wrote in love so deep I might drown, […] I wait all my life just to find my way back to you" (Granville Automatic track 8). "So much of the Civil War is told on these really epic terms," Judy Colia, the curator of the Brooklyn Historical Society's exhibit, remarks, "It was just as much about people keeping in touch at home and maintaining their relationships" (Bischof). Just as Granville Automatic, historical societies have endeavored to keep those sparks of thought alive despite the potential for collective amnesia among the American unconscious. As the *New York Times* comments about the Brooklyn exhibit: Thousands of these [letters] ended-up half-forgotten in attics and bureau drawers, a small stash comes to light in the exhibition which consists of just one little room with a lot in it—including letters, civil war souvenirs and explanatory texts—with everything as readily accessible as if in a well-packed suitcase (Cutter).

One of the most poignant of Granville's songs, "Grancer Harrison," is about "one of the most famous ghosts of Alabama," who wanted to be buried with his fiddle and dancing shoes, as he used to throw lavish parties at his farm and fiddled all night under the moon. "His wishes were carried out, and his grave is a large bed-shaped tomb (they say he hangs out there still)" (Granville Automatic track 9), Granville explains. Granville Automatic, in fact, shot one of their videos of that song at the Harrison Cemetery in Coffee County, Alabama. Apparently, the site has been blown up many times by those seeking gold under the coffin, and, as Granville underlines, "Through Grance's grave remains, the Mobile area sites of the deaths of his sons have fallen victim to weather and lack of funding" (Granville Automatic track 9). In Martin's article in the *Washington Times*, one of the descendants of Grancer, Robert Harrison, speaks appreciatively of Granville's mission to combat the disappearance of quotidian civil war memories but laments: "Their whole principle is about writing music about things that are disappearing [...] the landscape changes, other connections to the past disappear with development" (Martin).

While "acoustic shadows" may seem overwhelming at times to those trying to preserve or capture traces of memory from being covered over, efforts such as the ones coming from historical societies, museums, and especially creative artists such as Granville Automatic and Sally Mann, however, continue to fight the good fight for those who can fight no longer. As Martin reports on the origins of Granville Automatic's artistic vision:

> Many of the songs were inspired years ago when Elks and Granville Automatic vocalist Vanessa Olivarez lived in metro Atlanta, Moreland Avenue, across battlefields now covered by streets and stores and hoping the stories of the Civil War were not lost to history. "We're paving over a tragedy and we're not remembering it," Elkins said. (Martin)

Conclusion: The War on Oblivion

"The passage from memory to history has required every social group to redefine its identity through the revitalization of its own history," Pierre Nora writes in *The Realms of Memory*. "The task of remembering makes everyone his own historian" (Nora 638). If for Nora, "places of memory" within a nation are made up of "the events, holidays and monuments that give people their identity" (634), Sally Mann and Granville Automatic are all the more important and powerful in their messages of covering what has not been memorialized officially, or rather, the phantom-like absences from the common writings of history, especially in light of recent movements to take down monuments to Confederate soldiers or leaders throughout the South. They are able to capture and continue what may be invisible to many but are still relevant to contemporary society. If, according to Maurice Halbwachs, the "collective memory of a nation is represented in memorials .../Whatever a nation chooses to commit to physical or more significantly what not to memorialize is an indication of the collective memory" (Halbwachs 172), Mann and Granville, by focusing on what is indeed not memorialized but humanly important, help us hang on to our collective memories as a "land" before the waves of oblivion snatch them up for good.

Notes

[1] See Sally Mann's *Mother Land: Recent Landscapes of Georgia and Virginia.*

[2] See Debbie Messina's "Norfolk Ends Debate on Building's History."

[3] The historical novelist P.G. Nagle has also written extensively on Glorieta Pass, which she thought of as a space that historians have egregiously overlooked. Her novel *Glorieta Pass: A Novel of the Far Western Civil War* (New York: Forge Books, 1999) as well as other New-Mexican-Civil War-themed novels, feature both confederate and union everyday heroes.

[4] See *Hallowed Ground: Membership Magazine of the Civil War Trust* (www.civilwar.org/hallowed-ground-magazine/)

[5] In *Camera Lucida*, Barthes also connects photography with death, specters and their resurfacing through photography. As he sees it: "Photography is a kind of primitive theater, a kind of *Tableau Vivant*, a figuration of the motionless and made-up face beneath which we see the dead," Roland Barthes, *Camera Lucida: Reflections on Photography*, translated by Richard Howard (New York: Hill and Wang, 1981 32). Barthes divides photography into the "studium," e.g., the official historical or political interpretation of a photo, and the "punctum," the "wound" that reveals the most personal part of what is taken. It is the *punctum* that Sally Mann is drawn to in her photography.

Works Cited

Abbas, Akbar. *Hong Kong: Culture and the Politics of Disappearance.* Minneapolis: University of Minnesota Press, 1997.

A Place not Forgotten: Landscapes of the South, exhibit catalogue. Lexington, KY: University of Kentucky Art Museum, 1999.

Augé, Marc. *Non Places: An Introduction to Supermodernity.* Translated by John Howe, New York: Verso, 2009.

Barthes, Roland. *Camera Lucida.* Translated by Richard Howard, New York: Hill and Wang, 1980.

Bischof, Jackie. "Civil Remembered in Photos and Letters of Brooklyn Soldiers." *Newsweek*, April 4, 2015.

Blessing, Jennifer and Nat Trotman. *Haunted: Contemporary Photography/ Video/Performance.* New York: Guggenheim Museum Publications, 2010.

Burke, James Lee. *In the Electric Mist with Confederate Dead.* New York: Pocket Books/Simon and Schuster, 1993.

Burns, Ken. "A Conflict's Acoustic Shadows." *New York Times*, April 11, 2001.

—. *The Civil War.* PBS Home Video, 1990.

Cutter, Holland. "Brooklyn Historical Society: 'Personal Correspondents: Photography and Letter Writing in Civil War Brooklyn.'" *The New York Times*, June 2, 2016.

Granville Automatic. *An Army Without Music: Civil War Stories from Hallowed Ground.* Record release: August, 2015.

—. www.granvilleautomatic.com/lyrics.

Halbwachs, Maurice, *On Collective Memory.* Heritage Sociology Series, translated by Lewis A. Coser, Chicago: University of Chicago Press, 1992.

Hallowed Ground: Membership Magazine of the Civil War Trust. www.civilwar.org/hallowed-ground-magazine.

Mann, Sally. *Mother Land: Recent Landscapes of Georgia and Virginia.* New York: Edwynn Houk Gallery, 1997.

—. *Sally Mann.* New York: Gagosian Gallery, 2006.

Martin, Jeff. "Band Releases Album of Songs Inspired by the Civil War." *The Washington Times,* August 15, 2015.

Messina, Debbie. "Norfolk Ends Debate on Building's History." *The Virginian Pilot,* Oct 5, 2007.

Nagle, P.G., *Glorieta Pass: A Novel of the Far Western Civil War.* New York: Forge Books, 1999.

Nora, Pierre. *The Realms of Memory: Rethinking the French Past, Vol 1.* Conflicts and Divisions, translated by Arthur Goldhammer, New York: Columbia University Press, 1996.

Saltzman, Lisa. "What Remains: Photography and Landscape, Memory and Oblivion." Blessing, Jennifer and Nat. Trotman, *Haunted: Contemporary Photography/Video/Performance.* New York: Guggenheim Museum Publications, 2010.

Slouka, Mark. "Blood on the Tracks." *Harper's,* June 2, 2000, Volume 300 (1801).

Soderbergh, Steven (dir). *The Good German.* Warner Brothers. 2006.

Chapter 10

Literary Vagabonds and the Lure of the Open Road

Adrian Tait

Independent Scholar

Abstract: Nature writing has become ever more popular in Britain, and this chapter explores one of its literary roots in the wayfaring literature of the late nineteenth and early twentieth centuries. Pioneered by writers such as R. L. Stevenson, Kenneth Grahame, and G. M. Trevelyan, the literature of the open road encouraged its readers to venture out of the cities and back into the countryside, there to reconnect with the nonhuman, natural world as they walked, tramped, and rambled. Although now neglected, this literature anticipates modern environmentalist thinking in several key ways and, with it, the "new" nature writing. Siren-like, it also offers an escapist vision of "Nature" that ignores the natural and nonhuman world's complex entanglement with a threatening modernity. As the chapter concludes, the literature of the open road nonetheless encouraged later, and more politicized moves to preserve Britain's open spaces, and secure the right to roam them.

Keywords: Pan(theism), open road, new nature writing, modernity/ modernism, (re)enchantment

***

Over the last few years, the literary marketplace in Britain has been transformed by the startling popularity of what it is now customary to call "new" nature writing. As Mark Cocker has remarked, its emergence is "among the most significant developments in British publishing this century." Inevitably, however, some have questioned its newness, pointing out that it simply forms a part of a continuing and "rich history of nature writing" (Moran 49). Indeed, one of its several roots can be found in the wayfaring revival of the late nineteenth and early twentieth centuries, which in turn generated a substantial but now largely overlooked body of work by British writers such as R. L. Stevenson, Kenneth Grahame, and G. M. Trevelyan, all of whom escaped the city for the countryside whenever the opportunity presented itself. Rambling, walking, tramping; the names they gave it were various, but for all, the experience of walking, of exploring the natural world through walking, gave their lives a purpose and meaning that modernity systematically denied them. In turn, these writers sought to communicate their transformative experiences to a now largely urban readership in the hope of urging "folk into the open air, and once there, keep them glad they came" (Lucas ix). In this essay, I intend to revisit and, albeit briefly, survey this large if loosely defined literature of "the open road," as E. V. Lucas entitled it, and reconsider its importance in light of the extraordinary phenomenon that is now the new nature writing in Britain.[1] Focusing on the work of R. L. Stevenson, but also of a later generation of writers such as Grahame, Trevelyan, and the poets and essayists anthologized by E.V. Lucas in *The Open Road*, my aim is to reconsider the way in which their shared spirit of leisured, "literary vagabondage" informed early attempts to recover a sense of enchantment in the natural world, not by rooting oneself in it, but by moving through it; by freeing oneself from the (unnatural) imprisonment of town and city, and rediscovering in open skies, open roads, and open horizons new possibilities for freedom, no matter how temporary (Macfarlane 2013 20). The influence of these writers on the passion for rambling, walking, and wayfaring remains significant. It anticipates several aspects of recent environmental thinking. Moreover, much of the new British nature writing reflects its inspiration. But what this essay also asks is whether this literature, in fact, represents an escape from material reality rather than a re-immersion in it; whether, after all, the lure of the open road was and is a distraction from a changed and changing environment in which it is increasingly difficult to create a sustained and sustainable relationship between people and place. In an urban and automobilized world, what can nature writing (new or otherwise) do to assert our inextricable entanglement with the world?

In a chapter entitled "Wayfarers All," Kenneth Grahame interrupts his children's classic *The Wind in the Willows* (1908) to describe the Water-Rat's chance meeting with his wayfaring cousin, the Pied Piper-like Sea Rat. Entranced by the Sea Rat's tales of life afloat and the constant changes it brings, the Water Rat is persuaded to leave home and hearth. He is, however, intercepted by his devoted friend, the Mole. The Mole breaks the seafarer's spell and the Water Rat returns to the riverbank, where his mind once again settles into its usual rhythms and routines. Rat is, after all, "rooted" to a "familiar landscape and its small society" (Grahame 2005 99). This is a pastoral, tranquil world: self-sufficient, self-contained, and still closely tied to the senses, and the seasons; it is (to quote another of the novel's chapters) a *"Dolce Domum"* (sweet home).

For Grahame, however, this world was already an exercise in wish fulfillment. Sometimes gentleman clerk and later secretary of the Bank of England, Grahame's weekday life was circumscribed by the big city (Avery in Grahame 2005 x–xii). At week's end, however, Grahame's time was his own, and at the earliest available opportunity, he would flee the big city and spend his leisure "messing about on boats" or tramping country roads (Avery x). In this, Grahame was entirely typical. Born in 1859, he was part of the world's first generation to be raised in an urbanized nation where sprawling cities were swiftly becoming the norm. Confronted by the rise of the ever-expanding megalopolis, this generation increasingly resented the deracinated existence that city life seemed to assume. As the Victorian period gave way to the Edwardian, many longed not only for the freedom denied them by a now industrialized society but for a way to reconnect with older rhythms, older ways, and above all, to reconnect with nature. Some sought to return to and settle on the land. Others, perhaps recognizing that no such return was now possible, translated their urban angst into a desire to tramp the open road. "If it is your ill-luck to live in a city," wrote John Cowper Powys, "hasten into the country, at least once a week, and spend all your dreams during the other days in remembering that happy seventh-day excursion" (Powys 190). Many did so. Walking clubs sprang up everywhere, and "[b]y the end of the century rambling had become, for many people from all but the poorest sectors of society, a positive obsession" (Searle 605).

The defining statement of this leisurely pursuit is, perhaps, E. V. Lucas' anthology *The Open Road*, first published in 1899. Subtitled "A Little Book for Wayfarers," it perfectly caught the mood of the moment. Those who rambled also read: conveniently printed in pocketable form, *The Open Road* drew together the prose and poetry of dozens of different writers with the straightforward aim of providing "companionship on the road" (Lucas ix). The tone of the collection was modest, but the success of the anthology was astonishing. The book was already in its seventh edition when Methuen took over its publication from Grant Richards in 1905, and by 1948, Methuen had published a further forty-five editions. As its success suggests, Lucas's collection spoke for and to a significant section of a now largely urbanized population that, whether walking, tramping, rambling, or roaming, sought out ways in which to reconnect with the world beyond the city and, in so doing, recover a sense of itself that had been lost or always denied.

What, then, can we learn from the poetry and prose that Lucas so carefully collected? Significantly, the collection's epigraphs include an excerpt from William Wordsworth's "The Tables Turned," a poem in which Wordsworth apotheosized "Nature" (hence the initial capital) as a source of true wisdom and dismisses the "meddling intellect" (Lucas x). "Let Nature be your teacher," the poem advises its readers, for "[s]weet is the lore which Nature brings" (Lucas x). This emphasis on the beneficial influence of a benign "Nature" is characteristic of many poems and prose extracts composing the volume. The majority of the volume's seventeen sections (and they are generally the largest sections) focus on the natural world or natural phenomena, as their titles suggest: "Spring and the Beauty of the Earth," "Sun and Cloud, and the Windy Hills," "Birds, Blossoms, and Trees," "Garden and Orchard," "The Sea and the River," "The Reddening Leaf," "Night and the Stars." Of the remaining sections, the first bids "Farewell to Winter and the Town," and the second is entitled "The Road;" the last and shortest section is entitled "The Return" and consists of a single poem entitled "The Glamour of the Town." There is also a long sequence of poems and ballads about love, "The Lover Sings," a very brief section entitled "Companions," another entitled "Summer Sports and Pastimes," and a section on the theme of "Refreshment and the Inn," the thought of which was no doubt welcome to those tramping the open road. In addition, there is a section entitled "A Handful of Philosophy," which opens with another excerpt from the work of William Wordsworth. Significantly, Lucas entitles this excerpt "The World is Too Much With Us." In the excerpt, Wordsworth's narrator rails against the "sordid boon" of "[g]etting and spending" in a notionally Christian country and declares, "Great God! I'd rather be/ A Pagan suckled in a creed outworn" (Lucas 354). As we shall see, this twofold rejection of a materialist culture and conventional religious belief resonated powerfully with the literary vagabonds that are my subject in this essay. Finally, Lucas included a section entitled "A Little Company of Good Country People." It is the only section in the volume that relates directly to life in the country. It contains just over a dozen pieces with titles such as "The Barefoot Boy," "A Fair and Happy Milkmaid," "The Shepherd on the Farm," and "The Pretty Washmaiden." It offers an idealized vision of life in the country as a kind of pastoral, remote from the realities of rural poverty.

As this brief overview of the contents of *The Open Road* suggests, Lucas's collection concentrates on the experience of being out in and amidst "Nature": it is the destination to which the open road inevitably leads. This "Nature" is, moreover, a Romantic construct, not a Darwinian one. There is no room here for Tennysonian doubts about the natural world as a place of strife, conflict, and competition. Instead, the collection invokes Wordsworth (once again) to demonstrate that, as he puts it in "The Green Linnet," "birds, and butterflies, and flowers/ Make all one band of paramours" (Lucas 133). In this world, argues Stevenson in another of the collection's extracts, "all out-door creatures" are "kindly [...] and a sheep of Nature's flock" (Lucas 310). As these quotes suggest, the poetry and prose that make up the volume valorize the natural world as a place quite apart from city life but essential for human health and happiness. "Nature" is the source of the "wander-thirst" felt by these writers, as Gerald Gould puts it, and it is the locus of their city-bound dreams (Gould in Lucas 7). "[P]oor among the poor," says Ada Smith's narrator in the poem "In City Streets," she dreams of nature's largesse: in her mind's eye, blackberries are always ripe, pools are always clear, and the wind always soft, "[s]oughing through the fir-tops" (Lucas 6). These pieces are lyrical and often lofty in tone; their intention is to offer an elevated sense of the natural world as a place of great beauty but also as a source of solace and comfort and as something to be treasured in itself. In the poem "England," for example, E. (Edith) Nesbitt declares that even "a corner of land, a furze-fringed rag of a byway" is "in our hearts [...] sacred" (Lucas 55). Furze is the name popularly given to an evergreen shrub often found on wasteland (*OED*), which underlines the poem's intent: to persuade the reader of (an English) "Nature's" claim over him or her, no matter how humble or easily overlooked its manifestations may be. As its end-rhymes carry the reader forward, the poem rises to a rhetorical climax in a series of questions that insist on "Nature's" pre-eminence and on our obligation to love and venerate it:

> "Is not each bough in your orchards, each cloud in the skies above you,
> Is not each byre or homestead, furrow or farm or fold,
> Dear as the last dear drops of the blood in the hearts that love you,
> Filling those hearts till the love is more than the heart can hold?"
> (Lucas 55)

As Nesbitt's use of the word "sacred" also implies, there is a spiritual dimension to this experience. In another excerpt in the collection, Richard Jefferies describes his own feelings at being immersed in nature's sensorium in terms that also evoke its mystical possibilities. "Touching the crumble of earth, the blade of grass, the thyme flower, breathing the earth-encircling air," he reaches out to "the unutterable existence infinitely higher than deity" (Lucas 95).

Whilst Lucas's collection provides useful insights into what contemporaries regarded as the "joys of the road," to quote another poem in the anthology, *The Open Road,* it is not our only source of understanding for this kind of walking literature (Bliss in Lucas 19). One of the most influential Victorian wayfarers was, in fact, Robert Louis Stevenson (1850–94), whose work is excerpted no less than five times in Lucas's collection. Stevenson is today best known as the author of highly imaginative stories such as *Treasure Island, Kidnapped,* and the *Strange Case of Dr Jekyll and Mr Hyde,* but his essays played an important part in shaping the public's interest in the open road and influencing the way in which later writers such as Grahame responded to the experience of walking in the open air. Perhaps the most important of Stevenson's essays were "Walking Tours" and "Pan's Pipes," both published in

1876 and later collected in *Virginibus Puerisque* in 1881. Together, these essays set the terms for what Ernest Rhys called "the conscious art of the literary wayfarer, who is of the town, yet delighted with the wild," and they give a strong sense of what it was later, turn-of-the-century wayfarers hoped to find on the open road that they so lacked in the city (Rhys vi). Still more significantly, however, Stevenson's essays also point to some of the ways in which the literature of the open road anticipates our own thinking about the environment and what Karen Barad calls our "intra-actions" (or co-constitutive entanglements) with it (Barad 33).

As Stevenson explains in "Walking Tours," the most important prerequisite for the rambler is the simple freedom to roam without conscious plan or design. "[F]reedom," he wrote, "is of the essence; because you should be able to stop and go on, and follow this way or that, as the freak [mood] takes you" (Stevenson 247). The aim was not, Stevenson insisted, to hasten along any particular highway or byway: to do so risked exhausting oneself. In pointed contrast to other great Victorian walkers—most notably Leslie Stephen, whose idea of a quiet Sunday involved a walk of twenty miles or more—Stevenson did not believe in strenuous effort. The "overwalker," he wrote, simply sets out "to stupefy and brutalize himself" (Stevenson 246). By comparison, the "temperate walker" was able to savor the experience of being out of doors and in contact with the world about him or her; as Stevenson stressed, "you must be open to all impressions and let your thoughts take colour from what they see" (Stevenson 246–7). This was the key to "peace and spiritual repletion" (Barad 33).

What was it, therefore, that the leisurely, open-minded wayfarer was supposed to experience? The answer lies in Stevenson's own, strong sense of the more-than-human world as itself alive—of "the voice of things, and their significant look, and the renovating influence they bring forth"—and of the open road experience as a means of recognizing the depth of our entanglement with that world: for "[w]hat experience supplies is of a mingled tissue," he wrote (Stevenson 265). Stevenson's awareness of what we would today recognize as the agentiality of matter raises significant questions over "the nature of agency and its presumed localization within individuals," which in turn coincide with modern theories of new materialism, such as Barad's agential realism (Barad x). Indeed, Barad's theory has been deeply influential within the environmental humanities, not least because, as Serpil Oppermann and Serenella Iovino point out, it shares their concern with breaking down the divide between nature and culture (Oppermann and Iovino 12). Barad's sense of "the world's radical aliveness" is, however, couched in the language of posthumanist technoscientific practices and derives from quantum physics, a twentieth-century field of scientific research whose often startling revelations of the entanglement of subject and object substantially undermined the kind of classical physics that dominated nineteenth-century science, with its belief in matter as static and passive (Barad 33). No such revelations were available to Stevenson, for whom the "scientific spyglass" was blind to the agentiality of the "web of the world" (Stevenson 263). Nor did he feel the need for such scientific insights. Stevenson had his own explanation for the liveliness of matter, and it was rooted in antiquity: the agentiality of the material world was, he insisted, the manifestation of the enduring power of the demi-God Pan. To "all ductile and congenial minds, Pan is not dead," Stevenson declared in "Pan's Pipes," "but of all the classic hierarchy alone survives in triumph; goat-footed, with a gleeful and an angry look, the type of the shaggy world: and in every wood, if you go with a spirit properly prepared, you shall hear the note of his pipe" (Stevenson 264).

As John Boardman explains, the satyr-like demi-God Pan is first found in Greek mythology, and his name is closely associated with the bucolic (Boardman 26). Pan's name is a contracted form of the word meaning herdsman, and "the same root is found in the English word 'pasture;'" Pan's home is in Arcadia, which is itself the root of classical constructions of the countryside as a pastoral idyll (Boardman 27). As Greg Garrad emphasizes, this sense of the pastoral has "decisively shaped our constructions of nature," often problematically, since it is used to imply "an idealization of rural life that obscures the realities of labour and hardship" (Garrard 37–8). However, Stevenson's sense of what Pan is or might be derives from a different, and strictly speaking, mistaken understanding of his name's etymological origin in the Greek word *pan*, meaning "all"' (Boardman 26). For Stevenson, as he makes clear, Pan is the God of all "Nature," including our own, human nature: to Pan's music, Stevenson wrote, "the young lambs bound as to a tabor, and the London shop-girl skips rudely in the dance" (Stevenson 263). Pan is, in this sense, everywhere, and everywhere matter itself comes alive: for Stevenson, therefore, the open road was (like the open or "ductile and congenial" mind whose importance he stressed) a way of accessing that suprahuman reality.

Stevenson's enthusiasm for Pan—and his feeling for an animate or animistic nature—resonated with a later, turn-of-the-century generation that felt it could no longer find spiritual consolation in conventional Christian beliefs. For self-styled neo- or "New-Pagans," amongst them writers such as Kenneth Grahame, E. M. Forster, Saki, Arthur Machen, Rupert Brook, Richard Le Gallienne, and G. M. Trevelyan, "all nature [was] sacred" (Searle 607). Like Richard Jefferies, they believed that God or gods were alive but alive in nature and that nature was itself alive. "At the close of a well-trodden day," wrote G. M. Trevelyan, the walker might well "have strange visions and find mysterious comforts" (Trevelyan 66). "Hastening at droop of dusk through some remote byway never to be found again," he wrote, "a man has known a row of ancient trees nodding over a high stone wall above a bank of wet earth, bending down their sighing branches to him [...] to whisper that the place [...] had always been waiting for him to come by" (Trevelyan 66).

For these writers, as G. R. Searle contends, "Nature-worship merged into a mystical pantheism," and Pan was its symbol (Searle 607). Indeed, Pan makes his sometimes disturbing presence felt in a number of contemporary works, such as Forster's "Story of a Panic" (1903), Machen's "The Great God Pan" (1894), and several of Saki's stories, including "Gabriel-Ernest" (1910) and "The Music on the Hill" (1911). Much tamed, Pan even makes a surprise appearance in *The Wind in the Willows*, his "glad piping" leaving Mole and the Water-Rat properly awe-struck and generations of later readers, children and adults alike, thoroughly bemused (Grahame 2005, 83). What links these often very varied literary expressions of Pan's identity is, nevertheless, a "thread of pantheism and nature-magic," which was in turn closely linked to the immersive experience of taking to the open road (Cecil 129). Like Stevenson before them, writers such as Machen, Forster, Grahame, and Trevelyan were all great walkers, and they shared his insistence on the immediacy of experience and the need to immerse oneself in it. As a friend of Kenneth Grahame later said of him, Grahame would, when walking, "slowly become a part of the landscape and a word from him would come as unexpectedly as a sudden remark from an oak or a beech" (in Green 226). For these writers, there was no way of experiencing that immersion except on foot. In "The Romance of the Road," for example, Grahame talks of the "god-like intoxication of speed," but he draws a "dividing line—strictly marked and rarely overstepped —between the man who bicycles and the man who walks," seeing in them "an essential difference in minds" (Grahame 15). Indeed, one's state of mind was, as Stevenson had suggested, critical to this process of losing one's self in one's surroundings. As A. H. Sidgwick wrote in *Walking Essays* (1912), "[t]he attainment of such a feeling requires a certain receptivity and even passivity of mind" (Sidgwick 8). It cannot be grasped "by a conscious effort of discursive reason" (Sidgwick 8). "[A]ll you can do," added Sidgwick, "is to set your body fairly to its task, and to leave the intimate character of your surroundings to penetrate slowly into your higher faculties, added by the consciousness of physical effort, the subtle rhythm of your walk, the feel of the earth beneath your feet, and the thousand intangible influences of sense" (Sidgwick 8).

As Sidgwick's comments underline, the combination of an open mind and the embodied experience of walking made it possible to step outside a narrowly bounded sense of self and in so doing, experience the wider totality of which that self is simply a part. Then "is the quiet soul awake," wrote G. M.

Trevelyan; "for then the body, drugged with sheer health, is felt only as a part of the physical nature that surrounds it and to which it is indeed akin" (Trevelyan 78). For Trevelyan, seeking out this expanded sense of self—a sense of self that depended on first quieting the restless, reasoning mind—was an essential antidote to modern life, and it took the form of an imperative. As Sidgwick himself wrote (note the repeated, rhetorical emphasis on the word "must"), "[y]ou must lay aside for the time being that formal and conscious reasoning which (you fondly think) gives you your distinctiveness and individuality in ordinary life; you must win back to deeper and commoner things: you must become mere man upon the face of your mother earth" (Sidgwick 8–9).

These are remarkable observations, and it is only, perhaps, in retrospect, that we can recognize just how radical they were. The abandonment of conscious or reasoned thought, the surrender of self, and the emphasis on embodied experience all anticipate aspects of the new nature writing, such as those described by Macfarlane in his introduction to Nan Shepherd's *The Living Mountain* (an introduction reproduced in Macfarlane's *Landmarks*, 2015). Here, Macfarlane's discussion of Shepherd's "avidly sensual" work is framed by his recognition that her thinking was, in philosophical terms, "cutting-edge" (Macfarlane 2015 71). As he points out, she was writing in the 1940s, at the same time that the "French philosopher Maurice Merleau-Ponty was developing his influential theories of the body-subject" (Macfarlane 2015 73). But just as Merleau-Ponty was not the first phenomenological philosopher, so Nan Shepherd was not, in fact, the first writer to recognize the way in which walking might intertwine "the human body and the phenomenal world" (Macfarlane 2015 73). We can, in fact, find their thinking anticipated in the literature of the open road, a walking cult, as Peter Green remarked, that became a "philosophy of life" (Green 118). Indeed, the philosophical dimension of this literature of the open road looks forward to our own, more consciously environmental thinking in several notable ways.

Firstly, these writers share with some (if not all) forms of modern environmentalism a deep suspicion of urban modernity, industrial capitalism, and an uncritical faith in progress.[2] Secondly, and still more fundamentally, these writers quietly question the structures on which Western modernity has been raised, and in particular, individualistic notions of selfhood, the conventional, scientific construction of the universe as inert, and the "foundational contrast between *reason* and *nature*" (Pratt 41; emphasis in the original). As we have seen, their approach to walking represents a decisive rejection of the Enlightenment belief in human reason as a privileged—or as even as the sole—means of engaging with and understanding the world (Pratt 3). Moreover, their intention in walking was to dissolve the sovereign human self, another of the building blocks of Western society, and collapse what Val Plumwood has identified as the "logic of colonization" inherent in dualistic thinking, with its false opposition of human/ culture/ reason *versus* nature, and its insistence on the "hyperseparation" of subject and object (Plumwood 49). Furthermore, they recognized in nonhuman nature a vitality that was explicitly at odds with then-dominant scientific constructions of matter as passive and malleable. This thinking anticipates the work of Barad, Donna Haraway, Stacey Alaimo, and Jane Bennett, amongst others, all of whom share a strong sense of the world as one "populated by animate things rather than passive objects," even of the earth *as* alive (Bennett vii). Indeed, the open road belief in a living earth (or "mother") speaks directly to the Gaia hypothesis first advanced by James Lovelock, and now a profoundly influential if undeniably controversial part of environmental thinking (Pratt 132).

Thirdly, and in setting aside conventional thinking, these writers sought new ways of being. Through walking, they were able to set aside self and find in that loss the much greater gain, in a deeper sense of self as part of the whole. This was what Trevelyan described as "the harmony of body, mind, and soul when they stride along no longer conscious of their separate, jarring entities, made one together in mystic union with the earth" (Trevelyan 61). On the one hand, therefore, the work of these walkers anticipates phenomenonological philosophers such as Edmund Husserl, who rejected the abstractions of modern science, and reasserted the importance of embodied experience—of knowledge gathered directly, through the senses—as the only way in which to restore "a proper understanding of the world and our place in it" (Pratt 53). Through walking, wrote Husserl in an essay of 1931, the body in motion "experiences the unity of all its parts" even as it experiences this as the "continuity of self amid the flux of the world" (in Solnit 27). On the other hand, and reframed in the language of theories of new materialism, these walkers recognized that they were caught up in a "lively dance of mattering," entangled with the world in ways that undermine human exceptionalism (Barad 37). "Existence," as Barad remarks, "is not an individual affair" (Barad ix). This "identification of self with nature" is part of a long tradition of nature-mysticism—and as we have seen, this was the form it took in the work of writers such as Kenneth Grahame—but it is also a constitutive part of more modern, environmentally inflected thinking (Pratt 34). In particular, it overlaps with the deep ecological belief in the process of what Arne Naess called "self-realization," through which we come to realize that we are "in, and of, nature from the very beginning of ourselves" (Naess 82).

For Naess, as for Barad, realizing that we are entangled in complex, "constitutive relationships" is the first step towards a new kind of ethical expansiveness that includes rather than excludes the more-than-human and non-human worlds (Naess 82). "[I]f your self in the wide sense embraces [other beings]," wrote Naess, "you need no moral exhortation to show care [towards them];" it follows, as naturally as one would care for oneself (Naess 91). In other words, Naess argues, this recognition suggests a way of fundamentally rewriting humankind's attitude towards its environment. For Grahame and his fellow walkers, however, the reasons for seeking out this feeling of interconnectedness were more personal, even solipsistic. Walking the open road enabled them to feel fully alive and, at the same, recognize and respond to the liveliness of the world in which they were immersed. The result was, as Graham wrote in an essay entitled "The Romance of the Road," a "supernal, a deific, state of mind [...] felt at its fullness after severe and prolonged exertion in the open air" (Grahame 1898 16). Supernal refers to the heavenly, deific to the divine (*OED*), terms that once again invoke a mystical sense of communion with one's surroundings, made possible, as Grahame put it, by "this particular golden glow of the faculties" (Grahame 1898 16). As Peter Green points out, however, the experiences that Grahame and his fellow walkers describe were only ever temporary (Green 116–117). "[T]omorrow you shall begin life again," wrote Grahame of the walker who, taking his ease after a long day's tramping, considers all the possibilities that are now available to him (Grahame 1898 17). In reality, however, Grahame did not begin anew. Like Trevelyan, Machen, and others, Grahame drew back from the radical implications of his own experiences, just as, at the end of every weekend or holiday, he returned to his own life. The experience of the open road was simply an all-too-brief escape from the "deadness of urban life" (Green 117).

Here, we can perhaps draw a distinction between Grahame's generation and Stevenson, whose work they so admired (Green 116). In the poem "The Vagabond," which Lucas included in *The Open Road*, Stevenson offers a lyrical paean to a life spent wandering the byways:

"Bed in the bush with stars to see,
Bread I dip in the river -
There's the life for a man like me,
There's the life for ever." (Lucas 16)

Stevenson's speaker has rejected urban modernity and materialistic culture, and substituted a life of extreme simplicity. Stevenson was himself this kind of perpetual wanderer, although one who was also propelled by ill-health (he eventually settled in Samoa, where he died aged just 44). By contrast, Grahame, like his character the Water Rat, always returned to the same, settled, comfortable circumstances and the same privileged existence. Walking offered a chance, as W. H. Hudson put it in *Afoot in England* (1909), to slip "back out of this modern world," but the modern world always reclaimed its own (Hudson 31). Moreover, it is perhaps obvious that Grahame and his fellow walkers were themselves beneficiaries of that modernity. Whilst the modern world, in the looming shape of the megalopolis, might have made it necessary to go in search of the open road, modernity (in the form of modern means of transport and communication) had also made it possible. Those who escaped the city did so using a train, tram, and later tube, before reading – or writing – about their shared experiences in magazines and periodicals that rolled in ever-increasing numbers from ever-more efficient printing presses.

On the open road, at least, Grahame and his fellow writers could pretend that they were out of reach of modernity. The open road was empty and unpeopled, a dusty and half-forgotten pathway through a depopulated countryside that they might roam undisturbed, indulging their intensely felt but also individualistic experience of the moment. However, it was not long to remain so. *The Wind in the Willows* contains a memorable scene in which Toad, Mole, and the Water-Rat are themselves walking the open road, only to be overtaken (and nearly mown down) by modernism's latest manifestation, the motor-car, "immense, breath-snatching, passionate" (Grahame 2005 22–3). The first petrol-driven car made its British appearance in 1895; just over a decade later, in 1906, there were already 44,098 cars in the country (Pearsall 137). In turn, the sudden appearance of the motor car divided those who enjoyed the freedom of the open road. Many relished the possibilities it offered. Others were appalled, sensing in its dominion over the open road—*their* open road—the quintessential expression of what Paul Virilio would later call a dromocratic society, "ruled by movement and acceleration," which would reduce the world to what we now think of as an edgeland; for edgelands (write Paul Farley and Michael Symmons Roberts) "are to drive for, to, through," and cars are their "defining characteristic" (Paterson 5). The motor car was, Grahame's generation felt, another (and still more appalling) extension of the modernity they sought to escape. "We see that times change, machines multiply, cities outrun the dreams of a century ago," wrote Edmund Blunden, but still, "we lament [the] hurtling land-liners sweeping all before them in lanes where the partridge was safe with her brood all the sunny day" (Blunden 184). As C. E. M. Joad would later write in "A Charter for Walkers" (1931), roads had simply become "little ribbons of town thrusting ever further into the heart of England, weals left by the whip-lash of civilization upon the fair face of the land" (Joad 10).

As these edgelands multiplied and motor cars grew ever more common, the idyll of the open road came to seem like a thing of the past. For Joad, writing in 1931, it was now "manifestly impossible" to walk the highways and byways of Britain: "[a]s a result the whole literature of walking and walking tours, in which the English are richer than any other nation, in particular the essays of men like Stevenson and Hazlitt and W. H. Hudson, has become obsolete" (Joad 10). In his view, the pleasure that Grahame's generation had taken in the open road did not long survive the sudden arrival of automobility. But Joad's own words underline the fact that all was not lost. Driven from the thoroughfares by what A. G. Gardiner called the "hurry and vulgarity" of the motorist, walkers instead sought out those green roads, paths, and tracks where no car could ever venture (Gardiner 253). "The real initiate of Nature will naturally avoid the main highways," wrote John Cowper Powys (Powys 195). Increasingly, this later generation looked to uplands and mountains, where they might be "let loose [...] into the vast spaces of earth and sky," far from "the gross tribe of motorists [...] with their hoots and their odours" (Gardiner 252–253).

This, then, is where we might now say we find ourselves in the midst of a rhetorically persuasive resurgence of nature writing that seeks to persuade us that, beyond the reach of restless modernity, it is still possible to resurrect the enchanted relationships that the literature of the open road itself set out to find and describe. Today, however, the new nature writing sets out on its own journeys on foot, mindful of what Macfarlane describes as the "old ways" and of the historical precedent set over a century ago by anthologists like Lucas and writers like Stevenson (Macfarlane 2013, 13), As Macfarlane observes in his own paean to the sense that "a walk is only a step away from a story," "I've read them all, these old-way wanderers" (Macfarlane 2013 18, 21). The question is, however, whether the new nature writing shares the same weaknesses as the literature of the open road. For all its popularity, that literature was, as Ronald Pearsall acerbically remarks, the work of "townees" seeking "succour and inspiration amidst flora and fauna [and] gently decaying villages," and treating what they saw, not as a living and working world itself beset by wider historical forces, but as a picturesque projection of their own immersion in the moment (Pearsall 118). Similar criticisms have been leveled at the new nature writing. As Mark Cocker, himself a distinguished nature writer, has written:

> "A criticism of new nature writing, proffered by one of its most important exponents, Kathleen Jamie, is the predominance hitherto of white, upper-middle-class men. The "Lone Enraptured Male" was her telling phrase, which encompasses the notion that the nature writer is also an excursionist who visits, then retreats back to the city [...]"

For these excursionists, as Kathleen Jamie writes, it is a case of "[a]dventures, then home for tea." However, the most telling aspect of Jamie's critique lies in her recognition that these solipsistic encounters substitute an unpeopled, ahistorical concept of "nature"—and as she adds, "I think 'nature,' 'natural' and 'wild' are almost synonymous here"—for a lived-in reality, rich in stories. "There's nothing wild in this country," she insists; "every square inch of it is 'owned'; much has seen centuries of bitter dispute; the whole landscape is man-made, deforested, drained, burned for grouse moor, long cleared of its peasants or abandoned by them." What is lost, as she points out in her review of Macfarlane's *The Wild Places*, is a sense of all the other voices—"Welsh or Irish or differently accented English"—that make up our collective experience of living in a complex, historied (and herstoried) world: and it is only by ignoring those voices, as she adds, that the new nature writing can establish its communion with nature.

It is now a decade since Jamie offered her shrewd and insightful critique of work such as Macfarlane's, and new nature writing has continued to grow in popularity. It has also grown in stature, partly through Jamie's contributions of verse and prose, amongst them *Sightlines* and *The Overhaul* (both 2012). Nor is Jamie's a solitary, female voice in a sea of enraptured males: Jean Sprackland's *Strands: A Year of Discoveries on the Beach* (2013), Helen Macdonald's *H is for Hawk* (2014), Madeleine Bunting's *Love of Country: A Hebridean Journey* (2016), Melissa Harrison's *Rain: Four Walks in English Weather* (2016), Alys Fowler's *Hidden Nature: A Voyage of Discovery* (2017), and Jessica J. Lee's *Turning: A Swimming Memoir* (2017) are just a few of the many deeply invested works by British women writers that challenge the "uninterrogated [...] association of literature, remoteness, wildness and spiritually uplifted men." (One could and should add—white men. It is relevant to note that Lee, whose memoir I have just mentioned, is a Canadian-Chinese-British academic and environmental scholar living in Berlin, a combination that underlines the kind of cosmopolitanism that can also be found in new nature writing.) Moreover, whilst walking remains the preferred means of exploring nature, the new nature writing also encompasses scrambling, climbing, (wild) swimming, and kayaking, each offering different forms of embodied experience, often of corners of the country (such as the canals of Birmingham) from which nature would appear to have been banished. In fact, the new nature now draws together work inspired by, but also immersed in town and country and edgeland, and the hybridized spaces that blur these distinctions (see, for example, John Grindrod's *Outskirts: Living on the Edge of the Greenbelt*, 2017). Indeed, we might now wonder why it needs to be called "nature" writing at all: as Plumwood argued, the term "nature" implies that we are somehow distinct from it or that "nature" can only be found beyond the city limits, far out on the open road, when much of the new nature writing insists on collapsing these distinctions. Bob Gilbert's *Ghost Trees* (2018) is a case in point: whilst it is concerned with tracing the "whole history of [the London parish of Poplar] and its people through its trees," and whilst the work is packaged and marketed as nature writing, Gilbert sets himself the much larger, and more inclusive aim of reconnecting "with people, with the past, and with my surroundings," in all the many forms (human, non-human, more-than-human) they take (Gilbert 18, 19).

"Not everything in the forest is lovely," as Robert Macfarlane concedes in his own response to the criticisms of the new nature writing (Macfarlane 2019). "More voices need to be heard from ethnic-minority writers and from a wider range of identities and backgrounds" (Macfarlane 2019). Moreover, the "first-person voice [remains] strong," Macfarlane notes, "but it was also strong in Henry David Thoreau's *Walden* (1854), a founding text of modern environmentalism." (Macfarlane 2019). Perhaps it might therefore be said that the newest of British nature writing does indeed justify its claim to be new, at least insofar as it has distanced itself from, say, the literature of the open road, which was so exclusively "claimed [as Jamie puts it] by the educated middle classes on spiritual quests." But the diversity of the new nature writing should also alert us to the possibility that the literature of the open road so conveniently designated by E. V. Lucas when he put together his "garland of good or enkindling poetry and prose" was itself just a sample of a much more diverse response to a changing environment (Lucas ix). Even as Trevelyan, Grahame, and Sidgwick focused their walks on the countryside, there were others who, when walking, found in both country and city agential materiality that was at once exciting and frightening: much of Arthur Machen's now neglected fiction and non-fiction testifies to this ambivalent but transgressive sense of the "wonder, mystery, awe" that might be found in walking "places by the Gray's Inn Road" [in London] no less than in the remote hills of Machen's beloved Wales (in Coverley 49). Nor was "Nature" necessarily excluded from the "new [urban] world" that Machen described (Coverley 49). The work of Richard Jefferies is twice represented in *The Open Road*—once in a piece entitled "The Hill Pantheist," and once in a piece entitled "Bevis and the Stars" —and both excerpts highlight the wonder of immersing oneself in nature. In essay collections such as *The Open Air* (1885, later published as part of The Wayfarers Library), however, it is quickly apparent that Jefferies is attentive to the way in which nature may also be found in cities; along with essays about forests and wildflowers, *The Open Air* includes a long account of the birdlife Jefferies glimpsed in the suburbs, "Nature on the Roof," and a discussion of "Red Roofs of London," which emphasizes the way in which wind and rain create opportunities for wildlife to reassert itself. "If [sparrows] can find a gap [in those roofs]," wrote Jefferies, "they get in, and a fresh couple is started into life" (Jefferies 245). As Macfarlane notes, in a recently republished (2012) edition of Jefferies' *Nature Near London* (1883), Jefferies' essays reflect a "decisive motion" away from the city's center, yet he is always "alert to the unexpected ecologies of the edgelands" that are its concomitant (Macfarlane 2012).

At the very least, then, the work of the open road writers should be considered more broadly in terms of the analogous urban experience of those who, like Jefferies, wrote from a perspective that fully embraced the phenomenological intimacy of encounters with the natural and non-human, whilst equally able to establish this kind of rapport in urban and suburban spaces which were themselves by no means empty of the natural and non-human. In turn, a broader reading of the work of writers such as Machen suggests that the new nature writing should be seen as part of a wider picture that includes the long tradition of psychogeography, which through "the act of walking" (and in a "spirit of political radicalism") "seeks to overcome the process of 'banalisation' by which the everyday experience of our [urban] surroundings becomes one of drab monotony" (Coverley 14). Nor should we forget that, from the perspective of a now increasingly globalized society everywhere defined by automobility, the very act of walking was and is transgressive: intimate, immediate, alert to place in a way that the driver or passenger may never be.

There is, however, one final issue in relation to the open road and the literature it inspired, and more generally to nature writing wherever it springs up in the world. Through their elevated prose and lyrical verse, writers such as Stevenson and Grahame sought to persuade their readers of the beauty of nature, its wondrous diversity, and its exquisite complexity: they sought, in other words, to cast a spell over their readers, just as "Nature" (so often spelled with an initial capital) had cast its spell over them, through and during their long rambles. They sought and found enchantment and wanted their readers to share that sense of wonder. But the problem with this kind of writing is the same one that, today, Mark Cocker identifies in relation to new nature writing. It is, he writes, centrally concerned with "the idea of 're-enchantment,' a diffuse term that seems to mean whatever the author wishes. It usually involves clothing a landscape in fine writing, both the writer's own and that of other historical figures—Emily Brontë, Edward Thomas, and Nan Shepherd are good examples—so that the place is infused with fresh cultural meaning." As he adds, "[t]he problem with this formula is that landscapes [by which he means these literary constructions] readily persist when all that makes a place enchanting—the filigree of its natural diversity—has long since vanished." Even as we celebrate what remains of nature, Cocker contends, we are "creating one of the most denatured countries on the planet."

Cocker is making a case for a more sharply critical and politically engaged form of nature writing rather than "a literature of consolation that distracts us from the truth of our fallen countryside." This "literature of consolation" is, he contends, a distraction, a retreat, a form of escapism, the same points that have been leveled—for example, by Peter Green—at the literature of the open road (Green 117). Is it possible, therefore, that this kind of writing—a "project of re-enchantment" (to quote Cocker) that links the wayfarers of over a century ago with new British nature writing—was and is simply a lure, a siren song, a fantasy designed to compensate for, but in no way confront, the grim realities of industrialized modernity? As Macfarlane has replied, in terms that are equally applicable to the literary wayfarers of over a century ago, Cocker's argument takes too utilitarian a view of what writing should be for, or what it can do (Macfarlane 2019). "The best of the recent writing," he argues, "is ethically alert, theoretically literate and wary of the seductions and corruptions of the pastoral," and some of it "is kick-up-the-arse furious," but literary responses to nature need not be "noisily game-changing." To the contrary, literature may work indirectly and unobtrusively yet still "lead to activism and […] feed into policymaking" (Macfarlane 2019). The fact of Macfarlane's very public argument with Cocker is an instance of the way in which new nature writing has, in Britain, upped the rhetorical ante and encouraged vigorous debate about what literature is for and how best we should safeguard the environment. In a perhaps less emphatic way, the point can also be made of the literature of the open road, whose ostensible aims were so humble (of "providing companionship"), whose manners were so polite, and which never for a moment sought to incite a revolution (Lucas ix). In spite of its self-effacing air, however, that literature encouraged many to get out of the city and experience nature at first hand. Their experiences later led to the mass trespasses of the 1930s, when ramblers willfully trespassed on private land to secure the right of access to open country. In turn, their passion for the open air and for open spaces led to the belated creation of Britain's own national parks in the 1940s. But it is, perhaps, equally important that this literature of enchantment also played its part—a vital part—in furthering what we would now recognize as an unbroken tradition of two centuries of walking literature connecting William Hazlitt with Robert Macfarlane. With its insistence on the value of nature and on the importance of experiencing that nature, at first hand, this tradition is itself an act of resistance to a modernity that has consistently and persistently discounted the value of the non-human and more-than-worlds and sought to distance us from embodied relationships with them.

Notes

[1] *The Open Road* was the title Lucas gave to his 1899 anthology of poetry and prose. It went through numerous reprints in the decades that followed its first publication; my copy text is a reprint of 1905.

[2] Garrard includes a useful discussion of some of the major concerns within contemporary environmentalism, and is also careful to distinguish between its variants; see Garrard 18-36.

Works cited

Avery, Gillian. "Introduction." Kenneth Grahame, *The Wind in the Willows*. London: Penguin, 2005, vii—xii.

Barad, Karen. *Meeting the Universe Halfway: quantum physics and the entanglement of matter and meaning*. London: Duke University Press, 2007.

Bennett, Jane. *Vibrant Matter: a political ecology of things*. London: Duke University Press, 2010.

Blunden, Edmund. "The Englishman and His Nature Poetry." *Prose of Our Time*, edited by J. J. Ratcliff, London: Thomas Nelson, 1936, pp. 183–188.

Boardman, John. *The Great God Pan: The Survival of an Image*. London: Thames and Hudson, 1997.

Cecil, Robert. *Life in Edwardian England*. London: B. T. Batsford, 1969.

Cocker, Mark. "Death of the naturalist: why is the 'new nature writing' so tame?" *New Statesman*, June 17, 2015. Accessed March 3, 2019. http://www.newstatesman.com/culture/2015/06/death-naturalist-why-new-nature-writing-so-tame.

Coverley, Merlin. *Psychogeography*. Harpenden: Pocket Essentials, 2010.

Farley, Paul, and Michael Symmons Roberts. *Edgelands: Journeys into England's True Wilderness*. London: Vintage, 2012.

Gardiner, A. G. *Windfalls*. London: J. M. Dent, 1920.

Garrard, Greg. *Ecocriticism*. Abingdon: Routledge, 2012.

Gilbert, Bob. *Ghost Trees: Nature and People in a London Parish*. Salford: Saraband, 2018.

Grahame, Kenneth. "A Bohemian in Exile." *Pagan Papers*, London: John Lane - Bodley Head, 1898, pp. 129–143.

—. "The Romance of the Road." *Pagan Papers*, London: John Lane - Bodley Head, 1898, pp. 9–18.

—. *The Wind in the Willows*. London: Penguin, 2005.

Green, Peter. *Kenneth Grahame: A Study of his Life, Work and Times*. London: John Murray, 1959.

Hudson, W. H. *Afoot in England*. New York: Alfred A. Knopf, 1922.

Jamie, Kathleen. "A Lone Enraptured Male." *London Review of Books*, March 6, 2008. Accessed March 2, 2019. https://www.lrb.co.uk/v30/n05/kathleen-jamie/a-lone-enraptured-male.

Jefferies, Richard. *The Open Air*. London: J. M. Dent, n.s.

Joad, C. E. M. "A Charter for Walkers." *The Spectator*, July 24, 1931.

Lucas, E.V. *The Open Road: A Little Book for Wayfarers*. London: Methuen and Co Limited, 1915.

Macfarlane, Robert. "Introduction." Richard Jefferies, *Nature Near London*, London: Collins, 2012, xi-xxv.

—. *The Old Ways: A Journey on Foot*. London: Penguin, 2013.

—. *Landmarks*. London: Hamish Hamilton, 2015.

—. "Why we need nature writing." *New Statesman*, September 2, 2015. Accessed March 3, 2019. http://www.newstatesman.com/culture/nature/2015/09/robert-macfarlane-why-we-need-nature-writing.

Moran, Joe. "A Cultural History of the New Nature Writing." *Literature & History* 23: 1, 2014, pp. 49–63.

Naess, Arne. *The Ecology of Wisdom*. Edited by Alan Drengson and Bill Devall, London: Penguin, 2008.

Oppermann, Serpil, and Serenella Iovino. "Introduction: The Environmental Humanities and the Challenges of the Anthropocene." *Environmental Humanities: Voices from the Anthropocene*, edited by Serpil Oppermann and Serenella Iovino, London: Rowman & Littlefield International, 2017, pp. 1–21.

Paterson, Matthew. *Automobile Politics: Ecology and Cultural Political Economy*. Cambridge: Cambridge University Press, 2007.

Pearsall, Ronald. *Edwardian Life and Leisure*. Newton Abbot: David & Charles, 1973.

Plumwood, Val. *Feminism and the Mastery of Nature*. London: Routledge, 1993.

Powys, John Cowper. "Culture and Nature." *Prose of Our Time*, edited by J. J. Ratcliff, London: Thomas Nelson, 1936, pp. 189–195.

Pratt, Vernon, with Jane Howarth and Emily Brady. *Environment and Philosophy*. London: Routledge, 2000.

Rhys, Ernest (ed). *Modern English Essays: Volume Two*. London: J. M. Dent, 1923.

Searle, G. R. *A New England? Peace and War 1886 – 1918*. Oxford: Clarendon Press, 2004.

Sidgwick, A. H. *Walking Essays*. London: Edward Arnold, 1912.

Solnit, Rebecca. *Wanderlust: A History of Walking*. London: Granta, 2014.

Stevenson, Robert Louis. "Pan's Pipes." *"Virginibus Puerisque" and Other Papers*, New York: Charles Scribner's Sons, 1901, pp. 262–270.

—. "Walking Tours." *"Virginibus Puerisque" and Other Papers*, New York: Charles Scribner's Sons, 1901, pp. 245–261.

Trevelyan, George Macaulay. "Walking." *Clio, a Muse and Other Essays Literary and Pedestrian*, London: Longmans, Green & Co, 1913, pp. 56–81.

Part IV.
Dwellings of Enchantment:
Ecopoetics
of Reenchantment

Chapter 11

Ecopoesis and the Rewilding of the World: Kathleen Jamie, Jay Griffiths, and George Monbiot

Adrian Tait

Independent Scholar

Abstract: This chapter examines three examples of nature writing in Britain, and explores the way in which each embodies a form of ecopoesis, as an act of making that prompts readers to rethink their own interactions with the environment. In *Findings* (2005), Kathleen Jamie highlights the continuing presence of the nonhuman and natural in our daily lives, suggesting that the term "nature" itself creates a problematic distinction or divide. In *Feral* (2013), George Monbiot looks for ways in which to reconnect with our own inherent wildness, and go beyond that opposition of "nature" and "culture" to create more sustainable relationships with the nonhuman world. In *Wild* (2005), by contrast, Jay Griffiths focuses on Indigenous communities, in which the dualistic divide between "nature" and "culture" is itself seen as unnatural. Taken together, these works underline the importance of seeking out the wildness that can still be found, both within us and without.

Keywords: Ecopoeisis, wildness, wilderness, rewilding, new nature writing, (dis)enchantment

***

In their introductory discussion of the field of ecopoetics, Angela Hume and Gillian Osborne (2018) note "how capaciously poets and critics understand both the concepts of an ecological perspective and of poetics" (2). Nevertheless, both assume that the term ecopoetics relates exclusively to poetry and not to prose (2), even as they draw attention to the etymological origins of *poesis* in the Ancient Greek word ποίησις, meaning "to make" (2). The aim of this chapter is, therefore, to think differently about *ecopoesis* as an act of making that also encompasses prose and, in so doing, to relate ecopoesis to the problematic question of dwelling, or how best to live responsibly and sustainably in the midst of a growing, global environmental crisis. As an act of making, ecopoesis may be defined as the way in which words encourage, prompt, or compel us to reconsider our relationship to the environment, perhaps by speaking with or for the more-than-human world and, in so doing, remind us not only of our imbrication in it and responsibility for it but of the inherent wildness that connects human and non-human. Through words, ecopoesis creates a space within which it is possible to think differently about the relationships that link us to the environment and, in so doing, re-center those relationships—and resituate that wildness—within our understanding of everyday life.

Mindful that ecopoesis may refer to prose no less than to poetry, this chapter focuses on three examples of prose writing that themselves represent acts of ecopoesis, prompting the reader to rethink what is meant by "dwelling," by "nature," by "wildness," and by "wilderness": Kathleen Jamie's *Findings*, a collection of essays published in 2005; Jay Griffiths' *Wild*, published in 2006; and George Monbiot's *Feral*, published in 2013. All three works form part of what has in Britain been called "[t]he new nature writing" (Cowley 7), but their diversity is, in fact, an important part of their appeal. Jamie is concerned with the way in which what we call "nature" always has been an integral part of our daily lives, suggesting that the term is, as a number of (eco)critics have suggested, a problematic externalization of relationships that in fact constitute our very existence (see, in particular, Morton 1–8). Monbiot, by contrast, is concerned not with recovering an original, authentic relationship with the more-than-human world but with the ways in which we may nevertheless embrace a ferality that takes us beyond the false opposition of nature and culture; his work blends journalistic polemic with first-person nature writing and practical proposals for a way in which the developed world might recreate a more sustainable and satisfying relationship with the non-human world. Griffiths, on the other hand, is focused on those still surviving Indigenous communities for whom the opposition between nature and culture is an unwelcome Western imposition entirely at odds with their points of view. Whether or not these three works fit conventional definitions of "nature" writing, and whether or not they are truly "new" or even "British," they offer fresh ways of approaching the relationships that bind human beings to a world that can never simply be contained by (or reduced to) the word "nature." In turn, each offers important insights into the wildness that inheres within us.

With those considerations in mind, this essay explores some of the varied ways in which these very different examples of British nature writing might be said to re-wild–even re-enchant–our perspective on the earth, beginning with Kathleen Jamie's *Findings*.

Kathleen Jamie: *Findings* (2005)

In Britain, the rising tide of new nature writing has quickly risen to a flood: it encompasses a startling range of non-human and more-than-human subject matter, from watersheds, coasts, meadows, and woods, to birds, bees, and butterflies. The obvious question remains, "what, if anything, is 'new' about it?" Glancing back over the collection of nature writing that Jason Cowley assembled for *Granta* in 2008, Anna Stenning and Terry Gifford suggest that "[o]ne answer would be 'not much'" (Stenning and Gifford 1). Stenning and Gifford do, however, make an exception for a piece by Kathleen Jamie (born in 1962), entitled "Pathologies: A Startling Tour of Our Bodies," which was subsequently revised and published in her essay collection *Sightlines* in 2012 (Stenning and Gifford 1–4). At its heart, Jamie's piece is a deeply personal meditation on what "nature" really is, or is not, in the "foreshortened" way it is usually defined (Jamie 2012 23): "I'd come home grumpy, thinking, 'It's not all primroses and otters.' There's our own intimate, inner natural world, the body's weird shapes and forms, and sometimes they go awry. There are other species, not dolphins arching clear from the water, but the bacteria that pull the rug from under us" (23). As this quote highlights, Jamie is amongst the most interesting of recent British writers, perhaps because, in subtle, allusive, but beguiling ways, she engages with some of the central issues that beset this surge (or resurgence) in "nature" writing, and its sometimes prickly relationship to the kind of ecocritical scholarship that Stenning and Gifford also represent. Nor is Jamie averse to critical comment on those who, like herself, have been brigaded under the catch-all "British nature writing": Jamie wrote a notably critical review of Robert Macfarlane's *The Wild Places*, in which a "white middle class Englishman" and "Lone Enraptured Male" sets out in search of wilderness in Jamie's Scottish backyard (Jamie 2008 26). "There's nothing wild in this country," she points out: "every square inch of it is 'owned'" (Jamie 2008 25).

Jamie is a poet and essayist, and the first of her two collections of essays is entitled *Findings*. The eleven pieces in the collection variously describe her encounters with peregrines, ospreys, cranes, corncrake, salmon, and, in her closing essay, a "Cetacean Disco" of whales and dolphins (Jamie 2005 185). However, the essays also describe her visit to a neolithic burial chamber during the winter solstice, the view out across the skyline of modern Edinburgh, and a partner's pneumonia. These essays are not in any simple or simplistic sense about "nature," except in a much more expansive sense than the one to which readers may be accustomed. Nonetheless, the collection as a whole takes its title from an essay in which Jamie appears to follow what might be considered one of the more conventional tropes of nature writing: the "motif" of a turn to and return from "wilderness" (Garrard 67). In "Findings," Jamie hitches a ride to the remote Monarchs, where she walks the deserted islands—once peopled, now empty—in the company of two sound recordists. The recordists are, as she comes to appreciate, people who have learned to listen, closely, "alert to bird-cries, waves sucking on rocks, a rope frittering against a mast" (Jamie 2005 54). She herself makes something of a discovery: "[h]ead down into the rain and wind," she writes, "I didn't see the whale until I was next to it."

> It didn't startle me—it was too big and too dead to be startling … I thought about touching it, with just one finger, furtively, the way a gull pecks, and I wish now I had, because I've never touched a whale and probably won't get the chance again. I should have touched the skin, because it looked almost like black leatherette. The biggest leatherette sofa you can imagine, washed up on an empty shore. (Jamie 2005 57–8)

Whale as sofa: this act of "defamiliarisation," as Victor Shklovsky famously defined art's ability to recover "the sensation of life" (1965 12), is a reminder of the way that Jamie interrupts ordinary speech with sometimes startling metaphors that make a self-conscious claim on the reader's attention. Elsewhere in the essay, for example, Jamie comes across "five silver fishes, freshly abandoned by a wave" on a "flawless sandy beach … glittering and bright as knives presented in a canteen" (Jamie 2005 51).

Like the comparison that she draws between a whale's carcass and a leatherette sofa, the idea of a canteen of knife-like fishes is arresting, even amusing; it marks Jamie's reluctance to reverence or reify what she has found, even as it focuses the reader on the curious, perhaps even enchanting beauty of her discovery. But the comparison of whale and sofa also signals her uncertainty about how she should react to her discovery. "I didn't know quite what to do with myself," she observes (Jamie 2005 58); "some gesture seemed required and I didn't know what" (58).

Yet her words also constitute an act of remembrance, and the sudden and surprising connection she makes between the carcass and a sofa plays a pivotal role in constructing the "gesture" with which she frames this encounter. By comparing the whale to something so prosaic, Jamie tilts at the tendency to describe wilderness encounters in terms of "reverential awe" a tendency that ecocritics such as Greg Garrard link to New World constructions of wilderness as nature "in a state uncontaminated by civilization" (Garrard 79). At the same time, Jamie's comparison reduces the whale to the status of a piece of detritus washed up on the shore. That is also Jamie's point. The islands, whilst remote and unpeopled, are covered in litter: traffic cones, aerosol cans, shoes, rope, "shampoo and milk cartons," and "the severed head of a doll" (Jamie 2005 59). The islands "are a 21st-century midden" (66). As Jamie wonders, it may be that there is no untouched place, and nothing that humankind has left unaffected, the whale included. As she observes in an essay on "The Braan Salmon:"

> They say the day is coming—it may already be here—when there will be no wild creatures. That is, when no species on the planet will be able to further itself without reference or negotiation with us. When our intervention or restraint will be a factor in their continued existence. Every creature: salmon, sand martins, seals, flies. What does this matter? (Jamie 2005 79)

Jamie leaves her own question unanswered, but it has certainly been suggested that it matters a great deal. For example, Bill McKibben has argued that "*we have ended the thing that has, at least in modern times, defined nature for us–its separation from human society*" (1990 60; emphasis in the original). As William Cronon argues, however, this sense of nature's necessary "otherness"—and of wilderness as by definition pure and untouched—is itself problematic: in transforming wilderness into "the natural, unfallen antithesis of an unnatural civilization that has lost its soul" (80), this vision of what constitutes nature leaves no room for humankind; it erases any trace of an indigenous past and denies humankind the possibility of a future there. It may even be that these acts of insistent erasure are themselves forms of disenchantment: as Cronon adds, "[o]nly people whose relation to the land was already alienated could hold up wilderness as a model for human life in nature" (80). This is not, however, Jamie's own position. Jamie's is, by contrast, a peopled world, rich in stories and history; indeed, it is precisely this richness and depth that suggests how enchanting the world may be for those inclined to listen to all the myriad voices–human and non-human—that have always constituted it. Thus, and whilst essays such as "The Braan Salmon" and "Findings" reflect Jamie's questioning attitude towards humankind's impact on its environment, her essays quietly underline the extent to which even the most remote Scottish islands already have often ancient human associations: the tomb she describes at Maes Howe on the Orkneys is 5000 years old (2005 10). Moreover, traces of human involvement are to be found everywhere: walking the clifftops, Jamie writes that "[y]ou might call it a wild place, what with the Atlantic to one hand and peat bog to the other, but in each saddle between the headlands was evidence of some human intervention; an enclosure or a wall" (165). Furthermore, and whilst a place such as this might not be a "wilderness," since it reveals a long history of human involvement, its wildness is for Jamie real, and restorative: here, she writes, "language fails me" (164). "If we work always in words, sometimes we need to recuperate in a place where language doesn't join up, where we're thrown back on a few elementary nouns. Sea. Bird. Sky" (164). Were these words repeated, they might even make up a kind of incantation, but it is an integral part of Jamie's meaning that she does not do so: for Jamie, the *failure* of language to frame or contain these wild places reflects their vitality, their continuing independence.

Yet, Jamie also rejects the implication that her life away from these wild places is, to paraphrase Cronon's critique, otherwise corrupted or artificial (Cronon 80) or that there is no nature to be found in the midst of a supposedly "unnatural civilization" (Cronon 80). Many of the most moving sections in Jamie's essays relate to intimate and very human considerations: when Jamie retreats to the cliff-tops, for example, it is "to clear her head" (2005 164) after a series of family crises (involving old age and senility, illness, and accident) with which many readers will be familiar. There is nothing *un*natural about these incidents. Indeed, "nature" itself finds a way of creeping back into her life, "[b]etween the laundry and the fetching kids from school," as she writes in her essay on "Peregrines, Ospreys, Cranes" (Jamie 2005 39).

A reading of Jamie, therefore, leaves us with a sense of the wildness that survives even the (supposed) end of the wilderness and of the nature that circumvents humankind's impositions, even as that nature reminds us that we too are not—or not yet—entirely post-natural or post-human. In turn, Jamie's writing leads us to question whether wilderness is necessarily a space or place untouched by humankind, particularly when, as Garrard points out, "the ideal wilderness narrative posits a human subject whose most authentic existence is located precisely there" (78). Perhaps wilderness is itself a function of the wildness that Jamie also describes, a wildness that may be inherent in both our own natures and what we have become accustomed to calling "nature," a point that the British writer Jay Griffiths (born in 1965) raises in *Wild*.

Jay Griffiths: *Wild* (2006)

Wild is Jay Griffiths' second book and compared to *Findings* and *Feral*, it is the one that comes closest to ecopoesis as it is often defined, as a form of writing that is necessarily poetic, if not in itself poetry (Hume and Osborne 2–3). It is also concerned with the twofold sense of "wildness" identified by Jamie as a quality stubbornly knitted into our own being and present even in those landscapes that appear to have been managed, tamed, controlled, or subjugated by long human habitation. "In Looking for Wilderness," Griffiths explains, "I was not looking for miles of landscape to be nicely photographed and neatly framed, but for the quality of wildness, which—like art, sex, love, and all the other intoxicants—has a rising swing ringing through it" (Griffiths

1). "I was looking," she adds, "for the *will* of the wild. I was looking for how that will express itself in elemental vitality, in savage grace. Wildness is resolute for life: it cannot be otherwise" (Griffiths 1). That wildness also calls to Griffiths, in ways so emphatic that her book may usefully be read as a sustained response to this deep-rooted urge, as she seeks the objective correlative of "its urgent demand in the blood" (1). "I could hear its call," she writes in her lyrical opening paragraph:

> Its whistling disturbed me by day and its howl woke me in the night. I heard the drum of the sun. Every path was a calling cadence, the flight of every bird a beckoning, the colour of ice an invitation: come. The forest was a fiddler, wickedly good, eyes intense and shining with a fast dance. Every leaf in every breeze was a toe tapping out the same rhythm and every mountaintop lifting out of cloud intrigued my mind, for the wind at the peaks was a flautist, licking his lips, dangerously mesmerizing me ... This was the calling, the vehement, irresistible demand of the feral angel—*take flight.* (1)

This is not poetry, in the sense that it is not structured as verse, but with its use of alliteration ("the forest was a fiddler," "a toe tapping"), near-rhyme (the "drum of the sun"), alternating line lengths, and startling imagery ("the wind [as] flautist, licking his lips"), the passage is certainly poetic, even incantatory; it seems to carry the reader forward, propelling her or him with the same urgency that Griffiths herself feels. Moreover, the kind of language that Griffiths chooses is, here as throughout the book, deliberately intended to support her contention that the non-human world is never silent; we simply lack "the skills and experience" (31), as she elsewhere writes, to register its "luminous and tumultuous diversity" of languages (30). In turn, her own insistent personification of the non-human world, her imaginative evocation of its voices, and the urgent rhythms of her prose all reflect her desire not just to speak for but to carry across and communicate the wildness that she hears or, more exactly feels, deep in her being.

For those accustomed to Kathleen Jamie's restrained prose, Griffiths's impassioned rhetoric may come as something of a surprise. For some, this linguistic extravagance is unwelcome. In his review of *Wild*, Mark Cocker, who is himself a notable representative of the new nature writing in Britain, suggests that Griffiths's "prose necessitates a breathless high-altitude trek from peaks of great lucidity to troughs of repetition and hackneyed phrase" (Cocker). "One wonders," he adds, "why her editor didn't attempt to curb the excess or excise the duplication" (Cocker). A plausible reply is that Griffiths' rhetorical excess itself represents a "technique of defamiliarization," which similarly exists "to make one feel things" (Shklovsky 12). In other words, it is not (or not simply) the accidental by-product of Griffiths's own "exuberance," as Cocker suspects, but a device whose purpose is to challenge the reader's own linguistic horizons and the way those horizons limit what it is possible to think, see, and understand. As her opening passage makes immediately clear, challenging those horizons is integral to Griffiths's account of what constitutes "wildness."

Griffiths's book describes a seven-year odyssey inspired by her exasperation with the Euro-American tradition of writing about wilderness and constructing it as feminine and irrational (Griffiths 2006 41) without ever finding out about it from those who live there, "the Native or Indigenous people who have a different word for wilderness: home" (Griffiths 3). "To me, humanity is not a stain on wilderness as some seem to think. Rather, the human spirit is one of the most striking realizations of wildness" (Griffiths 4). Embarking on her own odyssey, Griffiths structures her elemental journey around the "four elements of ancient Greece, earth, air, fire, and water, but adding ice as if it were an element in its own right" (2); she traverses Amazonian rain forest (earth), West Papuan montane (air), the Australian outback (fire), and reaches an island off Sulawesi (water) before concluding her journey in the Canadian Arctic (ice). Throughout, Griffiths immerses herself in Indigenous culture, searching out "the quintessential coupling of wildness with life" (Griffiths 3). As Griffiths discovers, the lives and livelihoods of many of the Indigenous peoples she meets are under threat from the same kind of "ecological imperialism" (Garrard 133) that transformed North America's biota and decimated its Native American population during the years of European settler expansion (Garrard 132–133; Griffiths 95). Today, Griffiths argues, these threats take forms as various as mining, logging, and bioprospecting, or simply missionary efforts to impose alien ways of thinking. Many of these threats derive their supposed legitimacy from the assumption that "wilderness" is, in fact, "wasteland" awaiting improvement, or that indigenous homelands are, in fact, unpeopled, or that indigenous peoples are, in fact, uncultured (Griffiths 93); and yet, as Griffiths remarks of her experience in the Amazon, "the assault against nature is an assault against culture, hundreds of tribal cultures" (Griffiths 94). It is, in effect, the erasure of long-standing patterns of integrated human existence within a wider, non-human world and an assault on forms of dwelling whose sustainability is self-evident from their persistence over time.

Griffiths' emphasis on the distinctiveness, depth, and variety of tribal cultures underlines her belief in the importance of what anthropologists have termed Traditional Ecological Knowledge (TEK), cumulatively and locally acquired, often over generations (Berkes 1–2). Knowledge such as this points to the possibility of a more reciprocal and sustainable relationship with the more-than-human world. For this reason, and as Garrard points out, many deep ecologists and ecocritics have taken a keen interest in indigenous ways of life as exemplary forms of sustainable existence (Garrard 129). Garrard adds that "indigenous environmental virtue" (129) is usually linked not to a lack of modern technology or "low population densities" but to "animistic belief systems" (130), and it is noteworthy that Griffiths is herself deeply responsive to this aspect of Indigenous existence. Griffiths talks at length about the limitations of Western ways of knowing—a point elsewhere raised by Linda Hogan (3–4)—and, by contrast, the "telluric [earth-related] thought" of Indigenes who have learned to extend "their minds by learning from the minds of other creatures" (Griffiths 16). In turn, Griffiths writes about the allusive, elusive language that Indigenes have developed alongside "a whole way of knowing" (29). "In the Amazon," Griffiths notes, "people refer to the forest as a speaking world, relating, talking and communicating" (30). It is noteworthy that recent studies by writers such as Frans de Waal frankly acknowledge the historical tendency in Western science to "downplay animal intelligence" (3). De Waal adds that there is now a virtual "avalanche" of new evidence to suggest that "human cognition" is simply "a variety of animal cognition" and not, therefore, distinct from it (2016 4–5). As Peter Wohlleben adds, Western science is only now recognizing the extent to which forests constitute complex communities in which trees communicate and cooperate (7-9). Dualisms such as "nature" and "culture" are increasingly untenable, notes Philippe Descola, and "[m]any so-called primitive societies invite us to overstep that demarcation line" (xix). The work of anthropologist Eduardo Kohn is a relevant case in point: his own experiences amongst the Runa people of the Upper Amazon prompted his recognition that "seeing, representing, and perhaps knowing, even thinking, are not exclusively human affairs" (1), prompting him to reconceptualize the forest as "an 'ecology of selves'" (16) which is 'thus "animate" [and] also "enchanted"' (16). As Hogan remarks, "there are many other intelligences all around us" (2).

Rich in what they are and have, adds Griffiths (84), Amazonian people therefore "live in a landscape of meaningful social interaction between themselves and animals, characterized by reciprocity, restraint and respect" (68). It is a way of life at odds with Western enclosures and appropriations, of which the city and city life is itself a symbol (41). For forest people, she observes, home is the forest (68), not some walled and windowed imposition on it. They are simply interdependent with, inseparable from, and "inter-intelligent with their lands" (30).

Whether or not Griffiths attains this level of understanding—a state of grace that might enable her to interleave her own existence seamlessly with that of the animate world about her—is, perhaps, a moot point. Describing one trek into the rainforest, she describes the onslaught of ants, flies, and mosquitoes (Griffiths 48) and the impossibility of writing a word without being subjected to an insect attack. "I would," she observes, "write my notes in almost complete darkness, for the light of a torch would attract a thousand moths. A guide saw my difficulty and caught a firefly for me, gently looping a thin thread around its body and tying it to the tip of my pen so it glowed its gentle green light on my notebook" (49). It is a perfectly observed moment, and also a captivating, even enchanting one, which firmly underlines the close relationship between her guide and the non-human world; yet it also underlines Griffiths' own status as an outsider, for whom the intimate understanding of the indigenes must itself be captured and put down. When her guide ties the firefly to her pen, he does so without words, unaware that this moment—to him so unremarkable—will seem enchanting to the disenchanted; in this moment, language is itself unnecessary and a symptom only of Griffiths' own alienation.

Whilst a moment such as this seems to set Griffiths at a distance from the world she describes, she is nevertheless fiercely protective of that world and deeply contemptuous of those who would destroy it. She is particularly scornful of the missionaries who, she contends, seek to undermine indigenous intimacy with the non-human (Griffiths 77–8). But, claims Griffiths, missionaries do much more than this (81–90). Their contact with undiscovered peoples brings disease (75); they "willingly grease the path for logging and oil companies" (74); they extend the whole apparatus of Western life. "The spread of missionary activity is, in fact, the spread of capitalism" (87).

Griffith also stresses the fragility as well as the strength of a symbiotic relationship between indigenous people and place (Griffiths 90). It is, she explains, a co-dependency. When their lands are taken from indigenous people, so is the language "that arises in the interplay of mind and nature" (30). As we have seen, her own writing is an attempt to test the limits of English usage and, in so doing, capture something of what this interplay might mean, even at the cost of overwhelming the reader with its linguistic inventiveness, its emotionality, and its repetitions. But as Griffiths' own acts of ecopoesis suggest to the attentive reader, the challenge of finding a linguistic correlation for these conversations with the non-human world seems insurmountable only because we have also lost our sense of language as a function of lived experience. "All languages," she writes, "have aspired to echo the wild world that gave them growth" (29), and her impassioned prose and elevated tone reflect her desire not only to offer her own "echo-poetics,"[1] but to remind us that languages have their own roots in the embodied experience of ecological rootedness. Words and ideas emerge in relation to this embodiment, shaped and influenced by the need to communicate the practicalities of an existence firmly situated in place. Still more significantly, and as Griffiths' work announces from the outset (see above), that world itself seems to speak a truth that is both literal (the soundscape is constantly shifting, and its shifts speak of what is happening, from a tree-fall in the jungle to the tell-tale creak of sea-ice) and metaphorical (an understanding and an involvement so intimate and complete that it may indeed feel like a conversation). The corollary, as Griffiths also suggests, is that a terrible kind of silence descends on those who, after generations of this kind of lived existence, are suddenly deprived of it: "[t]o lose your land is to lose your language, and to lose your language is to lose your mind…" (30). Her descriptions of the slum towns that have sprung up along the fringes of the Amazon underline the horror of what she is describing: "a hideous wasteland" (40) that is psychic and spiritual as well as literal and physical (39–40; 88). It is a blunt reminder of the realities of language loss and of the full impact of losing one's place, dimensions of lived experience that are easily forgotten when Indigenous communities are displaced from their homes and homelands.

George Monbiot: *Feral* (2013)

Writer, journalist, and environmental activist George Monbiot (born 1963) shares Griffiths' view that the earth has been ransacked and its Indigenes all too often marginalized or brutalized. His book, *Feral*, opens with a first-person account of "the devastated land" (Monbiot 1) created by mining activity in the Amazon circa 1990 and the resulting "physical and cultural collapse" of Indigenous communities (3). A further point of contact between the two writers lies in a shared belief that "the dulled televisual torpor of mediated living" (Griffiths 5) is itself a root of the developed world's disenchantment. This is an increasingly mainstream argument. Worldwide, there is growing evidence that contact with nature and the natural—an immersion, even if only temporary, in green space—is somehow necessary for human wellbeing, a finding that seems to carry across socio-economic, gender, and cultural divides (Williams). For Griffiths, therefore, the problem is simply defined: "I was, in fact, homesick for wildness" (2). "We may think we are domesticated," she adds, "but we are not" (2). For Monbiot, this is itself a starting point: struck by the "smallness" of his life in rural Wales (5), he recognizes that he is "ecologically bored" (7). "We still possess the fear, the courage, the aggression which evolved to see us through our quests and crises," he writes, but our lives of necessary "restraint and sublimation" deny us the chance to use them (6–7). However, Monbiot also notes that he has "already lived beyond the lifespan of most hunter-gatherers:" "[w]ithout farming, sanitation, vaccination, antibiotics, surgery and optometry I would be dead by now" (7). Monbiot, therefore, sets himself on the challenge of escaping this "ecological boredom" without renouncing modernity in its entirety. In so doing, Monbiot engages head-on with the question that haunts environmentally aware nature writing such as his own: whether it will encourage readers to change the way they live and, in so doing, curb the excesses of capitalism, or simply substitute a fantasy of "nature" that is itself a form of compensation for what has been lost.

This is a point that leading writers in the field have repeatedly discussed. As Robert Macfarlane has argued, the problem is threefold. Firstly, readers of new nature writing in Britain are often more or less sympathetic to environmentalist arguments; as Macfarlane adds, it is a case of the converted speaking to the converted (Macfarlane 2009). Secondly, it may be somewhat optimistic to believe that "the glittering argument or stylistic turn ... will produce an epiphany in skeptical readers" (Macfarlane 2009). Thirdly, some readers "have long specialised in a disconnect between their nature romance and their behaviour as consumers" (Macfarlane 2005): "[m]any of those who diligently fill their bird-feeders drive to work in a 4x4" (Macfarlane 2005). If, as Macfarlane adds (2005), "[t]he problem is a failure of connection," the question, in turn, becomes, "what to do?"

Feral proposes an answer. Originally subtitled *Searching for Enchantment on the Frontiers of Rewilding* (2013), *Feral* outlines a practical approach to the mass restoration of ecosystems and highlights the ways in which, even in the densely-populated islands of the United Kingdom, it might still be possible to undo an elaborately constructed "landscape," and return it to something more inspiring than the artifice of a pastoral monopolized (and made possible) by the sheep Monbiot so pithily dismisses as "a white plague" (Monbiot 155). Invoking the principle of "trophic cascades," Monbiot argues that the reintroduction of key "predators and large herbivores can transform the places in which they live" (9). His aim is not, he stresses, to reconstruct the past but "to permit ecological processes to resume" and, by re-involving humans in it, to rewild human life (8–10). What is at stake, therefore, is a positive but also inclusive environmentalism that goes far beyond the "abstraction we call Nature" (12–13).

So where, exactly, are we to put all these wolves, lynx, wolverines, beavers, boar, bison, and (one day) elephants (Monbiot 11)? As Monbiot points out, the uplands of Wales are an ecological desert created and monopolized by sheep. Yet subsidized sheep farming ("a slow-burning ecological disaster") makes little economic sense (158). By contrast, a self-willed habitat would offer everyone an opportunity "to escape from ecological boredom;" it would, Monbiot argues, pay for itself with a new form of adventure tourism (178–179). The same case, he argues, can be made for the Scottish Highlands, where a handful of absentee landlords impose a habitat dominated by deer with the sole aim of ensuring that those so inclined amongst the very rich have something to hunt. The Highlands constitute a monoculture which, as Monbiot points out, prevents both ecological and economic regeneration (102). These uplands are in every sense impoverished, a pattern repeated across the United Kingdom.

Although Monbiot takes care to make economic sense of his rewilding proposals (178), their wider political ramifications are explored in little detail; even sympathetic critics have called Monbiot's proposals "a fantasy, a feat of science fiction" (Hoare). The problems are various: the rights of landowners appear to be inviolable; farmers are themselves conservative and resistant to change; many people have become profoundly attached to the rolling green uplands created by overgrazing. In particular, Monbiot's project assumes a *collective* political will that is largely absent from the British political stage. But as Monbiot stresses, we can hardly gainsay the enthusiasm numerous Britons feel for wildlife and wildness, as the work of Jamie and Griffiths also attests. Like a "genetic memory" (Monbiot 2013 34), something "resonates" (11).

Nonetheless, a project that seeks to restore "a more authentic relation to nature" (Heise 508) may itself be dismissed as a paradoxical expression of the alienation and reification that follows from modernism (Harvey 301–2). For it to have any meaning, the connection this kind of rewilding creates must be of an order sufficiently total and intense to rewrite the rules of life for those exposed to it. There is no room here for tidy notions of a tamed and compliant "Nature," set at a safe distance implied by the concept of adventure tourism. The broader point, as Timothy Morton and others have argued, is that cherished notions of "Nature" must themselves "wither away in an 'ecological' state of human society" (Morton 1). The "ecological imaginary" (Morton 1) must itself make a conscious move away from its emphasis on a distinct and separate "Nature."

Consequently, a project such as Monbiot's would, to be meaningful, necessitate a different kind of writing about the world in which we live. That need not mean the end of the "new nature writing," whose newness might, after all, inhere in its refusal to set nature (our own or non-human) apart from us: as Jason Cowley remarked, in the *Granta* edition of 2008, "[a]t present, the human animal lives in but often strives to be apart from nature" (12). Work like Jamie's both reflects and respects the manifold intersections of the human and non-human, as Deborah Lilley notes (25). Moreover, Griffiths' startling and intense use of language—or language as "echo-poetics"—is itself a template for an immersive language analogous to Monbiot's ferality, a language capable, in short, of reminding us of the wildness at work in the world, and of the enchantment, we have forgotten or so often overlook.

We might nevertheless strike a cautionary note over the impact, if any, of words themselves. Engaging and as enchanting as the new nature writing might be, it is questionable whether it can convert an indifferent majority to what remains a minority point of view; it might also be asked, apropos of

Monbiot's scheme, whether rescuing the affluent few from their ecological boredom can ever be enough to rescue a polluted world whose support systems (such as a viable climate) are under increasing pressure from humankind. It may be argued, after all, that the global spread of an industrialized, capitalistic society—and the neoliberal philosophy that underpins its latest and most virulent manifestation—lies beyond any form of intervention or control. Indeed, and whilst it is the affluent who bear the greatest responsibility for environmental depletion and degradation, their way of life has become the model to which the whole world, rich and poor, now aspires. It would be more accurate to say that neoliberalism has increasingly succeeded in making everyone complicit in its spread. But this is itself a reminder that we all have a role in deciding the future direction of society, as new social movements from the Confederation Paysanne to the Trade Justice Movement or Via Campesina are intent on reminding us. What we have made can be remade and remade through the percussive effect of individual choices. In this light, it is perhaps more obvious what these three very different works have to offer: in their very different ways, each plays a role in persuading the reader to join a broader societal shift towards a more sustainable way of life that revels in and relishes the world's continuing wildness.

Conclusion

As these three works suggest, the new British nature writing is, in fact, characterized by its cosmopolitanism rather than its parochialism, and by its diversity rather than its uniformity: in *Findings*, Jamie is focused on rewriting what is meant *by* "nature writing;" in *Feral*, Monbiot makes his case for new ways of living in our post-modern here-and-now that resituates us within and reconnects with us those vital ecological relationships; and in *Wild*, Griffiths writes not of Britain, but of worlds in which entirely different ways of living persist in the midst of a "nature" that refuses to be a mere backdrop to human activities of which it is and always be a part. More importantly, given its relevance to the volume of which this chapter forms just a small part, all three writers are engaged in *ecopoesis*, as an act of making that relates directly to the ecological relationships with which humankind is invariably entangled: all three use language as a means of clearing a space within which it becomes possible for the reader to pause and reconsider the nature of those relationships, and in so doing, recognize that they are integral to her or his being. In turn, it becomes clear that, since we are inseparable from those relationships, a concept of external "nature" is itself symptomatic of a kind of shared forgetfulness of that inseparability; no matter how or where we live, our relationship with place demands we take responsibility for its wider consequences.

Whilst this is a shared theme that quietly connects all three works, each writer uses language in a different fashion. Jamie's work is centrally concerned with the way in which what we externalize as "nature" in fact forms part of the quotidian, the everyday, just as human activities have long left their mark on that "nature"; her prose is often interrupted by poetic metaphors that force the reader to pause, re-evaluate what is being described, and in turn, reconsider their own relationships to the subject matter. Monbiot is a journalist; his métier is a persuasive argument, but in *Feral*, that argument is interrupted by interludes in which he describes his own acts of belonging and becoming within a more-than-human world, momentary *longueurs* that both exemplify what might be meant by dwelling, and prompt the reader to revisit their own experiences, their own attitudes, their own ecological relationships. Griffith's work is, perhaps, much closer to a definition of ecopoesis as writing concerned with re-enchanting the world, speaking for all those who dwell within it, and singing with those whose lives are still (even now, in the Anthropocene) closely and intimately involved in and speak with the non-human community. In Griffiths' work, there is less sense that words and language are what set us apart from and may sometimes conspire to keep us from recognizing our ecological relationships; rather, the passionate excess of her work is intended to correspond with—perhaps even embody as well as communicate—the wild life (or language) that she hears around her and she feels coursing through her. Nevertheless, all three works testify to the same impulse: in a post-modern world that offers an increasingly abstract and disembodied mode of existence, it is essential to remind ourselves of the vital but also enchanting wildness that still exists within us and within the world of which we form a part. As such, all three books form part of the same programmatic insistence on a rewilding of our perspective, just as all three constitute a sustained (and sometimes noisy!) demand that readers think critically about what it is to dwell meaningfully and, therefore, sustainably on this earth.

Notes

[1] I am indebted to Bénédicte Meillon for suggesting the term "echo-poetics," and for drawing attention to the incantatory dimensions of the prose with which I am here concerned.

Works cited

Berkes, Fikret. "Traditional Ecological Knowledge in Perspective." *Traditional Ecological Knowledge: Concepts and Cases*, edited by Julian T. Inglis, Ottawa: Canadian Museum of Nature/ International Program on Traditional Ecological Knowledge / International Development Research Centre, 1993, pp. 1–10.

Cocker, Mark. "Where the wild things are." *The Guardian*, June 9, 2007. https://www.theguardian.com/books/2007/jun/09/featuresreviews.guardia nreview7.

Cowley, Jason. "Editor's Letter." *Granta: The New Nature Writing*, n°102, 2008, pp. 7–12.

Cronon, William. "The trouble with wilderness: or, getting back to the wrong nature." *Uncommon Ground: Rethinking the Human Place in Nature*, edited by William Cronon, London: Norton, 1996, pp. 69–90.

Descola, Philippe. *Beyond Nature and Culture*. Translated by Janet Lloyd, London: University of Chicago Press, 2013.

Garrard, Greg. *Ecocriticism*. Abingdon: Routledge, 2012.

Griffiths, Jay. *Wild: An Elemental Journey*. London: Penguin, 2006.

Harvey, David. *Justice, Nature, and the Geography of Difference*. Oxford: Blackwell, 1996.

Heise, Ursula. "The Hitchhiker's Guide to Ecocriticism." *PMLA*, n°121 (2), 2006, pp. 502–516.

Hoare, Philip. "*Feral* by George Monbiot." Review of *Feral*, by George Monbiot. *The Guardian*, May 28, 2013. http://www.telegraph.co.uk/culture/books/scie nceandnaturebookreviews/10077216/Feral-by-George-Monbiot-review.html.

Hogan, Linda. "Writer's Interview." Interview. *Dwellings of Enchantment: Writing and Reenchanting the Earth*, International Conference on Ecopoetics, Perpignan, 22–25 June 2016. ecopoeticsperpignan.com/wp-content/uploa ds/2016/08/Linda-Hogan-Writers-interview.pdf.

Hume, Angela, and Gillian Osborne, eds. *Ecopoetics: Essays in the Field*. Iowa City: University of Iowa Press, 2018.

Jamie, Kathleen. "A Lone Enraptured Male." Review of *The Wild Places*, by Robert Macfarlane. *The London Review of Books*, n°30 (5), 2008, pp. 25–27.

—. *Findings*. London: Sort of Books, 2005.

—. *Sightlines*. London: Sort of Books, 2012.

Kohn, Eduardo. *How Forests Think: Towards an Anthropology Beyond the Human*. Berkeley, CA: University of California Press, 2013.

Lilley, Deborah. "Kathleen Jamie: rethinking the externality and idealisation of nature." *Green Letters: Studies in Ecocriticism*, n°17 (1), 2013, pp. 16–26.

Macfarlane, Robert. "Rereading: Robert Macfarlane on *The Monkey Wrench Gang*." *The Guardian*, September 26, 2009. https://www.theguardian.com/ books/2009/sep/26/robert-macfarlane-monkey-wrench-gang.

—. "Where the wild things were." *The Guardian*, July 30, 2005. https://www. theguardian.com/books/2005/jul/30/featuresreviews.guardianreview22.

McKibben, Bill. *The End of Nature*. London: Penguin, 1990.

Monbiot, George. *Feral: Rewilding the land, sea and human life*. London: Penguin, 2013.

Morton, Timothy. *Ecology without Nature: Rethinking Environmental Aesthetics*. London: Harvard University Press, 2007.

Shklovsky, Victor. "Art as Technique." *Russian Formalist Criticism: Four Essays*, translated and introduced by Lee T. Lemon and Marion J. Reis, London: University of Nebraska Press, 1965, pp. 3–24.

Stenning, Anna, and Terry Gifford. "Introduction (Twentieth-century nature writing in Britain and Ireland)." *Green Letters: Studies in Ecocriticism,* n°17 (1), 2013, pp. 1–4.

Waal, Frans de. *Are We Smart Enough to Know How Smart Animals Are?* London: Granta, 2016.

Williams, Florence. "This Is Your Brain on Nature." *National Geographic,* n°229 (1), 2016, pp. 48–69.

Wohlleben, Peter. *The Hidden Life of Trees: What They Feel, How They Communicate: Discoveries from a Secret World.* London: William Collins, 2015.

Chapter 12

Trauma and Ecological Re-alignment in Gretel Ehrlich's *A Match to the Heart*

Wes Berry

Western Kentucky University, USA

Abstract: In the medical memoir *A Match to the Heart*, lightning strike survivor Gretel Erhlich describes how trauma alienates her from the Wyoming landscape she'd lived in for many years and her subsequent attempts to seek refuge in places like coastal California. Erhlich's frenetic traveling takes her to several territories in the United States, where she searches for a place conducive to healing and describes the landscapes of those places with the eye of the nature writer. Her artful reversals of metaphor—using the language of land/nature/wilderness to describe the interiority of the human body—break down the conventional boundaries between "humans" and "environment," revealing that the body is a bioregion, a complex ecosystem within broader ecosystems. Ehrlich's language acrobatics mark her memoir as a unique contribution to the genre of environmental nonfiction dealing with the human body, sickness and healing, and interior/exterior landscapes.

Keywords: bioregional, body, ecopsychology, healing, memoir, medical literature, landscape, mental health, metaphor, place, poetics, trauma

***

It is presence, the being present, that is the important part of enchantment.

–Linda Hogan

At times […] landscape and human destiny are one. I am fascinated with how the landscape a person lives in affects him or her psychologically.

–Ron Rash

To be 'home' is first to inhabit one's own body.

–Deborah Slicer

Trauma can alienate a person from her own body, from other humans, and from the landscapes she inhabits. At the same time, a traumatic experience can bring a person into an increasingly intimate relationship with these landscapes. Such paradoxical responses to "the world" (call it "physical landscapes," "nature," the "more-than-human," or whatever term to indicate this still-rich world of organic material) by people experiencing trauma are explored in several contemporary memoirs. To varying degrees, authors experiment with language to establish links between the human body and exterior landscapes. In *Because I Remember Terror, Father, I Remember You*, Sue William Silverman discloses how the sexual abuse she suffered during childhood causes her to hate her own body while drawing her into a closer relationship with what she calls "nature," including rocks, birds, and the winds that touch her. "Nature" becomes, for Silverman, a vehicle of disembodiment; by projecting her imagination into elements of the exterior landscape, she distances herself from the sexual assaults by her father. In the memoir *Refuge*, Terry Tempest Williams explains how experiencing her mother's slow decline from ovarian cancer prompts the author to frequently visit the Bear River Migratory Bird Refuge north of Salt Lake City. The dual encounters with the dying mother and the endangered bird refuge, which is disappearing under the rising lake waters, teach Williams how to cope with loss by accepting systemic flux. She writes: "I could not separate the Bird Refuge from my family. Devastation respects no boundaries. The landscape of my childhood and the landscape of my family, the two things I had always regarded as bedrock, were now subject to change" (Williams 1991 40). In a similar vein, Philip Lee Williams, in his memoir *Crossing Wildcat Ridge*, details how undergoing heart surgery leads him to a more intimate relationship with his own body and also with the wildlife that lives around his home in north Georgia. These works of creative nonfiction blend ecological science, knowledge of Western medicine, and devotional language to show how particular dwellings are conducive to healing. Writing in a kindred genre but employing some tricky poetic acrobatics in reversals of conventional landscape metaphors, Gretel Ehrlich, in her ecological-medical memoir *A Match to the Heart*, explores how getting struck by lightning takes her on a journey into the "organscape" of her body—an enchanted dwelling intimately dependent on external landscapes for her well being.

To varying degrees, these writers explore links between their own bodies and the external landscapes they inhabit. In Silverman's memoir, exterior landscapes are the "other" that enables an imaginative separation from her body. She draws a clear distinction between body and landscape. Terry Tempest Williams, on the other hand, emphasizes links between the body and exterior landscape; she writes of a mother's body as a type of ur-landscape:

> What is it about the relationship of a mother that can heal or hurt us? Her womb is the first landscape we inhabit. It is here we learn to respond—to move, to listen, to be nourished and grow. In her body we grow to be human as our tails disappear and our gills turn to lungs. Our maternal environment is perfectly safe—dark, warm, and wet. It is a residency inside the Feminine. (Williams 1991 50)

Philip Lee Williams, however, approaches the forests and streams of North Georgia with a scientific, matter-of-fact attitude. Whereas Terry Tempest Williams appears eager to seek meaning in more-than-human nature, Philip Lee Williams displays an ironic skepticism. He marvels at the "beauty and purpose" of shelf fungi but maintains a critical distance in his contemplations. "If they look like ears, they also seem like labia, which I instantly and ridiculously relate to Mother Earth. Perhaps everything means more than itself, but I rarely demand that of the world. In its variety and delight, it can be only a shelf fungus. That's enough most of the time" (Williams 1999 101). The descriptions of human anatomy in *Crossing Wildcat Ridge* are comparably clinical, as Williams outlines the procedure of heart catheterization with scientific terms and a few metaphors, as when he calls the heart a "glorious engine" (40). We have scientific terms for the human body and customary terms for descriptions of "nature," and Williams seldom confuses the two.

A Match to the Heart, on the other hand, frequently mixes customary descriptions of "body" and "nature." The text is an investigation of what environmental philosopher Deborah Slicer calls "The Body as Bioregion." When talking about land issues, proponents of *bioregionalism* urge making land use policies based on the particular ecological requirements of particular places rather than on arbitrary political boundaries "to address matters of pressing environmental concern through a politics derived from a local sense of place" and "moving away from existing but for the most part arbitrary political boundaries (nations, states, counties, cities, etc.) in favor of those that emerged from a biotically determined framework, primarily based on natural communities or watersheds" (Lynch, Glotfelty, Armbruster 2-3). In *LifePlace: Bioregional Thought and Practice*, Robert L. Thayer Jr.'s definition speaks to the life support systems and ecological interconnectedness embedded in the term *bioregion*:

A bioregion is literally and etymologically a "life-place"—a unique region definable by natural (rather than political) boundaries with a geographic, climatic, hydrological, and ecological character capable of supporting unique human communities. Bioregions can be variously defined by the geography of watersheds, similar plant and animal ecosystems, and related, identifiable landforms (e.g., particular mountain ranges, prairies, or coastal zones) and by the unique human cultures that grow from natural limits and potentials of the region. (Thayer 3)

In "The Body as Bioregion," Deborah Slicer takes the hyper-local focus of bioregional thinking and applies it to the human body, reinforcing the idea that the interior "landscapes" of the body are complex ecosystems, our primary life-place:

The only bioregion that we can claim strict identity with is the body. A human body is sixty electrical jolts a minute, at rest; twenty-five feet of gut, containing a virtual hothouse of microbes, each with its own diet; ninety square yards of alveoli, all performing the elegant exchange of oxygen and carbon; a mind that blips continuously up and down an eighteen-inch rope of salty brain-stuff the thickness of a man's finger. To be 'home' is first to inhabit one's own body. We are each, as body, a biological ecosystem as complex, efficient, and as fragile as the Brooks Range, the Everglades, a native prairie. (Slicer 113)

Gretel Ehrlich's metaphor mixing in *A Match to the Heart* helps establish links between the landscape of an individual body and the expansive landscapes of earth and sky. Her difficult search for a dwelling conducive to healing speaks to a fundamental tenet of ecopsychology: place matters to mental health and, of course, to the well-being of other bodily systems.

No Rest for the Weary: Post-Traumatic Alienation from Place

Ehrlich's narrative begins with an occasion of wounding. After she is blasted unconscious by a direct lightning strike, she regains enough of her senses to rise to her feet. The earth is distorted, feeling under her feet "like a peach that had split open in the middle; one side moved up while the other side moved down and my legs were out of rhythm" (Ehrlich 1994 8). Her mind is addled. "I struggled to piece together fragments. Then it occurred to me that my brain was torn and that's where the blood had come from" (9). Ehrlich fortifies her narrative with the language of science. The electricity from the lightning resulted in ventricular fibrillation (cardiac arrest). She lists the damage to her body. Being "flung far" by the strike, she sustains "a concussion, broken ribs, a possible broken jaw, and lacerations above the eye"; paralysis below the waist and in her chest and throat; and "fernlike burns" covering her entire body (12). In the days following the strike, symptoms worsen: "As I lay on my back with my feet up, the world grew black and a deadly lethargy filled me so that I could not move or talk. Chest pains, both sharp and piercing as well as deep and aching, with the classic heart attack symptoms—clamminess, shortness of breath, pains down the left arm—kept me awake all night" (18). Feeling she is dying in her ranch house in Wyoming, Ehrlich relocates to her childhood home in California. This return is the first of several moves Ehrlich describes throughout her memoir as she seeks landscapes conducive to healing at various stages of recovery.

Ehrlich remembers the moment of regaining consciousness after the lightning strike as a dream, which she describes in impressionist language in the opening paragraph of *A Match to the Heart*: "Deep in an ocean. I am suspended motionless. The water is gray. That's all there is, and before that? My arms are held out straight, cruciate, my head and legs hang limp" (3). Ehrlich reads significance into her dream and vows to move to where she can expose herself to an oceanic landscape: "In my coming-back-to-life dream I had been crucified and suspended in the ocean. That's why, now, I wanted to live at the water's edge. Here, I would surrender to whatever swam through me: death nailed to life. Here, I would be restored" (65). The gesture is erotic, surrendering to a place as if to a lover. Following her intuitions, Ehrlich moves into a new abode, a beach house in Santa Barbara, after being released from the hospital. "Water puts out fire," she writes. "The restoration of my health depended on it. If I stopped following fire, simply stopped, perhaps fire would stop erupting all around me" (64). Ehrlich is suggesting here that she has "followed fire" in her hectic traveling lifestyle, and that perhaps settling near water—allowing peace to enter into her life by staying put and assimilating the rhythms of the shore—will help quench the fire. The lightning strike was just one of several encounters with fire Ehrlich experienced over a six-month period. First, a plane caught fire on a runway in Denver, and when Ehrlich leapt to the ground from the stairs, a fire engine nearly ran over her. A month later, the lobby of a hotel in Dallas "burst into flames" as Ehrlich entered. Soon after that incident, she was sent scrambling from a London tube, fleeing the threat of a bomb blast. A month later, a spruce forest erupted in Fairbanks as her plane landed. As a Japanese farmer-monk explains to Ehrlich, she has been "following fire" (28). In settling by the world's largest body of water, she hopes to reverse the process.

The survivor's slow process of healing and ecological re-alignment with a dwelling place takes place in this coastal California section. As her body strengthens, Ehrlich begins taking daily walks up and down the edge of the sea with her dog Sam. The house by the sea serves as her "refuge" and the sea as her "restoration" (106). Ehrlich learns from the sea that balance comes from flux (recalling Terry Tempest Williams learning from the disappearing bird refuge to accept death as part of life's regenerative process). From the sea, Ehrlich takes comfort in change. A storm assaults the coastline with huge waves that remove five vertical feet of sand; but a week after the storm, sand-bearing waves begin to replenish the deficit: "The coastline kept reforming itself—revising drafts of how it should be shaped, how many rocks, how deep the sand" (105), she writes, testifying to the miracles of the ecological patterns in this place.

Furthermore, literally immersing the body into an aqueous solution can have a soothing effect on one's physiology. Terry Tempest Williams explores this phenomenon in the "Water" section of *Desert Quartet*, her erotic poetics of landscape. In the depths of the Grand Canyon, Williams swims nude at an hour past dawn. She floats on her back and allows the water of Havasu to caress her:

> I dissolve. I am water. Only my face is exposed like an apparition over ripples. Playing with water. Do I dare? My legs open. The rushing water turns my body and touches me with a fast finger that does not tire. I receive without apology. Time. Nothing to rush, only to feel. I feel time in me. It is endless pleasure in the current. No control. No thought. Simply, here. My left hand reaches for the frog dangling from my neck, floating above my belly and I hold it between my breasts like a withered heart, beating inside me, inside the river. We are moving downstream. Water. Water music. Blue notes, white notes, my body mixes with the body of water like jazz, the currents like jazz. I too am free to improvise. (Williams 1995 23–24)

The skeptical reader might call this passage contrived—a piece of desired mysticism using overblown metaphor and similes—but if we take the author at her word, she's trying to explain a revitalizing experience. "Desire begins in wetness," Williams writes. "We are baptized by immersion, nothing less can replenish or restore our capacity to love. It is endless if we believe in water" (28).

Ehrlich too tests the restorative properties of water. Dwelling at the edge of the continent with the Pacific Ocean stretching before her—myriad intelligences lurking beneath its surface—Ehrlich is moved to ponder the fabulous intelligence beneath the surface of her skin (her first bioregion). She spends hours watching the ocean, and her observations lead her back into the body, into the brain—the "body within a body" (Ehrlich 1994 69). Her poetics of body processes mirror the exterior landscape of the Pacific coast, taking on the language of sea and shore. Ehrlich likens the synaptic gaps of the brain to a lake, the River Styx, and a sea, with the sea metaphors most prominent. The brain, she poeticizes, is like an ocean:

> Bodies of thoughts swim in the synaptic lake, sliding over receptors, reaching for the ones that live on the other shore. An interval of between 0.5 and 1 millisecond transpires before an impulse makes its way across the gap, as in the bardo where we pause between life and death, treading water in the oblivion of a gray sea [...]. Thoughts are swimmers that leap, arch, loop, wheel, dive, or dog-paddle in the synaptic gap, the body of water that is like the sea at the beginning of all things, the sea without light [...]. perhaps the body is maritime and the act of making memory is natatory—a continuous breaststroke though [sic] a fast current of electrochemical impulses, and the gap, like any sea, is a form constantly undoing itself into a formlessness that rises into shapes through which we can swim. (Ehrlich 1994 70–2)

Ehrlich's "nature writing" in this unusual memoir deals as much with the human body as with the external environments a body lives in. Interior/exterior landscapes are blurred and merged, a poetic modeling of wholeness that moves away from the unfortunate dualistic thinking—like seeing the body as separate from the soul, or the human as separate from nature as the word "environment" suggests (that which "environs" is seemingly outside the human)—that's contributed to our ecological crisis.

While Ehrlich's explorations of her health conditions and the potential harm or healing power of particular landscapes may not satisfy the skeptical, scientific mind, she builds readerly trust by rarely forcing conceits. Consider, for instance, her complex portrayal of spring. She is forced to move from her first coastal residence when the owner of it decides to return, and she moves back into the world of people—still on the coastline, but in a residential neighborhood rather than on the "lonely beach." With the coming of spring, Ehrlich gets a boost of energy. Thoreau ends *Walden* [1854] in spring with typical poetic flourish: "As every season seems best to us in its turn, so the coming in of spring is like the creation of Cosmos out of Chaos and the realization of the Golden Age" (Thoreau 208). Ehrlich's spring, however, brings both new enthusiasms—she begins to dream again after six months of blank nights—and health problems. She loses consciousness easily and suffers a painful knot in her chest. She feels lonely, cut off from people, and consequently is haunted by the sensuousness of the sea: "I groped in darkness and found I was bound to no one, by no one, and possessed no means of reproducing myself. It was hard to hold my head up, and the air around me seemed dark. The sea was a cauldron of passion and intimacy, which I hated that week. How maddening water's fluency was as I lay transfixed by dead brain cells" (Ehrlich 1994 115). In this scenario, Ehrlich's interior landscape shapes her perceptions of the exterior landscape. Because of her deteriorating physical condition, spring for her is no Golden Age, as she cannot participate fully in its pleasures.

Ehrlich's fickleness towards finding a place to live is surprising when viewed in the context of her book *The Solace of Open Spaces*, published a decade earlier. In that text, Ehrlich describes a similar sense of rootlessness and restlessness—a loss of enchantment, perhaps, experienced by many who lack attachment to particular places. In an attempt to reverse this feeling in her life, Ehrlich moves from urban California to Wyoming, where she works on ranches for the next seventeen years. There is a "ceremonial" feel to ranch life. "It's raw and impulsive but the narrative thread of birth, death, chores, and seasons keeps tugging at us until we find ourselves braided inextricably into the strand" (Ehrlich 1985 103). She goes on to explain a national sense of being cut off from this continuity: "We live in a culture that has lost its memory. Very little in the specific shapes and traditions of our grandparents' pasts instructs us how to live today, or tells us who we are or what demands will be made on us as members of society" (103). She writes of her generation's "shrill estrangement" from the past, how "we want to join up, but it's difficult to know how or where." Her feelings of loss stemming from this cultural discontinuity are similar to the sense of displacement she voices in *Match*. On the ranch, however, Ehrlich discovers ground and purpose. "On a ranch, small ceremonies and private, informal rituals arise. We ride the spring pasture, pick chokecherries in August, skin out a deer in the fall, and in the enactment experience a wordless exhilaration between bouts of plain hard work. Ritual [...] goes in the direction of life. Through it we reconcile our barbed solitude with the rushing, irreducible conditions of life" (103). The intimate contact with animal bodies, soil, birth and death, and the effluvia and rhythms of the earth experienced in ranching gives Ehrlich a sense of being connected. Being struck by lightning complicates all this, though, by making her feel alienated from Wyoming and from her own body.

A turning point in *A Match to the Heart* occurs when after nearly a year of living on the edge of the Pacific Ocean, Ehrlich decides to return to Wyoming. This move is the first of several relocations she undertakes during the next year. Rootlessness becomes a habit shaped by her interior geography; that is, Ehrlich follows her instincts about where to settle, if only temporarily, and these instincts are shaped by her fear of lightning. It does not take Ehrlich long after her "return" to realize she cannot resettle in Wyoming. The expansive, arid grasslands she embraces in *The Solace of Open Spaces* no longer comfort her; rather, "[c]hest pains and dizziness nagged at me: this was no longer my home and I knew I had to leave" (Ehrlich 1994 140). Accordingly, she departs in search of a place more suitable for her interior landscape. "I drove. Chest pains seemed linked to open spaces: the wider the land, the more intense the feeling of constriction" (140). Storms shape her path of travel. "Thunder worked like echolocation," she writes; "it told me where I was, where to go next, and lightning was the lamp that showed the way" (Ehrlich 1994 141). Buddhist teachings creep into Ehrlich's narrative, as she determines that the "so-called hero" of the road is one who masters "her own dissolution" (141), choosing surrendering to conquering, moving along with no determined route. Ehrlich poses a difficult question about her own rootlessness since she fails to find a dwelling appropriate for her well-being; she asks, "Was I a citizen of the underworld with a ferryman who had gone mad?" (141). The answer seems to be a resounding "yes," as Ehrlich continues her erratic journey in search of ecological alignment with a place.

For example, after Wyoming, she travels to Alaska, where landscapes are constantly shifting. Floating icebergs appear and then disappear; glaciers calve continually. It is a dynamic landscape dwarfing human life. Camped near the face of a glacier, Ehrlich feels as if she were "a fish feeding at the crumbling edge of the universe" (Ehrlich 1994 148). This section reads like journal notes or a travelogue with philosophical ponderings. About gazing out into the inlet before her campsite, watching icebergs inhabited by seals float toward the bay and then return with the tides, Ehrlich reflects: "This was the inlet of devotion and transparency where illusion washed back and forth, a place that could teach me to see" (150). In this case, Ehrlich sets up a scenario for learning from the land; instead of developing the theme, however, she makes a jump in space and time to North Carolina, where she attends the Third Annual Lightning Strike and Electric Shock Conference. The frenetic fragmentation of the narrative mirrors her hectic traveling lifestyle.

Lightning trauma has a paradoxical effect of drawing Ehrlich into the complexities of anatomy as never before but also of making her feel estranged from her body, as if in a constant state of limbo. Such alienation is the subject of her chapter about the conference in North Carolina. In a clinical tone, Ehrlich relates how lightning has dramatically changed the lives of people from all areas of the United States. One young man explains how his post-strike life has been complicated by depression. Another woman explains how she now feels estranged from her body: "My body doesn't belong to me anymore" (Ehrlich 1994 154), she says. Doctors explain the psychological effects of lightning strikes and electric shocks, including "postelectrocution syndrome," which is symptomatic of "depression, anxiety, panic, memory deficits, hypervigilance, exaggerated startle response, profound fatigue, restlessness, insomnia, impotence, night terrors" (155). Ehrlich maintains a critical distance in this chapter, limiting her personal commentary to a minimum and cataloging instead the numerous other lives affected by high voltage. She does not draw us back into her thoughts and feelings until the end of the chapter when, in a moment of post-conference reflection, she meditates upon her own estrangement from her body. In her motel room facing the Smoky Mountains, she opens the windows wide, sees moonlight on patches of dogwood, and ruminates upon her uncertain future: "I thought of those humans who had awakened after being hit [by lightning] and became shamans and healers, and wondered what this new life of mine would be, carved from a ruined body and a ruined marriage, and what special passageways I could hollow out as in a labyrinth of dead ends" (160).

On one level, Ehrlich shares with readers the fascinating information she discovers about the workings of the brain, heart, and the "geography of our psyche" (Ehrlich 1994 73). On another, she explains how uprooted she feels from her own body and from any particular exterior landscape. "My travels had taken me from Wyoming to Alaska to North Carolina to Wyoming" (162), she writes, and, without clearly explaining why, she adds, "It was time to go back to California" (162). Ehrlich is clearly befuddled, following hunches about where to travel next and yet wary of her decisions. No place seems to satisfy her. "Halfway down a Wyoming highway I stopped, turned around, drove back north, stopped, and headed south again. The evening before, I had laid a map of the world on the floor of a friend's house and spun a beer bottle around on it. Where it stopped, I'd go: Africa, Asia, the Arctic, Idaho. But I was barely well enough to drive to the next state" (162). As she drives away from Wyoming, the meandering highway mirroring her unsteady course, she affirms her alienation from herself and from the sensory stimuli of the earth: "There was no right way to go, no airborne fragrance luring me. I wanted to commit my body to some gravityless place. But that's what I had been doing anyway; for a year, I had been treading water in the gap—it was my swimming hole, my highway, my home away from home, and it looked like I would continue to do so. Turn back again or not, all routes led to limbo, were paved with the stuff of limbo" (163). Not trusting in a better alternative, Ehrlich returns to Santa Barbara, where a prolonged, powerful storm saturates the earth, shifting the land with waterfalls and mudslides and spilling dams. It seems Ehrlich is being chased by violent weather, as she was once "chased by fire"; but perhaps, as the Japanese monk once suggested to her, she is not being chased by fire but rather is still chasing it. The constantly shifting landscape of the coastal region causes Ehrlich to reflect on the connections between place and psyche. Floods, fires, and earthquakes are regularly transforming the coastal landscape, and therefore Ehrlich wonders if growing up in such a place fosters her nomadism. "I designed furniture that pulled apart, folded, and broke down into neat stacks. Since arriving in California, I had moved four times and it looked as if I would move again. Was it the land running under my feet or my feet running over the land?" (165). While acknowledging the adaptability of humans, Ehrlich admits her ability to adjust to new places is not what it used to be. She writes, "I began to understand the meaning of 'life sentence': my old life had been erased in one-thousandth of a second and now I was trying to fly with clipped wings" (166).

Spring comes to the California coast, and Ehrlich begins walking. Her descriptions of the regional vegetation are vibrant, and yet a somber tone underlies the narrative, as Ehrlich still feels out of sorts with the landscape. The following paragraphs are indicative of this disjunction between the lively spring landscape and Ehrlich's contradictory mood:

> In the curve of the coastline, a mother whale and her calf—California grays—fed and rested thirty yards from shore. After they left I walked up the hill through yellow alleys, under monumental bouquets that opened out into green parks, then tightened into black sage jungles with pom-poms of purple flowers skewered on long stalks, which, farther up, gave way to scattered oak trees.

> Back on the beach, fourteen vultures were pecking holes in the side of a dead seal and they flew up as I approached, welding together in the sky like a single black cape. Was this the hood that would flop over my head and send me down underwater? A vulture's sense of smell, not sight, directs it to prey. I hoped I was not giving off a wrong signal. (Ehrlich 1994 181)

She marks time with vegetative changes, mapped through her regular walks along the coast. Her observations are still keen when spring segues into summer, but her expressions of alienation belie her naturalist's eye. She notes that the "yellow robes" of wild mustard have turned to red, then brown, and that blossoms have dropped off yucca plants. "I was still trying to get my bearings," she explains. "My blood pressure had normalized but I groped along the path" (192).

On she gropes, seeking a connection with the California coast—the landscape of her birth—throughout the final pages of the memoir. She walks in an attempt to get into the rhythm of the coast. "Walking had become an obsession. It was the way I moved in the world, achieved some rudimentary intimacy with a place" (Ehrlich 1994 192). This intimacy, however, is elusive: "As I trudged, my feet planted themselves in vertigo. Where was I? Why was I there? No matter how far and often I walked, I was still living in exile from the ranching community that had been my home" (193). The narrative continues to build around Ehrlich's estrangement towards the present and future when, near the end of the memoir, she appears to gain inspiration from the ancient live oaks of the California coast. In a less-skillful writer's hands, this motif of rebirth through the venerable oak could appear as a cliché, but Ehrlich avoids the paradigm of easy healing. After noting the symbolism of oaks—they are "sacred trees, trees of peace, marriage trees" living for hundreds of years— Ehrlich suggests that they prompt her to make a decision: to stay or go, to try to establish roots or continue wandering. On the evening of the day, when she encountered live oaks during a walk, she gazes seaward. Her vision is hallucinatory, and its message open-ended: "the moon on water that night was a silver oak leaf folded on my tongue, and on it was written my fortune. Later, an eclipse—I watched it through open doors from my bed—covered those words, but I imagined myself as a tree pushing up through hard soil, or as a wanderer with a knapsack walking across the face of a blackened moon" (195). The images suggest the contradictory desires that tug Ehrlich in separate directions: the seeking-for-a-place and the impulse to travel on, the rooted oak, and the backpacking hobo.

The Language of Landscape

In the opening paragraphs of *A Match to the Heart*, Ehrlich unsettles her audience with impressionistic language, luring them into identification with a bardo state, a condition of being in between life and death, out of the body, with fluid boundaries:

> Deep in an ocean. I am suspended motionless. The water is gray. That's all there is, and before that? My arms are held out straight, cruciate, my head and legs hang limp. Nothing moves. Brown kelp lies flat in mud and fish are buried in liquid clouds of dust. There are no shadows or sounds. Should there be? I don't know if I am alive, but if not, how do I know I am dead? My body is leaden, heavier than gravity. Gravity is done with me. No more sinking and rising or bobbing in currents. There is a terrible feeling of oppression with no oppressor. I try to lodge my mind against some boundary, some reference point, but the continent of the body dissolves. (3)

This opening paragraph sets the tone for a memoir that unsettles narrative conventions throughout. The word acrobatics Ehrlich employs as she seeks to understand the connections between the self-regulating universe of the body and the external landscapes we live in make *A Match to the Heart* an atypical contribution to environmental writing.

Lying in a hospital bed three weeks after being struck down, Ehrlich gazes at the "pale container" of her body and wonders how she could have previously been so uncurious about it:

> If I held a match to my heart, would I be able to see its workings, would I know my body the way I know a city, with its internal civilization of chemical messengers, electrical storms, cellular cities in which past, present, and future are contained, would I walk the thousand miles of arterial roadways, branching paths of communication, and coiled tubing for waste and nutrients, would I know where the passion to live and love comes from? (Ehrlich 1994 27)

The body becomes, in Ehrlich's memoir, an ecosystem that, like the earth systems that envelop our bodies, must adjust to violent disruptions. Ehrlich's boundary-blurring prose prompts metaphoric connections between the bodily devastation caused by lightning strike and ecosystem collapse caused by the mining and burning of fossil fuels, clearcutting of forests, and overfishing of oceans. Ehrlich marvels that we know very little about the intimate workings of our bodies, "the delicate architecture of their organs and systems, or the varying weathers of their private, internal environments" (27)—an ignorance that prompts her to think, "It is no wonder we neglect the natural world outside ourselves when we do not have the interest to know the one within" (27).

Anne Whiston Spirn's *The Language of Landscape* (1998) reinforces the cultural aspects of landscape and also the interlinkings between landscapes of various scales:

> Landscapes are as small as a garden, as large as a planet. To a person the garden is a landscape, to a people the nation is [...]. Ice floes on a river, lake, or arctic sea, inhabited by birds and seals, are a landscape. Ice crystals on a winter window look like ice floes seen from the air, are uninhabited, yet to a poet a landscape of the imagination. *Landscape may be inhabited in imagination alone.* (18; my emphasis)

When Ehrlich envisions the interior landscape of the human body, she is inhabiting a landscape of the imagination; at the same time, since technology has allowed humankind fuller access to the systems beneath the skin, her artistic descriptions of interior landscapes are, on another level, literal. "There are landscapes within landscapes within landscapes," Spirn writes. Ehrlich's explorations into the body reinforce this layered nature of circulatory, endocrine, and neural systems within bodies and also prompts us to reflect on the interconnected layers of bioregions and ecosystems—the life places of water, soil, sun, seeds, air, and human and animal companionship.

Ehrlich's prose is layered with metaphor, reminiscent of such canonical American nature writing as *Pilgrim at Tinker Creek* by Annie Dillard and *Désert Solitaire* by Edward Abbey, and extraordinary in its ability to plumb the depths of the human body, as well as the clouds, the earth, and the cosmos. In *Walden*, Thoreau plumbs with his fishing line the depths of his neighboring pond and feels a tug from below the surface, "a slight vibration along it, indicative of some life prowling about its extremity, of dull uncertain blundering purpose there" (Thoreau 120). His enthusiasm reaches to the literal life underneath the water's surface and also to the life of the mind, and thus he fancies he might "cast [his] line upward into the air, as well as downward into this element, which was scarcely more dense. Thus [he catches] two fishes as it were with one hook" (121). Fishing becomes a metaphor for intellectual inquiry when one's thoughts wander "to vast and cosmogonal themes in other spheres" (121). Ehrlich likewise establishes links between the interior human landscape and the landscapes of the sky through reversals of metaphor. She describes a thunderstorm with the language of the human body: "The electricity inside a cloud sweeps back and forth, up and down, always seeking the path of least resistance, while the dynamics of convection works like a heart, pumping air and moisture up through the valve of the cloud and pushing electricity down through an artery" (Ehrlich 1994 32). On the other hand, the human body is signified in the language of exterior landscapes: "I wondered what the interior geography of my body looked like or if my inside could be read like illuminated manuscript," Ehrlich writes. She goes on to attempt a speculative reading of her interior landscape, boosted through her perusal of *Gray's Anatomy*. "I traced nervous systems, blood vessels, intestinal coils, musculature, spinal cords, and the convolutions of the brain. A body is a separate continent, a whole ecosystem, a secret spinning planet. The brain looks Vesuvian with its breaks and draws called 'gyri' and 'sulci,' its fissures and fjords" (51). She shows her doctor a picture of the brain, noting how it "sits on its spindle, like a globe, the nodding head tilting on its axis, how the nervous system is a series of branches sprouting from that *axis mundi*, how each thought passing through is a separate ecosystem" (51). She personifies waves and wind:

A wave is a disturbance on the surface of a body of water, a kind of derangement. Waves are born when wind drags itself across calm water and the friction pinches it up into ripples and wavelets, which later become waves. Wind, the ever-present gardener, thins out the smaller, weaker ripples by pressing them into whitecaps and in a saga of bathrhythmic [sic] natural selection leaves the larger wavelets to grow." (184)

As a wave approaches the shore, "its back is broken and the long-distance runner falls" (185). This constant entangling of traits associated with human and more-than-human nature forces us to think about how multiple meshworks, or lifeworlds, are intertwined.

Ehrlich spends much time exploring marginal territory—gray areas where the conventional touchstones we use to structure existence are less differentiated. She begins her memoir by representing such a "blurry" space, her narrative voice hovering between death and life, "suspended motionless" in a "deep ocean." She later discusses the concept of *bardo*, which in the *Tibetan Book of the Dead* refers to

> that wandering state between life and death, confusion and enlightenment, neurosis and sanity. The past has just occurred, and the future has not yet happened. In the bardo of the human realm we experience the body as illusory. Our relationship to our own existence and nonexistence is lukewarm... The bardo state occurs not only at the moment of death or the moment before death, but all during our lives; the bardo is the uncertainty and groundlessness we often feel. (Ehrlich 1994 40)

Sickness is a type of bardo, for it can remove one from a sense of linear time. "When you are sick, days lie together haphazardly, like empty containers: each one counts because it means you are still alive, but the details of the greater world are unclear. Sickness entails a hiatus, a gap in habitual activity, an interval during which one is suspended motionless" (44). Ehrlich also focuses on bardo states in exterior landscapes, places where life and death coalesce together, as in the ocean, where living fish, plants, and mammals mix with the guano of seagulls, salt, rotting life, and the detritus of the continents. The edge of the shore—another marginal area—contains tide pools, gaps of another kind, "an edge between batholith and lithosphere, ocean and earth." Tide pools are "ecotones, in-between places like those clefts in the brain and the rug-pulled-out limbos in our lives where, ironically, much richness occurs" (94). In her discussion of tide pools, Ehrlich uses the discourse of culture to describe nonhuman life forms. In doing so, she again calls into question language that would separate human existence from more-than-human nature. She compares the "splash zone" of tidal pools to "village life," where multiple life forms "all crowd together in urban densities," and she accordingly catalogs some of these neighbors: barnacles, anemones, jellyfish, starfish, sponges, hydroids, worms, chitons, algae, lichens. "Aggregate anemones often live in concentrations of three thousand individuals per square meter of rock; they are marine apartment dwellers" (95), she writes. Ehrlich's language reversals—using the terms of natural history writing, such as descriptions of land topography, to describe the interior of the human body, and using terms from human culture to describe nonhuman landscapes—catches us off guard and consequently forces us to evaluate the dichotomies in our vocabulary.

As Ehrlich's prose breaks down such dichotomies as human/nature, it also questions perceiving the mind and body as separate entities. Her approach to both the body and exterior landscapes, rather, is holistic:

> We are elaborate biochemical, electrical, emotional organisms with message systems so intricate no computer could begin to track what happens to the body when even a single thought registers there. Feelings change the chemistry of the body as surely as physical traumas do. We blush, we faint at the sight of blood. Cells are constantly sending messages and reacting to messages from neurotransmitters. The mind-body split is a meaningless, laughable idea. Neurons are strung along electrical paths like Christmas tree lights, dancing and blinking, tiny intelligent beings that illuminate the dark continent of flesh. (88)

This holistic view of the body is reinforced later in the memoir when Ehrlich is granted the privilege of observing open-heart surgery. Gazing into the chest cavity of a patient etherized upon an operating table, Ehrlich marvels at the "forbidden cities within" the epidermis, the "organscape" of the interior, which she characteristically describes with imagery of minerals and trees. The heart, lungs, and branching arteries are "marble-quarries, veined leaves, red pathways leading to dark recesses" (171). She carries the linkages between the body and landscape even further with references to Tibetan medicine, which describes the body as being made up of four groups of veins and arteries; one of these is the "*Sriid pa'i rata*," or "vein of the world," "reminding us how intimately we are connected to the entire cosmos"; another is the "*t'se gnas pa'y rsta*," or "life-sustaining vein," reminding us that the body is a self-regulating universe. Instead of dividing the body into several separate "systems," Tibetan medicine presents a holistic conception of the body. "About these arterial pathways the Tibetans say: 'They all meet in the heart and the mental activities and emotions go through the chamber of the heart which causes the heart to beat" (175).

Readers may find Ehrlich's memoir erratic, for she makes frequent narrative leaps in subject and place. Such form, although appearing to lack structure, may be more purposeful than one might first assume. As lightning has fragmented Ehrlich's existence—cut her off from the continuity of ranch life in Wyoming, where after several years she had begun to feel "braided to the strand"—so too is her narrative a patchwork of fragmented experience and frustrated philosophy. Chapter 24 of *A Match to the Heart* is a single paragraph that suggests a method for Ehrlich's fractured narrative. She explains a dream she had about the composition of her text:

> I dreamed that the shape of this book should be a convection cloud, a rising bubble swarming with up and down drafts of electricity, moisture, and air. Inside, the narrative would zigzag like lightning, and the pages would be laid end to end to resemble a tree trunk, a channel down which fire suddenly flows. Once the book had been read, the top of the cloud would explode, leaving the reader holding a burned shell. (161)

Elsewhere, Ehrlich observes "torn clouds" near the California coast that are shaped like body parts—elbows, foreheads, and insect legs—and reflects that "in their fast-footed skudding, they showed how our fragmented passions can be pieced together as stories" (168). Perhaps this is a philosophy of composition to justify a piece of literature that is "all over the place"; or maybe Ehrlich's zigzagging prose reflects landscapes that are constantly shifting (I'm reminded here of Gary Snyder's image of "Blue Mountains Constantly Walking" from *The Practice of the Wild*) and therefore may be considered a type of organic, ecopoetic co-composition within dwellings of enchantment.

"a whole intelligence at work"

Ehrlich admits the mysteries of the healing process. While there is no hard scientific evidence proving the healing power of particular external landscapes, she believes certain places help her recuperate at different points of her sickness, and she explores the spiritual elements of healing, such as in the dynamics of the patient/physician relationship. Contemplating her years living on a Wyoming ranch, where she and other ranch hands successfully tended sick animals through a minimum of professional medicine but with intimacy—talking with them, touching them, keeping their beds layered with fresh straw, playing Mozart in the sun sheds—Ehrlich vows to know more about the uncharted mystical elements of healing:

> I wanted to better understand what makes people—or animals—live or die, the intermix of physiology and psychology, and to chart the dynamics of the patient-healer relationship. I wanted to look under the skin and see how the heart worked, how all the systems of the body— nervous and circulatory—achieved their miraculous harmony (119).

After accompanying her cardiologist on his rounds at the hospital and observing how his positive attitude seemed to boost patients' recuperation, Ehrlich begins to revise her ideas of "the chemistry of healing." She realizes that the body has an ecology of its own, with myriad interactive checks and balances, as does the ocean. "How dynamic the human body is, the same dynamism as the ocean's, all the systems—circulatory, nervous, immune, endocrine—so vigorously interactive with the workings of the mind. From cell to psyche, there is a whole intelligence at work" (128).

Ehrlich closes her narrative with a note of praise for the healing powers of the Pacific coast and offers a cautious promise of rebirth as she packs saddle, spurs, and hound into her truck and turns towards Wyoming. For all her feelings of estrangement, Ehrlich admits that the coastal landscape has provided a type of refuge for her recuperation. Her interior landscape has adjusted to the coast better than to other places, especially Wyoming, with its now-terrifying open spaces. Still, she has an urge to return to ranch life and a hope of reclaiming her lost sense of cultural continuity. The night before her departure for Wyoming, Ehrlich lies awake listening to ocean waves and thinks "how the curve of the coastline here had sheltered and nurtured live-born sharks, humans, and migrating whales. Here, at the edge of the continent, time and distance stopped; in the lull between sets of waves I could get a fresh start" (199). While throughout the memoir she intimates that certain dwellings are conducive to one's health, she does not make an ultimate statement about the role of intimacy with or immersion within landscapes as an alternative medicine. Pills that regulate her heart, the comfort given by her dog Sam, a good steak with a glass of red wine, walks along the coast, stillness, *and* motion—all play a role in her slow healing from lighting-strike disorientation and attempt to again feel at home in her body and in this enchanted world.

Works Cited

Ehrlich, Gretel. *The Solace of Open Spaces.* New York: Penguin, 1985.

—. *A Match to the Heart.* New York: Penguin, 1994.

Hogan, Linda. Interview for *Dwellings of Enchantment,* 2006.

Lynch, Tom, Cheryll Glotfelty, and Karla Armbruster, eds. *The Bioregional Imagination: Literature, Ecology, and Place.* Athens: University of Georgia Press, 2012.

Rash, Ron. Interview for *Dwellings of Enchantment,* 2006.

Roszak, Theodore, Mary E. Gomes, and Allen D. Kanner, eds. *Ecopsychology: Restoring the Earth, Healing the Mind.* San Francisco: Sierra Club, 1995.

Silverman, Sue William. *Because I Remember Terror, Father, I Remember You.* Athens: University of Georgia Press, 1996.

Slicer, Deborah. "The Body as Bioregion." *Reading the Earth: New Directions in the Study of Literature and Environment*, edited by Michael Branch, Rochelle Johnson, Daniel Patterson, & Scott Slovic, Moscow: University of Idaho Press, 1998, pp. 107–16.

Spirn, Anne Whiston. *The Language of Landscape*. New Haven: Yale University Press, 1998.

Thayer, Robert L., Jr. *LifePlace: Bioregional Thought and Practice*. Berkeley: University of California Press, 2003.

Thoreau, Henry David. *Walden*. New York: Signet, 1980.

Williams, Philip Lee. *Crossing Wildcat Ridge: A Memoir of Nature and Healing*. Athens: University of Georgia Press, 1999.

Williams, Terry Tempest. *Refuge: An Unnatural History of Family and Place*. New York: Vintage, 1991.

—. *Desert Quartet*. New York: Pantheon, 1995.

Winter, Deborah DuNann. *Ecological Psychology: Healing the Split Between Planet and Self*. New York: HarperCollins, 1996.

Chapter 13

Laudato Si', "The Mass on the World," and Flannery O'Connor's Eucharistic Ecology

George Piggford
Stonehill College, USA

Abstract: Flannery O'Connor's short story "A View of the Woods," composed in 1956, articulates a Catholic and Eucharistic ecology that resonates with Pierre Teilhard de Chardin's notion of the Cosmic Christ and anticipates the integral ecology articulated by Pope Francis in his 2015 encyclical Laudato Si'. Francis was powerfully influenced by Teilhard's vision of a universal Eucharist, which evokes a connection to the natural world that is both physical and spiritual. O'Connor learned of the "christification" of nature through her own reading of Teilhard, notably *The Divine Milieu*, and her stories anticipate the worldwide implications of the Eucharist Teilhard envisions in "The Mass on the World." "A View of the Woods" calls its readers' attention to the Eucharistic qualities of nature and tells a tale of the failure of humans to enact an ethic inspired by an integral ecology. The story portrays human sacrifice and natural destruction while gesturing toward regeneration and the eventual divinization of the cosmos.

Keywords: Flannery O'Connor, "A View of the Woods," Pierre Teilhard de Chardin, Pope Francis, Laudato Si', Eucharist, Catholic ecology

***

> Praised be to you, my Lord, through our Sister Mother Earth,
> who sustains and governs us, and who produces various
> fruit with colored flowers and herbs.
>
> –Francis of Assisi, "The Canticle of the Creatures"
> (Francis of Assisi 113–114).

In *Laudato Si'*, the landmark environmental encyclical promulgated in 2015, Pope Francis contends that "nature cannot be regarded as something separate from ourselves or as a mere setting in which we live." For Francis, "we are part of nature, included in it and thus in constant interaction with it" (Francis 105 [#139]). *Laudato Si'*—literally, "Praise Be to You"—emphasizes the symbiosis between human beings and the natural world. This interconnectedness is rooted in longstanding Catholic approaches to creation most prominently associated with the medieval friar Francis of Assisi (1181–1226), but it also resonates with other spiritual and ecological traditions, both Christian and non-Christian. Paula Gunn Allen, for example, connects the "Virgin Morena (dark virgin)" that appeared to St. Juan Diego in 1659 with the Indian goddess Tinotzin, she who is "grandmother of the sun, grandmother of the light" (Allen 26). For Allen this figure is "quintessential spirit," which "pervades everything" and is "capable of powerful song and radiant movement" (Allen 13). Like St. Francis' "Sister Mother Earth," the Virgin Morena breaks forth through the soil and is "Heart of Earth," Corn Woman, the very spirit of generativity (Allen 26). Likewise, the Pope's recent encyclical provides an ecological picture of organic interrelatedness, similar to Allen's sacred hoop, and this interdependence of humans, all living beings, and even the nonliving world provides the foundation for what Pope Francis terms an "integral ecology."[1]

In addition to diverse influences within and outside Catholicism, *Laudato Si'* has been powerfully informed by Ken Wilber's "integral theory," the liberation theologian Leonardo Boff, and the American ecotheologian Thomas Berry. Most importantly, for the purpose of the present essay, Pope Francis' encyclical also owes a significant debt to the Jesuit mystic and paleontologist Pierre Teilhard de Chardin (1881–1955).[2] Teilhard is mentioned only in one note in the Pope's lengthy letter, subtitled "On the Care of Our Common Home," but its articulation of "universal communion" is modeled on the writing of the French priest, especially his "Mass on the World" (Francis 65 [#83]).[3] Teilhard originally composed that meditation on the cosmic implications of the Catholic Eucharist in 1923 in China's Ordos desert.[4] "In the steppes of Asia," with "neither bread, nor wine, nor altar," Teilhard imagines a Holy Communion that is worldwide and ultimately universal, when "the contours of [God's] body melt away and become enlarged beyond all measure" and "the world is caught in the descending radiance of the heart of God" (Teilhard 1960b 19, 34, 35).[5] In this mystical vision, the Earth and all life upon it become a consecrated Host held up to the cosmic God. Everything is holy, and in Teilhard's anagogical view, God's sacramental presence in nature is revealed, and all creation has become Christ. Neither Francis nor Teilhard would use the term "reenchantment" for this process; rather, Teilhard's view heralds the "divinization" or "becoming divine" of the natural world and the entire cosmos.

Such a cosmic theophany might at first blush seem to be far afield from the work of American regionalist Flannery O'Connor (1925–1964), with the vast majority of her stories rooted in the distinctive red clay of her native Georgia. Like Teilhard, however, O'Connor's view tended, at least on occasion, toward the mystical and the universal. This feature of her writing is most famously present at the end of the short story "Revelation," first published in 1964. That story concludes with the shocked Ruby Turpin's view from her pig-parlor of an all-encompassing and upended human social order accompanied by "invisible cricket choruses" (O'Connor 1971 509). The ultimate gesture of the story is a vision of the Communion of Saints representing racial diversity, varieties of ability, and all classes of society.[6] This "vast horde of souls" is "rumbling toward heaven" in a kind of cosmic communion line; all are "climbing upward" into the "starry field" of the visible universe. With its final word, "hallelujah"—from the Hebrew root "praise be to you Lord"—the story provides a hopeful vision of the ultimate fate of both its protagonist Ruby and diverse humanity (O'Connor 1971 508–509). A vision that includes humans, nature, and the cosmos not only echoes Teilhard's "Mass" but also anticipates the current Pope's emphasis on universal communion—the cosmos itself understood as the Body of Christ.

Given O'Connor's astringent and sometimes brutal realism, however, such a magnanimous vision is a rarity. More typical is "A View of the Woods," a short story that calls its readers' attention to the divine and Eucharistic qualities in nature but examines more closely the failure of human beings to enact an ethic inspired by what Francis calls an "integral ecology," which is spiritual and physical, as well as cultural, economic, and ethical (Francis 104 [#137]). Teilhard commented in his 1916 essay "Cosmic Life" that "there is a communion with God, and a communion with earth, and a communion with God through earth" (Teilhard 1968b 14). What of those, however, who fail to perceive and act on this presence of God in the natural world? In "A View of the Woods" O'Connor emphasizes not only that divinity dwells within nature but also that our own planet and all life upon it is the wounded and bleeding Christ, especially in the face of industrialization and exploitation aided by technology. It is in suffering that the world and human beings find their place within Christ's "Mystical Body" in a process that Teilhard, following Eastern Christian traditions, terms "divinization" (Teilhard 1960a 7).[7]

O'Connor's Infernal Machine

Critics have emphasized the sacred qualities of the natural world in O'Connor, at least since Louise Westling's important *Sacred Groves and Ravaged Gardens*, which deems O'Connor's "woods and pastures" to be "sacred precincts for the enactment of violent rituals intended to batter her characters into an awareness of their helplessness before God" (O'Connor 1985 156–157). This stress on the damage that humans inflict on nature, often aided by technology, is evident from the beginning of "A View of the Woods," which O'Connor completed by the end of 1956 (O'Connor 1979 175). In the opening scene of the story, we are introduced to a grandfather, Mark Fortune, and one of those grandchild doppelgängers familiar to us in O'Connor's work, in this case, Mr. Fortune's granddaughter, Mary Fortune Pitts. They not only look alike physically but also, as the narrator asserts early on, "the spiritual distance between them" is "slight" (O'Connor 1971 526). We meet them mutually staring at the toil of "two huge yellow bulldozers" moving soil in a "hole" that will eventually become the foundation of a fishing club at a new lake, modeled on Lake Sinclair, located just a few miles north of O'Connor's home of Andalusia and created by the State of Georgia and the Georgia Power Company in 1953.

The work of these bulldozers is not described in detail, except for a comment that they are "smooth[ing] out" the pit formed by a different contraption, called throughout the story simply "the machine" (O'Connor 1971 528). Despite what many critics of the story have claimed, this machine is not itself a bulldozer but what is called an excavator, which is explicitly distinguished in "A View of the Woods" from its two attendant bulldozers and, later, a cement mixer.[8] The machine is most likely a hydraulic excavator mounted with a backhoe, which consists of a heavy jointed arm and a bucket at the end designed to draw earth back towards the machine (Haddock 220). Such machines generally turn on a "swing" or swivel, which allows them to expel dirt at the edge of a deepening pit. They are propelled either on an endless caterpillar-like track or on vulcanized rubber wheels (Haddock 200).

The narrative begins "the week before" the scene with the bulldozers—with a description of Mr. Fortune and Mary Fortune's habit of watching the excavator dig huge wounds into the blood-red Georgia clay:

> Mary Fortune and the old man had spent every morning watching the machine that lifted out dirt and threw it in a pile…. He sat on the bumper and Mary Fortune straddled the hood and they watched, sometimes for hours, while the machine systematically ate a square red hole in what had once been a cow pasture…. 'Any fool that would let a cow pasture interfere with progress is not on my books,' he had said to Mary Fortune several times from his seat on the bumper…. She sat on the hood, looking down into the red pit, watching the big disembodied gullet gorge itself on the clay, then, with the sound of a deep sustained nausea and a slow mechanical revulsion, turn and spit it up. (O'Connor 1971 335)

The machine is consistently described in monstrous terms and with malevolent motives. It is, in fact, a mechanized version of Lucifer in Dante's

Inferno, not masticating history's greatest traitors in the lowest pit of hell but chewing up and spitting out the earth itself.[9] The excavator eats but is never satisfied; it can chew but never swallow. It "systematically" damages the land not for its own sustenance but for the sake of what Mr. Fortune calls "progress."[10]

As Mark Graybill noted, this version of progress represents the "commercial and technological exploitation of nature," but it also anticipates many of the arguments in Pope Francis' environmental encyclical (Graybill 12).[11] "When people become self-centered and self-enclosed," Francis argues, "their greed increases. The emptier a person's heart is, the more he or she needs things to buy, own, and consume" (Francis 148 [#204]).[12] For Francis, no amount of exploitative consumption can possibly nourish a human in the most meaningful sense. The repetitive scene of the excavator gluttonously "gorg[ing] itself on the clay" only to vomit it up immediately evokes the profound emptiness of this compulsion to consume.[13] There is clear evidence that for both the current Pope and Flannery O'Connor our global environmental crisis reflects and results from a deeper spiritual crisis and requires an "integral ecology," one that is concerned with cultural structures, economic justice, environmental awareness, and spiritual development (Francis 104 [#137]). Indeed, a key insight in the encyclical is that social justice and ecological justice are integrally related. Francis thus calls for both a "bold cultural revolution" and a worldwide "conversion" to "a loving awareness that we are not disconnected from the rest of creatures, but joined in a splendid universal communion" (Francis 88, 157–158 [#114, #220]).[14] The Pope's language of "the rest of creatures" indicates a sense of communion that encompasses not only human animals but also all living entities.[15]

The Cosmic Christ

The vocabulary that Francis uses to describe his Catholic ecology is directly indebted to the writing of Teilhard de Chardin, especially "The Mass on the World." O'Connor did not live to see the publication of that work in English in 1965, but many of its ideas are present, although in a muted fashion, in Teilhard's *The Divine Milieu*, which O'Connor read and reviewed in early 1961 (O'Connor 1983 106). Given that my main literary focus here is "A View of the Woods," published in 1957, I am not as interested in the influence of Teilhard on O'Connor as I am in their similar environmental and Eucharistic visions and their anticipation of the approach that Pope Francis advocates in *Laudato Si'*. Mark Graybill, whose work is central to an understanding of what he calls O'Connor's "deep ecology," comments perceptively that O'Connor's fiction is "not so much ... reflective of Teilhard's thought" as it is "complementary to it" (Graybill 6).[16] That is, even before she read his work, O'Connor, in her fiction and other writing, foresees Teilhard's cosmic vision.[17] When O'Connor finally turned to the controversial Teilhard in the early 1960s after a conversation with her editor Robert Giroux, what she found was a kindred intelligence and similar capacity for mystic vision.[18] This congruence is evident in a number of her letters and is perhaps best summed up in her review of *The Divine Milieu*. There, O'Connor declares: "It is doubtful if any Christian of this century can be fully aware of his religion until he has reseen it in the cosmic light which Teilhard has cast upon it" (O'Connor 1983 108). Teilhard's efforts to reconcile Christian belief and Catholic sacramentalism with both biological and cosmological evolution offered O'Connor fresh insight into the relationship between God and creation.

Teilhard's claims about the unifying and trans-historical qualities of the Catholic Eucharist are evident in the only passage that O'Connor marked in her own copy of *The Divine Milieu*, currently in the archive at Georgia College and State University in Milledgeville (Kinney 33–34). In it, Teilhard notes that every Mass includes a priest and words of consecration, which in his time were universally *hoc est corpus meum* ("this is my body"). Each Mass, however, points to something even larger. As Teilhard expresses it, "the great sacramental operation does not cease at that local and momentary event." He continues:

> Even children are taught that, throughout the life of each human being and the life of the Church and the history of the world, there is only one Mass and one Communion. Christ died once in agony. Peter and Paul receive communion on such and such a day at a particular hour. But these different acts are only the diversely central points in which the continuity of a unique act is split up and fixed, in space and time, for our experience. (Teilhard 1960a 102)

In every Mass, the transcendent God intersects with chronological human time, and the infinitely vast becomes present in the tangible, physical forms of bread and wine.

Further, for Teilhard, the Incarnation is "realized, in each individual, through the Eucharist." Every human being who approaches God through a Eucharistic meal becomes intimately close to Christ, a partaker of the divine nature. This sacramental experience is, in fact, universal, communal, and trans-historical: "All the communions of a life-time are one communion. All the communions of all men [and women] now living are one communion. All the communions of all, present, past and future, are one communion" (Teilhard 1960a 102). The Eucharistic meal, in other words, always takes its participants beyond a specific sacramental action towards divinization, what Teilhard also calls "christification," that is ultimately cosmic (Teilhard 1960a 101).[19] Daniel Scheid, in *The Cosmic Common Good,* builds on this central point when he declares: "Communion inheres into the makeup of the universe itself. It springs from and reinforces the intrinsic goodness of every individual species and creature" (Scheid 2016 75).[20] Mass connects the individual not only to the historical person of Christ—God in the flesh from a Catholic perspective—but also to the universal Christ. Mass makes, or ought to make, its human participants more profoundly aware of the communion inherent in nature and in the universe, and the sacrament performs a central role in the transformation bringing all of creation into the Body of Christ.[21]

Teilhard calls the universal Christ the "Omega Point" (Teilhard 1968a 257), which is, to borrow Ilia Delio's phrase, "the power of evolution ... who is within and ahead" (Delio 2015 93). Christ as Omega is the motivating force of the universe, the proper end of all human action, and the inevitable culmination of all processes of generation, both cosmological and biological.[22] It is this very idea that provided O'Connor with the title of her second collection of short stories, *Everything That Rises Must Converge,* a phrase inspired by Teilhard's vision in *The Phenomenon of Man* of evolution as a pyramidal cone, "whose apex is supported from below" (Teilhard 1968a 270). Kathleen Duffy points out in *Teilhard's Mysticism* that the act of creation is ongoing: "the world is continually being created, allured toward higher levels of convergence by the personalizing and unifying presence of Omega, the Cosmic Christ" (Duffy 118). In this formulation, Christian divinization was initiated at the events surrounding the crucifixion of Jesus of Nazareth, and it continues, in fact evolves, at every Eucharistic celebration. Christ is, in Duffy's rendering, the "inner face," the personal and spiritual quality of the evolutionary principle itself. The beginning of the cosmos anticipates the emergence of life on Earth and its natural environment, which provides the setting for God's incarnation as a human being. As stewards of our cosmic and global setting, we continue the process of christification in an effort that Teilhard calls "noogenesis," which refers to the evolution of the human mind into an ever more ethical (and Christ-like) relationship with the world.[23] Catholic Mass is here understood as facilitating this development of human awareness and the ongoing transformation of all matter and energy into the divine life.

As an orthodox Roman Catholic, it was for O'Connor of utmost importance that at every validly celebrated Catholic Mass, bread and wine are transubstantiated into the Body of Blood of Jesus Christ. One of her best-known quotations emphasizes this belief. In a 1955 letter to her friend Elizabeth Hester, O'Connor describes a dinner party in New York City that included a conversation about the Eucharist, "which I, being the Catholic, was obviously supposed to defend." When other guests proffered a symbolic interpretation of the sacrament, O'Connor replied, "Well, if it's a symbol, to hell with it" (O'Connor 1979 125). This insistence on physicality and the body of an incarnate divinity in Catholic Communion has unsettled many throughout history. The emphasis on the bread and wine, products of field and vine and of human labor, as truly Christ's Body and Blood is longstanding in the Catholic tradition. By the nineteenth and twentieth centuries, Catholic theology highlighted more than any other dogma the reality and primacy of the Eucharistic Sacrament as an outward sign not only of God's grace but of God's Real Presence and mysterious indwelling in the world.[24] Timothy Vande Brake has pointed out that there are environmental consequences to such an idea of the Eucharist: this Teilhardian and cosmic "view posits that God's real presence in the humble bread and wine of the Eucharist is God's continual affirmation that the world of things is very good," to be treated with utmost care and respect (Vande Brake 30).

A Eucharistic Ecology

It is at this point that a question arises, one pondered by both Teilhard and O'Connor, despite the latter's emphasis on Eucharistic transubstantiation: Why do only bread and wine become Christ? If these items might be transubstantiated, then why not everything? Why does divinization cease with processed wheat and fermented grapes? In 1923 at his archaeological site in the Ordos desert, the priest Teilhard woke up on a Sunday morning with no bread and no wine at hand. What he substituted in their place is recorded in "The Mass on the World."[25] Here, his Eucharistic theology is much more radical than what he expresses in *The Divine Milieu*, and in fact, encompasses all of the natural world, living and dying. In this mystical prayer, the Eucharist is freed not only from the walls of churches and the rites of the Mass but also from the specificity of the elements of bread and wine: "Over every living thing which is to spring up, to grow, to flower, to ripen during this day say again the words: This is my Body. And over every death-force which waits in readiness to corrode, to wither, to cut down, speak again your commanding words which express the supreme mystery of faith: This is my Blood" (Teilhard 1960b 23).[26] Here, Earth herself becomes the altar of sacrifice, and the Host is associated with the life-force of the natural world. It is, indeed, life or really rebirth—"to spring up, to grow, to flower, to ripen"—that transubstantiates the world, that makes it into the Body of Christ. The element of wine is associated with the "death-force" which becomes transubstantiated into Christ's Blood. With the sheen of nature, living and dying, on its surface, the world becomes a planet-sized Host lifted up to the God of the cosmos.[27]

Teilhard's approach to the Eucharist was too extreme for the Catholic authorities of the mid-twentieth century, and a *monitum* or "warning" was issued against his writing in 1962.[28] From a Catholic perspective, one danger of this approach is pantheism, a religious view that O'Connor emphatically rejects in a 1956 letter to Elizabeth Hester: "Remember that I am not a pantheist and do not think of the creation as God, but as made and sustained by God" (O'Connor 1979 126). Because a pantheistic conflation of creation with Divinity undermined his model of evolutionary spirituality, such a position was also disavowed by Teilhard, most clearly in *The Divine Milieu*. In that book, he insists that "the sojourner in the divine milieu is not a pantheist." This is so because pantheism offers "only fusion and unconsciousness" in its vision of "perfect universal union" (Teilhard 1960a 93). What Teilhard offers is, instead, a Christian and Catholic paradox of individuality that finds its distinctiveness in union with God: "*to be united* (that is, to become the other) *while remaining oneself*" (Teilhard 1960a 94).[29] Therefore, Christians may "plunge" themselves completely into the divine milieu—the natural world— "without the risk" of becoming a pantheistic monist, someone who perceives God and the cosmos to be one and the same (Teilhard 1960a 94).[30] Nevertheless, as his contemporary and fellow Jesuit, Henri de Lubac, notes, Teilhard's mysticism is sometimes misread in this fashion. Teilhard, for de Lubac, remains "the most outspoken opponent of pantheistic concepts of the Godhead" because he articulates so clearly the simultaneous transcendence and profound immanence of a God who is both "further than everything and deeper than everything" (de Lubac 22, 24). This understanding of God's presence in the natural world comports well with (1) the vision of the Jesuit order's founder, Ignatius of Loyola, with (2) de Lubac's theological interpretation of Teilhard and (3) the poetry of yet another Jesuit, Gerard Manley Hopkins. This last writer was especially influential upon O'Connor's mystical ecopoetics.

In *Hymn of the Universe* Teilhard admits that "like the monist I plunge into the all-inclusive One," but here the crucial distinction between "like" and "as" is most relevant. To be *like* a monist is to differentiate oneself through comparison. The Teilhardian mystic loses the human "ego" in the divine One only in order to "find in it the ultimate perfection of ... individuality" (Teilhard 1960b 26). By becoming Christ, in other words, we become most ourselves. This paradoxical formulation provides a striking echo of Hopkins' famous sonnet "As Kingfishers Catch Fire," in which the human person "acts in God's eye what in God's eye he is—Christ." Christ and the self are not (yet) one but are in a playful and powerful relationship, with the self undergoing a process of Christification: "Christ plays in ten thousand places, lovely in limbs and lovely in eyes not his" (Hopkins 129).[31] Likewise, the transubstantiated species of bread and wine retain their distinctive sensate qualities in orthodox Catholic theology. They become Christ while remaining in texture, taste, and materiality what they have always been. According to the *Baltimore Catechism*, which was the manual of faith for American Catholics of O'Connor's generation, these items become Christ's Body. However, "the color, the taste, and whatever appears to the senses" remain (Third Plenary Council 197 [Q. 885]). The Eucharistic elements are utterly transformed while remaining their distinct species, and according to Teilhard, the same is true of the human species understood as becoming the Body of Christ. Christ seeks to dwell everywhere in creation in a mode that is not possessive but perfecting. As Pope John Paul II has memorably phrased it, "We are asked to become one. We are not asked to become each other" (John Paul II 1988). Humans are to be found in nature, not lost in it; integrated, not obliterated.

Recent popes have come around to a view of the Eucharist comparable to Teilhard's, where the cosmos itself is envisioned as becoming Christ. John Paul II's encyclical *Ecclesia et Eucharistia* declares that "the Eucharist is always in some way celebrated *on the altar of the world*. It unites heaven and earth. It embraces and permeates all creation."[32] This language evokes Teilhard's notion of convergence at the Omega Point. Of all Catholic leaders, Pope Emeritus Benedict XVI has made the greatest effort to rehabilitate Teilhard's reputation and ideas. A 2009 homily features a repetitive emphasis on the main theme of "The Mass on the World":

> The role of the priesthood is to consecrate the world so that it may become a living host, a liturgy: so that the liturgy may not be something alongside the reality of the world, but that the world itself shall become a living host, a liturgy. This is also the great vision of Teilhard de Chardin: in the end we shall achieve a true cosmic liturgy, where the cosmos becomes a living host. (Benedict XVI 2009)

At the end of cosmic history, all creation will be transubstantiated; God will dwell in all as all. Only then will God complete the great poem, the Mass, or the Eucharistic liturgy. This process began with the creation of the cosmos itself, continued with the mystery of divine Incarnation, and moves forward even now. Pope Francis, echoing Teilhard, calls the Eucharist "an act of cosmic love" (Francis 168 [#236]). In his view, we are to care for our common home, which includes not only the natural setting of Earth but of the cosmos itself. We are to treat all reality as if it were, at least potentially, Christ.

The Failed Mystic

While it is true that Flannery O'Connor did not know "The Mass on the World," she did imagine at least the possibility of something similar, and the best evidence for this can be found in her most ecological of stories, "A View of the Woods." In that story, we find in Mr. Fortune a potential though ultimately failed mystic in the mold of Teilhard. This character expresses, in Christine Flanagan's phrase, "a malevolent desire for domination" and identifies with the monstrous, gluttonous excavator" (Flanagan 165). At the same time, Mr. Fortune's vision is frequently haunted by the Christ-like and even Eucharistic qualities of the pastures and woods that he is serially selling off and enabling the destruction of, all in the name of 'progress.' In the story, Mr. Fortune is provided an opportunity to become aware of the divinity of the natural world before him and, indeed, of its Christ-like qualities. He is invited into an attitude of "accountability to the environment," as Lawrence Buell puts it, but he turns away from the suffering Christ hidden in the woods in the name of an ultimately self-destructive "progress" (Buell 7). His failed eco-mysticism, his inability to perceive the divine indwelling in nature, will prove lethal both to Mr. Fortune and to his granddaughter Mary Fortune Pitts.

"A View of the Woods" begins and ends with a focus on the malevolent machine, the Earth-wounding excavator that serves as the agent of Mr. Fortune's will to progress, his primary instrument for developing the heretofore relatively undisturbed landscape of central Georgia. This project might helpfully be situated within what historian C. Vann Woodward memorably calls the "bulldozer revolution," a phrase meant to evoke the massive changes to the topography of the postwar South owing to an economic boom and the belated industrialization of this region of the United States (Woodward 6). A concurrent process was suburbanization, and creating artificial lakes, such as Georgia's Lake Sinclair, raised property values for newly lakefront parcels. These alterations to waterways and the land gave rise to infrastructure like the "paved highway" that Mr. Fortune imagines supplanting the "clay road" currently running in front of his home (O'Connor 1971 337). Once the road has been paved, Fortune "wanted to see a supermarket store across the road from him, he wanted to see a gas station, a motel, a drive-in picture-show within easy distance" (O'Connor 1971 337). Such structures would, in his imagination, comprise a new town: Fortune, Georgia. This legal renaming represents his desire not only to alter the environment around him but also to rechristen it as his namesake, thereby claiming permanent possession of his property.

Mark Fortune's favorite grandchild, Mary, begins the story as a proponent of her grandfather's notion of 'progress' and is also his double. As both of them sit on a car hood and watch the "disembodied gullet" of the excavator continue to "gorge" on the Georgian clay, the girl's face is described as "a small replica of the old man's" that "never lost its look of absorption" in the Earth-wounding work of the machine (O'Connor 1971 336).[33] When, however, Mr. Fortune makes the decision to sell "the lawn" or open field in front of the house where Mr. Fortune and Mary live with the rest of her family, the Pittses, the granddaughter rebels against him (O'Connor 1971 342). She is concerned that the gas station proposed for this parcel will take away the family playground and the area where their calves graze. Most importantly, it will obscure their view of the woods. What Mr. Fortune cannot or will not realize is the value of this undeveloped land across the road from "the lawn" (O'Connor 1971 342). His attitude toward property is economic and exploitative. In his disenchanted view, the land is valuable only for its potential to be developed and to bring to reality his destructive idea of a town named Fortune. Nevertheless, the woods have something to try to teach him about the importance of the natural world and its Christ-like and Eucharistic qualities if only he will grant them his sustained attention.

Not long after his argument with Mary, Mark Fortune rises after his afternoon nap and gazes at the woodlands across the lawn, but "Every time he saw the same thing: woods—not a mountain, not a waterfall, not any kind of planted bush or flower, just woods" (O'Connor 1971 348). Rather than perceiving the diversity of the natural scene, it appears to him as an undifferentiated whole, simply "woods." But in the afternoon light "woven through them," each "pine trunk stood out in all its nakedness" (O'Connor 1971 348). The sense of this description is that there is something vulnerable about each tree, something stripped bare, and, as we will see, something Christ-like. Nevertheless, Mr. Fortune seems incapable of peering deeply into this scene and recognizing the woods as something other than property to be owned and sold. In the language of Pope Francis, Mr. Fortune lacks an "integral ecology" that might help him to understand his interconnectedness not only to other human beings, especially those suffering and in need but also to the trees and the complex ecosystem into which human and nonhuman entities are "woven."[34]

Mr. Fortune rises out of bed a second time to gaze at the woods, but he is only "reconvinced of his wisdom in selling the lot" (O'Connor 1971 348). A powerful moment of mystic vision occurs, however, upon Fortune's third view of the woods. At this point, he begins to develop what Scott Slovic discerns in the writing of Henry David Thoreau, a "habit of attention" (Slovic 4–7):[35]

> The third time he got up to look at the woods, it was almost six o'clock and the gaunt trunks appeared to be raised in a pool of red light that gushed from the almost hidden sun setting behind them. The old man stared for some time, as if for a prolonged instant he were caught up out of the rattle of everything that led to the future and were held there in the midst of an uncomfortable mystery that he had not apprehended before.[36] (O'Connor 1971 348)

This blood-like "gush" of red light leads him to a more specifically Christian insight into the mysterious nature of the woods. He perceives the mystery "as if someone were wounded behind the woods and the trees were bathed in blood" (O'Connor 1971 348). The sense here is that the woods are suffering from the damage being inflicted on the nearby sections of land that Fortune has already begun to develop. Through the mysterious interconnectedness of the natural scene, these "naked" trees suffer from the damage being done elsewhere on Mr. Fortune's property. There is a hint of futurity here, thus a transcendence of diachronic temporality: "The road would soon be paved." These woods, too, will soon be cleared, and the "red trunks" rise up in the "black wood" in an effort to communicate that they are sacred precincts, that they are holy—that the world, in the words of Pope John Paul II, is an altar, and they are the sacrifice (O'Connor 1971 348).

To say that Christ is present in the woods and the trees comes as no shock to any traditional reader of "A View of the Woods." The woods, after all, "walk" like Christ "across the water" on the very first page of the story, and O'Connor herself affirmed that only "the woods" in the story are "pure enough to be a Christ symbol if anything is" (O'Connor 1971 335) (O'Connor 1979 190). As the trees are felled and the blood-red Earth is gouged out by the excavator, Mr. Fortune, despite his spiritual impoverishment, begins to perceive someone wounded and naked within and behind them. The woods are calling the stubborn and greedy Mr. Fortune to "A sense of deep communion with the rest of nature," which "cannot be real if our hearts lack compassion and concern for our fellow human beings" (Francis 70 [#91]). Such lack of compassion characterizes Mr. Fortune as he rejects a sense of integration with nature and thereby resists his own divinization. He is, if you will, the excavator gorging himself on the clay of his own property, eating and not being satisfied.

Near the end of the story, a violent encounter between grandfather and granddaughter occurs, as they are unable to agree on the fate of the woods. After Mr. Fortune finalizes the sale of the property, he is determined to whip Mary in punishment for her stubbornness and disobedience. As she fights back, she takes on qualities of the natural world itself: her "small rocklike fists" batter Mr. Fortune while "five claws"—that is, her fingers—dig into "the flesh of his upper arm" (O'Connor 1971 354–355).[37] Eventually, however, Fortune is able to get the better of the child. His behavior mimics the excavator's: he grips his hands "tight around her neck," lifts her head into the air, and beats Mary's head "hard against the rock that happened to be under it" (O'Connor 1971 355). He does this again and again. At this point, Mr. Fortune remembers that Mary is his "image," although now "conquered" by his act of hollowing out her skull (O'Connor 1971 355).

After murdering his granddaughter for her opposition to his project of developing the "lawn" and blocking a view of the woods, Fortune experiences a heart attack and is felled like so many of the pines on his own property. From his vantage point of lying prone on the earth, he looks up "helplessly along the bare trunks into the tops of the pines" (O'Connor 1971 356). Meanwhile, his heart enlarges or expands, and he imagines an escape across the artificial lake and into the distant woods of his earlier vision. The mysterious and divine qualities of the natural scene continue to beckon him. In his dying imagination, however, the "gaunt trees" close ranks and march "across the water and away into the distance" (O'Connor 1971 356). Similar to the beginning of the story, the woods walk across the (blood) "red corrugated lake" away from Mr. Fortune. Lying upon the red Georgian clay near his dead granddaughter, his only other company is the "huge yellow" excavator "gorging itself," as ever, "on clay" (O'Connor 1971 335, 356). There is a sense of blood sacrifice in this ending, an offering up of not only a Eucharistic sacrifice but also a human one. The work of the machine reaches its apex with violent death, which is perhaps the inevitable end of efforts to exploit and consume, to dam rivers, to replace lawns with gas stations and woods with fishing clubs. Such activities, taken to their extreme, destroy not only the ecological balance but also those we love and, finally, as in Mr. Fortune's case, our very selves.[38]

Signs of Hope

In her essay "The Nature and Aim of Fiction," likely written in early 1957, Flannery O'Connor invokes the habit of attention so important in the Thoreauvian tradition of American nature writing in order to avoid such self-destructive, even apocalyptic, attitudes toward the world. She also advocates for a sense of universal communion: "The longer you look at one object, the more of the world you see in it, and it's well to remember that the serious fiction writer always writes about the whole world, no matter how limited his particular scene" (O'Connor 1969 77). This attentiveness reveals for O'Connor, as it reveals at least momentarily for the reluctant Mr. Fortune, that "Christ plays in ten thousand places" and that to wound Earth is to do harm to the Body of Christ. When O'Connor makes the point that "the bomb that was dropped on Hiroshima affects life on the Oconee River," she means this both physically and spiritually (O'Connor 1969 77). It cannot be a coincidence that the Oconee is the river that was dammed to produce Lake Sinclair, fictionalized in "A View of the Woods." Everything is interconnected and thus affects every other element in the created order, and certainly, the massive damage wreaked on the natural environment by the dropping of the atomic bomb on Hiroshima on August 6, 1945, reverberated across the world and through time. O'Connor composed "A View of the Woods" eleven years after that event, and her blood-red Earth and suffering, Christ-like trees continue to bear the wounds of that atrocity and its own fearsome instrument of death.

If there is any hope at the end of O'Connor's ecological tale, it emerges ironically from the deaths of Mark Fortune and his granddaughter. Her grandfather was preparing Mary to carry on his work of "progress" after his death, but that legacy is arrested first by her rebellion, then by the old man's murder of his heir apparent. Their corpses thus become potential compost for the rejuvenation of the woods. Although Mr. Fortune drafted a secret will leaving his property in trust to Mary, it is her family, the Pittses, who are the most likely heirs at the story's conclusion. O'Connor's original coda indicates this: "Pitts [Mary's father], by accident, found them that evening. He was walking home through the woods about sunset. The rain had stopped, but the polished trees were hung with clear drops of water that turned red where the sun touched them" (O'Connor 1979 190).[39] Here, Teilhard's "life force," in the form of pure water, is combined with the "death force," as the drops turn a bloody red. It is surely no coincidence that this combination echoes the holy water mixed with Communion wine that is prepared for Consecration at every Catholic Mass.

Although O'Connor wrote to Elizabeth Hester that "I don't really think" this draft ending "does anything for" the story, the image combining life and death reaffirms the Eucharistic connotations of "A View of the Woods" and situates it within the broader Teilhardian vision of a "Mass on the World" (O'Connor 1979 190). For Teilhard, "everything around me is the body and blood of the Word," and he asks, echoing Christ in the Garden of Gethsemane, "How could I refuse this chalice"? This Communion is complete when "not only the life-bringing forces, but also those which bring death" converge in God's "special" and "vitaliz[ing]" love (Teilhard 1960b 28, 31). No doubt such mystical language would provide only cold comfort to the story's deceased protagonists, or really antagonists, and in any case, the published version of O'Connor's story ends with a pessimistic focus on the monstrous excavating machine. "A View of the Woods" finally provides its readers with only a very muted notion that the survivors who appreciate the woods might, in the end, inherit and perhaps find some way to preserve them.[40]

Conclusion

"A View of the Woods" poses a basic question: whose legacy will endure—Fortune or Pitts? To use the language of the present volume: what will it be—disenchantment and self-destruction or a renewed sense of the divine indwelling within the natural world? In the midst of their disagreement over selling the woods, the grandfather asks the girl, "Are you a Fortune ... or are you a Pitts? Make up your mind" (O'Connor 1971 351). When Mark Fortune and his granddaughter are engaged in their final argument, the old man insists that Mary accept her identity as a Fortune and disavow her immediate family, the Pitts. He wants her to surrender to his attitude and the idea that she, like her grandfather, is destined to become the namesake of Fortune, Georgia. Mary strenuously resists, saying emphatically, "I'm PURE Pitts." The rebellion against her grandfather's attitudes will lead to her violent death. Through this familial struggle, the story asks: will an attitude of possession and ultimately unsatisfying consumption continue to wound Earth in the name of development and "progress"? Or will a more integrated and Eucharistic "view of the woods" raise awareness about ongoing damage to God's creation, generate a renewed sense of wonder and praise, and lead to ameliorative action?

As Pope Francis has persuasively explained, establishing an integral ecology is no mean task. Many spiritual traditions, including the Roman Catholic, have sought to raise awareness of the divine indwelling in the created order and the entire cosmos for centuries. This is one of the legacies of Pope Francis' namesake St. Francis of Assisi. At the same time, a perception of human integration with nature—Paula Gunn Allen's "sacred hoop"—remains a profound challenge owing to attitudes of consumption championed by many Christians, along with the monstrous machines that have long seemed ascendant in the so-called "developed" world. Nevertheless, O'Connor, writing as a devout Catholic, is emphatic that wanton harm to any of God's creation is ultimately self-destructive, both individually and for the human species. For O'Connor and Pope Francis, as for Teilhard de Chardin, we are called not to exploit but to cultivate habits of attention, an ethic of care for the natural world, and participation in universal communion. In such ways, we welcome, rather than futilely resist, the divinization of the cosmos.

Notes

[1] The title *Laudato Si'* is taken from Francis of Assisi's "Canticle of the Creatures," composed c. 1224. (Francis of Assisi 1999, 113).

[2] Ryszard Sadowski has persuasively argued that, in addition to Francis of Assisi, Pope Francis' *Laudato Si'* is profoundly indebted to these three pioneers of integral ecology (Sadowski 76–81).

[3] On universal communion, see Francis 69–72 (#89-#92).

[4] Although Teilhard did not compose "The Mass on the World" until 1923, he had considered the theme of "perpetual communion" as early as 1906 while on retreat at Sidi Gaber in Egypt. See King 2005 2.

[5] This vision is echoed in *Laudato Si'*: "The ultimate destiny of the universe is in the fullness of God, which has already been attained by the risen Christ, the measure of the maturity of all things" (Francis 65 [#83]).

[6] Those in Ruby's vision include (1) whites and "black[s] … in white robes"; (2) the physically and mentally disabled, described as "freaks and lunatics"; and (3) different economic classes from the lower, pejoratively described as "white trash," to the upper, namely the "tribe" of the "respectable" and financially well-off (O'Connor 1971 508).

[7] For an insightful analysis of this idea in Teilhard in relation to Eastern Christianity, Maximus the Confessor, and Thomas Merton, see St. John 2011.

[8] On the nature, operation, and Dantean significance of the central excavating machine in "A View of the Woods," see Piggford 2018.

[9] Pertile points out that Dante's Lucifer "is a machine totally dehumanized and desensitized, that is to say, totally deprived of either emotions or intelligence" (Pertile 89). O'Connor studied *The Divine Comedy* as a graduate student at the University of Iowa and possessed a well-read copy of the Carlyle-Okey-Wicksteed translation; see Kinney 1985, 134–135.

[10] Davis perceptively notes that O'Connor's stories often "privilege the artifacts of science and industry by making these very things the new bearers of the sacred" (Davis 21), as, for example, the telescope in "The Lame Shall Enter First" (1962). In "View," however, it is the woods themselves that are portrayed as sacred and the excavator as a desecrator of this sacred space.

[11] Thomas Berry, in *The Great Work,* describes this idea of "progress" in industrialized North America as a "psychic compulsion" that "drove the commercial and industrial entrepreneurs as well as the scientists and engineers in their work." Such compulsion resulted from a transition from an agricultural, "organic economy" to an "extractive economy" (Berry 140, 138).

[12] A character similar to Mr. Fortune in "A View of the Woods" is Mrs. May in O'Connor's "Greenleaf" (1956). When Mrs. May gazes upon "green pastures" and "a black wall of trees" through a window in her home, she surveys property that she possesses, and that might bring her profit. More profoundly, she perceives nature only in relation to herself: "When she looked out of any window in her house, she saw the reflection of her own character" (O'Connor 1971 321).

[13] This scene foreshadows Young Tarwater's unhealthy relationship with food in O'Connor's 1960 novel *The Violent Bear It Away*. His true hunger is for Christ, the Bread of Life, so "city food only weakened him" (O'Connor 1960 161). On the Eucharistic qualities of this novel, see Srigley 2012 201–210.

[14] This emphasis on ecological conversion builds on comments by John Paul II, Benedict XVI, and the Ecumenical Patriarch Bartholomew. A 1990 speech by John Paul II calls for a new relation between humanity and the earth: "Faced with the widespread destruction of the environment, people everywhere are coming to understand that we cannot continue to use the goods of the earth as we have in the past" (John Paul II 1990, #1). In a 2007 address Benedict XVI unambiguously connects social justice to ecology: "The worsening scandal of hunger … reminds us of the urgent need to eliminate the structural causes of global economic dysfunction and to correct models of growth that seem incapable of guaranteeing respect for the environment and for integral human development" (Benedict XVI 2007). On the relevance of Bartholomew's environmentalism to Francis' integral ecology, see Francis 13–15 (#7–9).

[15] It is important to note here that Francis' vision of universal communion does not explicitly extend to nonliving entities, in contrast to Teilhard de Chardin and, later, Thomas Berry. For Berry, "Every being enters into communion with other beings," and such beings include "Trees … insects … rivers … [and] mountains," entities, that is, that are biological, chemical, and geological (Berry 4–5).

[16] For Graybill "deep ecology" emphasizes "biocentric equality"; that is, the value of nonhuman life is not dependent on its relative usefulness for human beings (Graybill 2). This ecological tradition is most closely associated with the Norwegian philosopher Arne Naess and with Bill Devall and George Sessions' *Deep Ecology* (1985).

[17] See, e.g., O'Connor's 1952 novel *Wise Blood* and its description of the night sky over the fictional city of Taulkinham: "The black sky was underpinned with long silver streaks that looked like scaffolding and depth on depth behind it were thousands of stars that all seemed to be moving very slowly as if they were about some vast construction work that involved the whole order of the universe and would take all time to complete" (O'Connor 1952 33). Here one finds a vision of a cosmos under perpetual construction, persistently, even consciously, evolving.

[18] See Gooch 2009 322–323. On the controversial nature of Teilhard's writing from the vantage of the Catholic magisterium, see below.

[19] Ilia Delio clarifies this term in an ecological context: "we are to 'christify' the world" (Delio 94); that is, human beings ought to become Christ-like in our own dealings with the earth and to become aware that Christ's conscious presence pervades the cosmos.

[20] Scheid borrows his notion of communion from Thomas Berry and applies it to the traditions of Catholic social thought and to ecology.

[21] Michael P. Murphy has most helpfully connected Teilhard's idea of cosmic liturgy to O'Connor's mystical realism: "human fallenness is divinely encompassed and consecrated in her fiction as if in a liturgical space—a literary sacramentality, like liturgy itself, which is both precise in its care and cosmic in its scope" (Murphy 53).

[22] For an illuminating exploration of the connotations of Teilhard's term "omega," which signifies "a unity both within and without evolution," see Grim 2016.

[23] In Teilhard's parlance, "noogenesis" refers to the process of evolving the "noosphere," "a human sphere of consciousness around and over the Earth" (Grim 2016, 1). According to Delio, this process is "psycho-social," and she characterizes the noosphere as "a planetary neo-envelope *essentially linked to the biosphere* in which it has its root, yet is distinguished from it. It is the natural culmination of biological evolution and not a termination of it" (Delio 109). For an exploration of the influence of Teilhard's notion of noogenesis on O'Connor, see Watkins 39.

[24] See, e.g., Paul VI's encyclical *Mysterium Fidei:* "No one can fail to see that the divine Eucharist bestows an incomparable dignity upon the Christian people. For it is not just while the Sacrifice is being offered and the Sacrament is being confected, but also after the Sacrifice has been offered and the Sacrament confected—while the Eucharist is reserved in churches or oratories—that Christ is truly Emmanuel, which means 'God with us.' For He is in the midst of us day and night; He dwells in us with the fullness of grace and truth" (Paul VI #67).

[25] Thomas M. King stresses that "The Mass on the World" is primarily a "prayer," which Teilhard "prayed daily when unable to offer Mass" (King xiii).

[26] In *The Divine Milieu* this "death-force" is associated with what Teilhard terms "passivities of diminishment," both external ("all our bits of ill fortune") and internal ("the darkest element and the most despairingly useless years of our lives") (Teilhard 1960a 81). For him, even "our failures, our death, our faults" can "be recast into something better and transformed" in God (Teilhard 1960a 136).

[27] Boff develops this theme of cosmic divinization in *Cry of the Earth, Cry of the Poor.* "We must transcend the anthropocentrism that is common in Christologies, for Christ has divinized and liberated not only human beings but all beings in the universe" (Boff 174).

[28] In 2017, the Pontifical Council for Culture unanimously requested that Pope Francis rescind this *monitum*, especially in light of recent popes' "explicit references" to his works in various speeches and documents, including *Laudato Si'*, see O'Connell. As of September 2019, the *monitum* remains in effect.

[29] Emphasis in the original.

[30] Lake is most perceptive on this point (Lake 234): "Teilhard actually argues that Christianity is the only religion that promotes unity in which no particularities are lost. Pantheism is his example of a 'seduction' that emphasizes unity at the expense of particularity." In contrast to such pantheism, Teilhard's position here might usefully be labeled panentheistic. Panentheism understands the divine as interpenetrating every part of the universe or "divine milieu" while simultaneously transcending it. Boff perceives that Teilhard's evolving cosmos "invites us to undergo the experience that underlies panentheism: at the slightest manifestation of being, at each moment, in every expression of life, intelligence and love, we are facing the Mystery of the universe-in-process" (Boff 154).

[31] On the shared "theological aesthetic" of "pied beauty" in O'Connor and Hopkins, see Bosco, esp. 103–104.

[32] In *Laudato Si'* Francis quotes this statement from John Paul II's 2003 encyclical, which stresses the "cosmic character" of the Eucharist. John Paul II does not refer explicitly to Teilhard, but this notion is unmistakably Teilhardian (Francis 168 [#236]).

[33] This diabolical work might be understood in terms of the central image in Leo Marx's 1964 book *The Machine in the Garden.* On this, see Piggford 2018 94.

[34] O'Connor's story stresses the damage being done to the natural world through technology and the physical and spiritual consequences of that damage. At the same time, the Christ-like qualities of the natural world also evoke suffering humanity's need for relief. This comports well with Leonardo Boff's approach to integral ecology from the perspective of liberation theology. For Boff, to hear the "cry of the earth" is to hear the "cry of the poor," and vice versa: "To hear these two interconnected cries and to see the same root cause that produces them is to carry out integral liberation" (Boff 112). Pope Francis refers to these dual cries in *Laudato Si'* (Francis 40 [#49]).

[35] Pope Francis associates such a "habit of attention" with the "gaze of Jesus": "The Lord was able to invite others to be attentive to the beauty that there is in the world because he himself was in constant touch with nature, lending it an attention full of fondness and wonder" (Francis 75 [#97]).

[36] This scene anticipates a comment by Thomas Berry about an early perception of a meadow in his native North Carolina: "The more a person thinks of the infinite number of interrelated activities that take place here, the more mysterious it all becomes" (Berry 13).

37 Mary is also described as "mechanically" battering her grandfather, a term evocative of the work of the excavating machine.
38 Pope Francis reminds his readers of the "little way" of St. Thérèse of Lisieux as a hopeful mode of being that might provide an alternative to such a self-destructive course: "An integral ecology is … made up of simple daily gestures which break with the logic of violence, exploitation and selfishness. In the end, a world of exacerbated consumption is at the same time a world which mistreats life in all its forms" (Francis 163 [#230]).
39 This coda is included in an editor's note. On Fortune's secret will, see O'Connor 1971 337.
40 Pitts himself is no admirable figure, especially in light of his abusive relationship toward Mary (O'Connor 1971 344). Mary's surviving parents and siblings, however, do at least appreciate the undeveloped woods. Although Mr. Fortune has sold the "lawn" to the devil-like Mr. Tilman for a gas station, the woods themselves will likely be passed along through Fortune's lawyer to the Pitts family (O'Connor 1971 352, 337).

Works Cited

Allen, Paula Gunn. *The Sacred Hoop: Recovering the Feminine in American Indian Traditions*. Boston: Beacon, 1992.

Benedict XVI. "Address to the Diplomatic Corps Accredited to the Holy See for the Traditional Exchange of New Year Greetings." Vatican City: Libreria Editrice Vaticana, 2007. Accessed 15 September 2019. http://w2.vatican.va/content/benedict-xvi/en/speeches/2007/january/documents/hf_ben-xvi_spe_20070108_diplomatic-corps.html.

—. "Homily of His Holiness Benedict XVI, Cathedral of Aosta." Vatican City: Libreria Editrice Vaticana, 2009. Accessed 15 September 2019. http://w2.vatican.va/content/benedict-xvi/en/homilies/2009/documents/hf_ben-xvi_hom_20090724_vespri-aosta.html.

Berry, Thomas. *The Great Work: Our Way into the Future*. New York: Three Rivers Press, 1999.

Boff, Leonardo. *Cry of the Earth, Cry of the Poor*. Translated by Phillip Berryman, Maryknoll, NY: Orbis Books, 1997.

Bosco, Mark. "O'Connor's 'Pied Beauty': Gerard Manley Hopkins and the Aesthetics of Difference." *Revelation and Convergence: Flannery O'Connor and the Catholic Intellectual Tradition*, edited by Mark Bosco and Brent Little, Washington, DC: Catholic University of America Press, 2017, pp. 99–117.

Buell, Lawrence. *The Environmental Imagination: Thoreau, Nature Writing, and the Formation of American Culture*. Cambridge, MA: Harvard University Press, 1996.

Davis, Doug. "Grace in the Machine: Technology and Transfiguration in Flannery O'Connor's Short Fiction." *Flannery O'Connor Review*, n°7, 2009, pp. 18-34.

Delio, Ilia. *Making All Things New: Catholicity, Cosmology, Consciousness*. Maryknoll, NY: Orbis Books, 2015.

de Lubac, Henri. *The Faith of Teilhard de Chardin*. Translated by René Hague, London: Burns & Oates, 1965.

Duffy, Kathleen. *Teilhard's Mysticism: Seeing the Inner Face of Evolution.* Maryknoll, NY: Orbis Books, 2014.

Flanagan, Christine. "From Earth to Eternity: Ecocritical Approaches to 'Greenleaf' and 'A View of the Woods.'" *Short Fiction of Flannery O'Connor,* edited by Robert C. Evans, Amenia, NY: Salem Press, 2016, pp. 159–173.

Francis. *Laudato Si': On the Care for Our Common Home.* Frederick, MD: The Word Among Us Press, 2015.

Francis of Assisi. *Francis of Assisi—The Saint: Early Documents, vol. 1.* Edited by Regis J. Armstrong. New York: New City Press, 1999.

Gooch, Brad. *Flannery: A Life of Flannery O'Connor.* New York: Little, Brown, 2009.

Graybill, Mark S. "O'Connor's Deep Ecological Vision." *Flannery O'Connor Review,* n°9, 2011, pp. 1-18.

Grim, John. "President's Corner." *The Teilhard Perspective, n°*49 (1), 2016, pp. 1–2.

Haddock, Keith. *Giant Earthmovers: An Illustrated History.* Osceola, WI: MBI Publishing, 1998.

Hopkins, Gerard Manley. *The Major Works.* Edited by Catherine Phillips, New York: Oxford University Press, 2002.

John Paul II. "Letter of His Holiness John Paul II to Reverend George V. Coyne, S.J., Director of the Vatican Observatory." Vatican City: Libreria Editrice Vaticana, 1988. Accessed 15 September 2018. http://w2.vatican.va/content/john-paul-ii/en/letters/1988/documents/hf_jp-ii_let_19880601_padre-coyne.html.

—. "Message for the Celebration of the World Day of Peace." Vatican City: Libreria Editrice Vaticana, 1990. Accessed 15 September 2019. http://w2.vatican.va/content/john-paul-ii/en/messages/peace/documents/hf_jp-ii_mes_19891208_xxiii-world-day-for-peace.html.

King, Thomas M. *Teilhard's Mass: Approaches to "The Mass on the World."* Mahwah, NJ: Paulist Press, 2005.

Kinney, Arthur. *Flannery O'Connor's Library: Resources of Being.* Athens, GA: University of Georgia Press, 1985.

Lake, Christina Bieber. *The Incarnational Art of Flannery O'Connor.* Macon, GA: Mercer University Press, 2005.

Murphy, Michael P. "Breaking Bodies: O'Connor and the Aesthetics of Consecration." *Revelation and Convergence: Flannery O'Connor and the Catholic Intellectual Tradition,* edited by Mark Bosco and Brent Little, Washington, DC: Catholic University of America Press, 2017, pp. 51–77.

O'Connell, Gerard. "Will Pope Francis Remove the Vatican's 'Warning' from Teilhard de Chardin's Writings?" *America,* November 21, 2017. Accessed 15 September 2019, https://www.americamagazine.org/faith/2017/11/21/will-pope-francis-remove-vaticans-warning-teilhard-de-chardins-writings.

O'Connor, Flannery. *Wise Blood.* New York: Harcourt, Brace & Co, 1952.

—. *The Violent Bear It Away.* New York: Farrar, Straus and Giroux, 1960.

—. *Mystery and Manners: Occasional Prose.* Edited by Sally and Robert Fitzgerald, New York: Farrar, Straus and Giroux, 1969.

—. *The Complete Stories.* New York: Farrar, Straus, and Giroux, 1971.

—. *Letters of Flannery O'Connor: The Habit of Being.* Edited by Sally Fitzgerald, New York: Farrar, Straus and Giroux, 1979.

—. *The Presence of Grace and Other Book Reviews.* Edited by Carter W. Martin, Athens, GA: University of Georgia Press, 1983.

Paul VI. *Mysterium Fidei.* Vatican City: Libreria Editrice Vaticana, 1965. Accessed 15 September 2019. http://w2.vatican.va/content/paulvi/en/encyclicals/documents/hf_p-vi_enc_03091965_mysterium.html.

Pertile, Lino. "Introduction to *Inferno.*" *The Cambridge Companion to Dante,* edited by Rachel Jacoff, 2nd ed., Cambridge: Cambridge University Press, 2007, pp. 67–90.

Piggford, George. "Flannery O'Connor's Excavator and Dante's Lucifer in 'A View of the Woods.'" *Flannery O'Connor Review,* n°16, 2018, pp. 93-110.

Sadowski, Ryszard. "Inspirations of Pope Francis' Concept of Integral Ecology." *Seminaire,* n°37 (4), 2016, pp. 69–82.

Scheid, Daniel P. *The Cosmic Common Good: Religious Grounds for Ecological Ethics.* New York: Oxford University Press, 2016.

Slovic, Scott. *Seeking Awareness in American Nature Writing.* Salt Lake City, UT: University of Utah Press, 1992.

Srigley, Susan. "Asceticism and Abundance: The Communion of Saints in *The Violent Bear It Away.*" *Dark Faith: New Essays on Flannery O'Connor's The Violent Bear It Away,* edited by Susan Srigley, Notre Dame, IN: Notre Dame University Press, 2012, pp. 185–212.

St. John, Donald P. "Contemplation and Cosmos: Merton on Maximus and Teilhard." *Teilhard Studies,* n°62, 2011.

Teilhard de Chardin, Pierre. *The Divine Milieu.* Translated by Bernard Wall, New York: Harper & Brothers, 1960a.

—. *Hymn of the Universe.* Translated by Bernard Wall, New York: Harper & Brothers, 1960b.

—. *The Phenomenon of Man.* Translated by Bernard Wall. Rev. ed., New York: Harper & Row, 1968a.

—. *Writings in Time of War.* Translated by René Hague, New York: Harper & Row, 1968b.

Third Plenary Council of Baltimore. *Baltimore Catechism (A Catechism of Christian Doctrine).* Number 3. Charlotte: TAN Books, 2010.

Vande Brake, Timothy R. "Thinking Like a Tree: The Land Ethic in O'Connor's 'A View of the Woods." *Flannery O'Connor Review,* n°9, 2011, pp. 19-35.

Watkins, Steven R. *Flannery O'Connor and Teilhard de Chardin: A Journey Towards Hope and Understanding About Life.* New York: Peter Lang, 2009.

Westling, Louise. *Sacred Groves and Ravaged Gardens: The Fiction of Eudora Welty, Carson McCullers, and Flannery O'Connor.* Athens, GA: University of Georgia Press, 1985.

Woodward, C. Vann. *The Burden of Southern History.* 3rd ed. Baton Rouge, LA: Louisiana State University Press, 2008.

Chapter 14

Haiku as the Ecopoetical Threshold of "Ice Riding on Its Melting"

Keiko Takioto Miller

Mercyhurst University, USA

Abstract: Owing much to the Western language of phenomenology as a vehicle, this essay will elucidate the structurally invisible operative unique to *haiku* craftsmanship. Transcending discursive treatments of its visible structure will bring us "onto the earth, making [us] belong to it, and thus brings [us] into dwelling" (Heidegger 1971 216). The author's focus is on the composition of *haiku*, based on her theory of the genesis of the archetypal language at the threshold of "ice riding on its melting," as phrased by Robert Frost. Its insistence on minimalism opens us to the "understanding of the ground as an element in our way of being." (Levin 1985 290). At such a source, where the sky touches the earth, the lofty human language must be silenced once again in order for its co-originating operative to find its own eco-somatic dwelling as poetry. Here, the ego and eco are no longer distinguishable.

Keywords: *haiku*, structural visible and invisible, archetypal language, operative, re-pair, *mono no aware*, sense-making, *suchness*, nature-culture threshold, *s'écarter de*, ontic, ontological

***

I chanced upon a phrase by Robert Frost in his 1939 essay "The Figure a Poem Makes": "Like a piece of ice on a stove the poem must ride on its melting." In its *suchness* the image seems to convey the quintessence of poetic language, echoing the Japanese aesthetics of *wabi-sabi* ("profundity in simplicity") and *mono no aware* ("pathos of nature"). It evokes a corporeal inkling of primordial happenings as a "structurally invisible" trace. As such, the poetic language is capable of not only transporting us spatio-temporally to the nexus of its genesis in the raw, but also re-emerging as an internal catalyst when we are confronted with a moral dilemma, including that which concerns our relationship with Mother Earth.

Haiku as a poetical form has been popularized in the West since its first onset owing particularly to the compactness and portability of its 5-7-5 syllabic triad. Like most modern made-in-Japan products, it is small, adaptable, and even adequate. Except for a few esoteric literary circles, however, the true and more universal craftsmanship of *haiku* seems little understood. Ironically when we, as humans, understand and come to terms with the nature of the language it demands of us, we begin to "poetically dwell in that [which we] build," as Heidegger suggests, for such a language is not arrogant and divisive. Rather poetry "admits man's dwelling into its very nature, its presencing being. Poetry is the original admission of dwelling" (Heidegger 225). In other words, here, the Heideggerian mode of living, or dwelling, seems to reflect a trace of an unspoken transaction between nature and humans that is critical to sustaining both existences as ethos.

For the Japanese poet Matsuo Basho (1644-1694), who had witnessed the existential *superflu* among his contemporaries of the Edo period, renouncing hedonism in order to travel afar and dwell in the wilderness was not an option. By eschewing material excess, he was able to reflexively rediscover the primordial spring source of all manifestations, including language. His perhaps most celebrated *haiku* below marks not only his auspicious arrival at the edge of an ancient pond but also his "admission of dwelling" ecopoetically upon hearing the sacred essence in the sound of a frog plunging into its depth:

> An old pond—
> A frog leaps in.
> The sound of water
>
> –Basho
> (Shirane 183)

Basho took just the first few verses of the thirteenth-century aristocratic poetic form *renga* and developed it into 5-7-5 syllable *haiku*. This may have been prompted by his realization that its popularized predecessor, *haikai*, had become infected with a contemporary earthiness that had turned vulgar. By shedding linguistic excess, the poet embraced his own existential death in the ontic world and began to "dwell in its very nature"—ontologically.

In her book, *Merleau-Ponty's Phenomenology of Perception: A Guide to Commentary*, Monika M. Langer exposes Descartes's eventual, if not ironical, self-recognition of "the tremendous disparity between his own dualistic thesis and his actual experience of the body" (Langer 59). Subsequently, she expounds on Merleau-Ponty's critical points: (1) that the experiencing body is immanently predisposed with speech, which is, in turn, imbued with "*gestural* [*significance*] […] rather than merely translating an already accomplished thought; (2) that such speech is also 'authentic'" (Langer 59). This implies further that in order for genuine communication to take place between a poet (the speaker) and an audience (the listener), there must exist a dynamic inter-subjective threshold in which belies "the existential significance [beneath] the conceptual significance of language" (Langer 59). Accordingly, genuine poetry as a form of speech must possess "an immanent significance" capable of evoking a kind of primordial "bodily presence" not yet accessible to the intellect, yet structurally present, however invisibly.

Moreover, Langer's most critical point for understanding ecopoetics is revealed in her claim that "[t]he dawn of language lies in emotional gesticulation [which] is simultaneously 'natural' and 'cultural'" (Langer 62). This means that in order for us to be able to practice ecologically aware and responsible communication, we need to pay a kind of linguistic homage to this primordially dynamic nexus where the earliest nature-to-culture shift occurred in humans, as we witnessed it in Basho's existential inquiry above. It is as if the "t" in the middle of the word "cul*t*ure" positioned itself as such to alert us that the health of a culture is to be sustained dynamically by upholding the original essence of this magical, if not sacred, *t*hreshold between "cult" (human) and "[na]*t*ure." As such, the "t" bears a semantic significance. The following is an imaginative thought experiment on my part to illustrate the process of how language, as a dynamic nature-cultural phenomenon, may have emerged.

Ascending into modern humans, imagine our earliest primate ancestors as foragers cohabiting with nature inter-subjectively as one. Their survival instinct relied exclusively on their keen senses, not yet cognizant of their natural environment as a categorical "other"—until an event of awe stole their attention. Neuroscience defines this attention as "an act of recognizing a perceived stimulus so that you could move that information to your working memory and decide what to do from there" (Anderson 519). It gave our ancestors an impetus for an executive action forcing them to organize an otherwise chaotic mass of their perceptual data into a more meaningful protolanguage. With reference to Kant, Patricia Kitcher expounds on this point in her book *Kant's Transcendental Psychology:*

> The core of Kant's analysis is that we cannot represent objects at all unless there is some process that can construct unified representations on the basis of the multiple contents of cognitive states occurring at different times through the mediation of different senses. Any possible explanation of object cognition must include an account of this process of connection or synthesis. Further, this process cannot be

governed by the unaided law of association. Synthesis must be carried out inside the mind, so it requires some mental faculty that has the power of synthesizing (Kitcher 81).

Imagine here a person in awe trying to anchor herself aground in nature. She is feeling her inner struggle through which to process an inventory of her perceptual data into an expression as a viable form of representing reality. The geographer John Wylie echoes this idea in his book *Landscape.* He states that "the couplet culture/nature signals the tensions at work within the concept of landscape" (Wylie 9), meaning that this feeling within is a sign of one's ethical call for an action to mediate between nature and culture reflexively. Allying with such phenomenologists as Martin Heidegger and Merleau-Ponty, Wylie argues "above all that the Cartesian perspective does not in fact truthfully describe lived, human experience—the human experience of landscape, for instance" (Wylie 147). More importantly, he quotes anthropologist Tim Ingold, who states, "[T]o suggest that human beings inhabit discursive worlds of culturally constructed significance is to imply that they have already taken a step out of the world of nature" (Ingold 156), in the first place. Therefore, setting our foot into untamed nature in this life allows one to linguistically practice a kind of *rapprochement* between the expression and the expressed, possibly resulting in the poet's riding merely on its operative tension. That the Japanese *haiku* poet Basho literally chopped off a good chunk of the lengthier *renga* poetry from centuries earlier and purified the gangrened *haikai* in his life in order to craft more austere poetic form *haiku* into mere 17-syllables suggests that the truth shown in brevity is sufficient unto itself. In this sense, *haiku* served as a transient literary vehicle, which allows its beholder to ride mindfully on the felt *t*ension between na*t*ure and cul*t*ure. As such, it can offer, in its deceptively humble form, a visceral means to reverse the flow of *qi* from nature-to-culture to culture-to-nature using our navel center, from which to help redirect ourselves more organically. To better understand this point, let us first examine how we have come to the tipping point of cultural excess in the first place, hence our burning desire to return to nature, however awkwardly. Ironically, the proof of this phenomenon is in our millennia-old anthropocentric pudding sediment settled above the primordial soup. In it, we have cruelly drowned the very name and essence of the realm we could have dwelled more ecopoetically—nature. The coming to terms with it of our cultural ways is long overdue.

That the Ainu, the indigenous settlers of the geographically isolated Japan, had had no vocabulary word for "nature" (*shi-zen* 自然) until it was first introduced by the Chinese in the 6th century AD, affirms Wylie and Ingold's view mentioned above. Furthermore, this premise holds the key to my hypothesis: The genesis of a word presupposes not only the embodiment of its phenomenal trace relationally through senses but also a certain degree of distancing from it, forcing its beholder to organize this phenomenon into a representative form, of which language is one. As such, by failing to maintain the trace inherent to the expression, we become disembodied from its organismic reality. For example, when our ancestors were met by a natural event of awe, e.g. lightening, a passage of seasons, an encounter with animals of prey, ingestion of poisonous vegetation, etc., they may have experienced a sudden cognitive shift, or the aforementioned "attention," away from the yet to be differentiated indigenous realm. Here by "indigenous" I mean non-dualistic wholeness. It is also unthinkable to imagine that this same event of differentiation could have been responsible for shaping our spatio-temporal relationality— past/present/future and there/here/over there, etc. The material legacies of our ancestors who had learned to access nature's resources provide evidence enough that they had learned at some point to conceive a better temporal space (future) in which to escape and heal themselves from their undesirable experiences (past) both physically and emotionally. In other words, by distancing ourselves from nature, we have created a warehouse of illusions; dwelling within the latter, we have been busying ourselves, categorizing according to preferences shaped by our experiences, often to the point of delusion. We then let such categories validate our so-called identity, hence the material accumulation, including that with which we peculiarly promote our "connection" to nature.

Let us further explore this point by focusing on the advent of tool invention. A tool embodies at once nature (materiality) and culture (design), suggesting that humans have undergone a process of objectifying nature as a resource to troubleshoot a dilemma at hand. Its existence presupposes its beholders having already distanced themselves far enough from nature to be able to reflexively reconstruct it mimetically using their somatic data gathered in nature. The word "to repair" already embodies the operative trace "re-pairing" unpaired dualities back into its quasi-original wholeness. Not surprisingly, in time, an ax or hammer would come to symbolize "operatively" a given group's coming together as a tribe or nation-state. One's increased reliance upon such tools may have inspired the idea of surplus in storage to ensure the group's survival in the future. That one can also build something new not only implies simultaneously past (brokenness) to be mended in the present (wholeness) but also the future (investment) to insure against possible brokenness by outdoing nature. It is this last step that demands our ethical inquiry regarding excess.

How much of our hardwired fear has driven our human species to become increasingly obsessed with storage for our future? With each technological advancement, including language, humans have deviated more towards an environmentally and aesthetically convenient but costly path away from an ontologically meaningful context, in which "the person is part and parcel of the process of coming-into-being of the world as a whole" (Ingold 168). The irony is that we have stored more voids in milliards of manmade jugs in our warehouse but with little or no rainfall to fill them to appreciate the operative essence of pouring from their spouts, much less their source. We have become ignorant of the Heideggerian ecopoetic operative evident in his phrase, "The thing things the world" (Heidegger 178). Yet, there are still ways to resurrect the critical threshold where the noun "tool" and verb "tool" co-emerged. Arriving at this nuanced point of tension through ecopoetic dwelling is imperative for us to navigate along a more sustainable trajectory away from the linear one. But first, it requires us to embrace the reality of climate change before we reach the tipping point of no return, which is predicted to be in 2030 by many scientists, including Dr. Anthony Ingraffea, the founder and advisor of the Cornell Fracture Group (Ingraffea Lecture).

In any case, nature has revealed its healing potential to humans through the cyclical passage of time, dissipating some of its harsher realities. Here, one is made aware once again of the "tension," but more reflexively this time, upon reflection from afar. It presupposes our willingness to take a good look at the size of our warehouse of accumulation fueled by insecurity. Only then can we transcend all dualities, moving towards the realm of *rapprochement*. Once there, in order to sustain a wheel in motion following the laws of nature, one must hold both ends of a fiber, threading it until one can intuit the right center to feel the nuanced culture-nature tension. This posture is likened to an image of ritual in the making.

Heidegger's following ritual-like description of "the thing" in his book *Poetry, Language and Thought* (Heidegger 169–170) reinforces Frost's idea of poetic image alluded to in his phrase "riding on the ice melting," and Japanese aesthetic nuance *wabi-sabi* ("pathos of nature") unique to *haiku* poetry: "How does the jug's void hold? It holds by taking what is poured in. [...] The word 'hold' is therefore ambiguous. [...] In the gift of water, [...] sky and earth dwell. [...] In the jugness of the jug, sky and earth dwell" (Heidegger 169). That a jug was made for pouring liquid reflects our ancestors' having embodied its happening when, in nature, the sky split open as an awesome event of thundering and lightning to pour its rain upon thirsty earth, promising a good turn of harvest. It presences itself symbolically as an auspicious item. Imbued with both material essence and functionality, it is particularly evocative at the very moment when its aqueous content emerges from its spout to touch its thirsty receptacle. Similarly, the very process of seeding and bearing fruit in nature is also re-enacted in the ritual of exchanging spirited drinks between a marrying couple in the presence of an officiator who is entrusted to offer it to them as a blessing from the source. In essence, phenomenology teaches us to take a grip on each experience, both visible and invisible, with both hands, as it were, here and now, without fear of attachment. For if we learn to ride the cycle, then things will return. For example, an ancient symbol of a feathered serpent conceals the archetypal essence that the sky and earth are cyclically in communication. The archaeologist Colin Renfrew further affirms this view: "[W]e must be quick to realize that symbol and reality are not easily separable. [...] the mind works through the body. To localize it exclusively within the brain is not strictly correct. [...] This [material engagement] is an approach that endeavors to transcend the duality implied in those long-standing contrasts between mind and matter, soul and body, or cognition and the material world" (Renfrew 98–103).

Accordingly, our ancestors may have eventually come to regard nature not only as a mere entity apart from themselves but simultaneously as an awesome potential source of both life and death in a constant cycle. Since different seasonal phenomena are shaped relationally as the earth's periodic responses to maintain its balance according to the ever-shifting positions of other celestial bodies, natural adversities are, to some degree, inevitable. However, failing to understand and respect this nuance, or sustain this delicate nature-culture balance, by our cultural insisting on living linearly against nature's curved trajectories could lead to an irretrievable kind of manmade devastation. One way is to begin dwelling ecopoetically in the use of words.

If a "thing things," does a word word, too? If so, then in what way does language function like a jug? Let us examine the sound of the interjection "ah" whose likeness is found in most, if not all, languages. It is at once onomatopoeic and symbolic: Onomatopoeic in that it mimics the sonic reality associated with an experience of awe or wonderment, and symbolic in that it, as an example of the aforementioned Langer's "emotional gesticulation," evokes the unknown beyond the scope of human cognition. It finds its way from somewhere deep within our cells, the storehouse of our memories. The same sound is anticipated to emerge from a newborn's mouth at birth as a vital sign of life. In the Buddhist seed mantra "*aum*" the sound /a/ occupies the honored place of marking life's entry as /m/ does so, marking its closure. The semantic linguist Deborah James, who defines "oh" as a signal of one's becoming aware of something, including that which calls for action, associates "ah" more with pleasure (James 38). Whatever the event of awe, "ah" is potently imbued with the "stepping one step out of nature" perspective while finding oneself caught in nature that Ingold refers to. In its simplest possible acoustic unit, this exclamation is nuanced with the known and unknown, capable of offering humans a momentary clear field, hence an action-directive. In this sense, it is tempting to view it as the oldest lexicon, which may have emerged when our ancestors detected a pattern in their perceptual data upon encountering an unforgettable, yet indescribable, pleasant or unpleasant occurrence. It is as though the event triggered one's inner surge of blood, sweat, and tears to fuel and mediate the Langian "emotional gesticulation" into the exhalation "ah." In this vein transcending the onomatopoeic "ah" directs one towards a practical solution while bathing us in the yet-to-be-realized mysteries of the universe. And to this day, this remains the same. How, then, does the crafting of *haiku* help us appreciate this mysterious *ah*-ness by dwelling poetically in the humble *suchness* of the here and now through rapprochement with nature within and without?

When we embody the invisible thread exposed in a moment's happening in nature, we have already entered into a subliminal realm. From here, we can then journey towards the co-originating source of all things. Accordingly, the threshold of an aesthetic experience (*suchness*) can also be a gateway towards ethicality (eco-dwelling), which is ontologically rooted in nature. It is reflected in the Japanese aesthetic term *mono no aware*. Though often translated as "pathos of nature," the phrase's other interpretation, "feeling of being moved by things," may be more relevant here. The phenomenologist David Abram refers to this threshold not only as "the subjective field of experience, mediated by the body" but also "a collective landscape, constituted by other experiencing subjects as well as by oneself" (Abram 37). *Haiku*, in this vein, offers a methodology to practice "rewilding"—to borrow the *Earth First*'s founder David Foreman's term— our awareness back to the primordial nature-human emerging point no longer accessible to the intellect alone (Frazer 2010, 356). By removing oneself spatio-temporarily from the ontic mode of mere utilitarianism or self-serving emotionality in the name of "our culture," one is given a chance to re-experience the Merleau-Pontian *chiasm*, or Bachelardian "reverberation," whereby to re-immerse oneself in nature ecopoetically. This is the realm of "sensemaking" based on the psychologist Todd E. Marshall, who mentions K.E. Weick's work on the subject:

> Sensemaking is a combination of "action and cognition together" (Weick 1995). Weick refers to this as "enactment." This speaks to the fact that individuals participate in their environment. As they are creating their environment, they are also making sense of it. People are making sense of dynamic environments "not some kind of monolithic, singular, fixed environment that exists detached from and external to those people" (Weick 1995 31). The individual is part of the environment through the process of co-constructing it with fellow sensemakers. This is why sensemaking is not just interpretation. Interpretation is about reading a "text." Sensemaking involves not only understanding the text but also creating the text. (Marshall, Retrieved in 2018).

Based on the above assumption, only to those who have embodied the essence and workings of experiences unique to the group are their narratives culturally meaningful, especially if they can trigger their "emotional gesticulation" welling up from within. Such a sensemaking realm presences itself dynamically at the culture-nature threshold, like "ah." If so, what is it about the language of *haiku* that is linguistically capable of summoning its diverse audience by defying such cultural barriers?

Conventionally *haiku* has been known to the world as a poetic form in brevity and simplicity expressed in seventeen syllables, further broken down into a triad of 5-7-5-syllable lines. It also contains elements of the season and even of surprise in the third line. However, to assume that the universality is met by simply obeying such a formula is to dismiss the deeper appreciation of what a *haiku* can do for humanity deprived of opportunities to re-wild themselves. In his *Anthology of Japanese Literature*, Donald Keene elucidates the art form by stating, "One of the ideals of the *haiku* was to have each word indispensable and inalterable, no doubt a product of the brevity of the form" (Keene 377). By "indispensable and inalterable," *haiku* poets are meant to discipline themselves to work intimately with the essence of language through "enactment." In other words, in the process of gleaning his/her words without sacrificing the aesthetics of "profundity in simplicity," the poet is made to appear him/herself to the earth namelessly. This humbling posture, in turn, causes him/her to present him/herself primordially to the exfoliated consciousness. No longer in need of holding onto one's warehouse of self-identity, it suffices that a simple hut in the woods lets one hut ecopoetically in its *suchness*.

If in search of aesthetics, one falls into solipsism; it can pose a danger of becoming narcissism. If everything has to be translated into the language of the senses, we cannot be freed. *As mentioned earlier, Haiku is an ecopoetic way of practicing ethicality rooted in nature.* Bachelard echoes this point in his reference to George Rouault's painting, "The oeuvre must redeem an impassioned soul." According to Bachelard, perspectives anchored in this soul "must participate in an inner light which is not a reflection of a light from the outside world" (Bachelard xxi). By one's centering through the austere practice of minimalism in form, it helps to illuminate one's vision of the circumference of infinite dualities radiating from nuances each word holds. Here, one must sacrifice one's cultural bias by choosing words from a lexically primitive ground before one's perceptions become proportionately heightened. Thus if, without any subjectivity, a *haiku* poem could coax its reader to return not only to the realm of its simple noun elements but also to their "ontologically oscillating" threshold activated by its verbs, then it has done its job of situating its reader in the dynamic word-emerging culture-nature nexus. Here it all simultaneously makes sense. This is the *topos* where one is given one's second chance to freely wet one's feet at the edge of a primordial river and reconnect with the earth as one remembers in its untainted rawness. Unfettered by solipsism, riding only on simple nouns and verbs in their infinite pairing, chanced in their *suchness* of the moment, can we freely return to our own autochthonous realm? This is the primordial common ground of understanding for all sentient beings. It is, in essence, the very life of *haiku* poetry. It is capable of "gesticulating" (emoting) another body subtly yet profoundly so as to empathize with the earth and its earthlings long displaced from their mutual operative center "T." Could this be a cure for the Sartrian excess or the crisis of *superflu* experienced by the protagonist Roquentin in Sartre's *La Nausée?*

According to Li Mai, the phenomenologist author of *Heidegger on East-West Dialogue: Anticipating the Event*, "'Stillness' indicates the region which gives hints and at the same time withdraws itself" (Mai 140). In a moment of pause where one takes a breath, e.g., "ah," it is possible to view the unknown trying to balance with the known. One finds oneself illuminated by shifting more towards the other, hence meeting at the elliptically merged center. This is where restructuring makes sense. Furthermore, as Langer points out, "[I]t ['T'] is a way of situating oneself in the world and concomitantly, structuring one's experience" (Langer 63), primordially from the onset of the first great crisis. In this sense, re-wilding is not the same thing as our having to go back to the primordial ground zero. Instead, it encourages us to reclaim internally, through bodily *rapprochement*, the pre-linguistic state of our ecopoetical nature-culture dwelling as a sensible choice.

For modern folks like us, who are drenched in materialism and verbosity, the journey of *haiku* writing is an ego-shedding path to the original truth. It is the third tenet of the Buddhist *Four Noble Truths*, which encourages an ontic reduction of everydayness in the Heideggerian sense. As Albert Einstein has said, "Everything should be made as simple as possible, but not any simpler" (Retrieved from "Quote Investigator" 2018). If only we could realize that reaching such a common ground is imperative in intercultural communication, we would not have to use hyperboles counterproductively to convince ourselves that this earth must be let to heal itself naturally to its simple self. Only then can we realize we must reduce ourselves to our simplest possible selves. In the earthly furrows, we meet our mutual ancestral gleaners with whom we become moved profoundly by nature's subtle ways within and without.

"Conversations with Kyorai" by Murai Kyorai is an important testimonial to the world about the original intention of the *haiku*. It was revealed during Master Basho's confession of his poem criticized by his old Master Shohaku. Basho praised his disciple Kyorai for understanding the secret of *haiku* upon the latter's transcending seasonal and geo-climatic boundaries mentioned in the poem and opening himself up to empathize with "one like yourself [Basho] who is living by the lake." "What truth there is in the poetry of a man who has been genuinely stirred by some sight of nature!" (Keene 378). "Genuinely stirred"—because in his embodiment of the ever-shifting structural invisible at work upon the "sight of nature," Basho was able to feel the reverberation of the *dharma*, which had long been denied behind the shadow of human construct. There in solitude, he was able to recollect the body's primordial memories of the original threshold of all emanating manifestations upon this Earth.

Let us plunge into the mystery held by the following *haiku* poems:
Little sparrows,
Step aside, step aside,
Master Horse is coming through

–Issa
(Shirane 941)

Hey, don't swat the fly!
He wrings his hands,
Wrings his feet

–Issa
(Shirane 941)

Counting fleabites
as she nurses
the child

–Issa
(Shirane 944)

Taking a midday nap
Feet planted
Upon a cool wall

–Basho

Stillness—
Sinking deep into the rocks
Cries of the cicada

–Basho
(Shirane 223)

Under the same roof
Women of pleasure also sleep—
Bush clover and moon

–Basho
(Shirane 230)

Kakibara Eiken notes: "[I]n poetry, the scene is always in the emotion, and the emotion is always in the scene." […] "Although it appears that the poem possesses absolutely no emotion, Basho has managed to suggest the emotion of quiet loneliness. This is what is called the overtones of poetry. Isn't it what haikai is all about?" (Haruo Shirane 194). Note, here the emotionality is closer to empathy rather than invested energy justifying one's action. The so-called "emotion of quiet loneliness" is less a subjective feeling of lack on the part of the poet than a subtle collective human memory of our once being separated from our Mother Nature long ago.

Peculiarly there exist two *kanji* ideographs 寂／淋 in Japanese for "loneliness." Despite the public's concern for social appropriateness in choosing one over the other, the general consensus indicates that either one is acceptable. However, based on the etymological construct of these *kanji* characters, the latter one 淋, in particular, draws my curiosity because of its ecopoetical elements both in parts as well as a whole. The character is composed of essentially the radical of "water" 氵, and "woods" 林, which is derived from two "trees" 木. The combination of these radicals suggests "loneliness" is found in the behavior of the water, which may have trickled out of our ancestors' eyes as tears upon being caught in the rain deep in the woods. He is hut-less and vulnerable. Since tears can manifest themselves upon experiencing either a lack of "other" or a fulfilling return of "other," their meanings are enigmatic by nature. In this sense, trees as a shelter in such a moment can evoke a sense of relief, rendering complexity to the meaning of "loneliness" assigned to this ideograph. In reference to the Native American Yaqui people, who dress deer antlers with wildflowers to perform the Yaqui Deer Dance in the spring at the edge of the forest, the poet Linda Hogan speaks of the forest as "a place of enchantment" (Hogan Ecopoetic Dwelling Conference). It is too familiar for our ancestors that the interspace between the wild and tamed is a nuanced threshold. It's one thing to re-enchant ourselves by choosing to live in a small cottage in a forest as Linda Hogan does. But her reverse *écartement* goes a few steps further. By letting wasps and hummingbirds naturally find their way into her house, she lets nature deconstruct the preconceived design and function of windows by humans and finds herself cohabiting with them, hence blurring the divide. She dwells in what Bachelard calls "the original state of reverie" (Bachelard xxi). Calling the wasps' buzzing her new alarm clock, she ambiguates the European colonial constructs and succeeds in her journey back to the primordial intersubjective threshold honored by the indigenous. It is where their existence in nature ("woods") emerged as essence, and essence reverberated into words. Such words, as hers, are imbued with spells of magic unreachable with modern intellect. It is in this subliminal space of enchantment where shamans dwell of old, including Hogan herself (Hogan Ecopoetic Dwelling Conference).

If, as Robert Frost says, "the poem should be like ice riding on its melting," then something in the likeness of *qi* must be given off (as do tears) as the ecopoetic happening. That is, its verbal form yields itself to its original essence. It resembles what Shirane calls in Basho's *haiku* poems as "suggested emotion" or "the overtones." When the ego is let go, its *qi* is channeled back into the threshold where life's happening undo itself as *suchness*. Here we are revealed in reverse of life emerging from its birth canal. The "overtone" is the "structurally invisible" element upon which we are able to "ride" intersubjectively, or even namelessly, as one. Heidegger calls this *suchness* "thingly or workly character," which "in the art work is like the substructure into and upon which the other, authentic element is built" (Heidegger 19–20). As if to summon us to dismount from the pile of our bad habits, Heidegger urges us: "[A]nswer to the question [,] 'What is the thing?' He condemns our having become "so familiar that we no longer sense anything questionable behind them" (Heidegger 22). Accordingly, for him, "The thing is the *aistheton*, that which is perceptible by sensations in the sense belonging to sensibility" (Heidegger 25). That is to say, the language of ecopoetry must be able to awaken our primordial senses simultaneously as they are being synthesized sonically into words. In this way, as Heidegger holds, we get "much closer than [to] all sensations"—"[to] the things themselves" (Heidegger 25). This is how we ride on the liminal Frostian ice-melting.

A silhouette
In the early dawn cold
Lighting a fire

–Basho
(Shirane 199)

The image in the poem above by Basho is poignantly moving. It is particularly so for me, since it is deeply embedded in my childhood memory even before I could reason. My grandfather was the keeper of the seed fire in my family. At bedtime, he would cover the dwindling charcoal ember buried in its own ashes now accumulated in the brazier which sat in our family's tea room. Every morning before anyone woke up, he would carefully expose the retained ember buried in the ashes and bring it to a pile of kindling wood outside to start a new fire in a clay pot all over again. Imprinted in my mind is my grandfather, who, squatting over the fire pit outside in the wintry darkness of early morning, relentlessly kept blowing the ember of potential ignition. Here, Basho's poem captures the fleeting moment of my grandfather's white breath turning into a growing flame lighting up his face, which, only a moment ago, was a lump of dark shadow in the feeble dawn's light. This is the "ice riding on its melting" moment. It's not so much that it lacks emotion. Rather, our heart is moved when it recognizes the primitive elements within us and without trembling inter-subjectively at the threshold of life. Here I neither possess my grandfather as my own nor my authorship of the poem. It suffices that the subtle essence of light and fire so moves us deeply in its primitive *suchness*.

On a cold January morning of my grandfather's funeral, the mourners followed the snowy footprints of the straw sandals worn by my eldest uncle. Clad in a ritual white *kimono* and *hakama*, he solemnly carried a ceremonial cedar tray upon which rested an unlit hand-plumed wooden torch. It was his turn to light up the wooden barrel casket now occupied by the corpse of his old man. As the sound of the flame in the cremation chamber made a thunderous crack, the Buddhist monks' chanting seemed to subside deeply into the bowel of the Earth.

Momentarily distracted, I stole a glimpse of a hunchbacked man who had snuck into the cremation hut from the dark woods behind. When I whispered to my aunt about him, she answered dutifully, "He is the man in charge of spending the night with Grandpa until his body turns into ashes tomorrow." I asked what his name was. She didn't know; after all, he was "only a *burakumin* (an untouchable)," as I would find out much later. But the image keeps knocking on my door in my reverie:

> The corpse now ablaze
> The hunchback's job's just begun
> A child steals his shadow

In the preface of his book, David Michael Levin reiterates Heidegger by stating, "Ontology has an ontic foundation" (23). The irony is that ontology is possible only to those who question the dysfunctionality (disconnect from *Dasein*) of our own banal (ontic) way of existing. Thus inspired to *s'écarter* from this ontic numbness, we find ourselves in the field of clarity. There our ecstatic *rapprochement* with the Being, or aforementioned Heideggerian "thingliness" or Zen *suchness*, rekindles and sustains the ontological self. Here, we must hear the calling of nature into its bosom.

The sustenance of the ontological self then requires our constant reverse-*écartement* from the ontically formed banal cultural identity in equidistance towards the nature-culture nexus. This must be done to avoid our eventual dangling in the void like an abandoned jug. Therefore, as Thomas M. Alexander emphasizes, by awakening the forgotten element, we need to be in contact with the process of the symbolic unconcealing of "'Mythos' in our understanding of the self and world" (Alexander 293). In other words, a *haiku* poet can be considered a shaman who posits him/herself in the "interspace" between worldliness and wilderness. As an "interbeing," (Nhat Hanh 1993) s/he "understands the world and himself as a metaphoric power as the possibility of significant relation" (Alexander 294). Using ecstasy and laughter, she aesthetically transcends all dualities by vertically upholding with its spine what's above and below the *omphalous* plane, the nexus of the natural and cultural. Seeing signs of unseen environmental disasters in recent decades, operating from such an ecopoetical axiom has become an ethical ethos.

Our modern world is a product of a long and relentless process of externalizing what we have internalized. It presupposes a history of our ancestors' exponential distancing, or "écartement," from having formerly immersed in nature. The language of *haiku* is pre-reflective. As it were, it gives off as a vapor from the subliminal space during the author's "*écartement*" from the ice riding on its melting. It is simultaneously *natural ena language* at the threshold of life's emergence. This is, as Langer mentions, "Underlying that reflective procedure which tears the subject away from its body and its world, we find a pre-reflective experience in which our body, things, and the world are immediately present and interrelated in a 'living connection,' just as are the part of our body itself" (Langer 70). This is the very core of Zen Master Dogen's book *Shobo Genzo*—to let one's ego disperse into the wind as one dares to hop onto the back of a running horse: "Know that if you authentically inherit one phrase, you authentically inherit one dharma. If you inherit one phrase, you inherit mountains, and you inherit waters. You cannot be separated from this very place" (Dogen 278). Riding on the Frostian ice melting is not the same thing as riding on the current glacier melting. The latter is an un-ecopoetical consequence of our having chosen to craft an easier way of life by using up our natural resources unempathetically. Einstein's last four words "but not any simpler" in his aforementioned quotes, seems to warn us of the karmic effect of living excessively. *Haiku* encourages an ecopoetic embodiment of living simply but not any simpler.

Works Cited

Abram, David. *The Spell of the Sensuous*. Vintage Books: New York, 1996.

Alexander, Thomas M. *The Human Eros: Eco-ontology and the Aesthetics of Experience*. New York: Fordham University Press, 2013.

Anderson, John R. *Cognitive Psychology and its Implications* (6th ed.). Worth Publishers, 2004. p. 519. Retrieved from http://byuipt.net/564/2013/08/23/cognition-sensory-memory/

Bachelard, Gaston. *The Poetics of Space: The Classic Look at How We Experience Intimate Places*. Boston: Beacon Press, 1958.

Dogen. *Treasury of the True Dharma Eye: Zen Master Dogen's Shobo Genzo*. Kazuaki Tanahashi, Editor. San Francisco: Shambala Publications, 2013.

Einstein, Albert. "Quote Investigator." Retrieved from https://quoteinvestigator.com/2011/05/13/einstein-simple/

Fraser, Caroline. *Rewilding the World: Dispatches from the Conservation Revolution*. New York: Picador, 2009.

Frost, Robert. "The Figure a Poem Makes." *Essay*, 1939. Retrieved from *http://www.mrbauld.com/frostfig.html*

Heidegger, Martin. *Poetry, Language, Thought*. Translated by Alfred Hofstadter, New York: Harper & Row Publishers, Inc., 1971.

Hogan, Linda. "Dwelling of Enchantment: Writing and Reenchanting the Earth" Writers' Interviews, 2016. p. 7.

Ingraffea, Anthony R. "The Science of Shale." Lecture at Mercyhurst University, October 27, 2015.

Ingold, Timothy. *The Perception of the Environment: Essays on Livelihood, Dwelling and Skill*. London: Routledge, 2000.

James, Deborah. *The Syntax and Semantics of Some English Interjections*. University of Michigan, Doctoral dissertation, 1973.

Keene, Donald, compiler. *Anthology of Japanese Literature: From the earliest era to the mid-nineteenth century*. New York: Grove Press, 1955.

Kitcher, Patricia. *Kant's Transcendental Psychology*. New York: Oxford University Press, 1990.

Langer, Monica. *Merleau-Ponty's Phenomenology of Perception: A Guide and Commentary*. Talahassee, FL.: Florida State University Press, 1989.

Levin, David Michael. *The Body's Recollection of Being: Phenomenological Psychology and the Deconstruction of Nihilism*. Boston: Routledge & Kegan Paul, 1985.

Mai, Lin. *Heidegger on East-West Dialogue: Anticipating the Event*. New York: Routledge, 2008.

Marshall, Todd E. "Sense Making." *R. David Lankes*. Retrieved from https://davidlankes.org/new-librarianship/the-atlas-for-new-librarianship/threads-2/mission/sense-making/

Matamala, Anna. "The Translation of *Oh* in a Corpus of Dubbed Sitcoms." *Catalan Journal of Linguistics*, n°6, 2007, pp. 117–136.

Merleau-Ponty, Maurice. *Phenomenology of Perception*. New York: Routledge, 1962.

Naht Hanh, Thich. *Interbeing: Fourteen Guidelines for Engaged Buddhism.* Berkeley, CA: Parallax Press, 1989.

Sartre, Jean-Paul. *La Nausée.* Translated by L. Alexander, New York, NY: New Directions Paperback, 2007.

Shaner, David. E. *The Bodymind Experience in Japanese Buddhsim: A Phenomenological Study of Kukai and Dogen.* Albany, NY: State University of New York Press, 1985.

Shirane, Haruo and Brandon, James. *Early Modern Japanese Literature: An Anthology 1600-1900,* New-York: Columbia University Press, 2002.

Writer's Corner

Poems by David Lloyd

Miraculous Body

I was thinking

about Provincetown,
the lawn to mow, forms to fill,

a reception to attend, and the rip
a jet bound for Iraq can make in a sky distended

with God's angers, opened
like an apocalyptic piñata

to deluge the earth with frogs, gnats,
locusts, viruses—everything

humans deserve—when a hawk screeched
by Limestone Creek, and a cardinal asserted himself,

and the sky remained
unripped, and it struck me

that in a few hours fireflies would perforate the dark,
that bats hadn't abandoned us,

that grass masks grasshoppers,
that slugs would not neglect

their nocturnal appointments,
that the tousled, deep-red bee balm

by the window where I write
might lure a hummingbird so close

I could reach and touch
his miraculous body, if he would let me.

(published in the journal *Stone Canoe*)

Open House

What say we give up?
Fling open doors and windows,
leave wide the chimney flue?

Pull down screens,
rip the tongue from the groove,
crowbar shingles from the roof?

Burn fly-swatters. Bury insecticides,
pesticides, and assault weapons
in a steel coffin.

No vacuuming. No sweeping.
No sponging—not even skin.

Let dust roll its ghostly basketballs
across a threadbare floor.

Let stars invade our space,
downpours on mattresses,
sunlight on sconces.

Welcome the field mouse to the cheese board,
cockroach to the carvery,
bedbug to the duvet,
snakes to the wine cellar.

Birds swoop without concussion.
Raccoons scour the stovetop with quick tongues.
And everyone drinks from the toilet.

Give over to the ant's carpentry,
the wood wasp's spelunking,
the nesting swallow's mud-packing,
the orb spider's corner wizardry—

What say we leave unmolested
that drip hanging from the tip
of the blade of grass?

(published in the journal *The Hopper*)

Beavermind

A low-tech lumberjack with all that treefelling, logrolling.
A sentinel, safeguarding stations of the pond.

Equipped for winter's depredations
with anchored bales in a pantry.

Family? Certainly! The kits
groomed and oiled, cavorting in shallow safety,
slapping mini tails like daddy or mommy
when they glimpse the voyeur in the brush.

Social? Absolutely! Welcoming
even the skulking muskrat to hearth and home.

But when is enough enough?
Enough wood gnawed, enough flowing dammed?
Enough birth? Enough forest abridged to meadow?
When does nightfall's memory of steel teeth and bullets,
skin and fur draped over heads and shoulders,
dim to midnight that cheerful, bucktoothed face?

Never, I'm afraid, for the beavermind knows
this and here, not that and there. Which is why
when bats touch our faces and clouds inch like continents
over our heads, we need the beaver:
gnawing trunks, stanching seeps in dams,
praying with dexterous paws.

The List

Mostly raccoons, woodchucks, squirrels, where we live.
Moles, snakes, toads, possums, hedgehogs, deer also.
And surprises—those having no truck with roads:
bats, sparrows, pheasants out of time and place.
We mourn our dogs and cats, but shrug at the wild,
lacking collars. Watch out: big ones can stand

their ground: bear, stag, cow, moose, elk, bison—they stand
and fall, fall and rise, dead then maybe alive....
And we drive on in our mobile spaces—wild
air banished; touch and wind screens, buttons; so
leatherish the seat, so cranked, "Rock This Place,"
rocking through fourteen speakers. The road

more traveled, the road-trip, *On the Road*;
road runner, Rhoades scholar, macadam to stand
your ground or back into if you've lost your place.
To coydogs: die! To songbirds: live!
Wyoming pronghorn, New York bobcat, also-
ran wolf, unlamented worm, formerly wild

parakeet, colobus monkey, newly wild
alligator flushed down a toilet—all crossing roads
that cross the Wild we bought and named—but also
claimed by them. For the flattened beaver, we stand
and salute. For the wounded penguin to live,
we donate. Arise, and go forth! We know a place

that cradles a crippled self, a place-
less place: water spigots, fish by the bucket, child-
proofed—keep on waddling: just please live!
We forgive the squashed skunk, and the turtle, road-
marooned, dogged, hard to know. Is he standing? Running? Helplessly armored but also

hoping, like those on this list I also
make of the night paraders out of place:
the drunk, the child, the stricken trying to stand;
the old, the blind, you, me—we all dance the wild

watusi with kangaroo, koala. Roads
know no fences, and no mercy—it's the live-

free-or-die wild card, vector and chance, so
dark, so radiant, this place that is the road
where we stand, where—for a while—we live.

This Unfamiliar Place

After a lifetime of absence,
I have returned to the earth
in autumn, at the end of the long day,
when warmth has risen through an empty sky.

I lie down on my stomach on that old unmade bed:
naked, cold, at the mercy of wind and leaves,
tendrils and pistils. Insects I can't see
and every creature I have neglected,
know me again, once confined
within windows and walls,
smelling only my own skin and hair,
the perfumed products of my hands.

Eyes, now, with nothing to read.
Fingers with no switches or instruments
or sharp edges to touch.
The pads of my feet
vulnerable to air, to beaks and seeds,
to all the specks that float about,
tiny touches, intimate violations.

I turn my head,
ear on the uncut grass.
I listen to the grinding of the plates,
the groans of faults,
the continent's infinitesimal drift,
the streaming of rock

and all down the length
of my neck and back and legs
I feel the damp chill of night-time
in this unfamiliar place.

(published in my poetry collection *The Everyday Apocalypse*. Three
Conditions Press, 2002)

Biographies

Chloé Angué

Dr. Chloé Angué is a high-school teacher and a doctor from the Université Paris Ouest Nanterre La Défense where she taught in Licence and Master and where she recently defended her thesis in comparative literatures entitled "Biblical Myths and Polynesian Myths: The Flexibility of the Imaginary of Conquest and Dream. Literary Images of Polynesia from the 17th to the 21st Century." Her research interests are postcolonial, area, and myth studies. She is passionate about Polynesian literatures, languages, myths, territory representations, and imaginary.

Wes Berry

Dr. Wes Berry is Professor of English at Western Kentucky University, where he teaches American literature with a specialization in environmental texts and regional writing, such as Southern literature. Inspired by various agrarian writers—and a childhood spent working on Kentucky farms—Wes and his wife Elisa grow much of their own food and tend a menagerie of creatures, including honeybees, sheep, rabbits, goats, and chickens. Home slaughtering and butchering, preserving fruits and vegetables, growing mushrooms, daily cooking—the "art of the commonplace"—draws them ever closer to their place near Kentucky's Green and Barren Rivers. Berry's ecocritical scholarship includes essays on Walter Inglis Anderson, Wendell Berry, Barbara Kingsolver, Anne LaBastille, Cormac McCarthy, Toni Morrison, and Annie Proulx. His recent over-indulgent gustatory research led to the publication of The Kentucky Barbecue Book.

Anne Cirella-Urrutia

Dr. Anne Cirella-Urrutia earned a Ph.D. in Comparative Literature at the University of Texas in Austin in 1998 and a DEA degree in Anglophone Studies from University Paul Valéry in Montpellier, France in 1993. Her research on children's literature and bande dessinée has appeared in international journals such as *Bookbird, Les Cahiers Robinson, Examplaria, Revista Española de Estudios Northeamericanos, Mots Pluriels, ChLA Quarterly,* and *Journal of American Studies of Turkey*. An ecocritical essay on children's author D. Mwankumi's picture books appeared in *Aspects Ecocritiques de L'Imaginaire Africain* (2013). She published a chapter entitled "World War I in *Bande*

Dessinée: La Semaine de Suzette and the Birth of a Breton Heroine at War" in *Humor, Entertainment, and Popular Culture during World War I* (2015) and an essay entitled "Heroes and Heroines of the Great War: The Aesthetics of Horror in *Bandes Dessinées*" in *La Première Guerre mondiale dans la mémoire intellectuelle, littéraire et artistique des cultures européennes* (2013). Cirella-Urrutia wrote many book reviews for *ImageText Interdisciplinary Comics Studies, The Journal of Graphic Novels and Comics, The French Review, Callalloo* and *L'Esprit Créateur*. An Adjunct Professor, Cirella-Urrutia has taught French at Huston-Tillotson University in Austin, Texas, since 2000.

Asis De

Dr. Asis De is Assistant Professor of English and Head of the Department of English Language and Literature, Mahishadal Raj College (Govt. Sponsored), Mahishadal, West Bengal, India. His research interests include the study of Identity negotiation in newer / diasporic cultural spaces with particular reference to postcolonial Anglophone fiction. He has completed both his Master's in Philosophies and Ph.D. from Jadavpur University, Kolkata. In a number of publications and conference presentations in India and in Europe (Belgium, Germany, and England), he has worked on the issues of cultural identity and transnationalism in Asian, Caribbean and African fictional narratives. He also teaches Anglophone Postcolonial Literatures, Dalit and Tribal Literatures, Cultural Studies and Diasporic Literatures in Post Graduate level since 2010. He is a Life Member of Indian Association for Commonwealth Literature and Language Studies (IACLALS) and regular member of Postcolonial Studies Association (UK), GAPS (Germany) and European Association for Commonwealth Literature and Language Studies (EACLALS).

Caroline Durand-Rous

Dr. Caroline Durand-Rous is a *professeur agrégé*. She holds a Ph.D. in American literature entitled "Reinvented Totems: Exploring Identities and Rewriting Oneself in Contemporary Native American Fiction." Her research focuses on Native American novels and how ambivalent totemic figures offer guidance to characters in disarray on the path to the discovery of hybrid identities. She has published articles in *L'Atelier, Textes et Contextes,* and *Transatlantica.* She has participated in European conferences held by the AFEA, the AIW, and the EASLCE where she presented her analyses of Louise Erdrich's *The Painted Drum,* David Treuer's *The Translation of Dr. Apelles,* and Eden Robinson's *Monkey Beach.*

Stephen Greenfield

Dr. Stephen Greenfield earned a Ph.D. at the University of Wolverhampton. His work explores the application of labyrinthine approaches to J.R.R. Tolkien's *The Lord of the Rings* and Philip Pullman's *His Dark Materials*, and how they relate to ecological readings.

Catherine Hoffmann

Prof. Catherine Hoffmann, formerly Senior Lecturer in English at the University of Le Havre (France) and a participant in the joint project "Echoes of the Pastoral" (University of Poitiers and Orléans), now retired, has published essays on Dermot Healy in *Style* (43.3, Fall 2009) and the collective volume *Writing the Sky: Observations and Essays on Dermot Healy,* under the title "Mister Psyche's Microcosmos" (Dalkey Archive Press, 2016). Her most recent essay, "Phatic, Polemical, and Metaleptic Addresses to Readers in William Gerhardie's *The Polyglots,*" appeared in *The Rhetoric of Literary Communication* (Routledge, 2022).

David Latour

Dr. David Latour has been a certified teacher for several years. Since September 2015, he has been teaching English for special purposes in the Science Department at the University of Orléans, in Bachelor's degree and Master's degree. In December 2014, he defended his Ph.D. thesis on "H.D. Thoreau's Ecological Ethics" (supervisor, Gérard Hugues, Aix-Marseille University). In June 2010, he published an article entitled "Henry David Thoreau ou les rêveries écologiques d'un promeneur solitaire" in the on-line journal *E-LLA.* His research fields include Transcendentalism, Nature writing, ecopoetics, Environmental Studies, and Animal Rights Theories.

Margot Lauwers

Dr. Margot Lauwers holds a Ph.D. in American literature and ecofeminism from the University of Perpignan where she taught business English, English language, technical and literary translation, as well as American civilization for eight years. She has been an Assistant Editor for *Ecozon@: European Journal of Literature, Culture and Environment* since 2016 and currently works as a literary translator: she has completed the translation to French of Carolyn Merchant's *The Death of Nature* (Wildprojects, Marseille, March 2020) and is in the process of finishing the translation to French of Susan Griffin's *Woman and Nature the Roaring Inside Her* (Éditions Le Pommier, Paris, March 2020).

David Lloyd

Prof. David Lloyd directs the Creative Writing Program at Le Moyne College in Syracuse, New York, USA. He is the author of nine books, including a novel, *Over the Line*, and his latest poetry collection, *Warriors*. His other books include two poetry collections—*The Everyday Apocalypse* and *The Gospel According to Frank*—and a fiction collection, *Boys: Stories* and a Novella. In 2000, he received the Poetry Society of America's Robert H. Winner Memorial Award, judged by W. D. Snodgrass. His articles, interviews, poems, and stories have appeared in numerous journals, including *Crab Orchard Review*, *Denver Quarterly*, and *TriQuarterly*.

Maxime Petit

Mr. Maxime Petit studied English at the Ecole Normale Supérieure de Lyon. He is presently a *professeur agrégé* at the Université Toulouse 1 Capitole in Southern France, where he teaches English for specific purposes and co-organises Point Doc, an annual documentary film screening event. His research focuses on literature and film.

George Piggford

Prof. George Piggford, C.S.C., is professor of English at Stonehill College in Easton, MA. He has published work on American and British literature in *Christianity & Literature, Cultural Critique, English Studies in Canada, The Flannery O'Connor Review, Modern Drama, and Mosaic*, as well as in volumes such as *Through a Glass Darkly: Suffering, Sacred, and the Sublime* (Wilfred Laurier P, 2010), *Revelation and Convergence: Flannery O'Connor and the Catholic Intellectual Tradition* (Catholic U of America P, 2017), and *The Hermeneutics of Hell* (Palgrave, 2017). In 2014 he was an NEH Summer Scholar at the Revisiting Flannery O'Connor Institute at Georgia College. In November of that year, he reflected on O'Connor and Teilhard de Chardin at the induction of O'Connor into the American Poets Corner at New York's Cathedral of St. John the Divine. At Stonehill, he has been a Farmhouse Fellow, a position that provides scholars with space to read, write, and reflect at an organic farm committed to extending food access to nearby communities.

Peter Schulman

Prof. Peter Schulman is a Professor of French and International Studies at Old Dominion University. He is Chevalier de l'Ordre des Palmes Académiques and the author of *The Sunday of Fiction: The Modern French Eccentric* (Purdue

University Press, 2003) as well as *Le Dernier Livre du Siècle* (Romillat, 2001) with Mischa Zabotin. He has edited a critical edition of Jules Verne's *The Begum's Millions* (Wesleyan University Press, 2005) and recently translated Jules Verne's last novel *The Secret of Wilhelm Storitz* (University of Nebraska Press. 2012), as well as a meditation on waves by Marie Darrieussecq, *On Waves* (VVV editions, 2014); *Suburban Beauty* by poet Jacques Reda (VVV editions, 2009) and *Adamah* by Celine Zins (Gival Press, 2010). He is currently co-editor in chief of a new journal on eco-criticism, *Green Humanities* with Josh Weinstein (Virginia Wesleyan College), and has co-edited the following books: *The Marketing of Eros: Performance, Sexuality and Consumer Culture* (Die Blaue Eule, 2003); *Chasing Esther: Jewish Expressions of Cultural Difference* (Kol Katan Press, 2007) and *Rhine Crossings: France and German in Love and War* (SUNY Press, 2004).

Adrian Tait

Dr. Adrian Tait is an independent scholar and environmental critic. A long-standing member of the Association for the Study of Literature and the Environment (ASLE-UKI), he has regularly published in its journal, *Green Letters*. He has also contributed to a number of other scholarly journals and to essay collections such as *Thomas Hardy, Poet: New Perspectives* (2015), *Nineteenth-Century Transatlantic Literary Ecologies* (2017), *Victorian Ecocriticism* (2017), and *Enchanted, Stereotyped, Civilized: Garden Narratives in Literature, Art and Film* (2018). He continues to explore the way in which nineteenth-century and early modern depictions of the environment anticipate but also challenge contemporary, ecocritical concerns.

Keiko Takioto Miller

Ms. Keiko Takioto Miller is an Assistant Professor of Japanese and French and the Director of Asian Studies Program at Mercyhurts University, Pennsylvania. She has been teaching Japanese language and culture at Mercyhurst College for 23 years, as well as volunteering in the community with English as a Second Language in Head Start, Literacy and Adult Education Programs throughout her career. Miller also is an active NPCA member.

Index

www.ingramcontent.com/pod-product-compliance
Lightning Source LLC
Chambersburg PA
CBHW072053020426
42334CB00017B/1492